Advanced Studies in Emerging Markets Finance

Series Editors

Irina Ivashkovskaya, Higher School of Economics, National Research University, Moscow, Russia

Joseph McCahery, Department of Business Law, Tilburg University School of Law, Tilburg, The Netherlands

Eugene Nivorozhkin, School of Slavonic and East European Studies, University College London, London, UK

Elettra Agliardi, University of Bologna, Department of Economics, Bologna, Italy

D1723834

The series offers insights into the broad range of finance concepts applied to the specific environment in emerging capital markets. The series presents a broad range of theoretical concepts, empirical analyses and policy conclusions regarding financial markets, financial institutions, and corporate finance. Giving a voice to scholars from emerging and developed countries, comparative studies analyze different financial markets as well as firms' performance in emerging and developed economies. There is a particular focus on the largest emerging economies, namely the BRICS countries.

More information about this series at http://www.springer.com/series/15606

Irina Ivashkovskaya • Svetlana Grigorieva •
Eugene Nivorozhkin

Editors

Strategic Deals in Emerging Capital Markets

Are There Efficiency Gains for Firms
in BRIC Countries?

 Springer

Editors
Irina Ivashkovskaya
Higher School of Economics
National Research University
Moscow, Russia

Svetlana Grigorieva
Higher School of Economics
National Research University
Moscow, Russia

Eugene Nivorozhkin
School of Slavonic and East European
Studies
University College London
London, UK

ISSN 2662-4281 ISSN 2662-429X (electronic)
Advanced Studies in Emerging Markets Finance
ISBN 978-3-030-23852-0 ISBN 978-3-030-23850-6 (eBook)
https://doi.org/10.1007/978-3-030-23850-6

This Springer imprint is published by the registered company Springer Nature Switzerland AG.
The registered company address is: Gewerbestrasse 11, 6330 Cham, Switzerland

Series Editors' Preface

The Springer series on Advanced Emerged Markets Finance is designed to promote leading-edge research on corporate finance and asset pricing in emerging markets. Given the initiative by the National Research University Higher School of Economics (HSE), Russia, to present the advances in the trends, the processes, and the performance in different areas of finance in specific framework of emerging markets, the Springer Series will include empirical research by leading scholars from around the world.

The scope of the series is comparative and interdisciplinary, and the focus is on studies between BRICS, between BRICS and developed economies, or new research advances in emerging markets finance. The series will be relevant to a number of social science disciplines including economics, finance, and management. It is also relevant to a wide variety of professionals in financial, business, and governmental institutions.

The volumes in this series will broadly address the effect of financial integration on corporate finance choices. They will address important topics in corporate finance from mergers and acquisitions to asset pricing anomalies in emerging capital markets. This series, in contrast to other fields of economics, will also focus on the unique interdisciplinary aspects of the topic. The volumes will examine various corporate governance and management issues as well as the impact of the institutional structure and regulatory environment on corporate financing behavior. In emphasizing the specific environment of emerging markets, researches will shed light on how capital structure has changed in emerging markets in the post-Great Recession period.

Research in emerging market finance has developed in several directions over the last three decades. One main theme examines the impact of financial integration on the financial decisions of firms. On the one hand, financial integration has provided a greater range of financing sources and altered the capital structure of some firms. On the other hand, there are market imperfections that exist in emerging capital markets. In this series, researchers will present evidence on the internal and external determinants for the speed of adjustment of capital structures, highlighting the peculiarities of financing decisions in different countries after 2009. Economists will apply insights from behavioral and asset pricing theory, in another volume in the series, to show empirically why emerging markets are informationally less inefficient than developed markets and shed light on the methods and tests for analyzing risks of investments in emerging markets.

Another line of research explores the state of practice in M&A in emerging markets. While most research on the determinants of M&A focuses on the effect of such strategies in developed countries, this series analyzes the performance of M&A transactions in both developed and emerging markets, taking into account the different drivers of the value creation process in both markets. This work assesses the impact of horizontal, vertical, and conglomerate deals of shareholder value across different industry sectors and after the Great Recession.

This series will explore a third line of emerging market finance research that focuses on the prominent role of risk in emerging capital markets. One major difference between developed and emerging markets is the need for emerging markets—due to the complicated features of their banking systems—to adapt and modify the methods and models of risk assessment. This series will describe the search for new models that target estimation, of both the probability of default and expected loss, for emerging market financial institutions. The theoretical and empirical work will show how regulators in Russia and BRICS have transformed these risk models and the respective rating systems at the regional and country level. This analysis also covers new methods of assessment of systemic risk and stress testing of financial institutions in BRICS.

In emphasizing that emerging markets present a major challenge to traditional economic models, economists rightly note that a strong interdisciplinary approach is required to address unanswered questions of corporate finance behavior in the capital markets of emerging markets. We would expect that this series will begin to provide new and useful insights into these important problems and provide insights for policymakers.

Tilburg, The Netherlands   Joseph McCahery

Preface

.

During the last few decades, emerging economies have become an increasingly visible and integral part of the global business environment. Economic and political reforms have led to a significant liberalization of the economic landscape and boosted economic growth in these countries. This unlocked massive market opportunities for foreign firms and facilitated the expansion of firms from emerging economies outside their home markets. Cross-border and domestic M&A activities involving emerging economies also played an essential role in optimizing the allocation of ownership rights and improving the overall economic efficiency of evolving market institutions.

Despite the existence of a rich body of literature on M&A and their successes and failures, relatively little is known about strategic deals in the specific environment of emerging capital markets, where there is still a lack of institutional strength and regulatory experience, and a deficit in experienced management teams. The imperfect institutional environment in these countries results in additional operational and investment risks, uncertainty, transaction costs, information asymmetry, and less efficient market mechanisms, which may influence the success of companies in realizing synergies and efficient integration. In addition, poor corporate governance, inadequate disclosure, and pronounced government intervention in business may also lead to different market reactions to M&A deals in emerging capital markets. In cross-border deals, additional factors that contribute to the puzzle of M&A performance in emerging economies include the specific accounting and tax rules used by many firms, substandard legal system practices, a lack of supporting elements such as lawyers, accountants, and advisers, cultural differences, corruption level, and little experience in cross-border deals which often leads to mistakes by emerging market firms in choosing and valuing target firms.

This book is an output of a research project implemented as part of the Basic Research Program at the National Research University Higher School of Economics (HSE University).

The authors offer comprehensive insights into the determinants and efficiency gains of strategic deals in emerging markets as a whole and BRIC countries in particular. Despite the fact that BRIC countries are a highly heterogeneous group, they are a major contributor to the global M&A market, which increases the interest in examining the trends and efficiency of M&A deals in these economies. The studies presented contribute to the relatively scarce literature on emerging market M&A by employing innovative methodology and utilizing new data sources. They also highlight the unique challenges involved in deriving empirical regularities in studying M&A activities in emerging markets, as these often involve firms from countries with diverse economic, institutional, and cultural environments, typically characterized by and involving a number of methodological issues affecting casual inferences.

Given the growing volume of deals in monetary terms and in their size in this specific segment of the world economy, research on M&A in emerging markets enriches our understanding of modern M&A cycles, the evolving motivations behind these strategic transactions in less developed economic environment, and their potential and limitations.

Chapter 1 provides a comprehensive introduction to the historical developments in the M&A markets of the four major emerging markets of China, India, Brazil, and Russia. We present a thorough review of market trends in terms of the regulatory environment, the volume and value of transactions, and other relevant metrics and key drivers. Chapters 2 and 3 shed light on the academic literature related to M&A activities in emerging and developed markets. Chapter 2 focuses on the methods used to estimate whether M&A deals promote efficiency gains or not. We discuss the instruments which assess the effects of M&A on a firm's operating performance and value. We know from studies exploring M&A activities that there is no consistent vision on the performance of these deals for acquirers. They often follow unproductive paths and demonstrate value destruction in many countries, industries, and periods. Chapter 2 discusses the main findings of previous empirical studies of domestic M&A first. Particular attention is paid to the significant differences in the economic and institutional environments between developed and emerging markets and their implications for the existing empirical results. Chapter 3 presents the analysis of the theoretical insights and empirical regularities related to cross-border M&A when firms from emerging markets go abroad. The analysis of cross-border M&A is a relatively new subject and has only recently received rigorous attention in academic research. Within this nascent literature, Chap. 3 pays particular attention to the emerging markets, which, in line with their growing role in the global economy, have become an increasingly important arena for cross-border M&A.

To understand more deeply the diversity among chapters on deals by emerging market firms, the authors add to the literature their meta-analysis in Chap. 4. This specific research technique provides an estimation of the explanatory power of one or another determinant included in the previous empirical models considering the diversity of the research. Given the quantitative analysis of accumulated samples from existing chapters, this study determines how different variables affect the performance of M&A deals on average in emerging capital markets. The meta-analysis techniques cover published articles based on samples from China, India, Brazil, Russia, Malaysia, South Africa, Argentina, Chile, Slovenia, and Poland. There are several meta-studies of M&A in developed capital markets, but the research presented in Chap. 4 is one of the first for emerging capital markets.

Based on the conclusions from the literature analysis in Chaps. 2–4, we examine the impact of M&A deals on company value in the long run. Chapter 5 offers an empirical analysis based on developed and emerging economies to compare the results of deals from Western European markets and different emerging capital markets, respectively. We introduce economic profit (residual income) as a performance measure to identify whether the transactions in developed markets create more value for shareholders than M&A in emerging economies over the three-year period surrounding the deals. We also adjust the models for industry trends and show that they affect the performance of M&A deals in emerging and developed countries, respectively. Particular attention is paid to the impact of the economic crisis of 2007–2008 on the performance of M&A.

While looking into the specific features of strategic deals in emerging markets, it is important to understand the scope of the premium paid. Chapter 6 examines three groups of factors: the acquirer's characteristics, the target's characteristics, and the deal's characteristics for a sample of M&A deals in BRIC markets. To measure the premium, the event studies method is used; therefore, the data on cumulative abnormal returns (CAR) are adjusted to the market movements in each country. We focus on three levels of acquired stakes ($>25\%$, $>50\%$, and 100%). The study contributes to a deeper understanding of the differences in the size of the premium between the countries and the interaction of the main determinants influencing the magnitude of the premium. The study looks beyond the stylized determinants of the premium's size and considers the crisis to be among the premium's drivers.

In line with the growing role of knowledge-based resources, M&A deals in emerging markets involve firms with these types of business models. The relevance of this issue is inherent to M&A, especially at the integration phase. These issues are presented in Chap. 7 based on a study of critical success factors in the M&A integration processes of consulting engineering companies in Brazil in the last 10 years. A practical application using two classical ordinal ranking methods was applied, and interviews with 23 executives active in consulting engineering in Brazil with experience in leadership, management, integration, and/or M&A processes are summarized. We focus on the success factors, the challenges, and the risks in the M&A activities of such firms and show how they are prioritized in the integration of the purchasing and acquired companies in Brazil to achieve their objectives and reach the forecasted synergies.

A detailed empirical analysis of the synergies is further developed in Chap. 8 with data on Russian M&A. We offer an innovative approach to synergy analysis and identify potential success factors to evaluate two types of operating and three types of financial synergies. The novel features include the use of a relatively long series of accounting data for Russian companies and covering private companies and small deals that make up the majority of the Russian M&A market. They contribute by estimating the structure of the operating and financial synergies for every deal and by testing potential success factors.

Regardless of the types of corporate diversification strategies in M&A activities, they are very important driving forces for performance. Academic chapters mainly concentrate on the effects of corporate diversification in mature markets, while the consequences in emerging capital markets have been less explored. Building on the existing literature, Chap. 9 provides evidence on whether various types of diversification strategies of companies in emerging markets have the potential to add value. Given the degree of underdevelopment of capital and product market institutions, a diversification strategy could offset some negatives and generate substantial benefits for the participating firms. Is there a diversification discount? Is it beneficial to diversify in such an environment? This diversification puzzle needs to be reexamined in the context of emerging market M&A. The analysis is in line with other studies which distinguish between related and unrelated diversification. In contrast, our research model adds a specific approach to single out and separately analyze horizontal, conglomerate, and vertical acquisitions. In the framework of this puzzle, it is especially important to measure the capability of fulfilling these institutional gaps by means of diversification in times of economic turbulence. We contribute to the existing literature by comparing the effects of corporate diversification on firm value during the pre- and post-crisis periods for the sample from BRIC countries.

The theme of corporate diversification continues in Chap. 10 which investigates the links between international corporate diversification and firm performance in BRIC countries. We apply a new approach by measuring performance using economic profit. Given the need to account for the cost of capital to calculate the residual income metrics for the firms from the sample, economic profit allows us to capture investment risk. The effects of international diversification are examined not only using operating profits but also using the opportunity cost of capital and the required rate of return as a fundamental value driver of the firm. The research model also accounts for the market value-based performance of the sample firms and therefore accounts for an investor's expectation-based evaluation of international diversification results. The empirical analysis is done on a sample of companies from BRIC countries that expanded abroad during the period 2005–2015.

Given the growing involvement of emerging market firms in the global M&A market, we believe that the evidence and discussions presented in this book will be of use for researchers, educators, and practitioners who are engaged in business communications in emerging markets and who are interested in a deeper understanding of the impact of M&A on company results.

Moscow, Russia   Irina Ivashkovskaya
Tilburg, The Netherlands   Joseph McCahery

Acknowledgments

We are deeply indebted to a large number of people; without their talent, input, and hard work, this book would not exist.

We are first of all grateful to Prof. Joseph A. McCahery from Tilburg University who is a member of the editorial board of the overall series "Advanced studies in emerging market's finance" for valuable comments, creative guidance, and help. We appreciate the substantial help and suggestions we received from Prof. Elettra Agliardi from the University of Bologna who is also on the editorial board of the series.

This book has benefited substantially from the input of our colleagues from Corporate Finance Research Center in National Research University Higher School of Economics (HSE): Associate Prof. Anastasia Stepanova and Associate Prof. Maria Kokoreva. We are grateful to the interns from this center, who helped with data collection: Ekaterina Tarasova, Ksenia Obukhova, Daria Morozova, Roman Vasilenko, Dmitry Andrienko, Elena Chvyrova, and Georgii Gorbatov. Special thanks are to Anna Gladysheva, lecturer of the Department of Applied Economics of the Faculty of Economic Sciences of HSE, for her advice.

We gratefully acknowledge the valuable comments that we received at the international conferences where we discussed our ideas and research results: European Financial Management Association (EFMA) Symposium in 2017, European Academy of Management (EURAM) annual meetings in 2016–2018, European Institute for Advanced Studies in Management (EIASM) in 2015–2016, Annual International Academic Conference on Economic and Social Development by HSE in 2015–2017, Spring Meeting of Young Economists (SMYE) by the European Association of Young Economists (EAYE) in 2014, World Finance and Banking Symposium in 2015, and Graduate School of Management of Saint-Petersburg University (GSOM) Emerging Markets Conference in 2017.

For help in coordinating the flow of paper, e-mail, and phone calls, we owe our thanks to our assistant Valeriya Mechel, administrator of the School of Finance of the Faculty of Economic Sciences of HSE and Anton Shilovsky, the analyst of the School of Finance.

We have a word of appreciation for the excellent support from Barbara Fess, Philipp Baun, Yvonne Schwark-Reiber, and their team members of Springer for the speedy and excellent publication of the book.

Moscow, Russia   Irina Ivashkovskaya
                                                                                         Svetlana Grigorieva

Contents

Part III Diversification Strategies via M&As: New Evidence from BRIC

Part I
Strategic Deals and Value Creation: The Lessons from Previous Research

M&As Trends in Emerging Capital Markets

Deng Junzhi, Rajesh Chakrabarti, Karla Motta Kiffer de Moraes, Luiz F. Autran M. Gomes, and Irina Skvortsova

Abstract To explore the trends in buying and selling the firms in emerging markets, this chapter introduces the key features in the strategic deals in the largest markets within BRIC group. The upward and downward trends in purchasing corporate control that constitute the waves in the M&As activities in these countries are shown. The authors underline the role of government regulations and enhancement of competition in these countries in structuring the M&As waves. The changes in the industrial profiles, as well as the dollar volume and the quantity of deals in BRIC are presented. Both domestic and cross-border deals made by Chinese, Indian, Brazilian, and Russian firms are summarized.

Keywords M&As waves · Domestic deals · Cross-border deals

1 Introduction

Despite the BRIC countries constitute rather heterogeneous group with different dominating trends in the economies, they represent the largest markets for strategic deals among the countries with emerging capital markets. The internal economic development, globalization, and competitive forces push the firms forward to find the targets to foster growth strategies and to enter new markets. What are the main trends in the strategic deals in each country from the BRIC group? Are there upward

D. Junzhi · I. Skvortsova (✉)
Corporate Finance Center, HSE, Moskva, Russia
e-mail: iskvortsova@hse.ru

R. Chakrabarti
Jindal Global Business School, Sonipat, Haryana, India

K. M. K. de Moraes
Arcadis NV Brasil, Rio de Janeiro, Brazil

L. F. A. M. Gomes
Ibmec School of Business and Economics Brasil, Rio de Janeiro, Brazil

© Springer Nature Switzerland AG 2020
I. Ivashkovskaya et al. (eds.), *Strategic Deals in Emerging Capital Markets*,
Advanced Studies in Emerging Markets Finance,
https://doi.org/10.1007/978-3-030-23850-6_1

and downward waves in mergers and acquisition's activity in their national deal's markets? Given the potential unique nature of cross-border deals based on various market imperfections, information asymmetries as well as differences in innovative capacities, emerging market's firms may be involved into rather contradictory transactions of purchasing control over foreign companies. How active are the firms from BRIC group in the global M&A when they are initiating cross-border deals?

In order to explore the patterns of relationship between the types of strategic deals and value creation effects for the firms in emerging markets, we start from the introduction to the main trends in buying and selling corporate control in the largest emerging capital markets. This chapter provides an overview of the key features in inward and outward strategic deals of Chinese, Indian, Brazilian, and Russian firms.

2   M&As in China: Trends and Evidence

2.1   The M&As Market in China

Since China entered the WTO, M&As deals initiated by Chinese firms have played a growing role in the worldwide market for corporate control. As the Chinese economy continues to open to global markets and internal capital market becomes more mature, the M&As activity has kept growing. To foster economic globalization, the Chinese government significantly improved commercial regulation standards, decreased the entry threshold for foreign investment, introduced new foreign financing policies for domestic enterprises and for developing international trade (Büttner and Meckl 2017). By 2016, China's global investment reached a historical peak, and the value of cross-border M&As in China exceeded that of the USA.

Figure 1 shows that in 2010–2018 M&A market activity in China has experienced a considerable increase of 106% in terms of value (in dollars) and 95% in terms of number. However, since 2017, Chinese government has started to introduce a series of stricter policies on outbound investment to tighten the capital outflows, which directly lead to the sharp decrease of outbound deals. Under the environment of shifts in regulation and US-China trade war, the value of M&A market in China continues to decline in 2018 (Bloomberg 2018).

Now China is under the period of transformation and upgrading from the biggest global manufacturer to an ambitious investor; most Chinese investors start to focus on the industries, which not only help them to achieve more synergies and expand their global business landscape but also enhance their global influence.

2.2   M&As Waves in China

Chinese M&As activity has experienced six major waves (see Table 1) with the periods of high growth and the periods of relative inactivity. Within the first wave

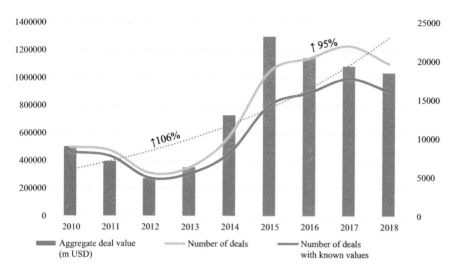

Fig. 1 Deal value and number of M&A in China from 2010 to 2018, in $ million

(1984–1992), many enterprises under the principle of "the separation of powers" generally developed a business model based on contracting and leasing operations. Most transactions were completed between state-owned enterprises (SOEs) and collective-owned enterprises, which were directly intervened in by local governments. During this period, horizontal mergers in the same or a similar industry dominated. However, most transactions were completed under the unclear property rights of this period (Bai Xinxi 2012).

Within the second wave (1992–1997), the Chinese government implemented market reforms which allowed the free flow of property rights and company restructuring. Since then, companies started using the stock market for M&As deals and contracts with intermediary agencies. M&A transactions increased both by value and by volume; stock purchase became one of the main types of payment for M&As. Unlike the pattern of M&As in the 1980s, more and more transactions took place between strong companies in order to achieve synergy effects. Cross-border transactions appeared and investment banks began to play an important role in M&A (Cai Yongming 2007; Bai Xinxi 2012).

The third wave (1997–2002) was based on the rapid development of the capital market in China. With a growing number of listed companies involved in M&As transactions, the types of deals became more diversified, and they gradually broke the regional, industrial, and ownership restrictions. M&As transactions were mainly based on the agreement of state-owned shares and A shares. However, in the late 1990s, there were many deals that were completed inappropriately due to the inadequate legal frameworks of M&As transactions. Since 2001, the Chinese government has been improving the legal environment, including accounting systems, exit mechanisms, and the distribution of assets. During this period, strategic

Table 1 Six waves of M&As in China

Period	1984–1992	1993–1997	1998–2002	2003–2005	2006–2015	2016 up to the present
Beginning of wave	The guidance of the principle of "separation of powers"	Deng Xiaoping's famous inspection tour to southern China in 1992	The progress in the transition to market economy	New laws and regulations about M&A were issued	The process of urbanization had been relatively accelerated	The "13th Five-Year Plan" Conference
Main types	Horizontal mergers	Equity acquisitions	Strategic acquisitions	Financial acquisitions	Equity acquisitions, equity assets	Financial and strategic acquisitions
Main type of payment	Cash/debt	Equity	Cash/equity	Cash	Cash/equity	Cash/equity
Key characteristics	Most companies were SOEs; under unclear property rights	The free flow of property rights and companies' restructuring were allowed	The deals became more diversified both in terms of sector and fields	Cross-border transactions growing rapidly	Chinese private companies entered the M&A market; the value of outbound M&A increase at a high speed	China sustains economic growth and stays on track with external financial liberalization

Source: Genfu and Linjiang (2001). Empirical Research on M&A Performance of Chinese Listed Companies. Economic Research, (1), pp. 54–61; Zhao XiuZhi (2016). The Process of Acquisition & Merger of Enterprises and Their Development, Journal of Beijing Union University (Humanities and Social Sciences); 4, No. 4, pp. 71–75

acquisitions became the mainstream for enterprises in order to enhance their core competencies in the market.

During fourth wave (2002–2005), the volume and value increased due to the new M&As laws and regulations. A new trend of cross-border transactions was pushed forward. Foreign and private capital became very active, and the role of financial intermediaries expanded (Zhao Xiuzhi 2016).

Within the fifth wave (2005–2008), China's economy entered a new stage of development, the process of urbanization accelerated and the Chinese government carried out reforms of the ownership structure in listed companies. In the new context of economic development, M&As transactions were associated with private offerings, asset transfer, and related transactions, which made the stock market more complicated. Private Chinese companies were slowly but surely entering the arena. With lower average costs and higher productivity, they began to challenge the SOEs in terms of product quality, market share, and M&As transactions.

With the acceleration of internationalization, the markets along the Belt Road offered huge development potential. Progress was made in the area of technology, real estate, financial services, and healthcare. Given the particular background of Chinese policy, SOEs played an active role in both domestic and cross-border M&As deals. The high-speed rail, nuclear power, telecommunications, and aviation sectors were the Chinese industries with the greatest M&As potential (White Case 2017).

2.3 What Is Typical for Current M&As in China?

Compared with other emerging countries, M&As market in China has several unique characteristics. Given its specific economic background, China has faced some serious obstacles including massive industrial overcapacity, high levels of corporate debt, and a frothy property market. Therefore, supply-side structural reform shapes everything from the government's efforts to reduce excess industrial capacity to initiatives designed to curb high levels of corporate debt has been proposed (The Economist Intelligence Unit 2017). Within the industrial sector, the Chinese government supports eight traditional industries (steel, coal, cement, glasswork, oil, petrochemical, iron ore, and nonferrous metals industries) to cut industrial overcapacity and accomplish the industrial transformation.

Since "Made in China 2025"[1](MIC2025) began to be prompted in 2015, Chinese companies have paid more attention to promoting innovation and high technology through R&D, enhancing brands and goodwill in the global market, and developing service-oriented manufacturing (US. Chamber of Commerce 2017). Therefore, some new technology sectors including information technology, new energy, new materials, biological medicine, agricultural technology and machinery, as well as

---

[1]"Made in China 2025" is an initiative to comprehensively upgrade Chinese industry.

insurance and other innovative financial services have performed well in M&As market (Deloitte 2017).

SOEs focus on the energy and natural resource sectors, while privately owned enterprises (POEs) prefer technological and innovative targets. Among SOEs in China, ChemChina, Hainan Airlines, State Grid, China National Petroleum Corporation have become the most active players in the global market for corporate control and have participated in many domestic and cross-border deals since 2006.

Figure 2a, b highlights the breakdown of M&As by industry in China in 2018.

The top three industries with the largest M&As deal number are IT, machinery manufacturing, and finance. Cloud computing, big data, software, and IT services are the hottest areas of M&A. In the last decade, the TMT (Technology, Media, Telecom) industry is growing at a fast-speed in China. Its output value has repeatedly reached new heights and made outstanding contributions to the rapid development of the Chinese national economy. Chinese internet giants BAT (Baidu, Alibaba Group, and Tencent Holdings) have been increasing their M&A activity each year. In 2018, one of the most famous transactions in China is Alibaba Group that acquired C-Sky Microsystems, which helped Alibaba in the layout of artificial intelligence.

Meanwhile, M&A transactions in traditional industrial sectors, which are closely related to the lifeblood of China's economy, such as machinery, metals, construction, and real estate, also made a good performance. In the context of policies "Made in China 2025" and "China's Belt and Road Initiative," Chinese manufacturing bidders aim to refresh their corporate image and restructure the global industrial and value chains by acquiring international targets. In 2018, the majority of transactions in the fields of high-end manufacturing related to semiconductors, sensors, robots, and new materials. For example, Chinese company Wingtech Technology as the world's largest smartphone contract manufacturer, the main distributor for Huawei Technologies, decided to acquire 75.86% share from Dutch semiconductor company NeNexperia for 3.63 billion USD for the purpose of entering into the goal market, opening the supply chain and obtaining the unique patent (Reuters 2017).

Chinese bidders are searching for higher-quality assets and shares in the global market. With the improvement of the regulatory environment, there will be more public deals and they will involve companies with rich experience.

2.4 Domestic and Cross-Border M&A Deals in China

Since China's 11th 5-year plan in 2006, cross-border M&As helped SOEs to gain more advanced technology, stronger management experience, and a higher global brand effect, to attract large equity funds from active overseas firms.

Figure 3 illustrates the dynamics in M&As domestic and cross-border deals. In 2013, the initiative "One Belt and One Road (OBOR)" was launched to create the

a

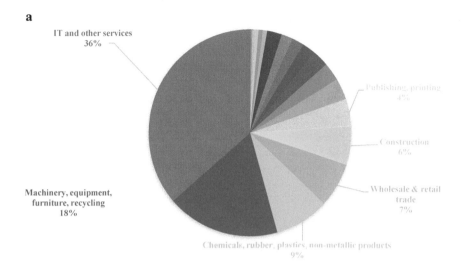

b

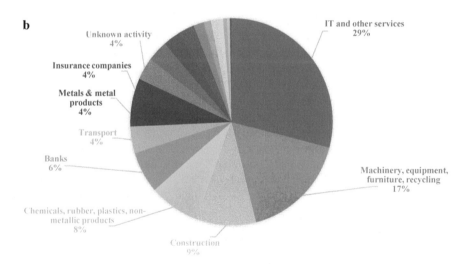

Fig. 2 Breakdown of M&A by industry in China in 2018. (**a**) Deal value and (**b**) Deal number

world's largest platform for economic cooperation, which mainly concentrated on South East Asia, West Asia, South Asia, Central Asia to Central and Eastern Europe (DealGlobe 2018). As a result, domestic and cross-border deals have demonstrated growth in deal values and number of deals. Privately owned enterprises (POE) and nonlisted companies also got a chance to enter into the M&As market in China.

Given the political reform and the support for M&A activity by the Chinese government in 2015, the domestic M&A transactions achieved a sharp increase and

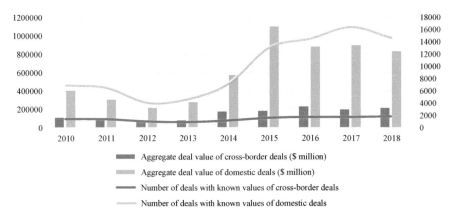

Fig. 3 Deal value and number of M&A transactions from 2010 to 2018 in China, in million US dollars

hit record highs both in terms of deal number and value. Then with the in-depth promotion of the "Belt and Road Initiative," the scale of overseas M&As activity by Chinese companies has been growing quickly during 2015–2016. However, the M&As market slightly slowed down mainly driven by tighter credit conditions and the changes in outbound investment policies in 2017. The policy-driven trend is that Chinese investors become more cautious about global trade uncertainties and focused more on the domestic M&As market. In 2015, the deal value of domestic transactions firstly broke the historical record in the last decade. In 2018, although Chinese bidders have faced financing difficulties, there are still big demands for investors to acquire new technologies by M&As, especially in the following fields such as advanced manufacturing, emerging information technology, and biological medicine (PEdaily 2018). The largest domestic M&A transaction in 2018 is that Alibaba Group Holding Ltd. spent $9.5 billion to get the full control of fast-growing food delivery startup Ele.me to enter to one of the most potential local service markets in China. In addition, under the influence of stock market volatility and the government's policies, domestic M&A transactions are seen as an important means of protecting capital and maintaining operations.

Starting with natural resources and energy in the early 2000s, the industrial profile of cross-border M&A deals enlarged in several stages. The first stage of cross-border M&As was related to Chinese SOEs investing overseas with the support of the government in upstream sectors including raw materials, oil fields, and mines. Then from 2005 to 2013, investors set their sights on sectors such as energy and basic materials, which were considered the most promising areas in that period. After 2013, with the rapid development of technology, cross-border deals in China became more diversified. Chinese bidders started to focus on developing international brands, introducing advanced technology, enhancing innovation capabilities, and increasing market share by M&As transactions (McKinsey's China Globalization Service Line 2017).

Chinese SOEs and POEs positively respond to the "going out" policy under the "Belt and Road Initiative," where mining, infrastructure, and gas became very important industries. From 2015 to 2017, Chinese investors have occupied a major position in the transactions completed by countries along the "Belt and Road." In 2017, private enterprises participated in 63% deals (DealGlobe 2018). There are some typical deals that represent the cross-border M&A activity along the "Belt and Road." In Russia, CEFC China Energy spends $9.25 billion to get 14% share of Rosneft Oil. In Myanmar, the syndicate consisted of China's CITIC Group, China Harbour Engineering, TEDA Investment, China Merchants Holdings (Hong Kong), Yunnan Construction Engineering Group), and Charoen Pokphand Group acquired 70% stake of Kyauk Pyu Port by $5.1 billion. In India, Shanghai Fosun Pharma invested $1.1 billion to hold 74% stake of the Indian pharmaceutical company GlandPharma (Reuters 2017). It is worth noting that Chinese players shift their attention from US market to emerging capital markets because of the complicated political and trade relationship between China and USA, which to some degree provides more chances for the countries along the "Belt and Road Initiative."

3 M&As in India: Trends and Evidence

3.1 The M&As Market in India

Given the financial sector reforms that started in 1991, M&As are reasonably new in India and yet, with 388 deals amounting to nearly $65 billion in 2016, India accounted for about 10% of M&As value in Asia (ex-Japan). Although less than a fifth of China's M&A in value, this was up 90% from $36 billion the previous year, (Mergermarket 2016). Figure 4 shows that in 2010–2018 M&As market activity in India has experienced a considerable increase of 30% in terms of value (in dollars) and 25% in terms of quantity, with a peak of value in 2017.

Figure 5 highlights the breakdown of M&As by industry in India in 2018. For each industry, the graph shows its share in total deal number in 2018 on the left, and its share in total deal value in the right. Apart from other services, top five industries by quantity of transactions are chemicals, rubber, plastics and nonmetallic products and machinery and equipment, construction, and wholesale and retail trade. Two of them are also among highest value industries, coupled with banking and post and telecommunications industry. Wholesale and retail deals, though high in number, reach only 3.7% of total deal value and are not included in the top five.

Given the steep rise of M&As volumes in India, several aspects of Indian M&As have been analyzed by researchers. In this paragraph, we look at domestic, inbound, and outbound acquisitions in the following three subsections.

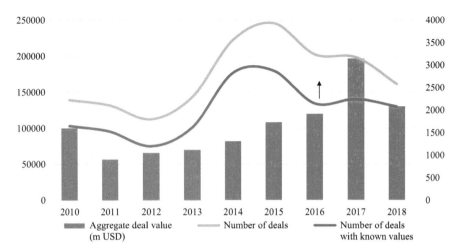

Fig. 4 Deal value and number of M&A transactions from 2010 to 2018 in India in million US dollars

3.2 Domestic M&A Activity

Which firms are more likely to initiate M&A activities? Empirical evidence shows that besides being larger, acquirers typically have higher cash flow, PE ratios, book value, liquid assets, and lower debt to total assets compared to target firms. The cash flow and net profit of target companies were on average about 25% and 19%, respectively, of the acquirers. The difference was less marked with long-term debt where the target's figures were about 80% of the acquirer's (Kumar and Rajib 2007). A drop in liquidity increased a company's chances of becoming a target.

How likely are hostile takeovers in India? Mathew (2007) examines the shareholding pattern of 500 Indian companies and predicted three reasons for a drop in hostile takeovers. A dominant position of founding shareholding; burdensome government approvals; and the provision in the Indian takeover code favoring promoters. Additionally, with higher growth in India and rising share prices, cheap targets are harder to find. This is different, however, during the slowdown phase of the business cycle.

Do M&As provide a likely entry route to India for foreign firms? Agarwal and Bhattacharjea (2008) focus on M&A regulations in India. Examining the Competition Act 2002 and its subsequent amendments, they find that as the entry barrier to India reduced owing to the free trade and cross-border economic cooperation agreements signed by India, new foreign firms are likely to enter the Indian market through acquisitions, reducing potential domestic competition in India. In their view, the ease of acquisition is likely to hurt innovation by small firms.

Do industry shocks affect merger activities? Agarwal and Bhattacharjea (2006) use a larger timespan, 1973–2003, and identified three subperiods of merger activities in India—a low-intensity period 1973–1988, a moderate-intensity period

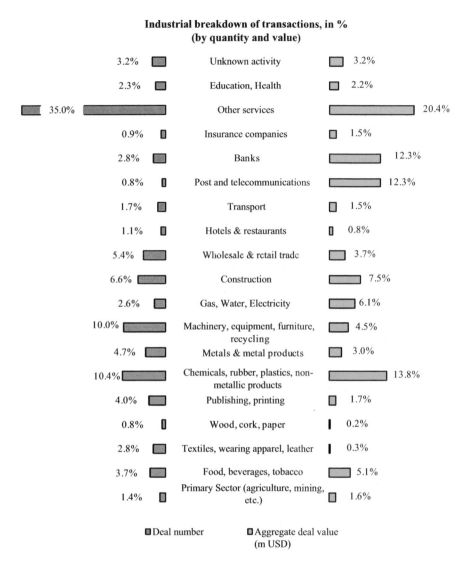

Industrial breakdown of transactions, in %
(by quantity and value)

	Deal number		Aggregate deal value
Unknown activity	3.2%		3.2%
Education, Health	2.3%		2.2%
Other services	35.0%		20.4%
Insurance companies	0.9%		1.5%
Banks	2.8%		12.3%
Post and telecommunications	0.8%		12.3%
Transport	1.7%		1.5%
Hotels & restaurants	1.1%		0.8%
Wholesale & retail trade	5.4%		3.7%
Construction	6.6%		7.5%
Gas, Water, Electricity	2.6%		6.1%
Machinery, equipment, furniture, recycling	10.0%		4.5%
Metals & metal products	4.7%		3.0%
Chemicals, rubber, plastics, non-metallic products	10.4%		13.8%
Publishing, printing	4.0%		1.7%
Wood, cork, paper	0.8%		0.2%
Textiles, wearing apparel, leather	2.8%		0.3%
Food, beverages, tobacco	3.7%		5.1%
Primary Sector (agriculture, mining, etc.)	1.4%		1.6%

☐ Deal number   ☐ Aggregate deal value
(m USD)

Fig. 5 Breakdown of M&A by industry in India in 2018 (deal number and value)

1988–1994, and a high-intensity period 1995–2001—demonstrating a wave in the clustering of mergers in a few industries.

The effects of acquisitions have received as much attention as the determinants. For instance, Pawaskar (2001) concludes that mergers do not create monopolies. Using a sample of 36 Indian mergers 1992–1995, he finds that a firm with above average industry performance acquiring a firm with lower than industry average profitability and size does not lead to any profitability improvement.

Beena (2008) analyzed financial ratios of acquirers in India, 1995–2000. She finds no improvement in postacquisition profitability ratios of acquirers. The capacity utilization ratio and R&D intensity decline after acquisitions. Acquirers typically raised dividends to win shareholder support after the acquisition. The financial structure also changes noticeably during the period, with a decline in external funding confirming the "pecking order" theory of capital raising.

Bhaumik and Selarka (2012) examine Indian M&As over half a century, 1954–2004, to analyze the impact of owner concentration on the post-M&A performance of firms. Their result suggests that the post-M&A performance of companies may improve if a significant portion of its ownership is in the hands of company directors but not if domestic promoters holding the largest share.

The Indian M&As landscape has also witnessed several major acquisitions of Indian companies by foreign MNCs as part of their entry strategy into India. A few of the landmark acquisitions in this category over the years include the 2004 IBM takeover of the BPO service provider Daksh e-Services valued at $130–170 million. In 2007, the Vodafone Group acquired the controlling interest of 67% held by Li Ka Shing Holdings in Hutchison-Essar for $11.1 billion and then bought out the remainder 33% from Essar Group for $5 billion. In 2008, Daiichi-Sankyo of Japan acquired, in two stages, the Indian pharmaceutical company Ranbaxy for $7 billion. The $12.9 billion Rosneft-Essar Oil deal, completed in 2017, provided a crude oil window out of Russia for the oil giant and much needed cash for the debt-strapped Essar group.

US-India cross-border acquisitions started around 1995, rose steadily till 2000, and then declined after the dot.com bubble burst, recovering its 2000 levels only in 2006. Karels et al. (2011), focusing exclusively on the US-India cross-border acquisition activity in both directions, note that US firms suffer significant losses on the announcement of Indian acquisitions of Indian targets, which realize significant gains on the announcement. The reverse is asymmetric. Publicly traded Indian acquirers of US targets realize insignificant or significant positive returns on their announcement of acquisitions of US firms, depending upon whether the targets are publicly traded or privately held, respectively. The gains for the publicly traded US targets are insignificant (Karels et al. 2011). Cash-rich firms were the frequent targets in cross-border acquisitions in India. In many cases, cross-border acquisitions contributed to an increase in acquirer's market value on announcement (Nagano and Yuan 2013).

Figure 6 illustrates the development of domestic and cross-border M&A market in India. The share of domestic deals, representing the majority of deals in India, has reduced slightly from 78.4% in 2010 to 77.8% in 2018. Their quantity has increased by 27.5% over last 8 years. The aggregate value of domestic deals has been fluctuating over 2010–2017, followed by a sharp increase in 2018. The number of cross-border deals has increased similarly, by 31.4% over 2010–2018, while the aggregate value increased by only 2.4%.

Of the three kinds of acquisitions, outbound ones, that is the acquisition of foreign targets by Indian companies, have by far captured the maximum research interest. Liberalization, starting in 1991, has effectively exposed the Indian market to foreign

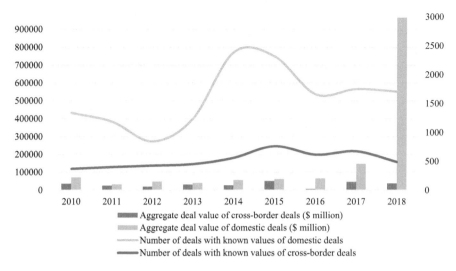

Fig. 6 Deal value and number of M&A transactions from 2010 to 2018 in India, in million US dollars

competition, gradually reducing the barriers to foreign investment in the country. Indian businesses, particularly large diversified Indian business groups, czars of their protected territories for decades, have been quick to realize that they have to change strategies to survive in the new setting. Some, like Reliance, have stuck to their "Indian game," leveraging their experience to take on the foreign competition in one of the fastest-growing large markets of the world. Others, especially India's revered Tata group, see the viability of their business on a global scale and have launched aggressive globalization initiatives. Their global expansion drives have typically used the M&A route to rapidly create a global presence at times buying iconic global brands like the Tetley Tea or the Land Rover Jaguar of the UK or a steel giant like Corus, much greater in size than its Indian acquirer.

Nayyar (2008) provides one of the earliest accounts of the new wave of outbound FDI and M&A. The share of developing countries as a source of FDI rose from 8.3% in 1990 to 13.5% in 2000 and fell to 11.9% in 2005. For India, the rise was even more dramatic, particularly in the new millennium, from $124 million in 1990 to $1859 million in 2000 and almost $10 billion in 2005. India's share in the total stock of outward FDI from developing countries rose from a negligible 0.08% in 1990 to 0.215 in 2000 and 0.755 in 2005. As part of India's GDP, it grew from negligible in 1990 to 1.25 in 2005. The count of MNCs headquartered in five selected developing countries—Brazil, China, Hong Kong, India, and Korea—increased from 2681 in the early 1990s to 14,762 in the early 2000s, by as much as 451%: a revealing statistics even after taking into account the base effect. The climb for India was even more dramatic, from 187 in the early 1990s to 1700 in the early 2000s, a more than eightfold increase. The vehicle of choice of this outward FDI was acquisitions.

Market access for exports seemed to be particularly important in the pharmaceuticals and automotive sectors. Horizontal, in part vertical, integration was particularly important in the steel (Tata Corus) and chemicals sectors. Service delivery seemed to matter most in IT, computer software, and business process outsourcing. The capture of international brand names (Tetley tea, Daewoo motors, Thomson SA, RPG Aventis) was particularly important in the consumer goods and pharmaceuticals sectors. Access to technology was key in the energy, telecommunications, semiconductor, and seed-technologies. Unlike the majority of acquisitions worldwide, but in keeping with India's domestic M&As experience, Indian overseas acquisitions yield positive abnormal returns on average. Returns are substantially higher for developed country targets (Gubbi et al. 2010). Gubbi et al. (2010) explain these returns in the international context using organization learning and the creation of dynamic capabilities. In developed country targets, Indian acquirers seek strategic assets denied to them at home by institutional and market constraints. The acquisitions are therefore part of a series of aggressive, risk-taking expansionary measures to achieve global competitiveness, often not path-dependent nor evolutionary, and they use acquisitions as a shortcut to capability. Hence, foreign acquisitions provide a significant, tangible value for emerging economy firms outweighing many of its challenges.

What helps Indian firms to venture out? Chittoor et al. (2015) argue that factors that help to reduce the perceived risks of overseas acquisitions play a critical role in encouraging acquisitions. They show that the prior experience of the CEO matters. Companies with large controlling shareholding, typically by the promoters, are more likely to make overseas acquisitions. The presence of a foreign institutional investor raises the chances too, presumably by helping companies to raise funds and increase knowledge about foreign targets. Business group affiliation plays a positive role in aiding a firm's internationalization from exports to FDI (Gaur and Kumar 2009). Are cross-border M&As asset augmenting or asset exploiting in their acquisitive behavior? The empirical evidence on Indian MNEs supports the conventional asset exploitation view (Buckley et al. 2016). Late liberalization and the large home market (Munjal et al. 2013) allow many Indian firms to earn monopolistic rents and, thus, home market features have shaped the firm-specific advantages of these acquirers. Several cases in M&A deals in India suggest that while Western companies use M&A to promote efficiency or immediate growth through cost reduction, emerging country giants, for example, Hindalco, acquire companies for more strategic reasons, to obtain technologies, competencies, and knowledge essential for their strategy. During the 2000s, Hindalco made a series of increasingly bigger and further-off acquisitions, leading to sizeable cross-border deals, each of which helped it acquire new competencies essential to its goal of global leadership by expanding its aluminum business, climbing up the value chain of products, and expanding its marketing reach around the world. Their key strategic approach toward finding the right "fit" for targets was identifying key weaknesses in their company and finding a target company capable of filling the gap. Given their clear long-term vision, they are prepared to give the target time to pay off.

4 M&As in Brazil

4.1 The M&A Market in Brazil

In line with globalization, Brazil unleashed a broad process of transformational change, breaking the paradigm of a nationalized and protected economy. The framework of changes was then complemented by macroeconomic fundamentals that have been modified, allowing currency stabilization, constitutional reforms of liberalizing direction, deregulation of markets, and therefore the predisposition to alliances, associations, and mergers and acquisitions. The twenty-first century brought changes of political power without changes in the economic strategy. The maintenance of the state-business disengagement strategy, economic openness, and the stimulation of FDI supported the growing M&As wave in Brazil that was only momentarily reversed due to the world crisis, but came back to hit record levels.

Figure 7 illustrates the evolution of M&As activity in Brazil over 2010–2018. Overall it has slowed down both in terms of deal quantity (−37%) and aggregate value (−71%) of deals. However, since 2016, there has been a period of slow recovery.

Research by PwC points out that the Brazilian market is dominated by smaller transactions on average about $100 million each, and they represent 73% of the 218 deals (PwC 2015). Table 2 highlights the variations in deal volumes compared to the changes in GDP. This was due to the presence of both political and economic uncertainties (increased inflation, public debt, low growth) and the decline in the Brazilian economy. When comparing the variation in the number of M&A and the variation of the Brazilian Gross Domestic Product (GDP), growth in both indexes in

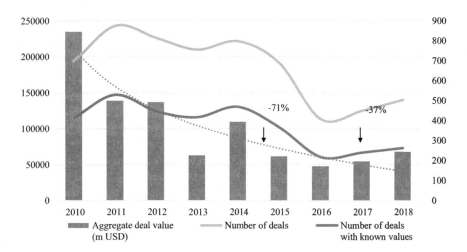

Fig. 7 Deal value and number of M&A in Brazil from 2010 to 2018, in million US dollars

Table 2 M&A and GDP variation

Year	M&A variation in Brazil (%)	GDP variation (%)
2006	47	4
2007	26	6,1
2008	−11	5,2
2009	0	−0,3
2010	24	7,5
2011	−6	2,7
2012	3	1
2013	5	2,3
2014	8	0,1
2015	−16	−3,8

Source: PwC (2015)

the years 2006, 2007, 2010, and 2012 to 2014. In 2008, the country continued to grow despite the global crisis that suggests that it has had a negative impact on the number of M&A in Brazil. In 2009, there was a slight negative change in GDP and the number of operations remained the same as in 2008. In 2011, there was a small positive change in GDP, but the number of transactions was reduced. In 2014 and 2015 M&As were concentrated in information technology, auxiliary services, finance, retail, and public services (PwC 2015).

With 51% of the transactions concluded in Brazil, the year of 2015 presented the leadership of foreign investments in the country, representing a 1% increase in relation to the number of transactions in the year 2014. This behavior possibly reflects the moment lived by the Brazilian economy, with political uncertainties and the depreciation of the Brazilian currency. Of the 310 operations with foreign investment, countries such as the USA, the UK, and Japan represent 48% interest in Brazilian assets. It should be noted that the majority acquisitions represent 46% of the transaction profile chosen by the investor in the Brazilian market, followed by minority purchases with 44% of the number of transactions disclosed in 2015.

Deloitte (2015) identified several factors for deal success, on the basis of interviews of more than 80 executives who performed M&As transactions in Brazil from 2012 to 2015. When asked about synergies, only 43% of the executives indicated that they had met their synergy goals, while 18% said they did not achieve them; 17% of the respondents were not sure if they had achieved their goals or had not set synergy goals. The executives reported that upon completion of the transaction, it took on average 2 years to achieve the integration synergy targets, while the US average was 6 months. The value of the transaction and the size of the target company or buyer, national or international operation, among others, had no substantial relationship with the success of the integration. Despite the trend toward greater maturity in how companies have been integrating in recent years (95% of respondents said they performed due diligence on the acquired company and involved external experts such as consultants, lawyers, and investment banks), 18% of the transactions were considered unsuccessful, and 35% of the respondents claimed not to have captured or measured synergies. An important aspect was the importance of assigning a project team with the appropriate skills after the completion of the transaction. Despite the invaluable role of external experts, nothing can replace the importance of having a strong and dedicated internal team to accelerate integration and leverage synergies.

Despite the decline in the number of deals in 2016, due to the uncertainties in the Brazilian economy, the technology subsector was, for the third consecutive year, the most active. In 2016, 202 transactions in this sector were recorded, representing an increase of 34% over the previous year. Deals in the financial and insurance, and Internet subsectors increased by 30% and 1%, respectively, compared to 2015. 2016 was also marked by the slowdown in these sectors of transactions involving the acquisition of Brazilian companies by foreign companies. There were 68 transactions compared to 82 in 2015. As in the previous year, US companies were the ones that invested most in Brazilian businesses in 2016.

Figure 8 illustrates the split of M&As activity by industry. For each industry, the graph shows its share in total deal number in 2018 on the left, and its share in total deal value in the right. Apart from other services, top five industries by quantity of M&As transactions are utilities, such as gas, water and electricity, chemicals, rubber, plastics and nonmetallic products, primary sector (agriculture and mining), machinery and equipment, and wholesale and retail trade. Highest value deals are in the primary sector and wholesale and retail trade, coupled with wood, cork, and paper sector, where only six deals make 10.5% of all deal values in Brazil in 2018. Other services, though representing 33% of all deals in number, only make 14% of deal value.

Figure 9 provides the data on the development of domestic and cross-border M&As market in Brazil. The share of domestic deals, representing the majority of deals in Brazil, decreased from 66.7% in 2010 to 59.7% in 2018. The aggregate value, as well as the number of domestic deals has been declining over the time period. The number of cross-border deals has also decreased, by 22% over 2010–2018, while the aggregate value decreased by 64%. After a general decline in 2016, however, M&As market was experiencing a slow recovery both in terms of value and deal quantity.

The Boston Consulting Group (BCG 2017) found that Brazilian publicly traded companies that made M&As in the last 20 years on average have a better return to shareholders than those who pursued organic growth alone. After analyzing more than a thousand M&As between 1995 and 2016 by 217 listed companies, they found that these companies had an average annual growth of 17.9% in shareholder return, compared to 14.6% for other companies. The companies that made M&As transactions had an average annual increase in net revenue of 16.3%, compared to 9.4% for the others. EBIDTA advanced on average 16.8% in the first group and 8.8% in the second.

Based on TTRecord (2017), in the first half of 2017, 300 transactions were announced, 5% above the volume registered in the same period of 2016, but a sharp recession and the subsequent stricter legal and regulatory scrutiny may slow M&As deals in Brazil, compounding the impact of the recession and political turmoil that is keeping buyers and sellers at odds over valuations. In recent months,

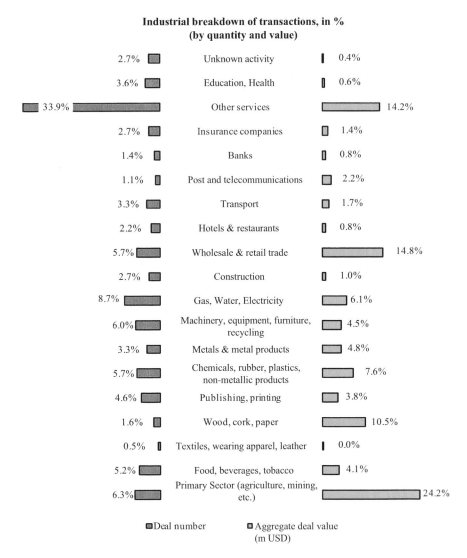

Fig. 8 Breakdown of M&A by industry in Brazil in 2018 (deal number and deal value)

trade unions and citizen advocacy groups have increased pressure on industry and federal auditors to stop state asset sales aimed at cutting Brazil's debt. More companies tapped antitrust authorities to review rival industry tie-ups, putting the brakes on several deals. For example, the Brazilian federal audit court (TCU) is asking for more transparent transaction terms. Legal and regulatory hurdles along with a growing call for compliance have become day-to-day features, making the M&As more challenging for buyers and sellers in Brazil.

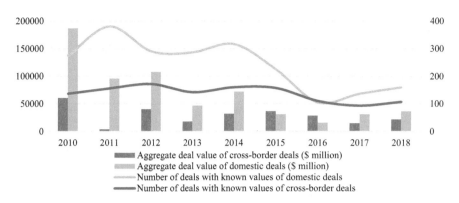

Fig. 9 Deal value and number of M&A transactions from 2010 to 2018 in Brazil, in $ million

5 The M&A Market in Russia

5.1 M&As Market in Russia

With vast natural resources and an ever-growing market, corporate takeovers in Russia have traditionally attracted domestic and foreign investors. However, the economic crisis in 2014, the Western sanctions imposed on Russia together with falling oil prices in the world markets have significantly changed the landscape of the Russian M&As market.

The M&As market in Russia is still very small as compared to the global market for corporate control: as of the end of 2018, its share is less than 1% in terms of the value and about 2% in terms of the number of deals announced. However, the Russian market generally resembles those of the emerging European economies. The number of deals announced in emerging Europe demonstrates slight growth after 5 years of decrease (2596 deals in 2012, 1985 deals in 2016 and 2093 in 2018) together with the growth worldwide (40,734 deals in 2012 and 48,577 deals in 2018) (Emerging Europe M&A Report 2016/17 2017; Emerging Europe M&A Report 2018/19 2019).

Figure 10 shows that the same trend can be seen in the Russian market: the number of the deals announced fell for the fourth successive year[2] although in 2018, the Russian market enjoyed the highest number of deals in Emerging Europe (Emerging Europe M&A Report 2018/19 2019). During the last 9 years, the average number of deals announced per year was 3084 with the highest number in 2010 (5412 deals) and the lowest in 2017 and 2018 (2261 and 1984 deals, respectively). In 2018, the Russian market announced 1984 deals, which is more than 60% lower than in 2010. On average, the number of transactions decreased 12% per year during 2010–2018. The drop in the market is expected to continue as the Russian

---

[2]The transaction volume figure refers to the number of deals announced irrespective of the fact whether or not a value of the deal is disclosed.

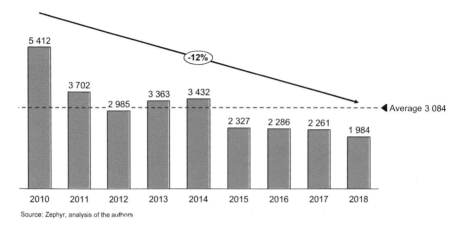

Source: Zephyr, analysis of the authors

Fig. 10 Number of mergers and acquisitions in Russia

Value of M&A transactions in Russia, in bln USD

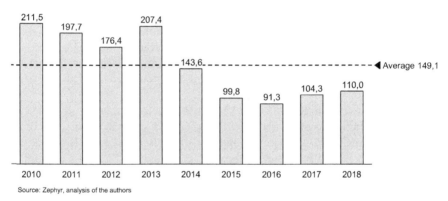

Source: Zephyr, analysis of the authors

Fig. 11 Value of M&As transactions in Russia, in $ billion

government has no large privatization plans till 2021 (Emerging Europe M&A Report 2018/19 2019). The M&As market is mainly driven by state-owned companies.

The known value of the transactions (see Fig. 11) decreased starting from 2013 by approximately 12% per year. In 2005, the share of the ten largest deals was more than 70% of the overall market; in 2015, their share did not exceed 40% of the market and, in 2016, was approximately 54%. The decrease of the volume may be explained by low commodity prices and limited access to financial resources in metallurgy and mining, economic sanctions against Russia and low oil prices, as well as governmental restrictions imposed on tariff growth in the energy and utilities sector.

Fig. 12 Key characteristics of the Russian M&A market

The distribution of the deals by sector became more homogeneous: in 2005, approximately 80% of the overall deals were in oil and gas, mining, and metallurgy sectors, and they were 65% in 2016 and already less than 30% in 2017. We can also observe growing interest in such sectors as agriculture, food, and manufacturing, which are actively supported by the localization program of the Russian government implemented against the imposed economic sanctions.

5.2   M&As Waves in Russia

Since 1992 when Russia began its transformation toward a market-based economy, we can identify five key waves in the Russian M&As summarized in Fig. 12. The market environment that evolved after privatization was aimed at the creation of the institute of private property in Russia. The first M&As wave is considered to last from 1992 to 1997, with the key motive of mergers and acquisitions being political rather than economic, which makes the value of the deals unrepresentative. This period gave birth to the majority of the largest Russian corporations such as Sibneft and Norisk Nickel.

The second wave or the wave of development (1998–2002) is characterized by property redistribution after the political and economic crisis of 1998 and the average value of deals was $5 billion per year. During this wave, the market witnessed unfriendly or hostile and speculative transactions (M&As in Russia 2012, 2013). Hostile acquisitions have a very different meaning in Russia: legislative gaps and numerous imperfections of M&As regulations, as well as corruption stipulated the predominance of illegal takeovers or raiding. Raiding could be implemented through political or judicial pressure or the use of force (Radygin and Jentov 2010). As a result, firms valued at $1 billion could be bought for only several million: for example, during the second wave, the largest in Russia automobile enterprise "ZIL" was acquired for $4 million dollars and the large transport machinery enterprise "Uralmash" for $3.72 million.

The third wave or the period of active growth (2003–2007) of the Russian M&As market began in 2003 when the total value was 18.5 billion. The period witnessed the active participation of governmental authorities in M&A transactions together with a gradual increase of transparency, specifically through the use of the stock market. One of the specific features of the M&As market in Russia during this period was the high number of transactions through the use of offshores.

Megadeals appeared during the third wave. The largest deal of this period was the deal that resulted in the creation of TNK-BP when the assets of the Tyumen oil company and the assets of British Petroleum in Russia and Ukraine were combined. By 2005, when the Russian market for corporate control evidenced the purchase of 73% of shares of large oil company Sibneft, the average annual value of the deal was $40.5 billion. The development of the Russian M&As market during this wave slowed down together with the international M&As market due to the global financial crisis.

The fourth wave (2008–2014) took place between the two crises (world financial and economic crisis of 2007–2008 and the Russian internal political and economic crisis of 2014). During this period, the volume of purchases of Russian assets by foreign players and domestic M&As dramatically shrank. This stage encouraged insider activities primarily by large shareholders and managers: for example, some Russian companies such as Norilsk Nickel or MTS repurchased their shares on the open market in 2008.

The fifth wave (2015 up to till present) is the contemporary period. The market has adjusted to the new economic conditions with limited access to foreign finance, low oil prices, and the ruble depreciation, resulting in relative increase in price of foreign assets for Russian investors. Given the plans and intentions of the Russian government, three industries are the most promising in terms of investment and M&As in the next several years in Russia: oil and gas, agriculture, and finance and banking (Russian M&A overview 2016, 2017).

5.3 What Is Typical for the M&As Market in Russia?

The industrial breakdown of the Russian M&As landscape resembles the structure of the national economy. The market is dominated by transactions in the primary sector of the economy involved in extraction of natural resources (See Fig. 13). The purchase of 9.9% of "Yamal SPG" of the Russian company Novatek by the Chinese company Silk Road Fund Co. was the largest deal in 2015. In 2016, the three largest deals were also in the oil and gas industry: the acquisition of 19.5% of Rosneft, the

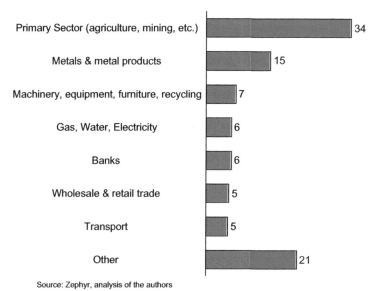

Industrial breakdown of transactions, 2018, in % (by value)

Sector	%
Primary Sector (agriculture, mining, etc.)	34
Metals & metal products	15
Machinery, equipment, furniture, recycling	7
Gas, Water, Electricity	6
Banks	6
Wholesale & retail trade	5
Transport	5
Other	21

Source: Zephyr, analysis of the authors

Fig. 13 Industrial breakdown of transactions

purchase of minority stakes of the Indian firm Essar Oil, and the privatization of Bashneft. In 2017, Glencore and the Qatari sovereign fund sold 14.2% of the shares of the oil company Rosneft that turned out to be the largest transaction in the Russian M&A market.

Internal restructuring is likely to stand behind transactions in the oil and gas sector. Russian players are likely to sell their shares to increase efficiency of operations and enhance competitiveness. Given decreasing expenditures on geologic exploration in most global oil and gas giants, partnerships with Russian firms present a good opportunity to substitute for oil and gas reserves and production (Russian M&As overview 2016, 2017).

Consolidation continues to drive M&As activity. In 2010, the majority of the transactions for industry consolidation took place in the telecoms and media, oil and gas, metallurgy, and mining sectors, which reflected the core specifics of the Russian economy. In 2016–2017, industry consolidation remained the key motive of transactions in the oil and gas, metallurgy and mining, construction, and real estate sectors, as well as technology and innovations. The situation with the telecommunication sector confirms the fact that the market is currently consolidated and its growth potential is significantly limited (Russia. Barometr uverennosti kompanij 2017).

Although this trend is likely to continue in the future, new opportunities may appear in some other industrial sectors, which are actively supported by governmental programs such as agriculture and services. The sanctions against food exports from European countries and the USA to Russia encouraged internal growth in the Russian agricultural sector, resulting in a 65% increase in M&A, compared to the previous period. In 2016, AFK Systema completed the acquisition of the vegetable producer "Yuzhniy" and the farm "Progress," and announced several additional transactions, which would give the company 100,000 ha of agricultural lands (Russian M&A overview 2016, 2017).

Transactions in various industrial sectors are characterized by certain features, which are typical for this specific industry in Russia. The majority of the acquisitions in metallurgy are vertical for the purpose of integrating primary producers with end-users of the manufactured products. The key goal of acquisitions in the food manufacturing or finance industries is diversification or entry into new markets.

Financing sources of the M&A market in Russia are mainly driven by Middle Eastern and Asian capital: in 2016, more than 80% of the deals were announced by investors from these regions. For example, during the last several years, investments from India tripled and as of the beginning of 2017 were $4,3 billion. We can also expect new investments from China in the context of China's ambitious Belt and Road Initiative under which China is planning to pour money into railroads, highways, energy, and other projects on the territory of Russia and territories of the former Soviet states such as Kazakhstan and Uzbekistan.[3] Western investors gradually increase their presence in the Russian market: in 2017, Schlumberger acquired 51% of the shares of Eurasia Drilling Company (Russian M&As overview 2017).

The low and insufficient level of information transparency, as well as nondisclosure of information regarding the value of deals have always been specific features of the market for corporate control in Russia. At present the transparency of the M&As market is gradually increasing. In 2005, information was available only for 30% of the deals; in 2014, this proportion increased to more than 70%. The increase could be explained by the improvement of corporate governance and financial information disclosure. However, the quality of financial information about the deals is still not sufficient; market participants are still trying to close deals without using financial expertise.

5.4 Domestic and Cross-Border Deals in Russia

The Russian market for corporate control has traditionally been dominated by inbound transactions. In 2012 and 2013, the share of domestic deals was 39 and 18%, respectively, in the total market of mergers and acquisitions in Russia (see Fig. 14). From 2014, the share of domestic deals gradually increased, although the volume of domestic deals in 2017 was close to the level of 2014. One of the major

---

[3]See, for example, Kottasova I. Russia gets investment from China while sanctions keep U.S. off limits. CNN money, July 7, 2017.

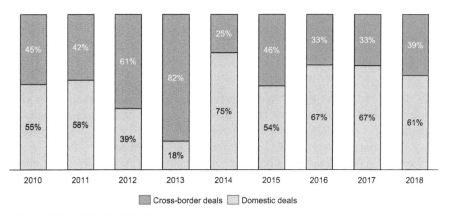

Fig. 14 Russian M&As market by transaction type, in percentage

reasons why domestic acquisitions dominate the market is the continuation of the imposed Western sanctions.

Trends of the last several years indicate that the interest of Russian investors is no longer aimed at the acquisition of inbound oil and gas assets. Russian investors are moving from oil and gas and metallurgy to other industries such as real estate and construction, agriculture, chemical. In 2017, there were about 20% domestic deals in the oil and gas sector compared to 93% in 2013. Local investors are currently focused on real estate and construction, energy and utilities, technology, and innovations. One of the reasons is the increased confidence with regards to the policies of the Russian government in these particular sectors.

The market for cross-border mergers and acquisitions seems to be recovering after the turbulence of 2014. The share of Russian assets acquired by foreign buyers is growing (approximately 34% versus 28% in 2016 and 2017 respectively). The share of foreign assets acquired by Russian firms decreased dramatically in 2012–2013, increased and remained unstable during 2014–2017. This indicates the uncertainty and caution of foreign investors with regards to the Russian M&As market (Russian M&As overview 2017).

The Russian oil and gas sector dominates the interests of foreign investors: the overall value of 2017 deals was about $14 billion. The same situation is true for the deals accomplished by Russian firms to acquire foreign assets although in 2017, the overall amount of transactions decreased to $0,5 billion. Foreign investors are also interested in the Russian construction, mining and energy, and utilities sector.

Russian firms acquiring foreign assets are mainly interested in assets in the innovations and technology, retail, and transportation industries.

6 Conclusion

The overview of the trends in the largest markets provides several important observations. The BRIC countries enjoyed the significant and even remarkable growth along with decline stages of M&As activity exploring different types of deals. The strategic deals in BRIC group tend to be undertaken in a pattern of waves mostly driven by a series of institutional and regulatory reforms by the governments of China, India, Brazil, and Russia. The origin of these waves differs from the firms in developed markets where they are mostly driven by the shifts in the competitive forces, the growing role of knowledge, and innovations.

Given the existence of M&As waves, at the current stage of this activity, the firms from BRIC group display rather different acquisition preferences. The Chinese firms mostly search for targets from developed markets as compared to other BRIC group firms. The firms from India prefer the targets from other emerging markets along with the firms from internal capital market. Russian firms are mostly focused on domestic targets. At the latest M&A wave, the preferences in industrial profiles that the firms follow in their strategies for the deals have changed. In the Russian domestic market, the firms are switching to real estate and construction, retail, energy and utilities, pharmaceuticals, and financial services sector. In their cross-border strategies, Russian firms are mainly focused on assets in the construction and telecommunication industries. Given the rapid development of technology, the Chinese firms became more diversified in domestic as well as in cross-border M&As deals. Their investments in high-tech businesses, financial institutions, manufacturing, and real estate grew rapidly compared to such traditional spheres of strategic deals, as energy production, and materials. Indian firms made a series of sizeable cross-border deals focused on new competencies to gain global leadership in aluminum business, consumer goods, and retail. Based on the key weaknesses in their companies, they searched for strategic assets capable to overcome domestic institutional and market constraints. Similar to the Chinese acquirers, Indian firms displayed aggressive and risk-taking strategies in new markets, which in many cases are not path-dependent.

In addition, the active participation of SOEs is the remarkable original feature of strategic deals in BRIC group. SOEs demonstrated significant roles in both domestic and cross-border M&As. In China, they have become the most active players in the global market. Chinese SOEs focus on the energy and natural resource sectors, as compared to the private firms, which exhibit preferences toward technological and innovative targets.

The current state of the art in M&As deals and their performance impact in the firms from BRIC group depend on the above-mentioned trends. The drivers behind the deals, the value creation effects, and the comparative picture in value creation or destruction between European and emerging markets and within the BRIC group itself are analyzed in the following chapters.

References

Agarwal, M., & Bhattacharjea, A. (2006). Mergers in India. A response to regulatory shocks. *Emerging Markets Finance and Trade, 42*(3), 46–65.

Agarwal, M., & Bhattacharjea, A. (2008). Are merger regulations diluting parliamentary intent? *Economic and Political Weekly*, 10–13.

BCG The Boston Consulting Group. (2017). *M&A "Made in Brazil": análise da geração de valor em duas décadas de fusões e aquisições no Brasil* (M&A "Made in Brazil": Analysis of the generation of value in two decades of mergers and acquisitions in Brazil). Retrieved from http://image-src.bcg.com/Images/M-A-Made-In-Brazil_tcm15-170565.pdf

Beena, P. (2008). Trends and perspectives on corporate mergers in contemporary India. *Economic and Political Weekly*, 48–56.

Bhaumik, S. K., & Selarka, E. (2012). Does ownership concentration improve M&A outcomes in emerging markets? Evidence from India. *Journal of Corporate Finance, 18*(4), 717–726.

Bloomberg. (2018). *Bloomberg China M&A dealer advisor ranking|China M&A market overall year-end* [online]. Retrieved from https://mp.weixin.qq.com/s?__biz=MzA5MDUyMjgyMw%3D%3D&chksm=8bf11244bc869b527a1252ae07bd99a8c048d9981581ac2390a5b5c57a8d3d38a20f01380117&idx=1&mid=2651842540&scene=0&sn=8a23265305cc655aa074e81cd4e27507

Buckley, P. J., Munjal, S., Enderwick, P., & Forsans, N. (2016). Cross-border acquisitions by Indian multinationals: Asset exploitation or asset augmentation? *International Business Review, 25*, 986–996.

Büttner, L., & Meckl, R. (2017). M&A due diligence in China—Institutional framework, corporate practice and empirical evidence. *American Journal of Industrial and Business Management, 7* (08), 998.

Chittoor, R., Aulakh, P. S., & Ray, S. (2015). What drives overseas acquisitions by Indian firms? A behavioral risk-taking perspective. *Management International Review, 55*(2), 255–275.

Deloitte. (2015). *Pesquisa de Integração Brasil 2015 – Entendendo os desafios para maximizar o investimento em M&A (Brazil 2015 integration research project - Understanding the challenges to maximize investment in M&A)* [online]. Retrieved from https://www2.deloitte.com/content/dam/Deloitte/br/Documents/mergers-acquisitions/Pesquisa-de-Integracao-Brasil-2015.pdf

Deloitte. (2017). *China M&A round-up: Keeping pace, marking milestone* [online], Volume 9. Retrieved from https://www2.deloitte.com/content/dam/Deloitte/us/Documents/mergers-acqisitions/us-csg-chinamaroundup-september2017.pdf

Emerging Europe M&A Report 2016/17. (2017). CMS, January 2017.

Emerging Europe M&A Report 2018/19. (2019). CMS, January 2019.

Feng, L. (2018). *DealGlobe. 2018 DealGlobe special report on China cross-border M&A* [online]. Retrieved from http://en.dealglobe.com/doc/2018/06/2018%20DealGlobe%20Special%20Report%20on%20China%20Cross-Border%20M&A.pdf

Gaur, A. S., & Kumar, V. (2009). International diversification, business group affiliation and firm performance: Empirical evidence from India. *British Journal of Management, 20*(2), 172–186.

Genfu, F., & Linjiang, W. (2001). Empirical research on M&A performance of Chinese listed companies. *Economic Research*, (1), 54–61.

Gubbi, S. R., Aulakh, P. S., Ray, S., Sarkar, M. B., & Chittoor, R. (2010). Do international acquisitions by emerging-economy firms create shareholder value? The case of Indian firms. *Journal of International Business Studies, 41*(3), 397–418.

Karels, G. V., Lawrence, E., & Yu, J. (2011). Cross-border mergers and acquisitions between industrialized and developing countries: US and Indian merger activity. *International Journal of Banking and Finance, 8*(1), 35–58.

Kumar, B. R., & Rajib, P. (2007). Characteristics of merging firms in India: An empirical examination. *Vikalpa: The Journal for Decision Makers, 32*(1), 27–44.

M&A in Russia. (2012). *KPMG*, March 2013.

Mathew, S. J. (2007). Hostile takeovers in India: New prospects, challenges, and regulatory opportunities. *Columbia Business Law Review, 2007*(3), 800–843.

McKinsey's China Globalization Service Line. (2017). *A pocket guide to Chinese cross-border M&A.*[online]. Volume 1(2). Retrieved from http://mckinseychina.com/wp-content/uploads/2017/04/McKinsey_A-Pocket-Guide-to-Chinese-Cross-Border-MA-English.pdf

Mergermarket. (2016). *Global and regional M&A: Q1-Q4 2016 including financial advisors.* [online]. Retrieved from file:///C:/Users/User/Downloads/Global_and_regional_MA_activity_during_Q1Q4_2016_including_financial_advisor_league_tables_0.pdf

Munjal, S., Buckley, P. J., Enderwick, P., & Forsans, N. (2013). The growth trajectory of Indian MNEs. In C. Brautaset & C. Dent (Eds.), *The great diversity - trajectories of Asian development.* Wageningen: Wageningen Academic Press.

Nagano, M., & Yuan, Y. (2013). Cross-border acquisitions in a transition economy: Recent experiences of China and India. *Journal of Asian Economics, 24*(C), 66–79.

Nayyar, D. (2008). The internationalization of firms from India: Investment, mergers and acquisitions. *Oxford Development Studies, 36*(1), 111–131.

Pawaskar, V. (2001). Effect of mergers on corporate performance in India. *Vikalpa, 26*(1), 19.

PwC. (2015). Relatório de Pesquisa: Fusões e Aquisições no Brasil: dezembro 2015,*Research Report: Mergers and Acquisitions in Brazil: December 2015.* São Paulo: PwC [online]. Retrieved from http://www.active-ma.de/wp-content/uploads/2017/01/china_market_spot light_2017.pdf

Radygin, A., & Jentov, R. (2010). Rynok slijanij i pogloshhenij: novye teoreticheskie podhody. *Jekonomicheskaja politika, 5*, 67–91.

Reuters. (2017). *Brazil's M&A delas may slow this year because of stricter due diligence.* Retrieved from http://www.reuters.com/article/us-brazil-m-a-outlook/brazils-ma-deals-may-slow-this-year-because-of-stricter-due-diligence-idUSKBN14Q097. Accessed 27 Oct 2017.

Russia. Barometr uverennosti kompanij. (2017). *E&Y, July 2017.*

Russian M&A Review. (2016). *KPMG*, April 2017.

Russian M&A Review. (2017). *KPMG*, March 2018.

Russian M&A Review – 2008-2012. (2013). *Deal financing and market structure. Gazprombank*, February 2013.

The Economist Intelligence Unit. (2017). *China's supply-side structural reforms: Progress and outlook* [online]. *1*(4). Retrieved from http://www.andrewleunginternationalconsultants.com/files/chinas-supply-side-structural-reform-1.pdf

Transactional Track Record. (2017). *TTR deal tracker.* [online]. Retrieved August 7, 2017, from www.TTRecord.com

US. Chamber of Commerce. (2017). Made in China 2025: *Global ambitions built on local protections. International trade and investment* [online]. Volume 9. Retrieved from https://www.uschamber.com/sites/default/files/final_made_in_china_2025_report_full.pdf

White Case. (2017) *China's rise in global M&A: Here to stay* [online]. Retrieved from https://www.whitecase.com/news/chinas-rise-global-ma-here-stay

Xinxi, B. (2012). Analysis on the development process of M&A of Chinese listed enterprises. *Securities & Futures of China, 5*(1), 31–32.

Xiuzhi, Z. (2016). The process of acquisition & merger of enterprises and their development. *Journal of Beijing Union University (Humanities and Social Sciences), 4*(4), 71–75.

Yongming, C. (2007). Division of Chinese enterprise M&A process. *Corporate Finance,* (12), 62–64.

How M&A Deals Influence Corporate Performance in Developed and Emerging Capital Markets: A Review of Empirical Results in the Literature

Svetlana Grigorieva

Abstract This chapter surveys the recent trends in the literature on the performance of M&A deals in developed and emerging capital markets. This literature is voluminous, diverse and challenging. We focus on the transactions within one country— domestic M&As—in particular focusing on the methods that the researchers use to estimate whether M&A deals promote efficiency gains or not. We discuss the research instruments which allow an assessment of the effects of M&As on firm operating performance and on firm value. Analysing the results of latest empirical studies, we reveal that target shareholders gain significantly in M&A deals. The evidence suggests that in most cases, acquiring shareholders receive negative or insignificant returns in the short run in developed capital markets, while in emerging economies, acquiring shareholders mostly gain in M&A deals. Operating performance analysis reveals mixed results in developed and emerging capital markets, while the analysis of papers which use value performance indicators shows the destruction of company value due to M&As in developed and emerging capital markets. The review also analyses studies that examine the relationship between different methods.

Keywords Mergers and acquisitions · Value creation · Company performance · Accounting measures · Economic profit · Capital markets · Developed markets · Emerging markets

1 Introduction

Nowadays, mergers and acquisitions (M&As) are a key strategy for many firms in their attempt to adapt to the rapidly changing conditions of the external business environment. Recent decades have shown a dramatic burst in the number and

S. Grigorieva (✉)
Corporate Finance Center, School of Finance at National Research University Higher School of Economics, Moscow, Russia

© Springer Nature Switzerland AG 2020
I. Ivashkovskaya et al. (eds.), *Strategic Deals in Emerging Capital Markets*,
Advanced Studies in Emerging Markets Finance,
https://doi.org/10.1007/978-3-030-23850-6_2

volume of M&As worldwide. This rising M&A activity has led to intensive research into the impact of M&As on company performance. Theoretically, potential sources of value creation in M&A deals are the opportunity to achieve synergy effects, the introduction of a new and more efficient management team as a result of the deal, the reduction of management freedom to use cash flows for negative NPV projects and the ability to react quickly to changes in the regulatory environment and in technological innovation (Sharma and Ho 2002). The main sources of value destruction in M&As, which lead to the inability to meet or exceed financial objectives, mainly include overpayment for targets as a result of the acquirer's overoptimistic valuation of synergies, agency problems, the slow pace of post-merger integration and poor strategy (DePamphilis 2012).

A substantial body of academic literature continues to investigate whether M&A deals lead to value creation or destruction, but we still know little about the effects of M&A deals on shareholder wealth in different countries and the sources of value creation in acquisitions (Calipha et al. 2010; Thanos and Papadakis 2012; Yaghoubi et al. 2016a, b). Remaining the one of the most popular corporate strategies, M&A deals far from increase the performance of merged firms (Calipha et al. 2010; Papadakis and Thanos 2010; Schoenberg 2006). Recent meta-analysis failed to explain the paradox of growing M&A activity and their high rate of failure, indicating that there is no significant correlation identified between the most studies variables, which seem to have the great influence on M&A success, such as previous experience in acquisition, mode of payment, industry relatedness, type of acquired company, and the M&A success (Calipha et al. 2010; Christofi et al. 2017). Academic researchers and practitioners continue to seek out the factors that influence M&A performance, but results are still inconclusive, indicating the need for further research into acquisition performance and factors that influence the overall success of M&A deals.

In contrast to the previous studies, this chapter deals with domestic M&A transactions. Since there are significant differences in motivations, outcomes, success factors, integration problems, information asymmetry and diversification between cross-border and domestic acquisitions (Bris and Cabolis 2008; Genç 2016), a separate analysis of these two types of deals is needed.

Previous research and reviews mainly concentrate on the analysis of M&A strategies in developed economies, as a majority of transactions in the past 100 years have been from these countries (Zhu and Zhu 2016), while there is less analysis of M&A transactions in emerging capital markets in empirical studies and reviews. Since the specific features of emerging markets, such as imperfect institutional environment, corporate governance practices, the decisive role of government in business, and less efficient capital market, may influence the relation between benefits and costs in M&A deals, it is interesting to compare the effects of M&A deals on corporate performance in developed and emerging capital markets. This chapter addresses this comparison and identifies the main findings of studies on M&A performance in developed and emerging capital markets in short—and long-run periods. We review the results of empirical studies that employ the most widely used methods to assess the performance of M&A deals: event studies and accounting studies (Zollo and Meier 2008; Krishnakumar and Sethi 2012), and also discuss the findings of recent papers using value measures instead of accounting ones to gauge the post-merger impact on shareholder value. Separate attention is paid to research applying several methods, which give the authors an opportunity to reveal the relationship between their results, in addition to simple measurements of M&A performance. Thus, our main contribution to the literature is to take a step towards analysing the performance of domestic M&A deals and understanding whether the effects of M&A deals on corporate performance on short—and long-time horizon are similar in developed and emerging economies.

This literature review is organized as follows: Section 2 summarizes the results of latest empirical studies, examining the stock market reaction to the announcements of M&A deals in developed and emerging capital markets. Section 3 reviews the findings of recent research papers, focusing on the consequences of M&A deals on operating performance in the long-term. Section 4 discusses the results of empirical papers employing value performance measures to assess the value effects of M&A deals in long-term. Section 5 discusses the relationship between different methods applied by researchers to assess the performance of M&A deals. Section 6 provides conclusion and an outlook for future studies.

2 Stock Market Reactions to the Announcements of M&A Deals in Developed and Emerging Capital Markets

Researchers use a wide variety of approaches to measure the impact of M&A deals on corporate performance. The most widely use one is short-term window event study method (Zollo and Meier 2008; Krishnakumar and Sethi 2012). Event studies examine the stock market reaction to M&A announcements and are based on calculating abnormal returns to shareholders. Abnormal returns mean that they exceed what investors normally expect to earn for accepting a certain level of risk. Abnormal returns are forward-looking as share prices usually reflect the present value of expected future cash flows. Consequently, large positive returns may reflect the expected synergy gains resulting from combination of target and acquiring companies (DePamphilis 2012). The high popularity of event studies may be explained by its several strengths (Lubatkin 1987; Krishnakumar and Sethi 2012; Thanos and Papadakis 2012). It directly measures shareholder value analysing stock performance. It is relatively easy to find the necessary data for publicly traded firms to implement this method. Event studies are not subject to manipulation by companies compared with methods using accounting measures to evaluate the impact of acquisitions on corporate performance. The method is simple in its implementation, allows the successful examination of cross-border deals, when the accounting standards of merged firms are different, and demonstrates the influence not only of the firm's actions but also of competitors in the market.

However, this approach has a significant implicit assumption that might be treated as a disadvantage. The use of an event study supposes that the capital market is efficient: investors are rational, they have access to all the necessary information about the company and the share price changes almost instantly in response to new available information (Martynova and Renneboog 2011). Furthermore, event studies measure market expectations of an M&A deal and not its actual performance, raising question about the ability of the market to perceive correctly information about future operating performance (Krishnakumar and Sethi 2012). This measure of performance can be used only for public companies and not for private ones. Finally, this method is more often used to catch only the short-term reaction of the stock market because of challenges connected with the requirement to eliminate the impact of other events in the analysed period. Despite the listed shortcomings, the use of short-term window event studies remains one of the main approaches used by researchers to measure the M&A performance. Below we present the results of recent empirical papers that test the impact of acquisitions on shareholder's value in developed and emerging capital markets.

2.1 Evidence from Developed Capital Markets

Stock market evidence strongly indicates that target shareholders gain significantly in M&A deals. Cumulative abnormal returns (CARs) vary between 7% and 42%, regardless of variations in the sample size, event window and time period (Maquieira et al. 1998; Eckbo and Thorburn 2000; Goergen and Renneboog 2004; Campa and Hernando 2004; Baran and Saikevičius 2015; Deshpande et al. 2016; Fatemi et al. 2017). Returns to acquiring firms are sometimes positive, sometimes negative and sometimes zero (Loderer and Martin 1990; Walker 2000; Moeller et al. 2005, 2007; Hackbarth and Morellec 2008; Hamza 2009; Krishnan et al. 2009; Chang and Tsai 2013; Mateev and Andonov 2016; Brander and Egan 2017).

Results of the recent major studies of short-run firm performance following acquisition announcements for bidding shareholders are summarized in Appendix 1. Scanning the columns of the Appendix 1 shows that the researchers are inconsistent about the impact of acquisitions on shareholder value in developed capital markets, but we may conclude that most studies suggest negative returns to shareholders or state insignificant stock market reaction to the announcements of M&A deals. Yaghoubi et al. (2016a, b) also indicate that abnormal returns for bidding shareholders are mostly insignificant, which is consistent with "Perfectly Competitive Acquisitions Markets" hypothesis. Despite examining the same periods and using similar event windows, researchers have arrived at contradictory results. Such divergence in research outcomes can be explained mainly by differences in sample selection procedures. For example, some authors examine only the largest deals, whereas others do not set such criteria. The divergence may also be due to the differences in methods that are used to generate normal returns for computing CARs.

The analysis of Appendix 1 shows that the observed returns for acquiring shareholders vary from −5.57% (Nnadi and Tanna 2014) to 6.14% (Maquieira et al. 1998). Researchers usually employ the standard market model to generate normal returns (Loderer and Martin 1990; Eckbo and Thorburn 2000; Gregory and O'Donohoe 2014; Brander and Egan 2017). Event windows for CAR calculation varied from the smallest comprising only 2 days to the largest accounting for 2 months. Several authors employ rather long windows, 120–365 days. Almost all researchers compute the abnormal returns with multiple time windows for robustness tests. Most researches are focused on US market, followed by studies examining M&As in Canada and European countries. The sample size varies from 50 (Healy et al. 1992) to 12,023 deals (Moeller et al. 2005). The analysed time period starts in last quarter of 1990s and ends in 2015.

The prevalence of negative and insignificant market reaction to M&A announcements, that we have observed analysing short-term window event studies, is reinforced by the results of empirical research based on long-term window event studies (Yaghoubi et al. 2016a, b). However, the implementation of long-term methods is not straightforward. The statistical reliability and limitations of this method have been a topic for debate in the academic literature for some time. As a result, many authors indicate that tests with a long horizon are highly susceptible to the joint-test problem, and have low power. As such, we should have more confidence in the results of short-horizon tests than in the results of long-horizon tests. According to Kothari and Warner (2007), "short-horizon tests represent the 'cleanest evidence we have on efficiency' (Fama 1991), but the interpretation of long-horizon results is problematic".

2.2 Evidence from Emerging Capital Markets

Our understanding of the performance of domestic M&A deals in emerging capital markets still lags significantly when compared with the vast body of knowledge for developed markets. Results from empirical studies examining the returns for target shareholders are in line with the general notion, that target firms' shareholders gain significant positive returns in M&A deals. Analysing acquisitions in Malaysia, BRIC countries and a group of different developing countries, previous research reveals that returns for target shareholders vary from 1.5% to 11.6%, see Table 1 (Mann and Kohli 2011; Rahim and Pok 2013; Zhu and Jog 2012; Ramakrishnan 2010; Kinateder et al. 2017). The most interesting question is about the benefits for bidding shareholders. In contrast to the mixed results that we observe for companies in developed capital markets, the research results in emerging economies are more consistent. Our review of 20 recent empirical academic papers allows us to state that M&A deals create value for acquiring firm shareholders in most cases (Table 1).

Researchers find positive returns around the bid announcement, which are statistically significant in most cases. The highest returns of 2.35% and 2.76% were

Table 1 Returns to target and acquiring shareholders in emerging markets in the short run

Study	Sample period, country, sample size	Event window	Acquirer abnormal returns (%)
Pop (2006)	1999–2005, Romania, 131 target firms	$(-1,1)$	0.4% for target firms
Mann and Kohli (2011)	1997– March 2008, India, 63 acquisitions	$(-1,1)$	8.26%*** for target firms
Trojanowski (2008)	1996–2000, Poland, 53 block transactions	$(0,1)$	1.16%** for acquirers
Tsung-Ming and Hoshino (2000)	1987–1992, Taiwan, 20 deals	$(-2,2)$	2.12%* for acquirers
Gregoric and Vespro (2009)	1999–2002, Slovenia, 15 block transactions	$(-10,10)$	0.16%** for acquirers
Chi et al. (2011)	1998–2003, China, 1148 deals	$(-2,2)$	0.27%* for acquirers
Bhaumik and Selarka (2012)	1995–2004, India, 123 deals	$(-1,1)$	0.8%** for group affiliated firms −2.4%** for non-group affiliated firms
Rahahleh and Wei (2012)	1985–June 2008, 17 emerging markets, 2340 deals		Statistically significant positive returns. Serial acquirers on average experience a declining pattern in returns with subsequent deals
Rani et al. (2012)	2003–2008, India, 398 deals	$(-2,2)$	2.35%** for acquirers
Sehgal et al. (2012)	2005–2009, BRICKS, 214 acquirers	$(-1,1)$	1.95% for acquirers
Kohli and Mann (2012)	1997–March 2008, India, 66 acquisitions	$(-1,1)$	1.19% for acquirers
Bhabra and Huang (2013)	1997–2007, China, 123 deals	$(-1,1)$	1.23%*** for acquirers
Gaur et al. (2013)	1993–2008, China, 1074 domestic and cross-border deals	$(-2,2)$	1.19%*** for acquirers Support for the growth probability hypothesis
Rahim and Pok (2013)	2001–2009, Malaysia, 180 targets and 196 bidders	$(-2,2)$	2.59%*** for target firms 0.34%*** for acquirers 2.25%*** for targets and acquirers
Zhou et al. (2015)	1994–2008, China, 825 deals	$(-2,2)$	0.83%*** for acquirers
Ramakrishnan (2010)	1996–2002, India, 34 deals	$(-10,10)$	11.6%* for target firms 0% for acquirers 3.4% for targets and acquirers
Black et al. (2015)	2000–2009, China, 415 deals	$(-1,1)$	2.76%*** for acquirers
Zhu and Jog (2012)	1990–2007, emerging markets, 1669 acquisitions	$(-1,1)$	1,5%*** for targets 0,5% for acquirers 0,6% for targets and acquirers
Pham et al. (2015)	2004–2013, Vietnam, 188 deals	$(-1;1)$	−0.28% for acquirers

(continued)

Table 1 (continued)

Study	Sample period, country, sample size	Event window	Acquirer abnormal returns (%)
Ma et al. (2016)	1998–2009, China, 364 acquisitions	$(-1,1)$	1.1%∗∗∗ for acquirers
Song et al. (2017)	1990–2008, China, 279 companies	$(-6,17)$	Acquirers have positive abnormal returns
Kinateder et al. (2017)	June 2006–2015, BRIC, 50 acquisitions	$(-1,1)$	0.39% for acquirers 3.41%∗∗∗ for targets
Grigorieva and Morkovin (2014)	2000–2012, BRICS, 247 domestic M&As	$(-1,1)$	0.84%∗∗∗ for acquirers

∗∗∗, ∗∗, ∗—1%, 5%, 10% level of significance

obtained for shareholders of Indian and Chinese firms (Rani et al. 2012; Black et al. 2015).

Similar to studies in developed markets, the most popular method employed to generate normal returns for acquiring firms in emerging economies is the standard market model (Bhabra and Huang 2013; Gaur et al. 2013; Ma et al. 2016; Song et al. 2017). Several authors used both market and market adjusted or CAPM models for robustness checks (Gregoric and Vespro 2009; Chi et al. 2011; Rahahleh and Wei 2012). The length of event windows is also similar. The size of the samples in emerging market papers is smaller than in developed ones, which may be explained by the short history of M&A market, the low liquidity of firms and the size of the acquired stake. The sample size of M&A deals vary from 15 to 2340 (Kinateder et al. 2017; Rahahleh and Wei 2012). The smallest research sample we observe in the study devoted to Slovenian transactions (Gregoric and Vespro 2009). Based on the sample of 15 deals studied during the period 2000–2001, the authors found positive abnormal stock returns following block transactions. Similar results were obtained by Trojanowski (2008) for a sample of deals in Poland in 1996–2000. Trojanowski (2008) found that cumulative average abnormal returns for block trades were about 1.16% and this result was statistically significant at the 5% level. In contrast to other papers, presented in Table 1, these two analyse block trades of between 5% and 25% of voting rights because under the law, "any acquisition of shares that, together with other shares, provides the buyer with 25% of the voting rights of a listed company is subject to a takeover bid" (Gregoric and Vespro 2009). Therefore, these studies examined only block transactions excluding mandatory bids.

Most research in emerging capital markets based on event study method is devoted to M&A deals in China, since Chinese activity catalysed M&A activity in emerging markets during recent years. Notwithstanding the rapid growth in number and volume of cross-border M&As in China in recent years, which has stimulated the increase in empirical research of the performance of such M&As, a significant part of the deals remain domestic, largely due to the pronounced government participation in business (Bhabra and Huang 2013). As mentioned above, the shareholders of acquiring firms earn high returns in Chinese M&A deals. The positive market reaction is explained in some research by the specific characteristics of the Chinese market such as the prevalence of M&A deals with state-owned enterprises (SOE), where the state continues to hold a controlling interest (Chi et al. 2011; Bhabra and Huang 2013; Zhou et al. 2015; Ma et al. 2016) and less capacity of targets in China to inflate the offer price, due to the unique Chinese tender rules (Song et al. 2017). Besides examining the market reaction to M&A deals in the short run, Chinese papers also calculate BHAR returns to analyse the effects of acquisitions in the long run (Chi et al. 2011; Bhabra and Huang 2013; Zhou et al. 2015; Black et al. 2015; Ma et al. 2016). Despite the analysis of the same market, these papers come to contradictory results. Bhabra and Huang (2013) and Zhou et al. (2015) find significantly positive returns with values of 46.43 and 23.36%, respectively, while Black et al. (2015) and Ma et al. (2016) state significantly negative long-term effects of M&A deals (-7.98 and -6.9%, respectively).

3 Long-Term Operating Performance of M&A Deals in Developed and Emerging Capital Markets

Accounting-based performance measures are the second most popular tool used by scholars to examine the performance of M&A deals (Zollo and Meier 2008; Krishnakumar and Sethi 2012). Researchers usually compare the accounting measures of merging firms before and after M&As to understand how operating performance has changed due to the deal. The focus ranges across profitability measures (such as ROA, ROE and ROS) and measures based on cash flow (such as operating cash flow to the total market value of a firm, to the book value of a firm or to sales) and proxies of cash flow (such as EBITDA or EBTDA adjusted for investments in working capital to book value of assets or sales). The most popular performance indicator is ROA (Thanos and Papadakis 2012). In order to isolate the impact of M&A deals on operating performance from economy-wide, industry trends, or a continuation of firm-specific performance before the merger, scholars usually make adjustments for industry trends, size and pre-M&A performance, by finding relevant benchmarks for each transaction and subtracting the median performance of benchmark firms from that of sample firms (Healy et al. 1992; Ghosh 2001; Papadakis and Thanos 2010; Rao-Nicholson et al. 2016). To test whether the operating performance of merged firms has changed as a result of the deals, change and/or intercept models are used (Healy et al. 1992).

The attractiveness of this method is that it measures the actual operating performance as reported in the financial statements and therefore best captures the synergies between firms (Hitt et al. 1998; Thanos and Papadakis 2012). However, there are several shortcomings of accounting-based measures; they reflect the past performance (Thanos and Papadakis 2012) and are dependent on the accounting standards and rules followed by companies, making, for example, it difficult to analyse cross-border M&As (Krishnakumar and Sethi 2012). They may be applicable only for deals at firm level, not to isolated ones, such as acquisitions (Thanos and Papadakis 2012). Factors other than acquisition may influence performance measures (Cording et al. 2010). The results might be influenced by different measures; applying different profitability-based measures or measures based on cash flows, researchers often come to different, contradictory results (Cording et al. 2010; Rao-Nicholson et al. 2016). This method does not measure changes in market value following M&A deals, while the main goal of firm is to increase shareholder value. And finally, management can manipulate accounting data in order to maximize its own benefits (Yook 2004; Krishnakumar and Sethi 2012).

The question of accounting performance improvements after M&A deals has been addressed by many researchers over the last decades, but the results are still inconsistent, in developed and emerging capital markets. We summarize the results of some of the latest studies which examine the performance of M&A deals in developed and emerging capital markets in Appendix 2. Studies where authors used performance measures based on cash flow in most cases suggest improved company performance following acquisitions (Healy et al. 1992; Switzer 1996; Rahman and Limmack 2004; Powell and Stark 2005; Carline et al. 2009; Ramakrishnan 2010; Shams and Gunasekarage 2016), while studies that used profitability-based measures indicate that mergers perform as well as relevant benchmarks, or merged companies experience a significant decline (Yeh and Hoshino 2002; Sharma and Ho 2002; Leepsa and Mishra 2012; Bhabra and Huang 2013; Boateng et al. 2017). This suggests that accounting rules may influence performance measurement and lead to contradicting results. The differences in results are also due to differences in national environments, differences in accounting standards, and differences in adjustment bases, sample size, sample period and statistical methodology (Sudarsanam 2003; Bruner 2004; Rao-Nicholson et al. 2016).

In developed capital markets, the researchers usually base their analysis on the sample sizes which varied from 36 to 859 (Sharma and Ho 2002; Cheng and Leung 2004; Heron and Lie 2002), while in emerging economies, the sample sizes are relatively lower and vary from 20 to 519 (Tsung-Ming and Hoshino 2000; Bertrand and Betschinger 2012). In developed markets, scholars in most cases examine both acquiring and acquired firms; make adjustments for industry trends and other characteristics, when comparing pre—and post-M&A performance; and employ change and intercept models to make the conclusion about the effects of M&A deals on company operating performance (Healy et al. 1992; Switzer 1996; Shams and Gunasekarage 2016), while in emerging markets, the researchers rather often analyse only acquirers, do not make adjustments for industry trends and other characteristics and employ change models to draw conclusions about long-term operating performance after M&A deals (Kumar and Bansal 2008; Mantravadi and Reddy 2008; Bhabra and Huang 2013; Rani et al. 2015). The most popular accounting-based measures in emerging country studies are profitability-based measures, whereas in developed countries, the most widely used indicators are indicators based on cash flow.

According to Panel B of Appendix 2, most research in emerging capital markets is devoted to Indian M&A deals. The economic liberalization and reforms initiated in 1991 have stimulated Indian companies to large-scale restructuring in conditions of reduced competition from multinational corporations and new opportunities (Kumar and Bansal 2008; Ramakrishnan 2010). Increasing M&A activity in India has led to an increase in research on the effects of M&A deals on corporate performance in the long run. "Analysing the operating performance of 118 acquiring firms in different industries in India 1991–2003, Mantravadi and Reddy (2008) find that mergers have a slightly positive impact on the profitability of firms in the banking and finance industry, while the pharmaceutical, textile, and electrical equipment sectors saw a marginal negative impact on operating performance (in terms of profitability and returns on investment). For the chemicals and agro-product sectors, mergers had caused a significant decline both in terms of profitability margins and returns on investment and assets" (Grigorieva and Petrunina 2015, pp. 379–380). These results are consistent with the outcomes of Pawaskar (2001) and are not in line with the outcomes of other studies, which mostly indicate improvements in operating performance following M&A deals or find insignificant results. Rani et al. (2012, 2015, 2016), in their several studies of M&A deals in India, document that domestic M&A deals create benefits for acquiring shareholders. Similar results were found by Kumar and Bansal (2008) and Ramakrishnan (2010); the latter found positive and statistically significant industry-adjusted differences between post—and pre-acquisition performance measures for a sample of 87 M&A deals in 1996–2002. Based on the sample of 115 M&A deals in manufacturing industries in 2003–2007 and 30 M&A deals in 1999–2002, Leepsa and Mishra (2012) and Kumar (2009) state no significant changes in performance following M&A deals.

4 Long-Term Value Performance of M&A Deals in Developed and Emerging Capital Markets

All the papers that we have discussed concentrate on analysing stock returns surrounding the announcements of M&A transaction or on examining the accounting data of acquiring firms. "The interpretation of results based on event studies is not straightforward. Accounting studies are criticized for their shortcomings in guiding shareholder wealth maximization (Yook 2004). Changes in commonly used book value measures (ROA, ROE, EBITDA margins, OCF to market value of assets, among others) do not allow us to assess the impact of M&As on company value. These measures ignore the cost of capital (Penman 2003). A company can earn a high accounting rate of return, but it may reduce shareholder value because its return on equity may be lower than a shareholder's required rate of return or opportunity costs. Another problem with accounting measures is the ability to manipulate them (Yook 2004). These and other shortcomings that we have discussed require another measure to assess value creation in M&A deals in the long-run. Some authors view the approach based on the concept of economic profit as an

Table 2 Value performance improvement of acquirers in post-acquisition period

Study	Sample period, sample size, country	Performance measure	Major findings
Sirower and O'Byrne (1998)	1979–1990; 41 US acquisitions	Event study; annual expected increases in EVA® (EVA® improvement after M&A deal—expected EVA® improvement)	EVA® reduces after acquisitions for most of the companies in the sample; high correlation between EVA® and short-term/long-term returns
Yook (2004)	1989–1993; 75 US acquisitions	Difference between post-merger and pre-merger EVA® of combined firms	Decline in EVA® after M&A deals
Guest et al. (2010)	1985–1996; 303 UK acquisitions	event study; accounting studies (ROE); residual income valuation model, RIV (difference between fundamental values of companies before and after M&A deals)	Negative market reaction; improvement in profitability (ROE); impact of M&As on fundamental value is slightly negative, but statistically insignificant
Ma et al. (2011)	1978–2002; 1077 US deals	RIV, BHAR	The intrinsic value of merged firms decreases on average in the 3 years following deal completion
Singh et al. (2012)	2005–2008; 17 acquisitions in India	Difference between post-merger and pre-merger EVA®, ROCE and EPS of combined firms	decline in EVA® and ROCE after M&A deals
Leepsa and Mishra (2013)	2003–2004; 2006–2007 29 M&A deals in India (manufacturing companies)	Difference between post-merger and pre-merger EVA® of combined firms	Insignificant decline in EVA® after M&A deals
Grigorieva and Petrunina (2015)	2003–2009; 80 deals initiated by companies from emerging capital markets	Economic profit, EBITDA and EBITDA adjusted to changes in WC to (1) BVassets, (2) sales	Decline in economic profit and operating performance indicators after M&A deals

alternative approach that can effectively solve the deficiencies of traditional accounting measures (Yook 2004; Guest et al. 2010; Sirower and O'Byrne 1998). There are only a few empirical studies that examine the performance of M&A deals using the concept of economic profit and employing such measures as economic value added (EVA®) and residual income under the residual income valuation model (RIV)" (Grigorieva and Petrunina 2015, p.380). We summarize the results of these studies in Table 2.

"Scanning the column of the sample examined by researchers yields the observation that authors analyse the performance of M&A deals only from the sample of companies from the USA, UK and India.

Based on a sample of 75 acquisitions in the USA in 1989–1993, Yook (2004) finds that acquisitions destroy company value. The median raw EVA® during the 5 years before the deal is –$3 million, while the median EVA® in the 5 years following the acquisition is –$27 million. When Yook takes into account industry dynamics, the difference becomes almost indiscernible. At the second stage of analysis, the author excludes the premium from a bidder's capital and reveals that industry-adjusted EVA® shows an insignificant improvement.

In contrast to Yook, Guest et al. (2010) use RIV, along with event study analysis and accounting studies, to assess the performance of 303 M&A deals in the UK in 1985–1996. Based on traditional accounting methods, the authors conclude that M&A deals result in a significant improvement in profitability (ROE). The estimate of α is +2.61%, and this value is significantly different from zero at the 1% level. However, the results from the event study and residual income analysis suggest a negative impact of M&A deals on company's performance. The authors find that over the month of announcement, the acquirer's abnormal return is -1.72%, and over the 36-month post-acquisition period, the buy-and-hold abnormal return is -15.61%. These results are statistically significant at the 1% level. The residual income approach reveals that the impact of M&As on fundamental value is slightly negative, but statistically insignificant.

Sirower and O'Byrne (1998) suggest a methodology for forecasting and evaluating post-acquisition operating performance. This methodology is based on EVA® and takes into account the market value of both companies in the few days before the deal and an acquisition premium. Based on the suggested methodology and also using event study analysis on a sample of the 41 largest US deals in 1979–1990, the authors find (1) a high correlation between the short-term returns and long-term returns, (2) a negative correlation between acquisition premium and both measures of shareholder returns and (3) a high correlation between EVA® and short-term returns (0.68) and EVA® and long-term returns (0.7). The authors conclude that the stock market's reactions to acquisitions carry important information that can be observed by boards of directors before the effective date of these acquisitions" (Grigorieva and Petrunina 2015, pp. 380–381).

Analysing Indian M&A deals, Singh et al. (2012) state the decline in EVA®A and ROCE, while Leepsa and Mishra (2013) observe insignificant change between the post—and pre-merger EVA® of combined firms.

To conclude, studies measuring long-term performance based on value indicators allow us to conclude that M&A deals destroy corporate value in developed capital markets. The limited amount of research in emerging countries does not allow us to make any ultimate conclusion about value effects of M&A deals.

5 Relationship Between Different Methods in Measurement of M&A Deals Performance

Several studies are based on multiple performance measures which may not be classified purely related to accounting measures, value measures or event studies. The application of multiple methods gives researchers an opportunity to reveal relationship between the results obtained by different methods, in addition to measurement of M&A performance. Moreover, one method identifies several effects, while it ignores others. The analysis of a different series of indicators demonstrates a more complete picture of the acquisition, provides with outcomes of the deal in various aspects such as market reaction, value creation, change in operating efficiency and others. As a result, employing a variety of methods allows authors to conduct research with a higher level of accuracy in their conclusions (Switzer 1996; Krishnakumar and Sethi 2012). Nevertheless, it is important to investigate correlation between different methodologies in order to understand whether the chosen methods can be treated as substitutes and whether it would be correct to use only one method to measure performance of M&A deals in developed or emerging capital markets.

Table 3 presents the results of studies that investigate the relationship between event studies and accounting studies, and event studies and the studies employing value-based performance measures.

Healy et al. (1992) were motivated by the hypothesis that market reaction is unable to determine whether an acquisition is efficient and creates economic gain for a company. However, authors find statistically significant positive relationship between post-acquisition operating performance and stock abnormal returns at the date of announcement. Results suggest that equity revaluation of combined firm is caused by market expectations regarding the deal efficiency for a company. Furthermore, investor expectations are efficient and they can correctly assess possible synergies. The same results are obtained by Switzer (1996), who conducts similar research with a small sample of the largest mergers and acquisitions. The author suggests that it is difficult to make a meaningful conclusion about M&A value creation without a significant number of deals. Switzer uses sample of 324 deals in 1967–1987 conducted in the USA. The results show that median industry-adjusted cash flow return improved by 1.97 percentage points which is statistically significant at the 1% level. Event study analysis indicates abnormal return equal to 1.01%, which is significantly different from zero at the 5% level. The paper provides additional evidence that shareholder's reactions to M&A deal include their expectations about deal performance and they can effectively perceive information regarding possible future operating performance. The author also concludes that results provided by Healy et al. (1992) were not biased by sample size. Similar results are found by Anand and Singh (1997) based on 289 deals in 1986–1992 from the USA in the most defence-dependent industries. The authors conduct their research regarding declining industries where mergers and acquisitions play the role of diversification into new market and consolidation within industry. They used the same

Table 3 Results of papers employing several methods simultaneously in developed and emerging capital markets

Researchers	Sample	Methods used	Result
Healy et al. (1992)	USA, 50 deals, 1979–1983	Event study and accounting-based measures	Positive relationship between methods
Switzer (1996)	USA, 324 deals, 1967–1987	Event study and accounting-based measures	Positive relationship between methods
Sirower and O'Byrne (1998)	USA, 41 acquisitions, 1979–1990	Event study and EVA®	Positive relationship between methods
Anand and Singh (1997)	USA, 289 deals, 1986–1992	Event study and accounting-based measures	Positive relationship between methods
Ghosh (2001)	USA, 315 mergers, 1981–1995	Event study and accounting-based measures	No correlation between methods
Cheng and Leung (2004)	Hong Kong, 36 deals, 1984–1996	Event study and accounting-based measures	No correlation between methods
Krishnan et al. (2009)	USA, 50 deals, 1992–1996	Event study and accounting-based measures	Positive relationship between methods
Guest et al. (2010)	UK, 303 deals, 1985–1996	Event study; accounting-based measures; residual income valuation model, RIV	Contradicting results from different methods
Papadakis and Thanos (2010)	Greece, 50 domestic deals, 1997–2003	Event study and accounting-based measures	No significant correlation between methods
Ma et al. (2011)	USA, 1077 deals, 1978–2002	RIV, BHAR	Positive relationship between methods

methodology as Healy et al. (1992) and reveal that target companies have significant positive stock abnormal returns (between 14% and 21%), while the acquirers' abnormal returns are statistically insignificant. Only deals with overlapping business units experience improvements in operating performance for declining industries. Nevertheless, Anand and Singh conclude that there are positive correlations between results obtained by event and accounting studies.

Ghosh (2001) found no correlation between results. Similar to Healy et al. (1992) and Anand and Singh (1997), Ghosh compared event study and accounting methodology on the sample of 315 M&As in the USA in 1981–1995. Krishnan et al. (2009) investigate whether market participants could correctly identify possible post-acquisition synergies at the date of the announcement by examining abnormal returns of acquirers and their main rivals relative to acquirers' operating performance after M&A deals. The authors use sample of 50 large US mergers and acquisitions in 1992–1996. Their results demonstrate a statistically significant positive association between acquirers' abnormal returns at the date of announcement and post-acquisition operating performance. Moreover, there is statistically significant negative relationship between main rivals' abnormal returns and subsequent acquirers' operating performance. These results show that market participants are able to effectively perceive M&A deal operating performance. These results are in line with the work of Sirower and O'Byrne (1998) who also concluded, as mentioned above, that the market reaction provides an unbiased opinion about the performance of an acquirer. However, in contrast to above-mentioned papers, this one compared event study and EVA® approach.

Unlike previous studies, Guest et al. (2010) obtain contradicting results from market-, accounting—and value-based performance indicators for the sample of UK deals. Papadakis and Thanos (2010) and Cheng and Leung (2004) do not reveal any correlation between stock returns and long-term operating performance on the sample of 50 Greek and 36 Hong Kong M&A deals, respectively.

Most of the mentioned papers state positive correlation between different methods and are based on the data from developed capital markets. Since the market efficiency hypothesis "works" better on these markets, the correlation between different approaches may differ in emerging markets. Yeh and Hoshino (2002) did not observe any correlation between the results using a sample of 20 M&As in Taiwan in 1987–1992. Singh et al. (2012) compare the results derived from accounting—and value-based performance measures on a sample of Indian M&A deals. They state that accounting—and value-based approaches are more reliable than event studies because the latter may be affected by market noise, rumours and market inefficiency as a whole. Thus, they did not use an event study approach in their work. Analysing ROCE, EPS and EVA®, they found that most of M&A deals were inefficient.

Krishnakumar and Sethi (2012) believe that the decision for choice of a method of evaluating the performance of M&As depends on the analysed capital market. The authors note that the methods used in developed markets may give poor results in emerging markets. They state that different methods are aimed for identifying different effects and do not capture all events followed by a transaction. For example, an event study focuses only on change in the market prices of companies and ignores all other indicators of merger efficiency.

In summary, the use of several methods will contribute to more accurate research on the performance of M&A deals. A significant number of researchers in developed and emerging capital markets based their research on several study methods (Healy et al. 1992; Bhabra and Huang 2013; Bhaumik and Selarka 2012; Ma et al. 2016), but there is a lack of papers that examine the relationship among different methods, especially in emerging capital markets.

6 Conclusion

This chapter provides an overview of the M&A literature with a view to understanding the performance of M&A deals. In contrast to previous reviews, we restrict the scope of the chapter to domestic M&A deals and present the comparative analysis of acquisition effects on company performance in developed and emerging capital markets. We focus our analysis on the papers that employ the most widely used techniques to assess the performance of M&A deals, such as event studies and accounting studies, and we also include in the analysis the papers that are based on value performance indicators, allowing the effects of M&A deals on company value in the long run to be tested. Our analysis permits us to make a number of conclusions. In respect to the stock market reaction to the announcements of M&A deals, the evidence suggests that target shareholders gain significantly in M&A deals in developed and emerging capital markets. The results for acquiring shareholders are generally mixed, but there tend to be negative or insignificant benefits from M&A deals in developed capital markets. Our results are consistent with the conclusions made by Yaghoubi et al. (2016a, b) and Tuch and O'Sullivan (2007) in their review of finance and accounting journals and also are in line with outcomes of Thanos and Papadakis (2012) in their review of managerial journals. Regarding the shareholders of the acquiring firms in emerging capital markets, we observe positive market reaction to the announcements of M&A deals in most cases.

Performance measured by accounting-based indicators is mixed in developed and emerging capital markets. The same conclusion was reached by Tuch and O'Sullivan (2007) for the effects of M&A deals on corporate operating performance in developed capital markets.

Our review of studies that are based on the concept of economic profit reveals the destruction of company value due to M&As in most cases in developed and emerging capital markets and also proves the importance of analysing market reaction to the announcements of M&A deals.

Despite the fact that there is a significant amount of research on M&A performance in developed capital markets, the results are still mixed, indicating the need for further research to understand this important company growth strategy. The literature on M&A effects on corporate performance in emerging countries is scarce despite the fast growth of the number and volume of M&A deals in these countries in recent decades. Research papers now cover M&A deals in only a few countries, leaving open the question about the influence of the country of origin of merged firms and specific features of emerging markets on M&A performance. Moreover, there is a lack of research papers in emerging capital markets on the relation between different methods used by researchers to assess the performance of M&A deals.

The existing literature in developed and emerging capital markets, mainly, gives us the picture about the market reaction to M&A deals (mainly in the short run) and operating performance of acquisitions in long-term period, rather than the value performance of M&A transactions in the long run, also opening a space for further research.

Acknowledgements I express my sincere thanks to research fellows Ekaterina Tarasova and Roman Vasilenko for their help with article search and table development.

Appendix 1. Returns to Acquiring Shareholders in Developed Markets in the Short Run

Study	Sample period, sample size, country	Event window	Acquirer abnormal returns (%)
Positive market reaction to the announcements of M&A deals			
Seth (1990)	1962–1979, developed markets, 104 tender offers	(−39; 0)	0.11∗∗ for total sample; 0.11∗∗ for related; 0.09∗∗ for unrelated
Maquieira et al. (1998)	1963–1996; 55 non-conglomerate US acquisitions; 47 conglomerate US acquisitions	(−60,60)	6.14%∗∗ for non-conglomerate; −4.79% for conglomerate
Eckbo and Thorburn (2000)	1964–1983; 1261 Canadian and US bidders	(−40,0)	1.71%∗∗ for Canadian
Kohers and Kohers (2000)	1987–1996, USA, 1634 deals	(−0, +1)	1.37∗∗ cash deals 1.09%∗∗ stock
Fuller et al. (2002)	1990–2000; 3135 US takeovers	(−2,2)	1.8%∗ for total sample of bidders; −1.0%∗ when target is public; 2.1%∗ when target is private; 2.8%∗when target is a subsidiary
Goergen and Renneboog (2004)	1993–2000; 158 European M&As	(−1,0)	0.7%∗∗∗
Moeller et al. (2005)	1980–2001; 12,023 US acquisitions	(−1,1)	1.1%∗ for total sample; 2.3%∗ for small acquirers; 0.1% for large acquirers
Conn et al. (2005)	1984–1998, UK, 4244 acquisitions	(−1,+1)	0.59∗∗∗ for total sample; 0.86∗∗∗ for private targets; −0.82 for public targets;
Faccio et al. (2006)	1996–2001, 17 Western Europe countries, 4429 deals	(−2; +2)	−1.4 for listed targets; 1.4∗∗∗ for unlisted targets
Hamza (2009)	1997–2005; 58 French takeover bids	(−20, −6), (−5,5), (+6,20), (−20,20)	7.33% ∗∗∗for the bidder with pre-bid blockholder position in the target (toe-hold); 0.40%∗∗∗ for bidders without toehold

(continued)

Study	Sample period, sample size, country	Event window	Acquirer abnormal returns (%)
Zaheer et al. (2010)	1990–1998, US, 503 acquisitions in high-tech industries	(−1; +1); (−5; +1); (−5; +5)	0.40; 0.76∗; 0.96∗
Martynova and Renneboog (2011)	1993–2001, 28 - European countries, 2419 deals,	(−1,+1)	0.72∗∗∗
Chang and Tsai (2013)	1990–2007; 4288 US M&As of privately held targets	from day 0 to 1, 2, 3, 5, 30, 60, 126 and 252 trading days from the announcement	Positive in short-run periods (+1.9%∗∗∗) and negative in long-run periods (10.9%∗∗∗)
Khanal et al. (2014)	2010–2012, USA, 38 deals	(−1; +1)	0.43∗
Favato et al. (2015)	2012–2014, USA, 90 deals	(−1; +1)	1.92∗∗∗
Hossain et al. (2016)	2005–2011, Australia, 139 deals	(−1; +1)	3.26∗∗
Baran and Saikevičius (2015)	2004–2013, EU-10 countries, 6967 deals	(0;1); (−5; 5); (−30;30)	3.8∗∗—19.4∗
Craninckx and Huyghebaert (2015)	1997–2007, developed Europe, 342 deals	(−1; +1)	0.11∗∗∗
Mateev and Andonov (2016)	2003–2010, 38 - European countries, 918 cross-border and 1903 domestic transactions	(−1; +1)	0.94∗∗∗ cross-border, 1.05∗∗∗ domestic
Fatemi et al. (2017)	2000–2014, Japan, 243 deals	(−1; +1)	1.55∗∗∗
Negative market reaction to the announcements of M&A deals			
Lang et al. (1991)	1980–1986, developed markets, 101 tender offers	(−5; +5)	−0.4∗∗∗
Servaes (1991)	1972–1987, developed markets, 704 mergers and tender offers	(−1,+1)	−1.07∗∗
Byrd and Hickman (1992)	1980–1987, USA, 128 deals	(−1, 0)	−1.2∗∗
Mulherin and Boone (2000)	1990–1999, USA, 281 acquisitions	(−1,+1)	−0.37∗∗∗
Mitchell and Stafford (2000)	1961–1993, USA, 366 deals	(−1, 0)	−0.14∗∗

(continued)

Study	Sample period, sample size, country	Event window	Acquirer abnormal returns (%)
Walker (2000)	1980–1996, USA, 278 deals	(−2; +2)	−0.84∗∗∗ for total sample; 0.03 for related; −2.97∗∗∗ for unrelated; 0.88 for cash; −4.16∗∗∗ for stock payment
Kiymaz and Baker (2008)	1989–2003; 100 largest US M&As	(−1,0), (−10,10), (−30, −1), (1, 30)	−1.65%∗∗∗
Akbulut and Matsusaka (2010)	1950–2006, USA, 4764 mergers	(−1,+1)	−0.6∗∗∗ for unrelated deals; −1.3∗∗∗ for related deals
Nnadi and Tanna (2014)	1997–2007, EU, 62 deals	(−5; +5)	−5.57∗
Fich et al. (2016)	1996–2008, USA, 2297 deals	(−1; 0)	−2.5∗∗∗
No significant market reaction to the announcements of M&A deals			
Loderer and Martin (1990)	1965–1984, CSRP database, 10,837 deals		1.72 over 1966–1968; 0.57 for 1968–1980; −0.07 for 1981–1984
Morck et al. (1990)	Compustat, 326 deals	(−2; +1)	−0.7
Healy et al. (1992)	1979–1984, USA, 50 largest US mergers during this period	(−5, +5)	−2.2
Agrawal et al. (1992)	1955–1987, USA, 927 mergers and 227 tender offers	12 months after the deal	−1.53
Schwert (1996)	1975–1991, USA, 666 deals	(−42, +126)	1.4
Eckbo and Thorburn (2000)	1964–1982, USA, 1846 deals	(0; +30)	−0.18
Leeth and Borg (2000)	1919–1930, USA, 466 acquisitions	(−1; 0)	2.43
Capron and Pistre (2002)	Developed markets, 101 horizontal deals	(−10; +1)	−0.34
Moeller et al. (2007)	1980–2002, USA, 4322 deals	(−1,+1)	0.8
Papadakis and Thanos (2010)	1997–2003, Greece, 59 acquisitions	(−1,+1)	−0.02
Harford et al. (2012)	1990–2005, USA, 3935 deals,	(−2; +2)	−0.036
Humphery-Jenner and Powell (2014)	1996–2008, EU and USA, 17647 deals	(−5; +5)	1.9

(continued)

Study	Sample period, sample size, country	Event window	Acquirer abnormal returns (%)
Gregory and O'Donohoe (2014)	1990–2005, USA, 169 cross-border and 119 domestic deals	(−2; +2)	−0.75 cross-border, −1.30 domestic
Zhang (2015)	2010–2014, USA, 635 deals	(−1; +1)	0.08
Chang et al. (2016)	1985–2008, USA, 760 deals	(−1; +1)	−2.0
Deshpande et al. (2016)	1990–2012, USA, 112 deals	(−2, +2)	−1.7
Brander and Egan (2017)	1985–2015, USA, 26428 deals	(−1; +1)	0.26

***, **, *—1%, 5%, 10% level of significance

Appendix 2. Long-Term Operating Performance of M&A Deals in Developed and Emerging Capital Markets

Study	Sample period, sample size, country	Performance measure	Performance measure adjusted for effect of	Major findings
Panel A. Evidence from developed capital markets				
Studies that find an improvement in post-acquisition operating performance				
Healy et al. (1992)	1979–mid-1984; 50 largest US mergers	Pre-tax OCF to TMV	Industry; controls for accounting method	Improvement
Switzer (1996)	1967–1987; 324 US acquisitions	Pre-tax OCF to TMV	Industry	Improvement
Parrino and Harris (1999)	1982–1987; 197 US deals	Pre-tax OCF to TMV	Industry	Improvement in case of changing management after M&A deals
Linn and Switzer (2001)	1967–1987; 413 US acquisitions	Pre-tax CF to TMV	Industry	Improvement
Heron and Lie (2002)	1985–1997; 859 US acquisitions	Operating income to sales	Industry, controls for possible mean reversion resulting from abnormal pre-event performance	Improvement
Powell and Stark (2005)	1985–1993; 191 UK takeovers	OCF to (1) TMV, (2) TMV adjusted for market reaction	Industry, size and pre-bid performance	Improvement

(continued)

Study	Sample period, sample size, country	Performance measure	Performance measure adjusted for effect of	Major findings
		to the takeover, (3) BV assets, (4) Sales		
Kruse et al. (2007)	1969–1999; 69 Japan mergers	Pre-tax CF to (1) MVT, (2) Sales	Industry, size	Improvement
Carline et al. (2009)	1985–1994; 81 UK mergers	Pre-tax OCF to TMV	Industry	Improvement
Guest et al. (2010)	1985–1996; 303 UK acquisitions	ROE	Industry, size	Improvement
Shams and Gunasekarage (2016)	2003–June 2011; 526 - Australian acquisitions	EBITDA to (1) TMV, (2) BV assets	Industry, size and pre-bid performance	Improvements for acquirers of private targets and deterioration for acquirers of public targets
Studies that find a deterioration in post-acquisition operating performance				
Clark and Ofek (1994)	1981–1988; 38 US deals with distressed targets	Pre-tax OCF to Sales	Industry	Deterioration
Yeh and Hoshino (2002)	1970–1994; 86 Japan acquisitions	ROA, ROE, sales growth, employment growth	Industry	M&As that involve keiretsu are followed by a significant decline in ROE and ROA; M&As involving independent firms do not
Pazarskis et al. (2006)	1988–2000; 50 Greek deals	Profitability, liquidity, Solvency ratios	–	Deterioration
Studies that find no significant changes in post-acquisition operating performance				
Ghosh (2001)	1981–1995; 315 US mergers	Pre-tax OCF to TMV	Industry, size and pre-bid performance,	No significant change
Sharma and Ho (2002)	1986–1991; 36 Australian mergers	Pre-tax CF adjusted for changes in WC to (1) BV assets, (2) BV equity, (3) sales, (4) number of shares	Industry, size	No significant change
Cheng and Leung (2004)	1984–1996; 36 partial	Different cash flow, accounting	Industry	No significant change

(continued)

Study	Sample period, sample size, country	Performance measure	Performance measure adjusted for effect of	Major findings
	mergers in Hong Kong	profitability, growth and lever-age ratios		
Kukalis (2007)	1995–2000; 80 US mergers	ROA, ROS, EBITDA/Net Sales	Industry	No significant change
Martynova et al. (2007)	1997–2001; 155 European acquisitions	EBITDA and EBITDA adjusted to changes in WC to (1) BVassets, (2) Sales	Industry, size and pre-bid performance	No significant change
Papadakis and Thanos (2010)	1997–2003; 50 Greek acquisitions	ROA	Industry	No significant change
Panel B. Evidence from emerging capital markets				
Studies that find an improvement in post-acquisition operating performance				
Rahman and Limmack (2004)	1988–1992; 113 Malaysian deals	Pre-tax CF adjusted for investments in WC to BV assets	Industry, size	Improvement.
Kumar and Bansal (2008)	2003; 74 Indian acquirers	WC, operating profit, profit before tax, EPS, ROE, D/E	–	Improvement.
Ramakrishnan (2010)	1996–2002; 87 Indian mergers	Pre-tax OCF to operating assets	Industry	Improvement.
Rani et al. (2012)	2003–2008, 398 Indian deals	ROE	–	Improvement.
Rani et al. (2015)	2003–2008; 305 Indian acquirers	14 ratios related to profitability, effi-ciency, leverage and liquidity	–	Improvement.
Ma et al. (2016)	1998–2009, 364 Chinese acquisitions	ROA, Sales/TA, OCF/TA	Industry	State-owned acquirers experi-ence a signifi-cantly larger performance improvement compared to non-state-owned acquirers.
Studies that find a deterioration in post-acquisition operating performance				
Tsung-Ming and Hoshino (2000)	1987–1992; 20 Taiwanese acquirers	ROA, ROE, finan-cial leverage, liquidity ratios,	Industry	Deterioration

(continued)

Study	Sample period, sample size, country	Performance measure	Performance measure adjusted for effect of	Major findings
		sales growth, operating expenses ratio		
Pawaskar (2001)	1992–1995; 36 Indian acquirers	Pre-tax CF to net assets	Industry, size	Deterioration
Mantravadi and Reddy (2008)	1991–2003; 118 Indian acquirers	6 different financial and operating ratios	–	Deterioration
Bertrand and Betschinger (2012)	1999–2008; 517 Russian domestic acquirers	Pre-tax CF to BV assets	Non-acquiring firm	Deterioration
Huang et al. (2014)	1998–2007; 91 Taiwanese IT acquisitions	Pre-tax OCF to TMV, different PM, total and fixed-assets turnover	Industry	Deterioration
Grigorieva and Petrunina (2015)	2003–2009; 80 deals initiated by companies from emerging capital markets	EBITDA and EBITDA adjusted to changes in WC to (1) BV assets, (2) Sales	Industry	Deterioration
Rao-Nicholson et al. (2016)	2001–2012; 57 ASEAN M&As	ROA, EBITDA/ Sales	Industry, size, pre-bid performance	Deterioration
Boateng et al. (2017)	2004–2011, 340 Chinese M&As	ROA	Size, book to market value	Deterioration
Studies that find no significant changes in post-acquisition operating performance				
Kumar (2009)	1999–2002; 30 Indian mergers	ROCE, ASTR, D/E	Industry	No significant change.
Leepsa and Mishra (2013)	2003–2007; 115 Indian deals	Different profitability, liquidity and leverage ratios	–	No significant change.
Bhabra and Huang (2013)	1997–2007; 123 Chinese acquirers	ROA, ROE, PM, Sales Growth	–	Operating performance remains statistically unchanged.

TMV total market value of assets, *BV assets* book value of assets, *BV equity* book value of equity, *ROE* return on equity, *ROA* return on assets, *ROCE* return on capital employed, *PM* profit margin, *EPS* earnings per share, *WC* working capital, *TA* total assets, *OCF* operating cash flow, *CF* cash flow, *D/E* debt to equity ratio, *ASTR* asset turnover ratio

References

Agrawal, A., Jaffe, J. F., & Mandelker, G. N. (1992). The post-merger performance of acquiring firms: A re-examination of an anomaly. *The Journal of Finance, 47*, 1605–1621.

Akbulut, M. E., & Matsusaka, J. G. (2010). 50+ years of diversification announcements. *Financial Review, 45*(2), 231–262.

Anand, J., & Singh, H. (1997). Asset redeployment, acquisitions and corporate strategy in declining industries. *Strategic Management Journal: Special Issue, 18*, 99–118.

Baran, D., & Saikevičius, D. (2015). Comparative analysis of mergers and acquisitions in the new member states of European Union. *Intellectual Economics, 9*(1), 1–7.

Bertrand, O., & Betschinger, M.-A. (2012). Performance of domestic and cross-border acquisitions: Empirical evidence from Russian acquirers. *Journal of Comparative Economics, 40*(3), 413–437.

Bhabra, H. S., & Huang, J. (2013). An empirical investigation of mergers and acquisitions by Chinese listed companies, 1997–2007. *Journal of Multinational Financial Management, 23*, 186–207.

Bhaumik, S. K., & Selarka, E. (2012). Does ownership concentration improve M&A outcomes in emerging markets? Evidence from India. *Journal of Corporate Finance, 18*, 717–726.

Black, E. L., Doukas, A. J., Xing, X., & Guo, J. M. (2015). Gains to Chinese bidder firms: Domestic vs. foreign acquisitions. *European Financial Management, 21*(5), 905–935.

Boateng, S., Bi, X. G., & Brahma, S. (2017). The impact of firm ownership, board monitoring on operating performance of Chinese mergers and acquisitions. *Review of Quantitative Finance and Accounting, 49*, 925–948.

Brander, J. A., & Egan, E. J. (2017). The winner's curse in acquisitions of privately-held firms. *The Quarterly Review of Economics and Finance, 65*, 249–262.

Bris, A., & Cabolis, C. (2008). The value of investor protection: Firm evidence from cross-border mergers. *The Review of Financial Studies, 21*(2), 605–648.

Bruner, R. F. (2004). *Applied mergers and acquisitions*. Hoboken, NJ: Wiley.

Byrd, J. W., & Hickman, K. A. (1992). Do outside directors monitor managers?: Evidence from tender offer bids. *Journal of Financial Economics, 32*(2), 195–221.

Ca_ipha, R., Tarba, S., & Brock, D. (2010). Mergers and acquisitions: A review of phases, motives, and success factors. *Advances in Mergers and Acquisitions, 9*, 1–24.

Campa, J. M., & Hernando, I. (2004). Shareholder value creation in European M&As. *European Financial Management, 10*(1), 47–81.

Capron, L., & Pistre, N. (2002). When do acquirers earn abnormal returns? *Strategic Management Journal, 23*(9), 781–794.

Carline, N. F., Linn, S. C., & Yadav, P. K. (2009). Operating performance changes associated with corporate mergers and the role of corporate governance. *Journal of Banking & Finance, 33*, 1829–1841.

Chang, S.-C., & Tsai, M.-T. (2013). Long-run performance of mergers and acquisition of privately held targets: Evidence in the USA. *Applied Economics Letters, 20*, 520–524.

Chang, X., Shekhar, C., Tam, L. H., & Yao, J. (2016). The information role of advisors in mergers and acquisitions: Evidence from acquirers hiring targets' ex-advisors. *Journal of Banking & Finance, 70*, 247–264.

Cheng, L. T. W., & Leung, T. Y. (2004). A comparative analysis of the market-based and accounting-based performance of diversifying and non-diversifying acquisitions in Hong Kong. *International Business Review, 13*, 763–789.

Chi, J., Sun, Q., & Young, M. (2011). Performance and characteristics of acquiring firms in the Chinese stock markets. *Emerging Markets Review, 12*, 152–170.

Christofi, M., Leonidou, E., & Vrontis, D. (2017). Marketing research on mergers and acquisitions: A systematic review and future directions. *International Marketing Review, 34*(5), 629–651.

Clark, K., & Ofek, E. (1994). Mergers as a means of restructuring distressed firms: an empirical investigation. *Journal of Financial and Quantitative Analysis, 29*(4), 541–565.

Conn, R. L., Cosh, A., Guest, P. M., & Hughes, A. (2005). The impact on UK acquirers of domestic, cross-border, public and private acquisitions. *Journal of Business Finance & Accounting, 32*(5–6), 815–870.

Cording, M., Christmann, P., & Weigelt, C. (2010). Measuring theoretically complex constructs: The case of acquisition performance. *Strategic Organization, 8,* 11–41.

Craninckx, K., & Huyghebaert, N. (2015). Large shareholders and value creation through corporate acquisitions in Europe. The identity of the controlling shareholder matters. *European Management Journal, 33*(2), 116–131.

DePamphilis, D.M. (2012). Introduction to mergers and acquisition, Chapter 1. In *Mergers, acquisitions and other restructuring activities* (pp. 3–50). New York: Elsevier.

Deshpande, S., Svetina, M., & Zhu, P. (2016). The impact of European commission merger regulation on US domestic M&As. *Journal of Multinational Financial Management, 36,* 1–15.

Eckbo, E., & Thorburn, K. (2000). Gains to bidder firms revisited: Domestic and foreign acquisitions in Canada. *Journal of Financial and Quantitative Analysis, 35,* 1–25.

Faccio, M., McConnell, J. J., & Stolin, D. (2006). Returns to acquirers of listed and unlisted targets. *Journal of Financial and Quantitative Analysis, 41*(01), 197–220.

Fama, E. (1991). Efficient capital markets: II. *Journal of Finance, 46,* 1575–1617.

Fatemi, A. M., Fooladi, I., & Garehkoolchian, N. (2017). Gains from mergers and acquisitions in Japan. *Global Finance Journal, 32,* 166–178.

Favato, G., Nurullah, M., & Cottingham, J. A. (2015). Impact of domestic acquisition on acquirer shareholders' equity: An empirical study on the US market. *Journal of Applied Finance and Banking, 5*(4), 33.

Fich, E. M., Nguyen, T., & Officer, M. S. (2016). Large wealth creation in mergers and acquisitions. *Journal of Financial and Quantitative Analysis, 64*(01), 192–224.

Fuller, K., Netter, J., & Stegemoller, M. (2002). What do returns to acquiring firms tell us? Evidence from Firms that Make Many Acquisitions. *Journal of Finance, 57,* 1763–1793.

Gaur, A. S., Malhotra, S., & Zhu, P. (2013). Acquisition announcements and stock market valuations of acquiring firms' rivals: A test of the growth probability hypothesis in China: stock market valuations of acquiring firms' rivals. *Strategic Management Journal, 34,* 215–232.

Genç, Ö. F. (2016). Comparison of international and domestic acquisition: A literature review. *Journal of Management and Economics Research, 14*(4), 128–149.

Ghosh, A. (2001). Does operating performance really improve following corporate acquisitions? *Journal of Corporate Finance, 7,* 151–178.

Goergen, M., & Renneboog, L. (2004). Shareholder wealth effects of european domestic and cross-border takeover bids. *European Financial Management, 10*(1), 9–45.

Gregoric, A., & Vespro, C. (2009). Block trades and the benefits of control in Slovenia. *The Economics of Transition, 17*(1), 175–210.

Gregory, A., & O'Donohoe, S. (2014). Do cross border and domestic acquisitions differ? Evidence from the acquisition of UK targets. *International Review of Financial Analysis, 31,* 61–69.

Grigorieva, S., & Morkovin, R. (2014). The effect of cross-border and domestic acquisitions on shareholder wealth: Evidence from brics acquirers. *Journal of Corporate Finance Research., 4* (32), 34–45.

Grigorieva, S., & Petrunina, T. (2015). The performance of mergers and acquisitions in emerging capital markets: New angle. *Journal of Management Control, 26,* 377–403.

Guest, P., Bild, M., & Runsten, N. (2010). The effects of takeovers on the fundamental value of acquirers. *Accounting and Business Research, 40*(4), 333–352.

Hackbarth, D., & Morellec, E. (2008). Stock returns in mergers and acquisitions. *Journal of Finance, 63*(3), 1213–1252.

Hamza, T. (2009). Determinants of short-term value creation for the bidders: Evidence from France. *Journal of Management and Governance, 15,* 157–186.

Harford, J., Humphery-Jenner, M., & Powell, R. (2012). The sources of value destruction in acquisitions by entrenched managers. *Journal of Financial Economics, 106*(2), 247–261.

Healy, P. M., Palepu, K. G., & Ruback, R. S. (1992). Does corporate performance improve after mergers? *Journal of Financial Economics, 31*, 135–175.

Heron, R., & Lie, E. (2002). Operating performance and the method of payment in takeovers. *Journal of Financial and Quantitative Analysis, 37*(1), 137–155.

Hitt, M., Harrison, J., Ireland, R. D., & Best, A. (1998). Attributes of successful and unsuccessful acquisitions of US firms. *British Journal of Management, 9*(2), 91–114.

Hossain, M. M., Heaney, R. A., & Koh, S. (2016). Director trading, or lack thereof, and acquiring firm performance: Evidence from Australian mergers and acquisitions. *Accounting Research Journal, 29*(3), 332–347.

Huang, H.-H., Chan, M.-L., Huang, I.-H., & Wu, K.-H. (2014). Operating performance following acquisitions: Evidence from Taiwan's IT industry. *Asia-Pacific Journal of Financial Studies, 43* (5), 739–766.

Humphery-Jenner, M., & Powell, R. (2014). Firm size, sovereign governance, and value creation: Evidence from the acquirer size effect. *Journal of Corporate Finance, 26*, 57–77.

Khanal, A. R., Mishra, A. K., & Mottaleb, K. A. (2014). Impact of mergers and acquisitions on stock prices: The US ethanol-based biofuel industry. *Biomass and Bioenergy, 61*, 138–145.

Kinateder, H., Fabich, M., & Wagner, N. (2017). Domestic mergers and acquisitions in BRIC countries: Acquirers and targets. *Emerging Markets Review, 32*, 190–199.

Kiymaz, H., & Baker, H. (2008). Short-term performance, industry effects, and motives: Evidence from large M&As. *Quarterly Journal of Finance and Accounting, 47*(2), 17–44.

Kohers, N., & Kohers, T. (2000). The value creation potential of high-tech mergers. *Financial Analysts Journal, 56*(3), 40–51.

Kohli, R., & Mann, B. J. S. (2012). Analyzing determinants of value creation in domestic and cross-border acquisitions in India. *International Business Review, 21*, 998–1016.

Kothari, S. P., & Warner, J. B. (2007). Econometrics of Event Studies. In B. E. Eckbo (Ed.), *Handbook of corporate finance* (pp. 3–36). North-Holland: Elsevier.

Krishnakumar, D., & Sethi, M. (2012). Methodologies used to determine mergers and acquisitions' performance. *Academy of Accounting and Financial Studies Journal, 16*(3), 75–91.

Krishnan, H., Krishnan, R., & Lefanowicz, C. (2009). Market perception of synergies in related acquisitions. *Academy of Strategic Management Journal, 8*, 99–119.

Kruse, T. A., Park, H. Y., Park, K., & Suzuki, K. (2007). Long-term performance following mergers of Japanese companies: The effect of diversification and affiliation. *Pacific-Basin Finance Journal, 15*, 154–172.

Kukalis, S. (2007). Corporate strategy and company performance: The case of post-merger performance. *The International Journal of Finance, 19*(3), 4475–4494.

Kumar, N. (2009). Post-merger corporate performance: An indian perspective. *Management Research News, 32*(2), 145–157.

Kumar, S., & Bansal, L. K. (2008). The impact of mergers and acquisitions on corporate performance in India. *Management Decision, 46*(10), 1531–1543.

Lang, L. H., Stulz, R., & Walkling, R. A. (1991). A test of the free cash flow hypothesis: The case of bidder returns. *Journal of Financial Economics, 29*(2), 315–335.

Leepsa, N. M., & Mishra, C. S. (2012). Post merger financial performance: A study with reference to select manufacturing companies in India. *International Research Journal of Finance and Economics, 83*, 6–17.

Leepsa, N. M., & Mishra, C. S. (2013). Wealth creation through acquisitions. *Decision, 40*(3), 147–121.

Leeth, J. D., & Borg, J. R. (2000). The impact of takeovers on shareholder wealth during the 1920s merger wave. *Journal of Financial and Quantitative Analysis, 35*(02), 217–238.

Linn, S. C., & Switzer, J. A. (2001). Are cash acquisitions associated with better postcombination operating performance than stock acquisitions? *Journal of Banking & Finance, 25*, 1113–1138.

Loderer, C., & Martin, K. (1990). Corporate acquisitions by listed firms: The experience of comprehensive sample. *Financial Management, 19*, 17–33.

Lubatkin, M. (1987). Merger strategies and stockholder value. *Strategic Management Journal, 8*(1), 39–53.

Ma, Q., Whidbee, D. A., & Zhang, A. W. (2011). Value, valuation, and the long-run performance of merged firms. *Journal of Corporate Finance, 17*(2011), 1–17.

Ma, M., Sun, X., Waisman, M., & Zhu, Y. (2016). State ownership and market liberalization: Evidence from China's domestic M&A market. *Journal of International Money and Finance, 69*, 205–223.

Mann, B. J. S., & Kohli, R. (2011). Target shareholder's wealth creation in domestic and cross-border acquisitions in India. *International Journal of Commerce and Management, 21*(1), 63–81.

Mantravadi, P., & Reddy, A. V. (2008). Post-merger performance of acquiring firms from different industries in India. *International Research Journal of Finance and Economics, 22*, 192–204.

Maquieira, C., Megginson, W., & Nail, L. (1998). Wealth creation versus wealth redistributions in pure stock-for-stock mergers. *Journal of Financial Economics, 48*, 3–33.

Martynova, M., & Renneboog, L. (2011). The performance of the European market for corporate control: Evidence from the fifth takeover wave. *European Financial Management, 17*, 208–259.

Martynova, M., Oosting, S., & Renneboog, L. (2007). The long-term operating performance in European mergers and acquisitions. In G. N. Gregoriou & L. Renneboog (Eds.), *International mergers and acquisitions activity since 1990. Recent research and quantitative analysis* (pp. 79–116). Cambridge, MA: Elsevier.

Mateev, M., & Andonov, K. (2016). Do cross-border and domestic bidding firms perform differently? New evidence from continental Europe and the UK. *Research in International Business and Finance, 37*, 327–349.

Mitchell, M. L., & Stafford, E. (2000). Managerial decisions and long-term stock price performance. *Journal of Business, 73*, 287–329.

Moeller, S. B., Schlingemann, F. P., & Stulz, R. M. (2005). Wealth destruction on a massive scale? A study of acquisition firm returns in the recent merger wave. *Journal of Finance, 60*, 757–782.

Moeller, S. B., Schlingemann, F. P., & Stulz, R. M. (2007). How do diversity of opinion and information asymmetry affect acquirer returns? *Review of Financial Studies, 20*, 2047–2078.

Morck, R., Shleifer, A., & Vishny, R. W. (1990). Do managerial objectives drive bad acquisitions? *The Journal of Finance, 45*(1), 31–48.

Mulherin, J. H., & Boone, A. L. (2000). Comparing acquisitions and divestitures. *Journal of Corporate Finance, 6*(2), 117–139.

Nnadi, M. A., & Tanna, S. (2014). Post-acquisition profitability of banks: A comparison of domestic and cross-border acquisitions in the European Union. *Global Business and Economics Review, 16*(3), 310–331.

Papadakis, V. M., & Thanos, I. C. (2010). Measuring the performance of acquisitions: An empirical investigation using multiple criteria. *British Journal of Management, 21*(4), 859–873.

Parrino, J. D., & Harris, R. S. (1999). Takeovers, management replacement, and post-acquisition operating performance: Some evidence from the 1980s. *Journal of Applied Corporate Finance, 11*(4), 88–96.

Pawaskar, V. (2001). Effect of mergers on corporate performance in India. *Vikalpa The Journal for Decision Makers, 26*(1), 19–32.

Pazarskis, M., Vogiatzogloy, M., Christodoulou, P., & Drogalas, G. (2006). Exploring the improvement of corporate performance after mergers–the case of Greece. *International Research Journal of Finance and Economics, 1*, 184–192.

Penman, S. H. (2003). The quality of financial statements: Perspectives from the recent stock market bubble. *Accounting Horizons, 17*, 77–96.

Pham, N., Oh, K. B., & Pech, R. (2015). Mergers and acquisitions: CEO duality, operating performance and stock returns in Vietnam. *Pacific-Basin Finance Journal, 35*, 298–316.

Pop, D. (2006). M&A market in transition economies: Evidence from Romania. *Emerging Markets Review, 7*, 244–260.

Powell, R. G., & Stark, A. W. (2005). Does operating performance increase post-takeover for UK takeovers? A comparison of performance measures and benchmarks. *Journal of Corporate Finance, 11*, 293–317.

Rahahleh, N. A., & Wei, P. P. (2012). The performance of frequent acquirers: Evidence from emerging markets. *Global Finance Journal, 23*, 16–33.

Rahim, N. M., & Pok, W. C. (2013). Shareholder wealth effects of M&As: The third wave from Malaysia. *International Journal of Managerial Finance, 9*(1), 49–69.

Rahman, R. A., & Limmack, R. J. (2004). Corporate acquisitions and the operating performance of Malaysian companies. *Journal of Business Finance & Accounting, 31*, 359–400.

Ramakrishnan, K. (2010). Mergers in Indian industry: Performance and impacting factors. *Business Strategy Series, 11*(4), 261–268.

Rani, N., Yadav, S. S., & Jain, P. K. (2012). Impact of mergers and acquisitions on returns to shareholders of acquiring firms: Indian economy in perspective. *Journal of Financial Management and Analysis, 25*(1), 1–24.

Rani, N., Yadav, S. S., & Jain, P. K. (2015). Impact of cross-border acquisitions' announcements on shareholders' wealth: Evidence from India. *Global Business and Economics Review, 17*(4), 360–382.

Rani, N., Yadav, S. S., & Jain, P. K. (2016). *Mergers and acquisitions (A study of financial performance, motives and corporate governance)*. Singapore: Springer.

Rao-Nicholson, R., Salaber, J., & Cao, T. H. (2016). Long-term performance of mergers and acquisitions of mergers and acquisitions in ASEAN countries. *Research in International Business and Finance, 36*, 373–387.

Schoenberg, R. (2006). Measuring the performance of corporate acquisitions: An empirical comparison of alternative metrics. *British Journal of Management, 17*(4), 361–370.

Schwert, G. W. (1996). Markup pricing in mergers and acquisitions. *Journal of Financial Economics, 41*, 153–162.

Sehgal, S., Banerjee, S., & Deisting, F. (2012). The impact of M&A announcement and financing strategy on stock returns: Evidence from BRICKS markets. *International Journal of Economics and Finance, 4*(11), 76–90.

Servaes, H. (1991). Tobin's Q and the gains from takeovers. *The Journal of Finance, 46*(1), 409–419.

Seth, A. (1990). Value creation in acquisitions: A re-examination of performance issues. *Strategic Management Journal, 11*(2), 99–115.

Shams, S. M. M., & Gunasekarage, A. (2016). Private public distinction of the target and the long run operating performance of acquirers. *Pacific Accounting Review, 28*(1), 38–58.

Sharma, D. S., & Ho, J. (2002). The impact of acquisitions on operating performance: Some Australian evidence. *Journal of Business Finance & Accounting, 29*, 155–200.

Singh, P., Suri, P., & Sah, R. (2012). Economic value added in Indian cross border mergers. *International Journal of Business Research, 12*(2), 160–164.

Sirower, M. L., & O'Byrne, S. F. (1998). The measurement of post-acquisition performance: Toward a value-based benchmarking methodology. *Journal of Applied Corporate Finance, 11*(2), 107–121.

Song, X., Tippett, M., & Vivian, A. (2017). Assessing abnormal returns: The case of Chinese M& A acquiring firms. *Research in International Business and Finance, 42*, 191–207.

Sudarsanam, S. (2003). *Creating value from mergers and acquisitions: The challenges, an international and integrated perspective*. Harlow: FT Prentice Hall.

Switzer, J. A. (1996). Evidence on real gains in corporate acquisitions. *Journal of Economics and Business, 48*, 443–460.

Thanos, I. C., & Papadakis, V. M. (2012). Unbundling acquisition performance: How do they perform and how can this be measured? In D. Faulkner, S. Teerikangas, & R. J. Joseph (Eds.), *The Handbook of Mergers and Acquisitions*. Oxford: Oxford University Press.

Trojanowski, G. (2008). Equity block transfers in transition economies: Evidence from Poland. *Economic Systems, 32*(3), 217–238.

Tsung-Ming, Y., & Hoshino, Y. (2000). The effects of mergers and acquisitions on Taiwanese corporations. *Review of Pacific Basin Financial Markets and Polices, 3*(2), 183–199.

Tuch, C., & O'Sullivan, N. (2007). The impact of acquisitions on firm performance: A review of the evidence. *International Journal of Management Reviews, 9*(2), 141–170.

Walker, M. (2000). Corporate takeovers, strategic objectives, and acquiring-firm shareholder wealth. *Financial Management, 29*(1), 53–66.

Yaghoubi, R., Yaghoubi, M., Locke, S., & Gibb, J. (2016a). Mergers and acquisitions: A review (Part 1). *Economic Studies in Economics and Finance, 33*(1), 147–188.

Yaghoubi, R., Yaghoubi, M., Locke, S., & Gibb, J. (2016b). Mergers and acquisitions: A review (Part 2). *Economic Studies in Economics and Finance, 33*(3), 437–464.

Yeh, T. M., & Hoshino, Y. (2002). Productivity and operating performance of Japanese merging firms: Keiretsu-related and independent mergers. *Japan and the World Economy, 14*, 347–366.

Yook, K. C. (2004). The measurement of post-acquisition performance using EVA. *Quarterly Journal of Business and Economics, 43*(3/4), 67–83.

Zaheer, A., Hernandez, E., & Banerjee, S. (2010). Prior alliances with targets and acquisition performance in knowledge-intensive industries. *Organization Science, 21*(5), 1072–1091.

Zhang, S. (2015). An analysis of wealth change of acquiring-firm shareholders in the recent technology mergers wave in US. *Organization Science, 38*(5), 1056–1067.

Zhou, B., Guo, J. M., Hua, J., & Doukas, A. J. (2015). Does state ownership drive M&A performance? Evidence from China: Does state ownership drive M&A performance? *European Financial Management, 21*, 79–105.

Zhu, P. C., & Jog, V. (2012). Impact on target firm risk-return characteristics of domestic and cross-border mergers and acquisitions in emerging markets. *Emerging Markets Finance & Trade, July–August 2012, 48*(4), 79–101.

Zhu, H., & Zhu, Q. (2016). Mergers and acquisitions by Chinese firms: A review and comparison with other mergers and acquisitions research in the leading journals. *Asia Pacific Journal of Management, 33*(4), 1107–1149.

Zollo, M., & Meier, D. (2008). What is M&A performance? *Academy of Management Perspective, 22*, 55–77.

Determinants of Cross-Border M&As and Shareholder Wealth Effects in a Globalized World

Eugene Nivorozhkin

Abstract We analyze theoretical insights and empirical regularities related to factors determining the cross-border mergers and acquisitions (M&As) and impact of M&As on shareholder value of acquires and targets. The analysis of cross-border M&As is a relatively new subject and only recently received rigorous attention in academic research. Within this nascent literature, the survey pays particular attention to the emerging markets, which, in line with their growing role of in the global economy, became an increasingly important arena for cross-border M&As. The existing evidence point out to prevailing challenges in studying cross-border M&As by emerging markets firms. The results are often contradictory and tend to focus on a single country falling short of formally testing existing theories or developing comprehensive theories for emerging economies. We show that the type of factors increasing the value enhancing effects of M&As tends to be similar to the factors affecting the likelihood of M&As transactions. The remaining methodological challenges for the existing studies are related to strong evidence with respect to nonrandom selection of acquisition targets, which, among other "selection issues," has important implications for choosing counterfactual evidence in order to appropriately compare pre- and postacquisition performance of firms.

Keywords Mergers · Acquisitions · Emerging markets · Shareholder value · Selection bias

1 Introduction

The global market for mergers and acquisitions (M&As) has been steadily expanding in the recent years, recovering from the slump caused by the Global Financial Crisis of 2008–2009, with both the number and the volume of transactions

E. Nivorozhkin (✉)
School of Slavonic and East European Studies, University College London, London, UK
e-mail: e.nivorozhkin@ucl.ac.uk

© Springer Nature Switzerland AG 2020
I. Ivashkovskaya et al. (eds.), *Strategic Deals in Emerging Capital Markets*,
Advanced Studies in Emerging Markets Finance,
https://doi.org/10.1007/978-3-030-23850-6_3

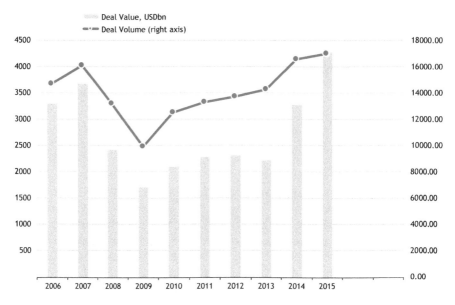

Fig. 1 Global M&As deals (Source: KPMG 2016)

reaching the record-high levels (see Fig. 1). Nevertheless, the value of global M&As transitions as a share of GDP tended to remain below the levels observed in the pre-crisis years. As in the past, the increasing number of the worldwide M&As could be attributed to the dynamic nature of international trade and the consolidations of industries and regions (Shimizu et al. 2004). Moreover, the increasing globalization of business has dramatically increased the opportunities and pressures to engage in cross-border M&As in a turbulent and continuously changing environment (Hitt 2000). While the majority of M&As involved two firms within the same country, the share of cross-border transactions value in the total value of M&As deal remained significant at 31% in 2015, similar to what was observed in 2011 and below the 39% observed in 2007 (KPMG 2016).

Given the increasing number of cross-border M&As and their growing importance in the global market, this survey will focus on factors determining the cross-border M&As activities—the issue which only recently received rigorous attention in academic research. We will also look at whether cross-border M&As transactions created wealth for firms' shareholders and whether the magnitude of this wealth creation and its distribution between acquiring and target firms' shareholders was different comparing to domestic M&As deals. The survey will pay particular attention to the emerging markets, which became an increasingly important arena for M&As, in line with their growing role in the global economy.

Understanding factors affecting the value and the volume of mergers and acquisitions is of great importance from both practical and academic perspectives. As many other mechanisms employed in the market-based economic systems, M&As are expected to contribute to efficient allocation of scarce resources in the economy by facilitating reallocation of control over companies, such that corporate assets are channeled toward their best possible use. Success or failure of combining companies through M&As to achieve certain strategic and business objectives is important not only for the companies themselves but also has important implications for workers, managers, competitors, communities, and the economy as a whole (Sudarsanam 2003). M&As are a multistage process characterized by a number of diverse problems and challenges for the firms involved. The historical developments in the market for corporate control indicate that the external context in which M&As take place is of crucial importance for understanding the issues affecting transactions. This external environment for the M&As transactions extends beyond purely economic considerations and includes political, sociological, and technological factors.

From the theoretical perspective, the foreign market entry of an acquirer is likely to be driven by desire to utilize its comparative advantage in exploiting market imperfections (e.g., Buckley and Casson 1976; Morck and Yeung 1992; Wilson 1980). The benefits of integrating acquirer's business with another firm are typically accrued through internalization, synergy, and risk diversification and expected to create wealth for both acquirer and target-firm shareholders (Kang 1993; Markides and Ittner 1994; Morck and Yeung 1991, 1992).

The empirical evidence reviewed in this chapter seems to indicate that overall the cross-border M&As are more likely to create value and produce gain for both parties involved in the transaction comparing to the domestic M&As, which are typically categorized by positive returns for the seller and negative or neutral returns for the buyer, with nonexisting or marginally positive combined returns.

The surveyed literature also provides strong evidence with respect to nonrandom selection of acquisition targets and highlights unique challenges represented by the cross-border M&As deals which tend to involve firms from the countries with different economic, institutional, and cultural environments.

The remainder of the article is organized as follows. Section 2 reviews factors associated with the occurrence of the cross-border M&As deals. Section 3 looks at what factors tend to important for success of M&As in terms of creating shareholder value. Section 4 offers concluding remarks.

2 Determinants of Cross-Border M&As

Historically, M&As activities tend to exhibit distinct wave patterns within countries and globally, with bursts in terms of both volume and value of transactions followed by periods of relative inactivity (Gilson and Black 1995). Although the determinants of M&As waves are still not fully understood, there are several stylized facts identified in the literature. The contextual developments accompanying M&As waves tend to affect the competitive advantage of firms or open up new markets. These developments typically include periods of high economic growth, episodes of recovery from economic recession and rising stock market, as well as discovery of new technologies (e.g., Gort 1969; Bannock 1990; Jensen 1997). Merger waves also tend to depend on the political, regulatory, institutional, and demographic changes (e.g., Bhagat et al. 1990; Shleifer and Vishny 1991; Mitchell and Mulherin 1996; Andrade et al. 2001). Importantly, the effect of various factors on M&As activities tends to vary across industries, and there is evidence of industry clustering of these activities (e.g., Mitchell and Mulherin 1996; Schoenberg and Reeves 1999).

Andrade et al. (2001) point out that while research on M&As activities has revealed a lot about their trends and characteristics over the last century, research success on the issue of why mergers occur has been more limited. A number of complementary economic theories have been able to explain some of the mergers over the last century and helped to understand the M&As drivers. The leading theories supported by empirical evidence highlighted factors such as efficiency-related reasons for M&As, which typically involve economies of scale or other "synergies"; attempts to create market power, for example, by forming monopolies or oligopolies; market discipline, exemplified by the removal of incompetent management of a target company; "empire building" incentives by acquirer management to "overexpand" and other agency costs; and diversification strategies, involving exploiting internal capital markets and managing risk for undiversified managers. Importantly, these reasons for M&As appear to be relevant only in certain time periods.

Andrade et al. (2001) argue that the historically observed merger waves and industry clustering of M&As activities in the USA, documented in Mitchell and Mulherin (1996), suggest that mergers are likely to occur as a reaction to unexpected (and hence largely unpredictable) shocks to industry structure, the view which is also consistent with the prevailing intuition of practitioners and analysts. To this extent, the results in Andrade et al. (2001) indicate that M&As activities in the USA in the 1990s continued to be clustered by industry and were increasingly and predominantly influenced by an industry shock represented by deregulation.

Although the dynamics of cross-border M&As tends to be similar to those of domestic M&As, they also involve unique challenges, as countries have different economic, institutional (i.e., regulatory), and cultural environments (Hofstede 1984; House et al. 2002). Cross-border M&As can facilitate access to new and profitable markets and expand the market for a firm's existing products. For example, international M&As are often used to maintain market share and avoid possible future threats, with suppliers strategically following the international expansion of their counterparties who could otherwise find alternative foreign suppliers with potential negative implications for the domestic market share of the existing supplier (Martin et al. 1998) Moreover, acquisitions of foreign firms often help the acquirer to obtain new knowledge and capabilities.

In general, country-, industry-, and firm-level factors, related to both to the acquiring and to the target firm, are important determinants of cross-border M&As. The important national and industry level factors are capital, labor, and natural resource endowments. Moreover, institutional variables such as the legal, political, and cultural environment also tend to play a crucial role. At the firm level, the important task is to identify and evaluate potential targets, so they can be effectively integrated with the acquiring firm in the postacquisition period to realize the potential value of investment.

A recent study by Erel et al. (2012) focuses on international factors influencing the decision of firms to merge. These factors include cultural or geographic differences, governance-related differences across countries, and imperfect integration of capital markets across countries. The authors use a sample of 56,978 cross-border mergers occurring between 1990 and 2007, and involving both public and private companies, to estimate the factors that affect the likelihood that firms from any pair of countries merge in a particular year.

A number of relevant factors appear to significantly explain the cross-sectional pattern of mergers. The first set of factors is related to attractive valuation of a target company as a motivation for cross-border merger, where currency and capital market valuation differences can arise due to imperfect integration between countries. The importance of changes in relative valuation, which are likely to lead to acquisitions, tends to be supported by positive effects of the 12-month real exchange rate return difference between the two countries' currencies and 12-month stock return difference of the country indices in local currency, with both indicators measured during the 12-month prior to the year of acquisition. The valuation effects are also supported by a positive effect of the difference in the country-level value-weighted market-to-book ratios between acquirer and target countries. That is, firms from countries whose currencies appreciated over the sample period are more likely to be purchasers of firms whose currency depreciated and superior equity returns and growth opportunities are likely to be indicative of lower cost of capital for the acquirer increasing the probability of cross-border transaction. Moreover, both the stock and currency return differences tend to have a larger impact on the likelihood of acquisition in situations where the acquiring country is wealthier than the target country. The currency effect also tends to be larger for country pairs for which the geographical distance between them is closer than the sample median. Finally, the effect of the valuation differences in country-level stock returns tends to be strongest when the target's country imposes constraints on capital account openness and hence the overall financial liberalization is low. Overall, the results suggest that the decision of cross-border M&As is affected by valuation, and that valuation has the largest impact on country pairs for which cross-border M&As are more probable for other reasons. Given that changes in valuation lead to M&As conditional on other reasons indicate that cross-border M&A should not be thought of as a pure financial arbitrage, as in this case, the marginal effect of valuation on M&As likelihoods would be approximately the same regardless of the countries involved. Overall, the results suggest that the impact of valuation on probability of acquisition occurs because of the wealth effect described by Froot and Stein (1991) rather than the mispricing effect discussed by Shleifer and Vishny (2003).

The second set of factors used by Erel et al. (2012) is related to the fact that the decisions to engage in cross-border M&As are likely to be affected by cultural differences between countries (e.g., language, religion, historical conflicts), which could increase the contracting costs involved in linking two firms across borders (e.g., Ahern et al. 2015). Nevertheless, the results reveal that sharing a common language or religion does not affect merger propensities when controlling for other factors. In fact, the common cultural background of countries could be indirectly captured by the positive effect of bilateral trade flows on cross-border M&As.

In addition to cultural distance, geographic distance between countries involved in cross-border M&As is also likely to affect the probability of transaction. Similar to the arguments of the "gravity" literature in international trade, physical distance can increase the costs of combining two firms (see Rose 2000). The results in Erel et al. (2012) provide strong support for this hypothesis. Geographic proximity clearly matters and other things equal, the shorter distance between two countries increases the likelihood of cross-border M&As.

The empirical evidence also indicates that taxes appear to affect cross-border M&A decisions, since acquirers are more likely to be from countries with higher corporate income tax rates than the countries in which targets are located.

Moreover, the potential for value creation through M&As, and hence the incentives to engage in transaction, is also likely to be affected by corporate governance factors. For example, acquisition could increase the legal protection of minority shareholders in target firms by extending to them some of the rights of acquiring firms' shareholders. In general, corporate governance arguments implies that firms in countries that promote governance through better legal or accounting standards will tend to acquire firms in countries with lower-quality governance (e.g., Bris et al. 2008).

The level of market development could also affect cross-border M&As. In that respect, developed-market acquirers are likely to obtain more benefits from weaker contracting environments in emerging markets (Chari et al. 2009). The positive effect between the quality of accounting disclosure systems of the acquirer and the target found in Erel et al. (2012) is consistent with governance arguments, because development and accounting standards are likely to be correlated with better corporate governance. The authors also investigate separately an issue related to the fact that the quality of accounting disclosure effect could be driven by the generally lower level of economic development of emerging markets included in the sample. The results for separate subsamples of developed and emerging country targets indicate that disclosure quality matters in each subsample, but the effect is indeed stronger when the target is from an emerging market.

The links between the corporate governance and cross-border M&As are explored in greater details in Rossi and Volpin (2004). The chapter studies the determinants of mergers and acquisitions around the world by focusing on differences in laws and regulation across countries. The sample includes 45,536 M&A deals announced between January 1, 1990, and December 31, 1999, and completed as of December 31, 2001, and covers 49 countries for which empirical measures of investor protection were available at the time of the study.

The authors focus on two competing hypotheses. According to the outcome hypothesis (La Porta et al. 2000), greater legal protection for investors generates more deals and stimulates competition among bidders. The effect of higher investor protection materializes from greater availability of financial resources for the acquirer and lower acceptable prices for the targets due to lower private benefits of control of their managers and owners. The alternative governance hypothesis (Manne 1965; Jensen 1986) points out that the cross-border market for corporate control tends to target firms with poor governance, and hence this hypothesis predicts a negative relationship between investor protection and M&As activity across countries.

The authors find that in general, the volume of M&As activity is significantly larger in countries with better accounting standards and stronger shareholder protection. Similar to Erel et al. (2012), it is also found that in cross-border deals, targets typically come from countries with poorer investor protection than their acquirers' countries. The result holds when the authors control for bilateral trade, relative GNP per capita, and cultural and geographical differences. According to the authors, the result suggests that cross-border M&As activity plays an effective role in worldwide convergence in corporate governance standards (Coffee 1999).

In particular, Rossi and Volpin (2004) find that as expected, the common-law origin of the target's country reduces the likelihood of a cross-border deal, as the common-law countries tend to better protect minority shareholders than do countries with civil law (Porta et al. 1998). They also show that raising the accounting standards and an increase in shareholder protection tend to significantly decrease cross-border deals, when the cross-border M&As activity is measured as the number of cross-border deals as a percentage of all deals with target in each country. This suggests that cross-border M&As play a governance role by targeting firms in countries with lower investor protection, providing support for the governance hypothesis. In contrast, all measures of investor protection tend to exhibit positive and significantly correlation with the M&As activity in the cross-country relationship between overall M&As activity and investor protection, providing evidence in favor of the outcome hypothesis.

The governance hypothesis is supported further when Rossi and Volpin (2004) study the pattern of cross-border M&As by controlling at the same time for the characteristics of target and acquirer countries, using as the dependent variable the number of cross-country deals for each pair of countries as a percentage of the total number of deals in a target's country. According to the results, only the quality of the investor protection in the acquirer country positively and significantly affects the volume of deals between two countries. The overall findings on the effect of shareholder protection suggest that countries with better governance standards (proxied by higher shareholder protection) export their standards to other countries via cross-border deals, and this supports the governance hypothesis. The results are also consistent with the outcome hypothesis as countries with a more developed capital market (proxied by higher accounting standards) seem to use their lower cost of capital for cross-border acquisitions. Somewhat puzzling, the effects of the investor protection variables of the target country tend to be insignificant, when the acquirer's country characteristics are controlled for.

Further evidence focusing on the difference in investor protection between acquirer and target presented in Rossi and Volpin (2004) reconfirms that the acquirer typically has stronger investor protection than the target in cross-border M&As. The governance hypothesis is also supported by the fact that richer countries are more likely to be acquirers and that the acquirer and target in cross-border M&As typically share the same language and religion and come from the same geographical area.

The cross-border M&As originating from emerging markets are growing in importance globally as they tend to be the largest part of outward foreign direct investment (OFDI) from emerging economies, which itself constitutes about one-third of global OFDI flows (UNCTAD 2014). The general perception is that international expansion of emerging market firms (EMFs) helps them to achieve important strategic objectives, such as the acquisition of technology, brand names, and natural resources (UNCTAD 2014).

Most of the literature on the determinants of cross-border M&As uses the global samples of firms' transactions. A study focusing specifically on examining cross-border M&As by EMFs is rare and contradictory and most often focuses on a single country falling short of formally testing existing theories or developing comprehensive theories for emerging economies (Deng 2013; Kothari et al. 2013). A notable exception to this is a recent chapter by Deng and Yang (2015) which conducts a comparative investigation of cross-border mergers and acquisitions by emerging market firms. The authors use a sample of M&As deals by firms from nine emerging economies which generated the highest number of transactions in 2000–2012. The countries covered are Brazil, China, India, Indonesia, Mexico, Russia, South Africa, Thailand, and Turkey.

The chapter seeks to apply and extend resource dependence theory (Hillman et al. 2009) to comparatively investigate major factors that determine the level of cross-border M&A by EMFs in developed and developing markets. The authors argue that the resource dependence logic of M&As helps to better understand the international expansion strategies of EMFs via cross-border M&As, but it is also conditional on institutional environment (i.e., government effectiveness) in a target's country. The authors effectively focus on four main hypotheses. First, the size of financial market in a target's nation is expected to positively affect the number of cross-border M&As initiated by EMFs in both developed and developing countries (Di Giovanni 2005; Nicholson and Salaber 2013). Second, the natural resources of a target's country are expected to be positively associated with the number of cross-border M&As by emerging market firms in each target's country (Pfeffer and Salancik 2003; Gaur et al. 2014). Third, the strategic assets of a target's country, such as superior marketing expertise, product differentiation, patent-protected technology, and managerial know-how, are expected to be positively related to the number of cross-border M&As by emerging market firms in each target's country. Finally, government effectiveness of the target's country is expected to be negatively associated with the number of cross-border M&As by emerging market firms in each target's country and also decrease the potential effects of the target's country market size, natural resources, and strategic assets on the likelihood of a transaction (Santos and Eisenhardt 2005; Das and Teng 2001; Dress and Heugens 2013).

As a dependent variable, Deng and Yang (2015) use the total number of complete M&As deals made by firms of the nine EMFs in each target's country each year. In terms of main explanatory variables, the ratio of stock market capitalization to GDP is used to represent the size of financial market, the natural resource endowment of the target's country is proxied by the ratio of ore and metal exports to merchandize exports, the total number of patent registrations (both resident and nonresident) in a target's country used as a proxy of strategic assets, while the government effectiveness of a target's country is measured by one of the six worldwide governance indicators developed by Kaufmann et al. (2011). The control variables used include the annual growth rate of GDP in acquirer's country, the total value of foreign exchange reserves in acquirer's country, the ratio of stock market capitalization to GDP in acquirer's country, the index capturing the difference between the national culture of acquiring firms and those of target firms (Kogut and Singh 1988), and the lagged number of M&As deals.

According to the results, factors affecting the level of cross-border M&As by EMFs in developed markets tend to be different from those in developing markets. The effects of resource dependence on cross-border M&As by EMFs and the moderating effects of target's government effectiveness on the M&As intensity are fully supported in the setting of developed markets and, to some extent, supported in the setting of developing markets. In particular, the effect of strategic assets is insignificant in the sample of developing markets M&As, and government's effectiveness in target's developing countries positively rather than negatively affects the relationship between the number of cross-border M&As and the level of natural resources of target's markets. The latter result is potentially explained by the large scale of acquisitions related to natural resources where higher government effectiveness of a target's country could help to legally protect acquirer's long-term interests (Kamaly 2007; Peng et al. 2008).

The effects of control variables indicate that EMFs are likely to undertake more M&As in both developed and developing markets when their home countries have bigger financial market size, have higher foreign reserves, and when they undertook more acquisitions in the previous year. It also appears that EMFs are likely to undertake more M&As in developing markets when these markets have small cultural distance with acquirer's countries.

Finally, Deng and Yang (2015) show that target's country factors attracting Chinese M&As are different from those attracting other emerging economies. The effects of natural resources endowment, strategic assets, and market size are insignificant for Chinese M&As in developing countries. Moreover, target's government effectiveness in both developed and developing countries positively rather than negatively affects the relationships between Chinese cross-border M&As and the size of financial market, the richness of natural resources, and strategic assets of developed countries. Thus, the authors conclude that one needs to be cautious in generalizing the determinants of Chinese M&As deals to other EMFs.

Shedding more light on the findings of Deng and Yang (2015), a recent study conducted by McKinsey & Co (Cogman et al. 2015) finds that an increasing number of emerging-market companies engage in cross-border M&As to acquire technology, brands, and know-how. This trend represents a shift from traditional focus on acquiring strategic and natural resources.

Rather interestingly, transaction's dominant strategic motive is identified indirectly by adopting measured based on median R&D intensity and intangible assets per industry (for asset-seeking motives), median sales growth per industry (for market-seeking motives), median staff cost per industry (for efficiency-seeking motive), and target company affiliation with natural resource industry (for natural resource-seeking motives). The industry measures for each year and each country were assigned to acquiring and target companies and the standardized difference between two companies involved was used to determine the dominant strategic motive of a deal. Out of 1095 emerging-market cross-border acquisitions completed in 2000–2013 and covered by the study, 56% of companies headquartered in emerging markets try to fill capability gaps caused by limited access to strategic resources, such as technology, management capabilities, or other intangible assets in their home markets. This is compared to 37% of companies in developed markets (69,657 acquisitions by companies from the OECD member-countries). The motive of tapping new markets and customers or sustaining existing markets accounts for 14% of emerging markets and 18% of developed markets acquisitions, while securing access to natural resources, such as raw materials and energy, accounts for 21 and 10%, respectively. The motivation of improving efficiency by accessing production assets, such as labor, at a relatively lower cost unsurprisingly results in the largest gap with only 2% of emerging markets companies versus 26% of developed market companies.

The breakdown of the 2000–2013 period into subperiods reveals a striking evolvement in motivation of EM companies. The proportion of deal volume motivated by strategic resources steadily decreases from 77% in 2000–2003 to 61% in 2004–2007, 56% in 2008–2009, and 44% in 2010–2013. The deals motivated by access to natural resources are on the rise throughout most of the period, reaching 31% of the total in 2008–2009 but subsequently declining to 18% in 2010–2013. In contrast, the volume of deals motivated by access to new markets rises dramatically from under 10% in 2000–2009 to 28% in 2010–2013.

The least common reason for the emerging-market companies' cross-border acquisitions is in pursuit of efficiency. The motivation behind these types of deals, which account for only 4% of the total in 2010–2013, typically includes low labor costs and specific government policies related to import barriers or investment incentives. Responding to these incentives emerging markets companies move manufacturing capacity to foreign markets by acquiring production-related companies abroad. Moreover, the growing share of efficiency-seeking M&As by emerging-market bidders mainly flows into other emerging countries, where production factors are comparatively cheap.

The evidence of nonrandom selection of acquisition targets presented in some of the chapters surveyed so far is further supported by Chari et al. (2012). The authors study acquisitions of US firms by firms located in emerging markets and find that the selected US targets tend to be characterized by relatively high levels of sales, employment, and total assets. This selection issue has important implications for choosing counterfactual evidence in order to appropriately compare pre- and postacquisition performance of target firms – the issue, which will be discussed in more detail in the next section.

3   Determinants of M&As Value Creation for Shareholders

The crucial issue in cross-border M&As transactions is whether they create wealth for firms' shareholders and whether the magnitude of this wealth creation and its distribution between acquiring and target firms' shareholders is different comparing to domestic M&As deals. From the theoretical perspective, the foreign market entry of an acquirer is likely to be driven by desire to utilize its comparative advantage in exploiting market imperfections (e.g., Buckley and Casson 1976; Morck and Yeung 1992; Wilson 1980). The benefits of integrating acquirer's business with another firm are typically accrued through internalization, synergy, and risk diversification and expected to create wealth for both acquirer and target-firm shareholders (Kang 1993; Markides and Ittner 1994; Morck and Yeung 1991, 1992).

Market reaction to M&As deal announcements tend to differ for cross-border and domestic M&A. The latter ones are typically categorized by positive returns for the seller and negative or neutral returns for the buyer, with nonexisting or marginally positive combined returns (Kaplan and Weisbach 1992; Carow et al. 2004). It has been argued that target shareholders gain from the acquisition because of the premium paid by the acquirer (Datta et al. 1992; Hansen and Lott 1996).

The existing evidence indicate that the cross-border M&As are more likely to create value and produce gain for both parties involved in the transaction. For example, Morck and Yeung (1992) examined 332 foreign acquisitions by US firms between 1978 and 1988 and found that the acquirer's abnormal returns were positively related to acquirer's R&D and advertising intensity, as well as its management quality. According to the authors, these factors represented information-based resources that allowed the acquirer to effectively internalize the assets of the target.

Markides and Ittner (1994) used a sample of 276 cross-border M&As by US firms between 1975 and 1988 and found positive association between acquirer's abnormal returns and acquirer's home currency strength, prior international experience, industry advertising intensity, industry concentration, business relatedness of two firms, and the relative size of the acquirer and the target firms' business.

Harris and Ravenscraft (1991) looked at M&As transactions where US firms were the targets of foreign buyers and find that target wealth gains were significantly higher in cross-border deals than in domestic acquisitions. Foreign companies paid about 10 percentage points (about 50%) more than domestic firms in noncash bid and premiums were positively related to R&D intensity of the industries, and the relative strength of the buyer's currency.

Kang (1993) studied M&As deals of 119 Japanese firms involving 102 US firms between 1975 and 1988. The results indicated that cross-border M&As created wealth for both acquirer and target firm shareholders. The acquiring firms' gains were positively associated with the relative strength of their home currency, and their overall level of debt and borrowings from financial institutions, suggesting that high leverage alleviates potential agency costs (Jensen 1986).

Datta and Puia (1995) studied shareholder value creation in 112 large cross-border M&As transactions undertaken by US firms between 1978 and 1990. In contrast to the previously reviewed studies, their results suggested that cross-border M&As, on average, do not create value for acquiring firm shareholders. The authors also found that M&As deals characterized by high cultural distance were associated with lower wealth effects for acquiring firm shareholders.

Manzon et al. (1994) focused on difference between tax systems of countries involved in cross-border M&As. The authors found that US acquirers' abnormal returns were higher when targets were located in high-tax countries, rather than low-tax countries. According to the authors, acquisitions that increased acquiring firms' ability to repatriate funds to USA resulted in a positive market reaction, while transactions that were likely to result in income that would trigger additional US taxes upon repatriation resulted in an unfavorable market reaction.

Cakici et al. (1996) examined shareholder wealth gains for 195 foreign firms that acquired US target firms during 1983–1992. Positive and significant abnormal returns were documented for foreign acquirers of the US targets but not for the US companies purchasing foreign firms. The changes in the US tax code did not appear to affect gains to foreign buyers of US firms. The authors also found that acquirer's abnormal returns were not affected by relative size of target to bidder, acquirer's overseas exposure, the target's R&D intensity, industry factors, or relative value of currency. The results suggested that competition among bidding firms for the same target decreases the returns to the acquirers.

In an attempt to reconcile the conflicting results of the previous research, Seth et al. (2002) analyzed factors that create or destroy value in cross-border M&As by focusing on different motives for acquisitions. The authors found that the value creating deals tend to be the ones focusing on synergies realized in combining firms' complementary assets. The documented sources of value creations were asset sharing, reverse internalization of valuable intangible assets, and financial diversification. The value-destroying deals were the ones where managers pursued their personal interest or made mistakes in the target evaluation process.

The importance of management qualities for value-creating M&As was reconfirmed by Servaes (1991). Using Tobin's q as a measure of managers' performance, the author found that M&As gains were the highest when firms with high Tobin's Q acquired firms with low Tobin's Q. In other words, better performing firms were more likely to make better acquisitions and more value was created from acquiring underperforming companies.

The increasing importance of emerging markets for the global economy and the growing volume of M&As transaction involving companies from these countries motivated a number of recent studies focusing on M&As' performance and its determinants in emerging markets (Lebedev et al. 2015).

Aybar and Ficici (2009) studied 433 acquisitions by multinational companies from emerging markets from 1991 to 2004 and found that abnormal returns for acquiring firms were on average negative. Nevertheless, abnormal returns were shown to be positively associated with the relative size of the target, private ownership of the target, and diversification motives of transactions. The value destruction was observed when the acquirer was from high-tech industry or the industry similar to a target. Consistent with the results of previous studies (Feito-Ruiz and Menéndez-Requejo 2011), the institutional development of a target's country was found to have a positive effect on abnormal returns for acquiring firms.

Gubbi et al. (2010) studied performance of 425 cross-border acquisitions of Indian firms between 2000 and 2007. The authors found support for the hypothesis that cross-border M&As create shareholder value for acquiring firms. According to the authors, international acquisitions helped to internalize resources that were difficult to trade through market transactions and were costly to develop internally, suggesting an important strategic aspect of value creation for emerging-economy firms. It was also shown that the value created for acquiring firms' shareholders was greater when the target firms were located in advanced economic and institutional environments.

Bhagat et al. (2011) looked at 698 cross-border acquisitions made by firms from emerging markets from 1991 to 2008. The authors documented positive abnormal returns for acquirers on the announcement day. The acquiring firms returns were positively related to the quality of corporate governance in the target country, suggesting that the acquirers voluntarily 'bootstraps' themselves to the higher governance standards of the target (Martynova and Renneboog 2008; Khanna and Palepu 2004).

Nicholson and Salaber (2013) studied 203 Indian and 63 Chinese cross-border deals over the period 2000–2010 and found evidence of significant shareholder wealth creation for acquiring firms. The authors found that Indian shareholders' gains were positively affected by small cultural distance with targets' countries, while Chinese investors benefited from the cross-border enlargement of manufacturing companies. Similar to the previously reviewed studies, acquisitions of firms from developed countries generated higher returns to shareholders.

Chari et al. (2012) analyzed 594 cross-border M&As deals from 1986 to 2006, where a developed-country multinational firm acquired majority control of a firm in an emerging market. The authors found that developed-market acquirers experienced positive and significant abnormal returns over a three-day event window and these abnormal returns for the same acquires were not observed when their targets were from the developed countries. The abnormal returns were found to be higher in the weaker contracting environment in the emerging market and in industries with high proportion of intangible assets.

Chari et al. (2012) study changes in the performance of US firms acquired by firms from emerging markets. The authors document significant improvements in the post-acquisition stock market and accounting-based measures of performance of publicly listed US targets. Nevertheless, the presented evidence highlights the importance of selecting an appropriate matched sample of control firms that were not acquired in order to correctly evaluate the changes in targets' post-acquisition performance by separating casual and selection effects in M&As. The propensity score matching approach employed to group together relatively similar acquired and non-acquired firms results in the 47–99% reduction in the bias for observable covariates. That is, the difference of means of selected covariates (e.g., sales, assets, employment, net income, debt, firm-age) between the two groups becomes statistically insignificantly only after implemented matching procedure, which in turn allows to appropriately evaluate changes in postacquisition performance and the effects of restructuring measures. The empirical results based on propensity score matching and difference-in-difference approach indicate an increase in profitability and efficiency improvements of acquired firms in line with the set hypothesis. The authors also document the positive and significant announcement period abnormal returns for the targets in the range of 8.9–9.7%, which is lower than what tends to be observed in domestic US M&As (Andrade et al. 2001).

4 Conclusions

The studies of the cross-border M&As deals only recently received rigorous attention in academic research. In this survey, we summarize the existing evidence on factors determining the cross-border M&As activities and look at whether cross-border M&As transactions tend to create wealth for firms' shareholders. A particular attention is paid to the evidence from the emerging markets, which became an increasingly important arena for M&As, in line with their growing role in the global economy. The dynamic and changing environment of the M&As activities of the emerging markets firms is clearly represented by a documented recent trend indicating a shift from traditional focus on acquiring strategic and natural resources toward acquisition of technology, brands, and know-how. The existing empirical evidence highlights unique challenges represented by the cross-border M&As deals which tend to involve firms from the countries with different economic, institutional, and cultural environments.

The reviewed chapters also provide strong evidence with respect to nonrandom selection of acquisition targets, which, among other "selection issues," has important implications for choosing counterfactual evidence in order to appropriately compare pre- and postacquisition performance of firms. A number of researches acknowledged that the empirical corporate takeover literature is plagued with largely unresolved econometric issues of endogeneity and self-selection, but corrections for self-selection are still relatively seldom discussed and implemented in empirical tests (e.g., Betton et al. 2008; Ahern 2009; Chari et al. 2012; Nivorozhkin et al. 2014). More research is this area is clearly warranted, and it would likely to have important implications on the existing results in the literature.

While following distinct wave patterns over time, the likelihood of the cross-border M&As deals tends to be positively (or nonnegatively) related to the attractive valuation of the target companies, more developed capital market of an acquirer's country relative to a target's country, geographical proximity between countries, and lower cultural differences between countries. The corporate governance factors also tend to play an important role. A weaker contracting environment of a target's country tends to increase the propensity of M&As deal involving a developed country's acquirer. To this extent, it appears that M&As activity tends to play an effective role in worldwide convergence in corporate governance standards. Nevertheless, when emerging market firms acquire firms in a developing country, the corporate governance proxies tend to have a positive effect on the number of M&As deals, particularly when conditional on some control variables, such as the industry of an M&As deal.

The cross-border M&As appear to be more likely to create value and produce gain for both parties involved in the transaction comparing to the domestic M&As. As the type of factors increasing the value enhancing effects tend to be similar to the factors affecting the likelihood of M&As transactions listed earlier, we again emphasize the importance of using an appropriate matched sample of control firms that were not acquired in order to correctly evaluate the changes in postacquisition performance by separating casual and selection effects.

References

Ahern, K. (2009). Sample selection and event study estimation. *Journal of Empirical Finance, 16*, 466–482.

Ahern, K., Daminelli, D., & Fracassi, C. (2015). Lost in translation? The effect of cultural values on mergers around the world. *Journal of Financial Economics, 117*(1), 165–189.

Andrade, G., Mitchell, M., & Stafford, E. (2001). New evidence and perspectives on mergers. *Journal of Economic Perspectives, 15*(2), 103–120.

Aybar, B., & Ficici, A. (2009). Cross-border acquisitions and firm value: An analysis of emerging-market multinationals. *Journal of International Business Studies, 40*(8), 1317–1338.

Bannock, G. (1990). *The takeover boom: An international and historical perspective*. Edinburgh: David Hume Institute.

Betton, S., Eckbo, E., & Thorburn, K. (2008). Corporate takeovers. In E. Eckbo (Ed.), *Handbook of corporate finance: Empirical corporate finance, Chapter 15* (Vol. 2). North-Holland: Elsevier.

Bhagat, S., Shleifer, A., & Vishny, R. (1990). Hostile takeovers in the 1980s: The return to corporate specialisation. *Brookings Chapters on Economic Activity: Microeconomics*, 1–72.

Bhagat, S., Malhotra, S., & Zhu, P. (2011). Emerging country cross-border acquisitions: Characteristics, acquirer returns and cross-sectional determinants. *Emerging Markets Review, 12*(3), 250–271.

Bris, A., Brisley, N., & Cabolis, C. (2008). Adopting better corporate governance: Evidence from cross-border mergers. *Journal of Corporate Finance, 14*(3), 224–240.

Buckley, P. J., & Casson, M. C. (1976). *The future of multinational enterprise*. London: Macmillan.

Cakici, N., Hessel, C., & Tandon, K. (1996). Foreign acquisitions in the United States: Effect on shareholder wealth of foreign acquiring firms. *Journal of Banking & Finance, 20*(2), 307–329.

Carow, K., Heron, R., & Saxton, T. (2004). Do early birds get the returns? An empirical investigation of early-mover advantages in acquisitions. *Strategic Management Journal, 25*(6), 563–585.

Chari, A., Ouimet, P. P., & Tesar, L. L. (2009). The value of control in emerging markets. *The Review of Financial Studies, 23*(4), 1741–1770.

Chari, A., Chen, W., & Dominguez, K. M. (2012). Foreign ownership and firm performance: Emerging market acquisitions in the United States. *IMF Economic Review, 60*(1), 1–42.

Coffee, J. C., Jr. (1999). Privatization and corporate governance: The lessons from securities market failure. *Journal of Corporation Law, 25*, 1.

Cogman, D., Jaslowitzer, P., & Rapp, M. S. (2015, July 13). *Why emerging-market companies acquire abroad*. McKinsey Insights.

Das, T. K., & Teng, B. S. (2001). Trust, control, and risk in strategic alliances: An integrated framework. *Organization Studies, 22*(2), 251–283.

Datta, D. K., Pinches, G. E., & Narayanan, V. K. (1992). Factors influencing wealth creation from mergers and acquisitions: A meta-analysis. *Strategic Management Journal, 13*(1), 67–84.

Datta, D. K., & Puia, G. (1995). Cross-border acquisitions: An examination of the influence of relatedness and cultural fit on shareholder value creation in US acquiring firms. *MIR: Management International Review*, 337–359.

Deng, P. (2013). Chinese outward direct investment research: Theoretical integration and recommendations. *Management and Organization Review, 9*(3), 513–539.

Deng, P., & Yang, M. (2015). Cross-border mergers and acquisitions by emerging market firms: A comparative investigation. *International Business Review, 24*(1), 157–172.

Di Giovanni, J. (2005). What drives capital flows? The case of cross-border M&A activity and financial economies. *Economic Systems, 28*, 281–300.

Dress, J., & Heugens, P. (2013). Synthesizing and extending resource dependence theory: A meta-analysis. *Journal of Management, 39*(6), 1666–1668.

Erel, I., Liao, R. C., & Weisbach, M. S. (2012). Determinants of cross-border mergers and acquisitions. *The Journal of Finance, 67*(3), 1045–1082.

Feito-Ruiz, I., & Menéndez-Requejo, S. (2011). Cross-border mergers and acquisitions in different legal environments. *International Review of Law and Economics, 31*(3), 169–187.

Froot, K. A., & Stein, J. C. (1991). Exchange rates and foreign direct investment: an imperfect capital markets approach. *The Quarterly Journal of Economics, 106*(4), 1191–1217.

Gaur, A. S., Kumar, V., & Singh, D. (2014). Institutions, resources, and internationalization of emerging economy firms. *Journal of World Business, 49*(1), 12–20.

Gilson, R. J., & Black, B. S. (1995). *The law and finance of corporate acquisitions (University Casebook).* New York: Foundation Press.

Gort, M. (1969). An economic disturbance theory of mergers. *The Quarterly Journal of Economics*, 624–642.

Gubbi, S. R., Aulakh, P. S., Ray, S., Sarkar, M. B., & Chittoor, R. (2010). Do international acquisitions by emerging-economy firms create shareholder value? The case of Indian firms. *Journal of International Business Studies, 41*(3), 397–418.

Hansen, R. G., & Lott, J. R. (1996). Externalities and corporate objectives in a world with diversified shareholder/consumers. *Journal of Financial and Quantitative Analysis, 31*(1), 43–68.

Harris, R. S., & Ravenscraft, D. (1991). The role of acquisitions in foreign direct investment: Evidence from the US stock market. *The Journal of Finance, 46*(3), 825–844.

Hillman, A. J., Withers, M. C., & Collins, B. J. (2009). Resource dependence theory: A review. *Journal of Management, 35*(6), 1404–1427.

Hitt, M. A. (2000). The new frontier: Transformation of management for the new millennium. *Organizational Dynamics, 28*(3), 7–17.

Hofstede, G. (1984). *Culture's consequences: International differences in work-related values* (Vol. 5). Thousand Oaks, CA: Sage.

House, R., Javidan, M., Hanges, P., & Dorfman, P. (2002). Understanding cultures and implicit leadership theories across the globe: an introduction to project GLOBE. *Journal of World Business, 37*(1), 3–10.

Jensen, M. C. (1986). Agency costs of free cash flow, corporate finance, and takeovers. *The American Economic Review, 76*(2), 323–329.

Jensen, M. C. (1997). The modern industrial revolution, exit and the failure of internal control mechanisms in chew. In C. Donald (Ed.), *Studies in international corporate finance and governance systems: A comparison of the US, Japan, & Europe.* New York: Oxford University Press.

Kamaly, A. (2007). Trends and determinants of mergers and acquisitions in developing countries in the 1990s. *International Research Journal of Finance and Economics, 8*, 16–30.

Kang, J. K. (1993). The international market for corporate control: Mergers and acquisitions of US firms by Japanese firms. *Journal of Financial Economics, 34*(3), 345–371.

Kaplan, S. N., & Weisbach, M. S. (1992). The success of acquisitions: Evidence from divestitures. *The Journal of Finance, 47*(1), 107–138.

Kaufmann, D., Kraay, A., & Mastruzzi, M. (2011). The worldwide governance indicators: methodology and analytical issues. *Hague Journal on the Rule of Law, 3*(2), 220–246.

Khanna, T., & Palepu, K. G. (2004). Globalization and convergence in corporate governance: Evidence from Infosys and the Indian software industry. *Journal of International Business Studies, 35*(6), 484–507.

Kogut, B., & Singh, H. (1988). The effect of national culture on the choice of entry mode. *Journal of International Business Studies, 19*(3), 411–432.

Kothari, T., Kotabe, M., & Murphy, P. (2013). Rules of the game for emerging market multinational companies from China and India. *Journal of International Management, 19*(3), 276–299.

KPMG. (2016, March). *Cross-border deals tracker.*

La Porta, R., Lopez-de-Silanes, F., Shleifer, A., & Vishny, R. W. (2000). Agency problems and dividend policies around the world. *The Journal of Finance, 55*(1), 1–33.

Lebedev, S., Peng, M. W., Xie, E., & Stevens, C. E. (2015). Mergers and acquisitions in and out of emerging economies. *Journal of World Business, 50*(4), 651–662.

Manne, H. G. (1965). Mergers and the market for corporate control. *Journal of Political Economy, 73*(2), 110–120.

Manzon, G. B., Jr., Sharp, D. J., & Travlos, N. G. (1994). An empirical study of the consequences of US tax rules for international acquisitions by US firms. *The Journal of Finance, 49*(5), 1893–1904.

Markides, C. C., & Ittner, C. D. (1994). Shareholder benefits from corporate international diversification: Evidence from US international acquisitions. *Journal of International Business Studies, 25*(2), 343–366.

Martin, X., Swaminathan, A., & Mitchell, W. (1998). Organizational evolution in the interorganizational environment: Incentives and constraints on international expansion strategy. *Administrative Science Quarterly, 43*, 566–601.

Martynova, M., & Renneboog, L. (2008). Spillover of corporate governance standards in cross-border mergers and acquisitions. *Journal of Corporate Finance, 14*(3), 200–223.

Mitchell, M. L., & Mulherin, J. H. (1996). The impact of industry shocks on takeover and restructuring activity. *Journal of Financial Economics, 41*(2), 193–229.

Morck, R., & Yeung, B. (1991). Why investors value multinationality. *Journal of Business, 64*, 165–187.

Morck, R., & Yeung, B. (1992). Internalization: An event study test. *Journal of International Economics, 33*(1–2), 41–56.

Nicholson, R. R., & Salaber, J. (2013). The motives and performance of cross-border acquirers from emerging economies: Comparison between Chinese and Indian firms. *International Business Review, 22*(6), 963–980.

Nivorozhkin, E., Holmén, M., & Rana, R. (2014). Do anti-takeover devices affect the takeover likelihood or the takeover premium? *The European Journal of Finance, 20*(4), 319–340.

Peng, M. W., Wang, D. Y., & Jiang, Y. (2008). An institution-based view of international business strategy: A focus on emerging economies. *Journal of International Business Studies, 39*(5), 920–936.

Pfeffer, J., & Salancik, G. R. (2003). *The external control of organizations: A resource dependence perspective.* Palo Alto, CA: Stanford University Press.

Porta, R. L., Lopez-de-Silanes, F., Shleifer, A., & Vishny, R. W. (1998). Law and finance. *Journal of Political Economy, 106*(6), 1113–1155.

Rose, A. K. (2000). One money, one market: the effect of common currencies on trade. *Economic Policy, 15*(30), 08–45.

Rossi, S., & Volpin, P. F. (2004). Cross-country determinants of mergers and acquisitions. *Journal of Financial Economics, 74*(2), 277–304.

Santos, F. M., & Eisenhardt, K. M. (2005). Organizational boundaries and theories of organization. *Organization Science, 16*(5), 491–508.

Schoenberg, R., & Reeves, R. (1999). What determines acquisition activity within an industry? *European Management Journal, 17*(1), 93–98.

Servaes, H. (1991). Tobin's Q and the gains from takeovers. *The Journal of Finance, 46*(1), 409–419.

Seth, A., Song, K. P., & Pettit, R. R. (2002). Value creation and destruction in cross-border acquisitions: an empirical analysis of foreign acquisitions of US firms. *Strategic Management Journal, 23*(10), 921–940.

Shimizu, K., Hitt, M. A., Vaidyanath, D., & Pisano, V. (2004). Theoretical foundations of cross-border mergers and acquisitions: A review of current research and recommendations for the future. *Journal of International Management, 10*(3), 307–353.

Shleifer, A., & Vishny, R. W. (1991). Takeovers in the '60s and the '80s: Evidence and implications. *Strategic Management Journal, 12*(S2), 51–59.

Shleifer, A., & Vishny, R. W. (2003). Stock market driven acquisitions. *Journal of Financial Economics, 70*(3), 295–311.

Sudarsanam, S. (2003). *Creating value from mergers and acquisitions: The challenges: An integrated and international perspective.* Singapore: Pearson Education.

UNCTAD. (2014). *World investment report 2014: Investing in the SDG: An action plan.* New York, Geneva: UNCTAD.

Wilson, B. D. (1980). The propensity of multinational companies to expand through acquisitions. *Journal of International Business Studies, 11*(1), 59–64.

Meta-analysis of M&As Studies in Emerging Markets

Anna Baranovskaya and Margarita Stemasova

Abstract Mergers and acquisitions (M&As) are a specific type of investment and many such transactions are made each year. Recently, the role of emerging capital markets has significantly increased in the M&As market. The growing number of transactions and increasing volumes has generated a lot of research devoted to the effectiveness of M&As. Unfortunately, the conclusions are substantially different. A meta-analysis summarizes the results of previous research and gives an estimation of the explanatory power of one or another determinant included in empirical models considering the diversity among the research. This study determines how different variables affect the performance of M&As deals on average in emerging capital markets. This research is one of the first in this area for emerging capital markets, although there are several studies of developed capital markets, mainly the US market. The study was conducted on a sample of 26 articles about M&AS performance in emerging capital markets. The sample covers articles published from 2003 to 2014. Countries in the selected articles include China, India, Brazil, Russia, Malaysia, South Africa, Argentina, Chile, Slovenia, and Poland. For the analysis, we have chosen the most popular among research determinants of the M&As effectiveness: the method of payment, the size of the acquirer, the deal size, cross-border deals, private target company, ROE, industry relatedness, SOE target (state ownership in the target company), ROA, and the financial leverage of the acquirer. This analysis allows conclusions to be drawn about differences in the explanatory power of different determinants, which has practical application for further research. The strongest drivers of performance for emerging capital markets are method of payment, acquirer size, ROA, and industry relatedness.

A. Baranovskaya (✉) · M. Stemasova
NRU HSE, Moscow, Russia

© Springer Nature Switzerland AG 2020
I. Ivashkovskaya et al. (eds.), *Strategic Deals in Emerging Capital Markets*,
Advanced Studies in Emerging Markets Finance,
https://doi.org/10.1007/978-3-030-23850-6_4

Keywords Meta-analysis · Mergers and acquisitions · Emerging markets · Capital
markets · M&As performance

1 Introduction

The industrial development of emerging markets has been a powerful driver of
mergers and acquisitions (M&As). Past decades have shown an increase in M&As
activity, both in terms of the number of deals and the market value involved in these
deals. The share of emerging markets in the global volume of M&As has increased
from 5% to nearly 25% since the beginning of 2000s according to Bloomberg and
Thomson Reuters data. This increase in the number of M&As deals, both in
developed and emerging markets, has led to an increase in research on the impact
of M&As on company performance. For past decades, there has been a growing
body of research on the determinants of M&As performance. However, there is still
no consensus about the key factors of success and the reasons why M&As often fail.

In this study, our primary goal is to determine how different factors affect the
performance of M&As deals in emerging capital markets. A meta-analysis summarizes the results of previous research and gives an estimation of the explanatory
power of different determinants included in the empirical models, taking into
account the diversity among different researches. Further, meta-analysis is less
influenced by biases and measurement errors in particular chapters.

The current research contributes by:

- Developing criteria and methodology for the selection of research for meta-
analysis
- Identifying the determinants of M&As performance in nonfinancial sectors in
emerging capital markets
- Choosing an approach and estimating the degree of impact of identified determinants on M&As performance
- Developing a model, identifying the influence of chapter characteristics on the
explanatory power of a particular determinant in M&As deals
- Identifying factors influencing the results of investigations of M&As performance

The practical application of results includes the identification of grounds for and
tendencies of M&As deals and the determinants of M&As performance, which are
vital for management and boards of directors to improve the financial feasibility of
M&As strategies and the company's value growth because of M&As.

Authors mainly focus on worldwide samples of research, while implementing
meta-analysis methodology (Homberg et al. 2009; King et al. 2004; Stahl and Voigt
2003). However, this question has not been examined previously on a sample of
studies based on the data from emerging capital markets.

We use a large sample of 26 articles, which allows us to qualitatively estimate the
explanatory power of the determinants of M&As deals. Within the research, we
looked through all chapters and articles devoted to M&As performance in emerging

capital markets, which gives an estimation of the determinant's influence more accurately. The sample helps to determine whether the results of research and explanatory power of parameters depend on article characteristics itself (year of publication, methodology used, etc.).

In line with other studies, we include in our sample articles, which assess the performance of M&As deals using event study analysis, and in contrast to them, we also analyze articles, which used accounting studies. This allows us to compare the results and show whether there is a difference when using different dependent variables. As in many previous chapters, only market indicators were used. In addition, we consider all event windows for market indicators, which give a full estimation.

We examine the most popular determinants of the M&As performance such as the method of payment, the size of the acquirer, the deal size, cross-border deals, private target company, ROE, industry relatedness, SOE target, ROA, and the financial leverage of acquirer.

The remainder of this chapter is organized as follows: Section 2 is devoted to a literature review of meta-analysis research and on M&As performance investigations; Section 3 describes the sample of articles and chapters used for analysis; in Sect. 4, the used methodology is represented; and, finally, Section 5 provides research results.

2 Literature Review

There is a large amount of research devoted to M&As performance. This section contains a brief analysis of the main M&As trends, research perspectives on M&As performance, and the level of available knowledge on the problem. In addition, a brief review of meta-analysis on the topic is provided.

M&As influence different aspects of company performance, such as costs, profitability, and the enterprise value; however, the focus of this chapter is on market and accounting methods measuring company performance.

2.1 Economic Explanation

According to the Cournot model, if two companies merge in the presence of a third company, there will be two companies in the market. As a result, the output and profit of the merged firms will be lower than the total output and profit of the firms before merger.[1] The fact that this theory suggests mergers to be unprofitable for

---

[1]See, for instance, L. Pepall, D.J. Richards, G. Norman, 2005, Industrial Organisation, Contemporary theory and practice, Thomson, 2005, pp. 358–391.

companies, while M&As deals are widespread both in developed and in emerging markets, is called "the merger paradox." So much research investigates the success factors of M&As deals and particularly the significant factors for the combined company's performance.

This paradox exists in cases when the company after the merger is compared with a company with no such experience and there is an assumption that they are comparable. If we omit such an assumption, we notice that the company may become a Stackelberg leader after the merger and register higher profits afterward. M&As deals are also successful in cases when the company becomes diversified and operates in different industries.[2]

Huck et al. (2003) provide an alternative explanation for merger profitability. They assume that a company after a merger should not be considered as a separate company, but as a combination of the two previous companies, as if they are affiliates led by interconnected management. The key element of such a union is fast and free information flow between the two companies and the absence of any barriers. The market becomes a hybrid for such companies, where one company becomes a Stackelberg leader, the other a follower. As a result, such a merger is advantageous for both companies and is characterized by profitability growth and an increase of competitive advantages in comparison with other market players.

2.2   Trends in M&As Deals

There is a changing trend in motives for M&As. We can observe the intention to win market power, diversification, entry into new markets, the divestment of assets, market discipline, and, finally, hostile takeovers. All these motives have been more or less popular in the past depending on particular external drives (e.g., the introduction of antitrust law, strong government interventions) and economic conjuncture as a whole.

Studies demonstrate that since the 1990s, M&As have become a way to weaken government intervention. The number of international deals has significantly grown due to the increased competition following globalization processes.

Another feature of M&As is waviness. Early research about waves of M&As identified that such waviness is caused by economic, regulatory, and technological shocks. Later studies found that there were various reasons common for all waves, in spite of a great number of factors influencing such wave effect. For instance, M&As waves traditionally occur during recovery periods after a serious economic crisis. They also tend to occur during sharp credit expansion, caused by growing external capital markets and booms on stock markets. M&As at the end of a wave usually demonstrate poor results and are ineffective, which may explain the inconsistences

---

[2]L. Pepall, D.J. Richards, G. Norman, 2005, Industrial Organisation, Contemporary theory and practice, Thomson, 2005.

among research on M&As performance. Such waves usually end up with continuous decline on stock markets and in the economy as a whole.

2.3 Determinants of M&As Performance

There are many different factors influencing M&As performance included in the empirical research. However, a meta-analysis approach requires focusing on the particular determinants which are the most popular among the studies in the sample. We identified such determinants of M&As performance (see Table 1).

2.3.1 Method of Payment

Studies show different effects of this determinant: negative in Ladkani and Banerjee; positive in Du and Boateng (2014), Chi et al. (2011), Chirkova and Chuvstvina (2011); and insignificant in Rahahleh and Wei (2012), Zhou et al. (2012), Bhabra and Huang (2013), Nurhazrina and Pok (2013), Kohli and Mann (2012).

It can be concluded that payment by cash has a positive effect on stock prices or will have no effect at all. This may be because samples of M&As deals are often significantly biased toward cash payments, which can distort the influence of this determinant.

2.3.2 The Size of Acquirer

The determinant "size of acquirer' was found in 77 model specifications among 13 articles from our sample. Authors usually use a natural logarithm of the total revenue or book value of assets as a proxy for measuring the acquirer's size. In half of our sample, this determinant has a negative effect on the M&As performance, while in the other half, it shows a positive effect. The following chapters report a negative effect on M&As performance: Rahahleh and Wei (2012), which considers 17 countries from emerging markets; Rahim et al. (2013) which studies Malaysian M&As; Bhaumink and Selarka (2008), etc. A positive effect is reported in studies by Zhou et al. (2012), which studies Chinese M&As; Bhagat et al. (2011), which considers eight emerging countries.

Studies show the size of the acquirer has contrasting influences on M&As performance. A positive effect was obtained mostly for Chinese and Russian samples. This can be explained by the fact that larger companies benefit more from mergers due to monetary aspects and administrative resources. The negative impact may be caused by the fact that very large companies may be less capable of growing more.

Table 1 Determinants of M&As performance in emerging capital markets and hypotheses of research

Determinant	Proxy	Number of model specification	Hypothesis
Method of payment	Equal 1 if the deal was paid by cash, and 0—if it was used anther methods (stock or mixed method).	66 model specifications among 26 articles	Hypothesis № 1: method of payment has high explanatory power on the performance of mergers and acquisitions.
The size of acquirer	Total revenue or book value of assets	77 model specifications among 13 articles	Hypothesis № 2: the size of acquirer has high explanatory power on the performance of mergers and acquisitions.
Deal size	Announcement value of the deal	18 model specification in 6 articles	Hypothesis № 3: the deal size has high explanatory power on the performance of mergers and acquisitions.
Cross-border deal	Equal 1 if deal is a cross-border deal and 0 in otherwise	18 model specifications in 4 articles	Hypothesis № 4: the 'cross-border deal' has high explanatory power on the performance of mergers and acquisitions.
Private-target deal	Equals 1 if the target company is a non-public, and 0 otherwise	32 model specifications 5 articles	Hypothesis № 5: the 'public-target' has high explanatory power on the performance of mergers and acquisitions.
ROE (return on equity)	The amount of net income returned as a percentage of shareholders' equity of target company	11 model specifications in 4 articles	Hypothesis №6: ROE has high explanatory power on the performance of mergers and acquisitions.
Industry relatedness	Equals 1 if the buyer and the target company operating in similar industries, 0— otherwise	64 model specifications from 15 articles	Hypothesis № 7: Industry has high explanatory power on the performance of mergers and acquisitions.
SOE (state-owned enterprise)	Equals 1 if in the ownership structure of the target company's present share of the state, and 0—otherwise.	27 model specifications in 8 articles	Hypothesis № 8: SOE has high explanatory power on the performance of mergers and acquisitions.
ROA (return on assets)	The amount of net income returned as a percentage of total assets of acquirer company	37 model specification in 5 articles	Hypothesis № 9: ROA has high explanatory power on the performance of mergers and acquisitions.
Financial leverage	Debt/equity	34 model specifications in 6 articles	Hypothesis № 10: Financial leverage of acquirer has high explanatory power on the performance of mergers and acquisitions.

2.3.3 Deal Size

A negative influence of deal size was shown in: Bhagat et al. (2011), Dakessian and Feldmann (2013), and a positive influence in Ladkani and Banerjee (2013).

A negative impact was found using large samples of developing countries, so it can be concluded that deal size has a negative effect on M&As performance. This is because large deals require borrowed funds, which may hinder the further development of the combined company.

2.3.4 Cross-Border Deals

Authors usually note a negative impact of cross-border deals on M&As performance (Bhabra and Huang 2013). Usually, cross-border deals are investigated independently from other deals. Therefore, it is impossible to make a firm conclusion about the impact of this factor. Cross-border deals can increase the stock value or reduce the performance after an M&As.

2.3.5 Private Target

Private-target determinant means publicity of the target company. It is also a dummy variable that equals 1 if the target company is a nonpublic and 0 otherwise. This variable was studied in 32 model specifications in five articles from the total sample. In most articles, private targets have, in general, a negative impact on the performance of the deal. However, in 30% of cases, it has a positive impact. This can be explained by the fact that the activity of listed companies is more transparent, so the deal is less risky. At some points, the buyer benefits from acquiring a private target company because of the liquidity discount, but this is true only for the short-term horizon (Nicholson and Salaber 2013).

2.3.6 ROE

ROE was found in 11 model specifications in four articles in our sample. It usually negatively influences M&As performance. This determinant is a proxy of investor expectations about the expected return.

2.3.7 Industry Relatedness

Industry relatedness is a dummy variable that equals 1 if the buyer and the target company operate in similar industries, and 0 otherwise. This variable can be observed in 64 model specifications in 15 articles of our sample. It is the third most common variable in studies. Authors generally note a positive impact of this variable on M&As performance; however, some studies observe a negative impact (Nurhazrina and Pok 2013; Kohli and Mann 2012). This may be because the acquisition of a company operating in a similar industry is a factor for company growth and can be positively interpreted by the market; however, it can also be a sign of lack of diversification, which, in turn, can be negatively interpreted by the market.

2.3.8 SOE

In most studies this determinant has a positive effect on the performance of M&As deals (Du and Boateng 2014; Chi et al. 2011; Nicholson and Salaber 2013; Gaur et al. 2013) as companies with state participation are more stable and less susceptible to market fluctuations. Moreover, SOEs give political and economic advantages to the firms and this will be reflected in stock prices.

2.3.9 ROA

ROA was found in 37 model specification in five articles. Authors found a positive effect on M&As performance. This determinant is usually used as an accounting profitability measure.

2.3.10 Financial Leverage

Financial leverage usually has a positive impact on M&As performance (Yen et al. 2013; Gregoric and Vespro 2003; Zhou et al. 2012). A high level of financial leverage might induce more control by lenders and make managers more selective in M&As deals. Therefore, managers will try making only "high-quality" deals. However, often results are insignificant.

We assume, therefore, that the most common determinants in the studies have a high explanatory power.

In addition, we formulated the following hypothesis: Research results do not depend on the characteristics of the articles, such as the number of countries in the sample, the year of publication, the analysis method used, or the use of different measures of performance. This hypothesis is based on the fact that the sample comprised almost entirely of articles published in journals cited in Scopus, meaning that these articles were influenced by some selection procedures and reviews, so our sample could be biased. We test this hypothesis using meta-regression analysis.

2.4   Meta-analyses of M&As Performance

The results of research on M&As performance do not give a general view of profitability or a company's market value after the deal. The only thing we can be sure of is that the motivation and popularity of M&As deals differ over time and demonstrate waviness. However, a number of factors are similar in the majority of articles about M&As performance. Therefore, we conclude that there are particular determinants influencing M&As performance.

Meta-analysis allows us to reveal different determinants and their generalized influence and explain which articles provide results that are more valid. In other words, we are able to identify whether the choice of the methodology or the number of countries in the sample significantly affects the results of research.

There are a limited number of publications or working chapters on the meta-analysis of M&As deals. In particular, M&As deals in developing market have not been studied. Authors (e.g., Homberg et al. (2009), King et al. (2004), Stahl and Voigt (2003), Datta et al. (1992)) usually include articles from developed countries in the sample or do not limit the sample and analyze all available works. Another key feature of the meta-analysis of M&As is the small sample size (no more than 100 articles). Some authors (e.g., van Geuns 2009) analyzed deal performance from three different points of view (effect-areas): the impact on costs, the impact on profits, and the impact on stock prices. van Geuns (2009) analyzes these effect-areas separately, exploring the impact of region, sector, cross-border deals, the type of buyer, previous experience with similar transactions, the time period, the value of the transaction, the level of significance of the model. The overall effect on costs is a cost increase after the deal, the overall effect on profits is profit decline, and the overall effect on stock prices is an increase in stock prices.

In addition, the results are significantly influenced by the characteristics of the study. For instance, the results are different in studies with significant results and those with insignificant results. Moreover, study characteristics, such as the length of the post-merger period, region, the ranking of the journal where the study is published, etc., are found to be significant.

Homberg et al. (2009) also use regression analysis to study 67 articles and similar factors: industry of target and acquirer, cultural similarities, technological similarities, and similar sizes of companies. They apply the approach of Hunter and Schmidt (2000) to their research, finding that similarity of industry and technology has a positive effect on the result of the transaction, while the cultural similarities and comparable company's size had a negative impact.

Finally, King et al. (2004) conducted one of the most important meta-analysis (93 articles in the sample). They investigate the variables for which the correlation coefficient with the dependent variable was available. They used the approach of Borenstein (1997) for calculating the effect size. They found that the average performance of the acquiring company is negative for M&As. Characteristics of the article do not affect the explanatory power of variables.

In this chapter, we attempt to contribute to existing literature about M&As deals by using the approach of meta-analysis. We conducted the meta-analysis on a sample of articles on M&As deals in emerging capital markets.

3 Sample

Twenty-six articles were selected as the sample for meta-analysis. We employed multiple search techniques to identify empirical research that included financial M&As performance. For M&As performance, we observed accounting measurement of performance and market measurement of performance. Firstly, we searched articles from databases, such as Web of Science and Scopus, by key words: for "performance"—performance, efficiency, value creation, bidder returns, abnormal returns; for "M&As"—M&As, merger, acquisitions, merger and acquisitions; for market location—emerging markets, developing countries and each country separately; for method—abnormal returns, event study; cross-border as specific researches. Other search strategies included screening conference proceedings and reviews of articles on emerging markets, conducting internet search using standard search engines such as Google. We required that the articles contain regression analyses for determining M&As performance and have t-statistics or standard errors of b-estimation. We investigated articles with different valuations of M&As performance and different measures of the same determinants to make samples more representative. We also used all model specifications from each article. Our final sample consists of 26 articles covering a total of 21,824 M&As deals.[3]

The sample includes articles published from 2003 to 2014; however, the deals they cover occurred between 2000 and 2013 as most M&As deals in emerging capital markets took place during this period. Some works, such as about the markets of India and China, cover the period of the 1990s. The countries in the sample included China, India, Brazil, Russia, Malaysia, South Africa, Argentina, Chile, Slovenia, Poland, with the BRICS countries being the most common. The samples included intra- and international M&As deals. OLS was the most popular methodology because of its simplicity and effectiveness (Table 2).

4 The Methodology

The meta-analysis followed Hunter and Schmidt (1990) and Lipsey and Wilson (2001). Our methodology consists of (1) calculating the effect size, (2) calculating the standard error of effect size, (3) calculating weights and testing for homogeneity, and (4) conducting a meta-regression.

---

[3]We calculated this number of deals by adding all deals in samples, not excluding recurring.

Table 2 Sample description

№	Authors	Year of publication	Journal	Article	Number of deals	Countries	Period	Dependent variable
1	Rahahleh, Wei	2012	Global Finance Journal	The performance of frequent acquirers: evidence from emerging markets	2340	17 Emerging markets (Brazil, China, Greece, HongKong, India, Malaysia, Mexico, New Zealand, Norway, Philippines, Poland, Portugal, Russia, Singapore, South Africa, South Korea, and Taiwan)	1985–2008 (June)	CAR
2	Du, Boateng	2014	International Business Review	State ownership, institutional effects and value creation in cross-border mergers & acquisitions by Chinese firms	468	China (cross-border deals)	1998–2011	SCAR
3	Chi, Sun, Young	2011	Emerging Markets Review	Performance and characteristics of acquiring firms in the Chinese stock markets	1148	China	1998–2003	CAR
4	Nicholson, Salaber	2013	International Business Review	The motives and performance of cross-border acquirers from emerging economies: Comparison between Chinese and Indian firms	266	China (63), India (203) (Cross-border)	2000–2010	CAR
5	Bhaumink, Selarka	2008	Working Chapter	Impact of M&A on firm performance in India: Implications for concentration of ownership and insider entrenchment	86	India	1995–2002	CAR

(continued)

Table 2 (continued)

№	Authors	Year of publication	Journal	Article	Number of deals	Countries	Period	Dependent variable
6	Gaur, Malhotra, Zhu	2013	Strategic Management Journal	Acquisition announcements and stock market valuations of acquiring firms' rivals: a test of the growth probability hypothesis in china	1074	China	1993–2008	CAR
7	Zhou, Guo, Hua, Doukas.	2012	European Financial Management	Does State Ownership Drive M&A Performance? Evidence from China	825	China	1994–2008	CAR/BHAR
8	Bhagat, Malhotra, Zhu	2011	Emerging Markets Review	Emerging country cross-border acquisitions: Characteristics, acquirer returns and cross-sectional determinants	698	Brazil, China, India, Malaysia, Mexico, Philippines, Russia, and South Africa	1991–2008	CAR
9	Harjeet S. Bhabra. Jiayin Huang	2013	Journal of Multinational Financial Management	An empirical investigation o fmergers and acquisitions by Chinese listed companies, 1997–2007	136	China	1997–2007	CAR
10	Nagano, Yuan	2012	Journal of Asian Economics	Cross-border acquisitions in a transition economy: The recent experiences of China and India	953	China and India	1999–2006	CAR
11	Narayan, Thenmozhi	2014	Management Decision	Do cross-border acquisitions involving emerging market firms create value Impact of deal characteristics	151	Emerging markets	1999–2007	Deflating EBITDA by BVA
12	Wu, Xie	2010	Procedia Social and Behavioral Sciences	Determinants of Cross-Border Merger & Acquisition Performance of Chinese Enterprises	165	China (cross-border)	2000–2006	ROA

	Author	Year	Journal	Title	Sample	Country	Period	Measure
13	Grigoreva, Morkovin	2014	Journal of Corporate Financial Research	The effect of cross-border and domestic acquisitions on shareholder wealth: evidence from BRICS acquirers	364	BRICS	2000–May 2012	CAR, BHAR
14	Yen, Chou, Andre	2013	Emerging Markets Finance & Trade	Operating Performance of Emerging Market Acquirers: Corporate Governance Issues	98	Emerging Markets	1998–2006	OCFR
15	Vuong, Napier, Samson	2013	International Journal of Business and Management	Innovation as Determining Factor of Post-M&A Performance: the case of Vietnam	212	Vietnam	2005–2012	Success probability
16	Dakessian, Feldmann	2013	Brazilian Administration Review	Multilatinas and Value Creation from Cross-Border Acquisitions: An Event Study Approach	607	Argentina, Brazil, Chile, Colombia, Mechico, Peru, Venezuala	1989–2011	CAR
17	Bertrand, Betschinger	2011	Working chapter	Performance of Domestic and Cross-border Acquisitions: Empirical Evidence from Russian Acquirers	2051	Russia	1999–2008	ROA
18	Nurhazrina M.R.	2013	International Journal of Managerial Finance	Shareholder Wealth Effects of M&As: the Third Wave from Malaysia	376	Malaysia	2001–2009	CAR target SR, CAR target LR, CAR acquirer SR, CAR acquirer LR
19	Kohli, Mann	2011	International Journal of Commerce and Management	Target shareholders' wealth creation in domestic and cross-border acquisitions in India	106	India	1997–2008	CAR
20	Chirkova, Chuvstvina	2011	Journal of Corporate Financial Research	Acquisition of Private and Public Targets: Abnormal Return in Emerging Markets	128	Emerging capital markets	2000–2008	CAR

(continued)

Table 2 (continued)

№	Authors	Year of publication	Journal	Article	Number of deals	Countries	Period	Dependent variable
21	Gregoric, Vespro	2003	Working Chapter	Block Trades and the Benefits of Control in Slovenia	15	Slovenia	2000–2001	Post-trade block premium, Pre-trade block premium
22	Pop	2006	Emerging Markets Review	M&A market in transition economies: Evidence from Romania	131	Romania	1999–2005	CAR
23	Trojanowski	2008	Economic System	Equity block transfers in transition economies: Evidence from Poland	53	Poland	1996–2000	CAR
24	Gubbi, Aulakh, Ray et al.	2010	Journal of International Business Studies	Do international acquisitions by emerging-economy firms create shareholder value? The case of Indian firms	315	India (cross-border)	2000–2007	CAR
25	Rani, Yadav, Jain	2013	Procedia Economics and Finance	Impact of corporate governance score on abnormal returns and financial performance of mergers and acquisitions	155	India	2003–2008	CAR
26	Grigoreva, Troitsky	2012	Journal of Corporate Financial Research	The Impact of Mergers and Acquisitions on Company Performance in Emerging Capital Markets	61	BRIC	2005–2009	EBITDA/SALES

We calculated effect size and the standard error of this effect size by applying Fisher's Zr-transformation (Hedges and Olkin 1985):

$$ES_{Zr} = .5\ln\left[\frac{1+r}{1-r}\right] \tag{1}$$

$$se = \sqrt{\frac{1}{n-3}} \tag{2}$$

where *ES* is the effect size, *r* is the correlation coefficient (Pearson correlation coefficient), *se* is the standard error of the effect size, and *n* is the number of observations.

The effect size shows the strength of the impact of the determinants on the total result, in our case on the performance of M&As. It is impossible to determine what the direction (positive or negative) of this impact is. The effect size is compared with 1 to identify the impact. When the effect size is larger than 1, this means there is a strong influence. When the effect size is less than 1, but close to it, then impact is moderate. When the effect size is much less than 1, the impact is a low.

For calculation of r-coefficient, we used t-statistics or standard error for b-estimation for each determinants and number of observations in a sample in each model specification during the following calculation (Borenstein et al. 2009):

$$r = \frac{t}{\sqrt{N}} \tag{3}$$

$$t = \frac{\beta}{st.e.\beta} \tag{4}$$

where *r* is the correlation coefficient, *t* is the t-statistic, *N* is the number of observations, β is the beta-coefficient, and *st. e. β* is the standard error of the beta-coefficient.

We calculated weights of each effect size and tested this average for homogeneity. If the null hypothesis of homogeneity is rejected, the distribution of effect sizes is assumed to be heterogeneous, and then we used a random effect model for calculating the average effect size.[4]

We determine how an article's characteristics influence the published result using a meta-regression. We conducted the meta-regression only for determinants with a large number of observations.

For the regression analysis, we used the following features of articles:

---

[4]Fixed effect (FE) model assumed that all of the variability between effect size is due to sampling error.

Random effect (RE) model assumed the variability between effect sizes is due to sampling error plus variability in the population of effects (Pigott Terri 2012). FE and RE models are the same as for panel-data analysis.

- Methodology: 1 if in the article was used OLS method, 0 otherwise
- Year of publication—the absolute value
- Country: 1 if the article researched more than 1 country, 0 if only one country
- Working: 1 if the study is a working chapter, 0 if it is a published article
- CAR: 1 if CAR was used as a measure of M&As performance, 0 if an accounting measure was used

We used meta-analysis techniques for the 10 determinants described above. Our analysis can be divided into three parts. First, we examined the effects on performance in general without reference to the measurement methods. Next, we showed how much each parameter explains the M&As performance depending on different measurement methods (market or accounting). Finally, we make meta-regressions for 3 determinants to identify which characteristic of articles affect the explanatory power of a determinant. Meta-regressions allow an evaluation of whether the quality parameters of the article may influence on its results.

- Step 1: "the common performance" means that we did not differentiate the measurement methods. We calculated the effect size in terms of a fixed-effect (FE) and a random-effect (RE) model. We calculated the aggregate effect size for all determinants. This leads to a conclusion about the strength of the effect of a particular determinant on the performance of M&As deals, and the effect size for each article separately and the weight of each item in the final sample. In addition, this analysis can compare different models and decide which one is the most suitable for this case.
- Step 2: We used two methods of performance measurement in articles included in the sample. The most common method in our sample is the market method (cumulative abnormal return—CAR). We also used accounting methods, but with different proxies. Therefore, we studied the impact on the market method for all the determinants and the impact on the accounting methods for the determinants with a suitable number of observations. In this case, we have operated the same way as in the previous part of the analysis. We compared the FE and RE models to decide which is more suitable and which total effect size is in a sample.
- Step 3: For the three determinants with the largest number of observations (represented in the greatest number of articles and specifications), we conducted a regression analysis to identify which characteristics of the article have the greatest impact on the explanatory power of a specific determinant. We also divided the regression analysis into two parts: an analysis of "the common performance" and a market measurement of performance and an accounting measurement of performance separately.

5 Results of the Meta-analysis

The results are represented in a summary table (see Table 3) and are further described in more detail for each determinant. First, we provide the results of the effect size calculations and the homogeneity test. Then we consider the influence of determinants on performance, measured by market and accounting methods. For determinants, such as method of payment, buyer size, and industry relatedness between acquirer and target company, the results of meta-regressions are provided.

Table 3 shows the effect sizes for all the determinants for different subsamples (for performance (without separating the method of measurement), performance, measured by market method and performance, measured by accounting methods, if possible). The effect size is calculated by using two models: FE and RE. Table 3 shows the homogeneity test results for each subsample.

Analyzing the results of the research, represented in Table 3, we notice that almost all chosen determinants significantly explain M&As performance. The results for "the common performance" (without separating the effect of chosen performance

Table 3 Research results

Determinant	Fixed-effect	Random-effect	Number of obs.	Homogeneity (p value)
Method of payment	1.04***	1.04***	66	0.01
Method of payment (CAR)	1.04***	1.05***	52	0.13
The size of acquirer	1.08***	1.04***	77	0.00
The size of acquirer (CAR)	0.91***	0.91***	30	0.00
The size of acquirer (accounting parameters)	1.09***	1.09***	47	0.00
Deal size	0.91***	0.92***	18	0.00
Cross-border deal	0.972*	0.97*	18	0.98
Private (CAR)	0.99	1.00	32	0.00
ROE	0.92**	0.88*	11	0.00
Industry relatedness	0.99	1.00	64	0.08
Industry relatedness (CAR)	0.99	0.99	49	0.02
Industry relatedness (accounting parameters)	1.01	1.01	15	0.83
SOE	0.99***	1.00	27	0.00
SOE (CAR)	1.07***	1.07***	20	0.97
ROA	1.22***	1.19***	37	0.00
ROA (accounting parameters)	1.23***	1.23***	30	0.14
Financial leverage	0.97***	1.01	34	0.00
Financial leverage (CAR)	0.93***	0.93	14	0.37
Financial leverage (accounting parameters)	1.112	1.112	20	0.97

***Significant at the 1% level
**Significant at the 5% level
*Significant at the 10% level

measurement) are similar to those that represent the results for market measurement of performance.

5.1 Method of Payment

The total number of empirical models, which examine the influence of the method of payment as a measurement of deal performance, is 66, which is the second most in our sample.

The results show that for both models (FE and RE), the effect size is the same: 1.035 and significant at 1% (see Table 3). The homogeneity test shows that the null hypothesis about homogeneity is rejected at 1% significance level, which is a sign of sample heterogeneity. Therefore, we choose the RE model, as it describes such cases more precisely.

The results of the RE model demonstrate the high explanatory power of method of payment as a determinant of M&As performance. Payment in cash significantly influences the M&As performance. This influence is due to the fact that information about the method of payment is usually available and reliable. In addition, this factor has a significant effect, if payment was other than by cash.

At the second stage, we consider the influence of the method of payment on market measurement of performance in particular way. This subsample consists of 52 observations, which means that market method of performance measurement is used in 52 models. Both FE and RE models provide significant and similar results. The effect size for FE model is 1.00, and for random effect model it is 1.05. We cannot reject the null hypothesis of homogeneity at any significance level. Moreover, we can conclude that for market measures of performance, the method of payment has higher explanatory power than for "common measurement of performance" (without considering the method of measurement). So, hypothesis 1 is not rejected. The method of payment, therefore, has a greater impact on the market measurement of performance than on the accounting measurement. This may be because the market measurement of performance measures the short-term performance, and the accounting measurement of performance measures long-term performance. Therefore, the choice of method of payment is more significant in the short term.

At the third stage, we conduct a regression model for the total sample and the different methods of performance measurement separately. The results of the regression analysis for this determinant are shown in Table 4, which shows that we obtain significant results for all determinants, except working and methodology, which were deleted because of collinearity. The use of CAR as a measurement of performance increases the explanatory power of the effect size and positively influences the research results. This supports the previous results of the effect size for "common measurement of performance" and market measurement of performance. Therefore, the study of the influence of the payment method on M&As performance measured by the market method will be larger than when using accounting indicators. The

Table 4 Meta-regression for method of payment on total sample

ES	Coef.	ST.E.	95% interval	
Country	−0.03∗	0.02	−0.06	0.00
Year	0.03∗∗∗	0.01	0.01	0.05
CAR	0.09∗∗∗	0.03	0.04	0.14
cons	−55.78∗∗∗	17.83	−91.42	−20.15
Number of observations	66			
R^2 adj	71.42%			

∗∗∗Significant at the 1% level
∗∗Significant at the 5% level
∗Significant at the 10% level

Table 5 Meta-regression for the method of payment for market measurement of performance

ES	Coef.	ST.E.	95% interval	
Country	−0.03	0.02	0.07	0.01
Year	0.02∗∗	0.01	0.00	0.04
cons	−44.99∗∗	16.6	−82.38	−7.61
Number of observations	52			
R^2 adj	63.37%			

∗∗∗Significant at the 1% level
∗∗Significant at the 5% level
∗Significant at the 10% level

Table 6 Meta-regression for the method of payment for accounting measurement of performance

ES	Coef.	ST.E.	95% interval	
Country	−0.33∗∗∗	0.09	−0.53	−0.14
Year	0.24∗∗∗	0.05	0.12	0.36
cons	−479.89∗∗∗	107.58	−716.67	−243.11
Number of observations	14			
R^2 adj	100%			

∗∗∗Significant at the 1% level
∗∗Significant at the 5% level
∗Significant at the 10% level

explanatory power in more recent studies is higher than in later ones, which is shown by positive beta-coefficient for the *year* variable. When research was conducted later, there was more information about the deal. Finally, the use of cross-country samples in research lowers the explanatory power of the method of payment as a performance determinant. This can be explained by the sample, collected from different markets, being heterogeneous (for instance, it may have more observations for one country and less for another one). Moreover, the specifics of markets and deals in different countries also differ.

We also conducted a regression analysis for the different measurement methods of performance (see Tables 5 and 6). For market measurement of performance (see

Table 5), we obtain similar results for the variables *year* and *country*, which influence the explanatory power of the method of payment positively and negatively, respectively. However, for the variable *country* the result is not significant. This may be explained by the sample covering different countries. It is better to use the market method, as it better smoothes out possible specific differences between countries.

We also conducted a similar analysis for the accounting measurement of performance (see Table 6). In this case, the results are the same as for the total regression. The variable *country* is significant at 1% significance, which means that it is not reasonable to compare accounting proxies in different markets, as there are specific features in the measurement of such parameters, because of different accounting standards. Accounting parameters are strongly influenced by market mechanisms of a particular country, existing conjunction, and legislation.

Thus, the method of payment has high explanatory power for M&As performance. However, it is better to use market measurement of performance for cross-country research.

5.2 The Size of Acquirer

The size of the acquirer was used in 77 model specifications (see Table 3). At the first stage, we calculated the effect size for the RE and FE models, and tested for heterogeneity.

The FE model shows much stronger explanatory power compared to the RE model (Table 3). However, the test for heterogeneity allows a rejection of the hypothesis of homogeneity, so we have to choose the RE model. The effect size for the acquirer size is 1.036, which also shows the high explanatory power of a variable.

At the second stage, we examined the effect of the acquirer size for market measures of performance separately. In this case, the subsample is homogeneous and the RE and FE models are equivalent. There is no difference in the effect size for the two models. This value is less than 1, indicating the moderate explanatory power of a variable.

For the accounting method for measuring the performance, the effect size is the same as for the performance without separating the measurement approach (the accounting and market methods together). The subsample is heterogeneous, so we choose the RE model. The effect size for this subsample is 1.087, indicating a very high degree of explanatory power.

Larger companies have a more stable market position and deal more easily with risks and problems. It usually indicates the ability to generate gains through economies of scale, scope, knowledge exchange, and brand development.

At the third stage, we conducted a regression analysis for the total sample, and for different methods of measuring the performance alone. The regression results are presented in Table 7.

Table 7 Meta-regression for the determinant of the size of acquirer on the total sample

ES	Coef.	ST.E.	95% interval	
Working	−0.03	0.03	−0.08	0.02
Country	−0.03	0.02	−0.08	0.01
Year	0.03***	0.01	0.02	0.05
Methodology	0.05	0.04	−0.02	0.13
CAR	−0.1885***	0.0208	−0.2299	−0.1469
cons	−68.9925***	11.005	−90.9359	−47.0491
Obs.	77			
R^2 adj	97.29%			

***Significant at the 1% level
**Significant at the 5% level
*Significant at the 10% level

Table 8 Meta-regression for the determinant of the size of acquirer on the 'accounting' sample

ES	Coef.	ST.E.	95% Interval	
Working	0.01	0.03	−0.05	0.08
Country	−0.02	0.05	−0.13	0.08
Year	0.03***	0.01	0.02	0.05
cons	−65.96***	14.75	−95.7	−36.22
Obs.	47			
R^2 adj	1.00%			

***Significant at the 1% level
**Significant at the 5% level
*Significant at the 10% level

The regression analysis showed that for explanatory power of the acquirer, size is influenced by the publication year of the article. The later a study was done, the greater the explanatory power of a variable. This can be explained by more data being available for recent studies. In addition, the use of a market-based approach to performance measurement also increases the explanatory power of the variable. The point is that market measurement better reflects the market situation and provides a less biased estimation than accounting measures of performance. The other determinants, such as the number of countries in the sample, the research methodology, and the publication status, do not significantly affect the explanatory power.

The results obtained for the subsample with accounting methods are in Table 8. The subsample covers 47 observations. The year of publication is a significant factor affecting the explanatory power of the acquirer size using the accounting method for performance measurement, while the publication status and the number of countries in the sample were not significant.

Next, we conducted a regression analysis also for the subsample with the market measurement of performance. The results of the analysis are presented in Table 9.

The regression analysis for the subsample for the market measure of performance reveals that the methodology selection does not affect the explanatory power of acquirer size. As for the method of payment, if a study is being conducted on a

Table 9 Meta-regression for	ES	Coef.	ST.E.	95% interval	
the determinant of the size of acquirer on the 'market' sample	Working	−0.12**	0.04	−0.20	−0.03
	Country	−0.04*	0.02	−0.08	0.00
	Year	0.02**	0.01	0.01	0.04
	Methodology	0.05	0.03	−0.02	0.12
	cons	−48.76**	17.84	−85.5	−12.03
	Obs.	30			
	R^2 adj	100.00%			

***Significant at the 1% level
**Significant at the 5% level
*Significant at the 10% level

sample of several countries, the explanatory power of variable decreases. This may be because for different countries, different sizes of companies are typical and such a sample can be heterogeneous. The year of publication, as in previous cases, positively and significantly affects the effect size.

5.3 Deal Size

Deal size was used in 18 model specifications of all the articles in our sample. Most of the observations used CAR as an M&As performance measure. Therefore, for this variable, we considered the case for the overall performance as a division into two small subsamples is not appropriate.

The subsample for this determinant is not homogeneous, since the hypothesis of homogeneity is rejected (see Table 3). Therefore, the RE model gives the most correct result although both models give practically the same significant results. The effect size is 0.915, indicating the moderate explanatory power of a variable.

The deal size has a significant, but not a strong effect on the M&As performance. This may be because the samples could contain one of the largest transactions in the market and the effect of including this determinant is underestimated since the sample is limited.

5.4 Cross-Border Deal Dummy

The sample for cross-border dummy consists of 18 models. At the first stage of our analysis, we obtain same effect size for the FE and RE models (see Table 3). A homogeneity test shows that we cannot reject the null hypothesis of homogeneity, so both models (FE and RE) are appropriate to estimate the effect size. The models provide results with the same 12% significance level. A cross-border dummy moderately explains M&As performance.

The cross-border dummy has an average effect on M&As performance. Such deals are usually investigated separately, so the effect of including such deals in the total sample is leveled. Nevertheless, this factor influences the performance of transactions, and the inclusion of this determinant will improve the explanatory power of the model.

As there are a small number of observations, there is no need to divide the sample into two subsamples or conduct regression analysis.

5.5 Public Target Company Dummy

The sample for the public company dummy (equals 1 if public and 0 otherwise) consists of 32 observations. All observations are represented for market measures of performance. None of the articles or working chapters where the influence of this variable was studied used the accounting method of performance measurement.

The sample is heterogeneous at the 1% significance level, so it is better to use the RE model to estimate the effect size. The effect size is 1, which shows the high explanatory power of the variable. This means that deal performance highly depends on the type of the target (public or private). These two types of companies disclose information differently, and this may influence the investor and market expectations.

Other stages of analysis were not conducted for this determinant for the same reasons as for cross-country dummy.

5.6 ROE

ROE was only used in 11 model specifications of all the articles in our sample. The results show (Table 3) that ROE has a moderate impact on the performance of M&As. The overall impact in the FE model is 0.92 (5% significance level) and in the RE model is 0.88 (10% significance level). The test for homogeneity rejects the null hypothesis of the homogeneity of the sample. Therefore, we must choose the RE model according to which the impact of the determinant is moderate.

The range between the smallest and the largest effect-size in the sample is from 0.44 to 1.60. The weights of all the observations are distributed about the same, which indicates the homogeneity of the result. Thus, the interval for each effect-size is not broad.

The separation of the sample using only accounting methods or CAR is impossible in this case because of small number of observations.

5.7 Industry Relatedness

Industry relatedness was used in 68 model specification in 28 articles. This determinant is one of the most widespread among the studies. Consequently, we consider it separately for the subsample of accounting methods of performance measurement and CAR. At the first stage, we calculated the effect size for the RE and FE models, and also did a test for heterogeneity.

The results do not show (see Table 3) that the same industry buyer and target has a significant impact. However, the overall average impact on the fixed-model is 0.998 (not significant result at any reasonable level of significance), on the model of random-effect 1.000 (not significant result at any reasonable level of significance). The test for homogeneity rejects the null hypothesis of homogeneity of the sample at 10% significance level. Consequently, it is impossible to combine the results into one overall effect. It is therefore necessary to consider two subsamples.

At the second stage, we examined the effect of industry relatedness for accounting measures of performance separately. In the subsample of only accounting measurement of deal performance we also found nonsignificant results both in the FE and RE models. Similar nonsignificant results were observed for the subsample of market measures of deal performance.

At the third stage, we conducted a regression analysis for the total sample despite the insignificant results at the previous stage. The impact of industry relatedness is not influenced by the study year, the number of countries in the sample, or the use of accounting or CAR methods to measure performance. This suggests that the results obtained by researchers are independent and homogeneous, although it is impossible to say how, on average, this determinant affects the performance of deals.

This can be explained by the fact that companies, operating in related industries, can benefit from synergy after the deal, while unrelated companies may face many risks, connected to the new industry, market, and competitors. Therefore, the effect of industry relatedness is controversial and is not able to fully explain the deal performance.

5.8 SOE

This determinant was found in 27 model specifications from 28 articles. The results (see Table 3) show that this determinant has a significant impact on the performance of M&As on average for the sample of articles. However, this effect size is equal to 0.987 for the FE model, significant at the 1% level (the result for the RE model is insignificant). The sample is heterogeneous at the 5% level of significance. When the RE model is insignificant and the sample is heterogeneous, we cannot observe the overall effect size of the sample.

Despite the small number of observations, we decided to study the results in the separated sample. When using only CAR (20 observations), there is a significant result for both the FE and the RE models, which is the same and is 1.070, thus the influence is stronger than for the whole sample as a whole. This sample is homogeneous, so it can be considered using both models. Therefore, when CAR was used as a measurement method of M&As performance, it will be significant influence for SOEs in emerging capital markets.

The company's participation with SOE in M&As deals is reflected in the market measure of the performance of such transactions. State involvement is important for the market, because such transactions will either be large enough or have certain advantages, although state companies can be over- or undervalued, which is also important for the market.

5.9 ROA

ROA is observed in 37 modifications of models in 28 articles and working chapters. The results show that the determinant significantly influences deal performance on average among the whole sample of studies. The effect size for the FE model is 1.223 (significant at 1%) and for the RE model is 1.198 (significant at 1%). The sample is heterogeneous, so it is necessary to consider the RE model, where the impact is slightly smaller, but still significant.

The range between the smallest and largest effect sizes is not that great in the sample, and the confidence intervals for separate observations are not wide. The weights among all the observations are distributed almost identically, which is the sign of the homogeneity of the final result.

At the second stage, we analyze the subsample with accounting measures of performance. The size of the subsample is 30 observations. We obtain the same effect size for the FE and RE models, which is 1.226 (significant at 1%). The subsample is homogenous (significant at 15%), so we can use both models (with the same results). This result exceeds the result for the total sample, so the explanatory power of ROA is higher when using accounting methods of performance measurement.

More profitable companies have more resources available to benefit from raising further capital and making investments. However, sometimes, this relationship can be negative, because managers of more profitable companies make riskier investments.

5.10 Financial Leverage

Financial leverage is observed in 34 modifications of models among the studies. At the first stage, we calculate the effect size for the RE and FE models and test for homogeneity. The results show that this determinant significantly influences deal performance (see Table 3). The effect size is 0.967 for fixed model (significant at

1%). The result for the RE model is not significant. The sample is heterogeneous, so we should consider the RE model for the effect size calculation. However, the effect size is not significant, so we divide the sample into two subsamples.

At the second stage, we separately study the impact of financial leverage on M&As performance, measured by the market method and the accounting method. The accounting method gives a significant positive result for the FE model, and the RE model. The sample is homogenous, so we can use both models.

A similar situation is observed for market method of performance measurement (CAR). In this case, the average effect size is 0.929 for the RE and FE models. Both models can be considered, as the subsample is homogenous. Therefore, the explanatory power is higher for accounting measures than for market measures (CAR). This is because market measures of performance are usually measured in the short term and the financial leverage indicator may not be known at the time of the deal. Thus, financial leverage is more appropriate to use as a determinant of performance, measured in the long term.

6   Conclusion

Meta-analysis is a tool for summarizing the obtained results by many researchers on one particular problem. The application of meta-analysis in economic chapters is limited, as the methods of research vary from study to study. Nevertheless, conducting such an analysis is possible taking into account a number of limitations and assumptions.

There have been a limited number of studies devoted to the meta-analysis of M&As performance in emerging markets. These studies allow a summarizing of the results obtained using different samples and with the use of different methods of performance measurement. Therefore, we can draw conclusions about the impact of different performance determinants. Moreover, it is possible to identify the dependence between the results and parameters of the studies themselves.

We studied M&As performance in emerging markets, using a meta-analysis methodology. We identified and analyzed the most widespread determinants of M&As performance, such as the method of payment, the size of the acquirer, the deal size, cross-border deals, private target company, ROE, industry relatedness, SOE (state ownership of the target company), ROA, and the financial leverage of acquirer. These determinants were chosen because required data was available in the selected articles. In addition, researchers often receive significant results for these determinants.

Our analysis shows that it is impossible to identify a significant average effect size for some determinants (industry relatedness, SOE) because of sample heterogeneity. In contrast, for other determinants (method of payment, acquirer size, and public company), an effect size was identified. There are differences in the effect sizes when we use different methods of deal performance measurement. For instance, for the method of payment, it is better to use market measures of performance, while for the acquirer size, accounting measures of performance are better.

This chapter also demonstrates the influence of article characteristics on the explanatory power of chosen determinants. All the studies apply different methodologies and use different data, which obviously influences the results. We examine such article characteristics as publication year, type of the study (article or working chapter), country, and method of performance measurement. The year of publication is significant almost for all determinants which we ran regression for; this can be explained by data availability. Recent studies had more data available and their authors could use more deals and broader period. Furthermore, country dummy (equals 1, if there are more than 1 country) is negatively significant, which can be explained by differences between countries and markets. When one country is considered, the factors influence the same way within one particular market.

Our analysis allows conclusions to be drawn about differences in the explanatory power of different determinants which has practical application for further research. It will give researchers the opportunity to select deals with available information on main performance determinants at the stage of sample collection. Further, the study of the impact of other determinants will be possible along with the introduction to the model of control variables, i.e., determinants that influence deal performance in emerging markets. The strongest drivers of performance are such variables as method of payment, acquirer size, ROA, and industry relatedness for emerging capital markets.

References

Bertrand, O., & Betschinger, M.-A. (2011). *Performance of domestic and cross-border acquisitions: Empirical evidence from Russian acquirers.* Working chapter.

Bhabra, H. S., & Huang, J. (2013). An empirical investigation of mergers and acquisitions by Chinese listed companies, 1997–2007. *Journal of Multinational Financial Management, 23*(3), 186–207.

Bhagat, S., Malhotra, S., & Zhu, P. (2011). Emerging country cross-border acquisitions: Characteristics, acquirer returns and cross-sectional determinants. *Emerging Markets Review, 12,* 250–271.

Bhaumink, S. K., & Selarka, E. (2008). *Impact of M&A on firm performance in India: Implications for concentration of ownership and insider entrenchment.* Working Chapter.

Borenstein, M. (1997). *Comprehensive meta-analysis.* Englewood, NJ: Biostat.

Borenstein, M., Hedges, L., Higgins, J., & Rothstein, H. (2009). *Introduction to meta-analysis.* Chichester: Wiley.

Chi, J., Sun, Q., & Young, M. (2011). Performance and characteristics of acquiring firms in the Chinese stock markets. *Emerging Markets Review, 12,* 152–170.

Chirkova, E., & Chuvstvina, E. (2011). Acquisition of private and public targets: Abnormal return in emerging markets. *Journal of Corporate Finance Research, 5*(3), 30–43.

Dakessian, L. C., & Feldmann, P. R. (2013). Multilatinas and value creation from cross-border acquisitions: An event study approach. *Brazilian Administration Review, 4,* 462–489.

Datta, D. K., Pinches, G. E., & Narayanan, V. K. (1992). Factors influencing wealth creation from mergers and acquisitions: A meta-analysis. *Strategic Management Journal, 13,* 67–84.

Du, M., & Boateng, A. (2014). State ownership, institutional effects and value creation in cross-border mergers & acquisitions by Chinese firms. *International Business Review, 11*, 430–442.

Gaur, A. S., Malhotra, S., & Zhu, P. (2013). Acquisition announcements and stock market valuations of acquiring firm's rivals: A test of the growth probability hypothesis in China. *Strategic Management Journal, 12*, 215–232.

Gregoric, A., & Vespro, C. (2003). *Block trades and the benefits of control in Slovenia*. Working chapter.

Grigoreva, S., & Morkovin, R. (2014). The effect of cross-border and domestic acquisitions on shareholder wealth: Evidence from brics acquirers. *Journal of Corporate Finance Research, 8* (4), 34–45.

Grigoreva, S., & Troitsky, P. (2012). The impact of mergers and acquisitions on company performance in emerging capital markets. *Journal of Corporate Finance Research, 6*(3), 31–43.

Gubbi, S. R., Aulakh, P. S., Ray, S., Sarkar, M. B., & Chittoor, R. (2010). Do international acquisitions by emerging-economy firms create shareholder value? The case of Indian firms. *Journal of International Business Studies, 41*(3), 397–418.

Hedges, L. V., & Olkin, L. (1985). *Statistical methods for meta-analysis*. Orlando: Academic Press.

Homberg, F., Rost, K., & Osterloh, M. (2009). Do synergies exist in related acquisitions? A meta-analysis of acquisition studies. *Review of Managerial Science, 3*(2), 75–116.

Huck, S., Knoblauch, V., & Müller, W. (2003). On the profitability of collusion in location games. *Journal of Urban Economics, 54*(3), 499–510.

Hunter, J. E., & Schmidt, F. L. (1990). *Methods of meta-analysis: Correcting error and bias in research findings*. Beverly Hills, CA: Sage.

Hunter, J. E., & Schmidt, F. L. (2000). Fixed effects vs. random effects meta-analysis models: Implications for cumulative research knowledge. *International Journal of Selection and Assessment, 8*(4), 275–292.

King, M. D. R., Dalton, D. R., Daily, C. M., & Covin, J. G. (2004). Meta-analysis of post-acquisition performance: Indications of unidentified moderators. *Strategic Management Journal, 25*(2), 187–200.

Kohli, R., & Mann, B. J. S. (2012). Analyzing determinants of value creation in domestic and cross border acquisitions in India. *International Business Review, 21*, 998–1016.

Ladkani, R., & Banerjee, A. (2013). *Emerging markets bidder returns and the choice of payment method in M&A: Evidence from India*. Midwest Finance Association Annual Meeting Chapter.

Lipsey, M. W., & Wilson, D. B. (2001). *Practical meta-analysis*. Thousand Oaks, CA: Sage.

Mann, B. J. S., & Kohli, R. (2011). Target shareholders' wealth creation in domestic and cross-border acquisitions in India. *International Journal of Commerce and Management, 1*, 63–81.

Nagano, M., & Yuan, Y. (2012). Cross-border acquisitions in a transition economy: The recent experiences of China and India. *Journal of Asian Economics, 10*, 66–79.

Narayan, P. C., & Thenmozhi, M. (2014). Do cross-border acquisitions involving emerging market firms create value impact of deal characteristic. *Management Decision, 8*, 1451–1473.

Nicholson, R. R., & Salaber, J. (2013). The motives and performance of cross-border acquirers from emerging economies: Comparison between Chinese and Indian firms. *International Business Review, 22*, 963–980.

Nurhazrina, M. R., & Pok, W. C. (2013). Shareholder wealth effects of M&As: The third wave from Malaysia. *International Journal of Managerial Finance, 7*, 49–69.

Pigott Terri, D. (2012). *Advances in meta-analysis*. New York: Springer.

Pop, D. (2006). M&A market in transition economies: Evidence from Romania. *Emerging Markets Review, 7*, 244–260.

Rahahleh, N. A., & Wei, P. P. (2012). The performance of frequent acquirers: Evidence from emerging markets. *Global Finance Journal, 10*, 16–33.

Rahim, K., et al. (2013). Determinants of cross border merger and acquisition in advanced emerging market acquiring firms. *Procedia Economics and Finance, 7*, 96–102.

Rani, N., Yadav, S. S., & Jain, P. K. (2013). Impact of corporate governance score on abnormal returns and financial performance of mergers and acquisitions. *Procedia Economics and Finance, 5*, 637–646.

Stahl, G. K., & Voigt, A. (2003). *Meta-analysis of the performance implications of cultural differences in mergers and acquisitions: Integrating strategic, Financial, and Organizational Perspectives.* Working Chapter.

Trojanowski, G. (2008). Equity block transfers in transition economies: Evidence from Poland. *Economic System, 3*, 217–238.

van Geuns LLM, L.S.J. (2009). *Meta-analysis on the effects of mergers and acquisitions. Influences on the cost, profit and stock price Effects analysed.* Thesis Economics of Markets, Organisations, and Policy.

Vuong, Q. H., Napier, N. K., & Samson, D. E. (2013). Innovation as determining factor of post-M&A performance: The case of Vietnam. *International Journal of Business and Management, 18*, 25–31.

Wu, C., & Xie, N. (2010). Determinants of cross-border merger & acquisition performance of Chinese enterprises. *Procedia Social and Behavioral Sciences, 2*, 6896–6905.

Yen, T.-Y., Chou, S., & Andre, P. (2013). Operating performance of emerging market acquirers: Corporate governance issues. *Emerging Markets Finance & Trade, 3*, 5–19.

Zhou, B., Guo, J., Hua, J., & Doukas, A. J. (2012). Does state ownership drive M&A performance? Evidence from China. *European Financial Management, 1*, 1–26.

Part II
Strategic Deals and Value Effects: New Empirical Evidence

Post-acquisition Value Effects of M&A Deals: A Comparative Analysis in Developed and Emerging Capital Markets

Svetlana Grigorieva and Svetlana Kuzmina

Abstract This chapter contributes to the literature on M&A performance by examining the impact of M&A deals on company value over the long run in developed and emerging economies. Examining a sample of 153 and 125 deals from Western European and emerging capital markets respectively, 2002–2013, and employing economic profit as a performance measure, we find that transactions in developed markets create more value for shareholders than M&As in emerging economies over the 2-year period surrounding the deals. After adjustments for industry trends, economic profit significantly decreases for firms in emerging capital markets, taking negative values, while for companies in developed markets, we observe insignificant improvements in economic profit values following acquisitions. These results indicate that companies in emerging capital markets cannot achieve the planned synergies, integrate successfully, and improve the performance of the combined firms. We find that industry and geographical diversifications influence the performance of M&A deals in emerging and developed countries, respectively. We also find that the effects on company value differ for stock and cash deals and for high- and low-tech transactions in both markets. By testing the impact of economic crisis of 2007–2008 on the performance of M&A deals, we reveal that the adjusted economic profit does not differ significantly between pre- and post-crisis M&As.

Keywords Mergers and acquisitions · Value creation · Economic profit · Company performance · Emerging capital markets · Developed capital markets

S. Grigorieva (✉)
Corporate Finance Center, School of Finance, National Research University Higher School of Economics, Moscow, Russia
e-mail: sgrigorieva@hse.ru

S. Kuzmina
Corporate Finance Center, National Research University Higher School of Economics, Moscow, Russia

© Springer Nature Switzerland AG 2020
I. Ivashkovskaya et al. (eds.), *Strategic Deals in Emerging Capital Markets*,
Advanced Studies in Emerging Markets Finance,
https://doi.org/10.1007/978-3-030-23850-6_5

1 Introduction

This chapter focuses on mergers and acquisitions (M&As) in developed and emerging capital markets. We examine post-acquisition value effects of M&A deals and reveal the drivers of M&A performance. Initially, developed markets were the main field of corporate acquisitions. However, globalization, saturation, the consolidation of world markets, and toughening competition have forced developed market companies to search for growth in emerging economies. In recent decades, these processes have also encouraged emerging market companies to be active participants in M&A deals as acquiring firms. M&As in emerging markets are challenging due to the high level of operating and investment risks; uncertainty; the lack of supporting elements such as advisers, accountants, and lawyers, which are key players in acquisitions; weak corporate governance; and less efficient market mechanisms. These specific features of developing countries may influence the post-acquisition performance of merged firms and therefore raise the question about the value effects of M&A deals.

There is no consensus in the literature about acquirer performance after M&A deals. Companies in developed or emerging markets either experience negative or no gains from acquisitions (Ghosh 2001; Sharma and Ho 2002; Yook 2004; Martynova et al. 2007; Papadakis and Thanos 2010; Guest et al. 2010; Bertrand and Betschinger 2012; Rao-Nicholson et al. 2016) or increase their performance through M&A deals (Healy et al. 1992; Powell and Stark 2005; Kumar and Bansal 2008; Grigorieva and Troitskiy 2012; Grigorieva and Grinchenko 2013; Rodionov and Mikhalchuk 2015; Zaremba and Plotnicki 2016).

Although there is a significant amount of research on M&A performance, more research is needed to help to understand this important strategy and to provide recommendations to strategists which enable them to succeed in acquisitions (Hitt et al. 2012). Some authors suggest examining emerging market deals to understand whether the country of origin of acquirers and specific features of emerging markets influence M&A performance (Rao-Nicholson et al. 2016; Thanos and Papadakis 2012).

There are two widely used approaches employed by researches to measure long-term performance of M&A deals: accounting studies and long-term window event studies (Zollo and Meier 2008). While examining long-term market reactions to M&A deals is a popular approach, the former allows the measurement of the post-acquisition performance directly. Nevertheless, the analysis of commonly used book value measures (such as ROE, ROA, EBITDA margins, and OCF to market value of assets) of merged companies before and after acquisitions shows us how the operating performance has changed but does not provide information about the impact of M&A deals on company value. There are only a few studies examining the impact of M&A deals on corporate value over the long run. These mostly analyze deals in developed markets (Sirower and O'Byrne 1998; Yook 2004; Guest et al. 2010; Singh et al. 2012; Kan and Ohno 2012; Leepsa and Mishra 2013). Thus, the literature in developed and emerging capital markets now, mainly, gives us a picture of the operating performance of M&A deals in long-run period, rather than value performance of M&A transactions (Yook 2004; Grigorieva and Petrunina 2015).

Our study contributes to the literature on the influence of M&A deals on company value in the long run in several ways. First, we provide a comparative analysis of the post-acquisition value effects of M&A deals in developed and emerging capital markets. Second, we examine the performance of M&A deals based on an economic profit model. Third, we examine how deals, completed in pre- and post-crisis periods, influence M&A performance. Fourth, we compare the performance of M&A deals in high- and low-tech industries.

The remainder of this chapter is organized as follows: Section 5.2 summarizes the related literature and gives the hypotheses. Section 5.3 describes the sample selection procedure. Section 5.4 provides a discussion of the results, and Sect. 5.5 concludes.

2 Literature Review and Hypotheses Development

Theoretical arguments suggest that M&A deals may have both value-enhancing and value-reducing effects. "A potential benefit of M&A deals is the achievement of operating and financial synergies (The Synergy Theory). Other benefits are connected with a new and more efficient management team as a result of the deal (The Market for Corporate Control Theory), reduced management freedom to use future cash flows for negative NPV projects, particularly for non-equity purchased acquisitions (The Free Cash Flow Theory) and a rapid adjustment to changes in the regulatory environment and technological innovation (The Strategic Realignment Theory) (Sharma and Ho 2002). On the other hand, the disadvantages which reduce M&A gains include systematic overpayment for targets as a result of the acquirer's overoptimistic evaluation of synergies (the Hubris Theory), agency problems, difficulties at the people and process levels (Rao-Nicholson et al. 2016) and diversification" (Grigorieva and Petrunina 2015).

In line with Switzer (1996), Hamza (2009), and Martynova and Renneboog (2011), we suppose that bidder companies in developed capital markets are able to increase shareholder value through M&As due to the strong legal and institutional environment and greater management experience compared to emerging markets (Bruner et al. 2002). Developed countries have higher transparency in financial reporting and corporate governance, reducing the risk of bad investment decisions based on insufficient information about potential target and management self-interests (La Porta et al. 2002). Consequently, companies are able to reach operating synergy, increase asset productivity, and reduce associated costs.

In emerging capital markets, the puzzle of M&A performance is more specific. An imperfect institutional environment increases operational and investment risks, uncertainty, transaction costs, information asymmetry, government intervention, and less efficient market mechanisms, making it difficult for firms to achieve synergies and integrate efficiently. The probability of positive value effects of M&As is likely to be lower in emerging markets than in developed ones. Moreover, the acquisition of firms from developed capital markets by firms from emerging economies may also lead to value-reducing effects. According to Narayan and Thenmozhi (2014), emerging market firms often make mistakes when choosing and valuing targets because they lack experience in cross-border M&As and they are often smaller in size and pay high premiums because of their limited bargaining power. Taking into account these arguments, we expect that:

H1 *M&A deals in developed markets create more value for shareholders than M&A deals in emerging economies.*

A significant amount of research has focused on understanding the factors that drive M&A performance. According to Hitt et al. (2012), the most popular determinants of M&A performance are target size, industry relatedness, mode of payment for M&As, the acquisition experience of the acquiring company, and firm performance before the deal. In recent years, a great deal of attention has also been paid to cross-border deals, which have become a widely used strategy in the changing competitive landscape (Moeller and Schlingemann 2005; Boateng et al. 2007; Narayan and Thenmozhi 2014; Lebedev et al. 2015). Companies from emerging markets are beginning to play an increasingly important role in cross-border M&A deals both as acquirers and as targets. The value of cross-border M&As made by firms from emerging markets has increased from 15.5% in 2010 to 27.1% in 2015 of the world's total value of cross-border M&As (Thompson Reuters report 2015). In a review of the M&A literature, Shimizu et al. (2004) and Hitt et al. (2012) suggest that further empirical research on cross-border M&As especially initiated by companies from emerging economies is needed. Such research would provide a valuable source of information about M&A deals and their performance in different institutional, culture, governance, and regulatory environments. Research in recent years has also started to analyze the impact of economic crises on M&A performance, opening the space for further discussion of this question in different regions (Wan and Yiu 2009; Rao-Nicholson et al. 2016; Lebedev et al. 2015). Recent studies have also shown that the type of acquired resources may influence M&A performance. In the last decade, acquisition in the field of high technology has become a popular strategy, which obviously relates to the penetration of high tech in each industry, stimulating additional investments in innovation (EY report 2015).

In this chapter, we suggest several hypotheses to test whether the most popular determinants of M&A performance in the literature influence the post-acquisition value effects of M&A deals.

Method of Payment
Managers tend to pay with cash (equity) when they believe that shares are undervalued (overvalued) (Myers and Majluf 1984; Loughran and Vijh 1997). Therefore, payment by cash may signal manager expectations that performance will be higher after the deal. The free cash flow theory states better performance for deals paid in cash since debt financing reduces the agency problem and monitors manager efficiency. In competing bids, a cash offer enables faster deal closures,

capturing synergies (Berkovitch and Narayanan 1990; Rao-Nicholson et al. 2016. Other authors indicate another advantage of cash deals: allowing the replacement of a poor management team for better results in the future (Denis and Denis 1995; Ghosh and Ruland 1998; Parrino and Harris 1999). In cross-border deals, target companies would prefer cash as a mode of payment when acquirers belong to emerging markets due to high stock market volatility which makes the stocks of acquirers an unattractive offer for the target shareholders (Kohli and Mann 2013). On the other hand, when deciding on the method of payment, a potential acquirer takes into consideration other investment opportunities. If a company has a sufficient number of lucrative investment projects, it will be more prone to use stock, which will save cash and avoid a debt increase (Theory of investment opportunities, see Martin 1996; Dong et al. 2006). Stock deals enable the company to diversify risks between the shareholders (Hansen 1987) and alleviate the asymmetric information problem, especially in case of markets with imperfect information. In cross-border M&As with a higher level of uncertainty than in domestic ones, stock deals may create more value for shareholders than cash deals (Dutta et al. 2013).

Analyzing the results of previous empirical research in developed capital markets, we may conclude that better performance is mostly achieved in cash M&A deals (Ghosh 2001; Haleblian et al. 2009; Hitt et al. 2012), providing us with opportunity to hypothesize that:

H2a *M&A deals paid for by cash show better performance than deals paid for by stock in developed capital markets.*

In emerging capital markets, the results are mixed (Boateng and Bi 2014; Kohli and Mann 2013). Taking into account the high level of uncertainty and capital constraints in emerging capital markets, we suppose that:

H2b *M&A deals paid for by stock show better performance than deals paid for by cash in emerging capital markets.*

Cross-Border/Domestic Acquisitions

Transnational deals are motivated by a variety of factors, and their motivation differs from those of domestic M&As. These factors include growth by market expansion, utilization of lower raw material and labor costs, the extension of technology, applying a firm's brand name or intellectual property in new markets, tax and currency arbitrage, and the benefits of geographic diversification. These deals are more complex due to the additional risks connected with differences in the political and economic environment, corporate culture, organization, accounting, law, and tax rules between the countries of the acquirer and the target company (Sudarsanam 2003; Bruner 2004). The literature offers conflicting evidence about the effects of cross-border M&A deals on firm value.

Moeller and Schlingemann (2005), for example, examine a sample of M&A deals in 1985–1995 and find that US companies that acquire foreign targets compared to those that acquire domestic firms experience significantly lower returns and operating performance. Gugler et al. (2003) do not find any significant difference between the performance of cross-border and domestic deals. Moreover, Dutta et al. (2013), analyzing domestic and cross-border deals by Canadian companies in 1993–2002, find positive abnormal returns for acquirers in two types of deals and prove that the market favors cross-border acquisitions over domestic M&As. Analyzing M&A deals where developed market firms acquire emerging market targets, most research indicates that such acquisitions provide more gains for shareholders than M&As where targets are from developed markets (Francis et al. 2008; Chari et al. (2010); Narayan and Thenmozhi 2014). Hence, we assume that:

H3a *Cross-border M&A deals show better performance than local deals in developed capital markets.*

In emerging capital markets, the results are also mixed. Kohli and Mann (2012) examine 268 M&A deals in 1997–2008 and find that cross-border M&A deals create significantly higher gains than the domestic ones in India. De Beule and Sels (2016) also indicate performance improvements for Indian firms. Bhagat et al. (2011), based on the sample of 678 cross-border M&A deals in 1997–2008, find a positive market reaction to the announcements of M&A deals for companies from BRICS, Malaysia, Mexico, and the Philippines. "Analysing the similar time period Al Rahahleh and Wei (2012) also prove positive effects of cross-border M&A deals for acquirers from 17 developing countries. A negative market reaction is found by Aybar and Ficici (2009) and by Bris and Cabolis (2008) for deals, initiated by companies from Asia, Latin America and Africa. Deshpande et al. (2012) state insignificant announcement returns for developing country acquirers with targets in any country" (Grigorieva and Petrunina 2015, p. 385).

Following Bris and Cabolis (2008) and Aybar and Ficici (2009) and taking into account the fact that developing market firms have limited experience in cross-border deals and in many cases overpay for target companies because of limited bargaining power in cross-border M&As (Narayan and Thenmozhi 2014), we expect that:

H3b *Local M&A deals show better performance than cross-border deals in emerging capital markets.*

Industry Relatedness
According to empirical results in developed countries, the prevailing opinion among financial researchers is that corporate diversification destroys value and diversified firms trade at a discount (Berger and Ofek 1995; Lang and Stulz 1994; Fukui and Ushijima 2007). Frequently, the internal capital market and high agency costs are viewed as sources of this value loss. On the contrary, in emerging capital markets, the diversification strategy may be attractive for firms. These markets are as a rule characterized by a dominance of diversified companies. The specific features of emerging markets, to some extent, can affect the performance of an integration strategy. In developed countries, well-organized capital markets, competitive product markets, and labor markets, and a high level of contract enforcement, guarantee similar rules of play both for diversified and focused firms. In these conditions, the benefits of integration may be reduced. On the contrary, in an imperfect institutional environment and with weak contract enforcement, diversified firms may be of value.

They can mimic the beneficial functions of various institutions that are present in developed markets and thereby create a potential source of value growth for integrated firms (Khanna and Palepu 1997; Fauver et al. 2003; Grigorieva and Petrunina 2015). However, severe market imperfections, which increase the potential agency costs resulting from higher information asymmetry, can lead to value destruction in firms that undertake such strategies (Lins and Servaes 2002; Bertrand et al. 2002; Lu and Yao 2006). Moreover, improvements in the institutional environment with time may also contribute to the reduction of attractiveness of a diversification strategy in emerging economies (Lee et al. 2008). Thus, we suppose a similar effect of diversification on M&A performance in developed and emerging capital markets:

H4a *Focused M&A deals show better performance than diversified deals in developed capital markets.*

H4b *Focused M&A deals show better performance than diversified deals in emerging capital markets.*

The Impact of the Crisis in 2007–2008 on the Value Effects of M&A Deals
We expect that post-crisis deals perform better than pre-crisis deals. There are several reasons supporting this hypothesis. First, following a crisis, acquirers usually have less cash to finance mergers and acquisitions, "meaning that each opportunity for acquisitions faces more scrutiny and, as a result, decisions on transactions are more balanced. Moreover, during the crisis, prices fall considerably, meaning that it is possible to buy good companies on the cheap" (Grigorieva and Petrunina 2015, p. 386). Wan and Yiu (2009) state that a crisis suggests the firms have opportunities to perform better in the future. The authors argue that during a crisis, companies may change their resources and capabilities via M&As in order to better adapt to the changing conditions and improve their performance. Analyzing M&A deals in ASEAN countries in 2001–2012, Rao-Nicholson et al. (2016) find that acquisitions completed during the financial crisis are more profitable than those completed before and after it. In this study, we compare the performance of M&A deals in pre- and post-crisis periods and hypothesize that:

H5a *Post-crisis M&A deals perform better than pre-crisis deals in developed capital markets.*

H5b *Post-crisis M&A deals perform better than pre-crisis deals in emerging capital markets.*

Type of Acquired Resources
Since 1990, there has been a substantial increase in M&A activity in high-tech industries due to the need to acquire firms to obtain new skills and new technical and technological knowledge (Rossi et al. 2011). The expansion of M&A deals in high-tech sectors has led to an increase in research on the performance of such deals. The results of empirical papers are controversial, and analyzing short-term returns of merged firms and changes in post-acquisition performance in developed markets, some authors document performance improvements following M&A deals (Benou and Madura 2005; Dutta and Kumar 2009; Mithas et al. 2012: Canace and Mann

2013; Lusyana and Sherif 2016), while others find negative or no gains from M&A deals in high-tech industries (Datta et al. 1992; Porrini 2004; Sears and Hoetker 2014).

In emerging capital markets, the question about M&A performance in high-tech sectors is much less explored. A limited number of empirical studies also show contradictory results. Based on the sample of 422 M&As initiated by companies from Asia and Latin America in 1991–2004, Aybar and Ficici (2009) find a negative market reaction to the acquisitions of high-tech targets. Bertrand and Betschinger (2012), on the contrary, document positive influence of M&As on corporate performance for high-tech acquirers from Russia. Concentrating on the comparative analysis of high- and low-tech deals, the latest papers reveal that market reacts more favorable to high-tech acquisitions in different emerging capital markets (De Beule and Sels 2016) and BRICM countries (Yoon and Lee 2016).

Regardless of the high uncertainty surrounding high-tech deals, we expect that they will positively affect M&A performance as the acquisition of technology is critical within the innovative economy providing companies with a competitive advantage and value growth both in developed and emerging capital markets (Porrini 2004; Aybar and Ficici 2009; Yoon and Lee 2016; De De Beule and Sels 2016).

H6a *High-tech M&A deals show better performance than low-tech deals in developed capital markets.*

H6b *High-tech M&A deals show better performance than low-tech deals in emerging capital markets.*

3   Methodology and Data

3.1   Performance Measures

In contrast to existing studies, we examine the post-acquisition value effects of M&A deals in developed and emerging capital markets. Our study involves a two-step procedure. At the first stage, we assess the impact of M&A deals on shareholder value based on economic profit and measure and compare the performance of M&A deals for companies in developed and emerging capital markets. At the second stage, we try to reveal the main factors that influence post-acquisition performance of M&A deals.

The rationale for using value-based performance measures to evaluate the post-acquisition performance is that it takes into account investment risk, which is embedded into the cost of capital, allowing an understanding of whether the planned synergies, which are the most common motives for M&A deals (Thanos and Papadakis 2012), really create value for shareholders. Following Sirower and O'Byrne (1998), Yook (2004), Singh et al. (2012), and Leepsa and Mishra (2013), we use economic profit to assess post-acquisition value effects of M&A deals in long-run period:

$$EP = (ROCE_t - WACC_t) \times CE_{t-1} \tag{1}$$

where $ROCE_t$ is the return on capital employed at period t, $WACC_t$ is weighted average cost of capital at period t, and CE_{t-1} is capital employed at period $t-1$.

To examine the changes in performance of the combined firms after M&A deals, we use the standard change model (Switzer 1996; Martynova et al. 2007; Yook 2004; Papadakis and Thanos 2010). Following Papadakis and Thanos (2010), we choose a time frame of $(-2;+2)$ since 2 years after a deal are critical to its success and in many cases enough to finish the integration process. Furthermore, extending the observation beyond 2 years following M&As would substantially reduce our sample size due to the unavailability of complete financial information. We exclude from our analysis the year the M&A deal took place, also following previous researchers (Martynova et al. 2007; Yook 2004; Papadakis and Thanos 2010).

Taking into account that the difference between pre-merger and post-merger performance may also be in part due to economy-wide and industry factors, or to a continuation of firm-specific performance before the merger (Healy et al. 1992), we make an adjustment for industry trend (Healy et al. 1992; Yook 2004; Papadakis and Thanos 2010). We use the performance of industry-median firms as a benchmark (Yook 2004). The industry median is identified from the pool of all companies which belong to the same industry in Bloomberg database as the sample firms (acquirers/targets) in the year prior to an M&A deal.

Industry-adjusted economic profit is measured by comparing both acquiring and target firms with other firms that operate in the same industry:

$$EP_{i,t}^{ind} = EP_{i,t} - \left(\frac{IndustryEP_t}{IndustryCE_{t-1}} \right) \times CE_{i,t-1} \tag{2}$$

where $EP_{i,t}$ is firm i's EP in year t, $CE_{i,t-1}$ is firm i's capital employed at the end of year $t-1$, $IndustryEP_t$ is the industry median EP in year t, $IndustryCE_{t-1}$ is the industry median capital employed at the end of year $t-1$, $\left(\frac{IndustryEP_t}{IndustryCE_{t-1}} \right)$ is the median EP created per dollar of capital in a particular industry during year t, and $\left(\frac{IndustryEP_t}{IndustryCE_{t-1}} \right) \times CE_{i,t-1}$ is the industry's median EP for a firm of the same size (Yook 2004).

Raw and industry-adjusted EPs are calculated before and after M&A deals, and the Wilcoxon signed rank test is employed to test whether the change in EP of the merged firms is statistically significant following M&A deals (Martynova et al. 2007; Yook 2004; Rao-Nicholson et al. 2016).

To reveal the determinants of post-acquisition performance, at the second stage of our analysis, we also employ a change model and the Wilcoxon signed rank test for significance.

Table 1 Sample selection procedure

Step #	Sample selection criteria	Number of deals	
		DM	EM
1	M&A deal is completed	984	536
	Acquirers and targets are listed firms		
	Acquirers and targets have the same accounting standards		
	Companies from financial and regulated industries are excluded		
	The stake after acquisition is above 51%		
2	Acquirers and targets initiated only one deal during the analyzing period	530	401
3	Financial data is available for analyzing period (−2, +2)	153	125

3.2 Sample Characteristics

Our study focuses on M&A performance in both developed and emerging capital markets in 2002–2013. We concentrate on less examined in academic literature Western European M&A deals and deals initiated by firms from different emerging capital markets. To define a list of developed and emerging economies, we use the IMF classification, which comprises 25 Western European and 19 emerging markets. The details of each deal were extracted from the Bloomberg database. We include domestic as well as cross-border deals and use the criteria presented in Table 1 to construct the sample.

Descriptive statistics of our final sample, including 153 and 125 M&A deals initiated by companies from Western European and emerging markets, are presented in Appendices 1 and 2. Panel A show a decrease in M&A activity in post-crisis years in developed capital markets but an increase in number of deals in emerging markets, which correspond to the overall M&A trends. The industry breakdown of both subsamples is similar: consumer and industrial sectors have the largest number of deals (Panel B). Panel C state that about 51% of deals in developed markets was initiated by acquirers from the United Kingdom (40 deals), Germany (20 deals), and France (19 deals). In emerging capital markets leaders by number of deals are China (18 deals) and India (17 deals). A significant part of the Malaysian deals in our sample is explained by the rapid growth of acquisitions initiated by Malaysian firms in pre-crisis period. For the method of payment, more than half of the deals both in developed and emerging capital markets use cash (Panel D). Emerging market companies are more active in cross-border deals (70%) compared with developed ones (50%) (Panel E). Regarding M&A strategies (Panel F), the sample is divided between diversifying (70%) and focusing (30%) deals equally in developed and emerging capital markets. Panel G shows that 49% and 71% of deals in developed and emerging markets, respectively, involved high-tech acquisitions.

In Appendix 3, we provide the descriptive statistics for pre- and post-acquisition value performance measure for companies in developed and emerging capital markets.

4 Results and Discussion

4.1 Value Effects of M&A Deals in Developed and Emerging Capital Markets

To test our hypothesis that M&A deals in developed markets create more value for shareholders than M&A deals in emerging economies, we calculate the differences between pre-acquisition and post-acquisition economic profit for companies from both markets and compare the results, using the Wilcoxon ranked test for significance. Table 2 shows the levels of economic profit for merged firms in developed and emerging capital markets. Economic profit is measured in two ways, before adjustments for industry trend (raw EP) and after (industry-adjusted EP) and is calculated for the 2 years before and the 2 years after deal completion. The final line in each panel is aggregate median for the associated 2-year period.

Our findings from Table 2 indicate that M&A deals in developed countries have a positive impact on both raw and industry-adjusted performances for merged firms. Though most estimates are not significant, the increase in raw economic profit by $12.3 million in the period $[-1;+1]$ is significant at the 15% level. These results are consistent with the effects obtained by Yook (2004), who finds a slight but insignificant improvement in economic profit after the exclusion of acquisition premiums from an analysis of the US market. The results from our empirical analysis are also similar to findings obtained by Guest et al. (2010) who analyzed UK acquisitions in 1985–1996 and found statistically insignificant value effects of M&A deals.

Table 2 Raw and industry-adjusted economic profit for merged firms in developed and emerging markets; all EPs are in millions of dollars

Year relative to completion	Developed markets		Emerging markets	
	Raw EP	Industry-adjusted EP	Raw EP	Industry-adjusted EP
Panel 1: Pre-acquisition performance				
−2	63.0	8.7	28.2	−0.7
−1	64.2	12.3	31.3	7.6
Medians	76.4	11.1	41.6	8.9
Panel 2: Post-acquisition performance				
+1	97.0	11.0	32.8	−4.4
+2	89.6	16.5	40.3	−0.5
Medians	117.2	19.6	41.7	−3.0
Panel 3: Difference between pre-acquisition and post-acquisition indicator				
−2, +2	19.2	9.8	4.6	−0.9^d
−1, +1	12.3$^+$	16.1	2.0	−4.6**
Medians	17.0	23.1	2.5	−1.1*

***,**,*,+Significance at 1%, 5%, 10%, and 15% using Wilcoxon ranked test which shows that the post-M&A performance is significantly different from pre-M&A performance
a,b,c,dSignificance at 1%, 5%, 10%, and 15% using Wilcoxon ranked test which shows that industry-adjusted change in performance is significantly different from raw change in industry performance

Table 3 Comparison of value effects of M&A deals in developed and emerging capital markets; all EPs are in millions of dollars

Year relative to completion	Raw EP			Industry-adjusted EP		
	Developed markets	Emerging markets	Z-value	Developed markets	Emerging markets	Z-value
Difference between pre-acquisition and post-acquisition indicator						
−2, +2	19.2	4.6	−0.1	9.8	−0.9	−0.1
−1, +1	12.3+	2.0	−0.9	16.1	−4.6**	−1.8*
Medians	17.0	2.5	−1.0	23.1	−1.1*	−1.2

***,**,*,+Significance at 1%, 5%, 10%, and 15% using Wilcoxon ranked test which shows that change in M&A performance in developed markets is significantly different from change in M&A performance in emerging capital markets

According to the results for emerging markets, the differences in raw economic profit are statistically insignificant (Panel 3), while differences in industry-adjusted economic profit are negative and significant at 5 and 10% levels for 2-year window (−$4.6 million) and for median values (−$1.1 million), respectively. These results indicate that industry effects eliminate the deterioration of value following M&A deals in emerging capital markets. Our results are consistent with findings of Singh et al. (2012), and Leepsa and Mishra (2013), who analyze Indian M&A deals.

Our results from Table 3 show that there is a significant difference (at 10% level) in value effects of M&A deals in developed and emerging capital markets for the 3-year period (Table 3).

Adjusted economic profit for developed market firms increases by $16 million, while for emerging-market companies, it drops to −$5 million level, indicating that firms from Western Europe are more successful in achieving planned synergies and integration due to lower levels of risk and perfect institutional environment. The results are consistent with hypothesis H1.

4.2 Determinants of Value Effects of M&A Deals in Developed and Emerging Capital Markets

This section focuses on the analysis of the main factors that influence the value creation process in M&A deals. Changes in value performance adjusted for industry effects for different subsamples of deals in developed and emerging capital markets are presented in Table 4.

First, M&A deals paid by stock provide significantly (at 10% level) better value performance improvements than cash deals in developed capital markets only when a 2-year period around the deal is examined. This result does not support our hypothesis H2a. In our sample, almost half of the deals are cross-border ones, indicating that stock payment may be more preferable due to the high level of uncertainty in such deals and opportunity to share the risk between the shareholders of merged firms. Analyzing equity-financed versus cash-financed deals in emerging

Table 4 Determinants of changes in value performance adjusted for industry trends for firms in developed and emerging economies; all EPs are in millions of dollars

Year relative to completion	Developed markets			Emerging markets		
Difference between pre-acquisition and post-acquisition EP						
	Stock	Cash	Difference	Stock	Cash	Difference
−2, +2	24.4	13.3	0.1	6.5	−3.2	1.4
−1, +1	188.7	26.1	−1.8*	−0.1[a]	−10.3	2.0*
Medians	13.3	37.8	0.0	26.8[b]	−6.2	2.0**
	Cross-border	Local	Difference	Cross-border	Local	Difference
−2, +2	31.7	−6.3	−1.7*	−1.6	−4.4	−0.7
−1, +1	26.9	1.5	−1.0	−18.6	−11.3[b]	−1.2
Medians	37.8	0.9	−1.4	−49.4	−2.8[d]	−1.2
	Diversified	Focused	Difference	Diversified	Focused	Difference
−2, +2	−1.4	30.4	0.6	−6.2	0.9	2.3**
−1, +1	19.8	10.7	−1.1	−12.3	−20.1[b]	−0.2
Medians	28.9	13.3	−1.0	−13.1	−14.9[d]	0.9
	Post-crisis	Pre-crisis	Difference	Post-crisis	Pre-crisis	Difference
−2, +2	30.4	0.6	−0.7	3.1	−2.8	−0.5
−1, +1	53.7	9.0	−1.3	−2.8	−8.8[b]	−0.1
Medians	33.1	14.7	−0.3	6.0	−2.2[c]	−0.7
	High-tech	Low-tech	Difference	High-tech	Low-tech	Difference
−2, +2	0.6	39.0	1.5+	−3.0	−7.7	−0.7
−1, +1	10.7	23.8	0.2	0.1	2.0[b]	−1.1
Medians	0.9	43.7	2.1**	25.2	−5.1[a]	−1.8*

***,**,*,+Significance at 1%, 5%, 10%, and 15% using Wilcoxon ranked test which shows that change in M&A performance for stock, cross-border, diversified, post-crisis, and high-tech deals is significantly different from corresponding change in M&A performance for cash, local, focused, pre-crisis, and low-tech deals

a,b,c,dSignificance at 1%, 5%, 10%, and 15% using Wilcoxon ranked test which shows that the post-M&A performance is significantly different from pre-M&A performance for different subsamples

markets, we also find that stock transactions perform better than those paid in cash. The results are statistically significant at 10% and 5% levels for 2-year period and median values, respectively, supporting our hypothesis H2b.

Second, developed market companies experience better performance improvements following cross-border M&As than local deals. We find a significant difference (at 10% level) in economic profit values between these two types of deals for the 4-year period (Table 4), which favors hypothesis H3a. For the sample of deals in emerging markets, we find that adjusted economic profit does not differ significantly for cross-border and local deals, which does not allow us to accept the proposed hypothesis H3b.

Third, comparing the performance of diversified and focused deals in developed capital markets, we reveal that there is no difference between these two types of deals. This result is consistent with Martynova et al. (2007) who also examined European M&A deals. The results for emerging market companies suggest that focused transactions erode firm value. The differences between pre- and post-acquisition economic profits for the subsample of focused deals are −$20.1 million and −$14.9 million for the 2-year period and median values, respectively. These results are statistically significant at 5 and 15% levels, respectively. Our findings also show that for the 4-year period, focused deals perform on average better than diversifying transactions. Industry-adjusted economic profit is −$6.2 million in transactions with low similarity (diversifying) and $0.9 million in focused deals. The difference is statistically significant at 5% level for the 4-year window. The results are consistent with hypothesis H4b for deals in emerging markets and do not allow us to accept the proposed hypothesis H4a for companies in developed capital markets.

Fourth, Table 4 also reports economic profits classified by the time of the M&A deal completion, during the pre- or post-crisis periods. The lack of significance of the results provides no support for hypotheses H5a and H5b. Our results also indicate that changes in performance due to M&As in emerging capital markets for the subsample of deals completed during the pre-crisis period are negative (−$8.8 million and −$2.2 million) and statistically significant at 5% and 10% levels for 2-year period and median values, respectively, indicating that such deals decrease value for shareholders. Rao-Nicholson et al. (2016) also find a statistically significant, negative impact of pre-crisis deals on M&A performance, but in contrast to us, they examine the operating performance of corporate acquisitions. They reveal that post-crisis deals benefited from a higher increase in performance than pre-crisis ones.

Finally, we split the samples of M&A deals in developed and emerging capital markets into high-tech and low-tech deals. Using the classification of industries based on NACE Rev 1.1 codes, suggested by Eurostat and OECD, we reveal the deals with high- and low-tech targets. Our results for developed market companies indicate that low-tech deals outperform high-tech transactions, which contradicts hypothesis H6a. According to the results in Table 4, median industry-adjusted economic profit is $47.3 million for non-technological and $0.9 million for technological M&As. The difference is statistically significant at 5% level and indicates that low-tech deals generate more value for shareholders than high-tech ones. Technological deals, regardless of their attractiveness for acquirers, may not lead to value creation for several reasons: (1) a high level of uncertainty surrounding such deals, (2) difficulties with the integration of non-technological divisions of target firms (Chakrabarti et al. 1994; De Man and Duysters 2005), and (3) a lack of disclosed information about the acquired technology because of intellectual property protection, which complicates the adaptation of technology and its integration with other company resources and, as a result, leads to additional costs. The lack of complete information and the high costs of innovative developments contribute to an overestimation of technological companies (Puranam et al. 2006). Some authors also argue that the inefficiency of high-tech deals is because in most cases acquirers are forced to purchase in addition to the desirable technologies unimportant and inapplicable functional units and know-how, which neutralize the positive effects (Hennart and Reddy 1997; De Man and Duysters 2005).

Comparing the value effects of high- and low-tech deals in emerging markets, we find the opposite results, which are consistent with hypothesis H6b, assuming that high-tech M&A deals show better performance than low-tech transactions. The results shown in Table 4 indicate that adjusted economic profit is −$5.1 million for low-tech and $25.2 million for high-tech firms. The difference is statistically significant at 10% level for median values.

5 Concluding Remarks

This chapter tests whether M&A deals create value to shareholders in developed and emerging capital markets. The research will help managers to justify a company's expansion via M&As and create value after the deal.

We contribute to the literature by comparing M&A performance for companies in developed and emerging economies over the long run, using economic profit as the value performance measure. In line with other studies, we examine the influence of the most popular deal characteristics on acquisition performance, such as mode of payment and geographic and industry diversification, and, in contrast to most of them, we analyze whether post-crisis and high-tech transactions outperform pre-crisis and low-tech acquisitions in developed and emerging capital markets.

Based on a sample of 153 M&A deals in Western European markets and 125 deals initiated by firms from different emerging capital markets in 2002–2013, we find that after adjustments for industry trends, economic profit significantly decreases for firms in emerging capital markets. For the companies in developed markets, we observe statistically insignificant improvements in economic profit values following acquisitions. These results indicate that companies in emerging capital markets cannot achieve planned synergies, integrate successfully, and improve the value performance of the combined firms. This means that managers should focus more on the post-merger integration process to realize potential synergies and create value for shareholders. Comparing the effects of M&A deals on company value in both markets, we reveal that transactions in developed markets create more value for shareholders than in emerging economies for the 2-year period surrounding the deals. The difference in the results may be explained by the imperfect institutional environment in emerging capital markets which prevents companies extracting the benefits of M&A deals. Companies in emerging capital markets have limited experience in cross-border M&A deals, which accounts for a significant part of our sample, and they may make mistakes in choosing and evaluating target firms (Narayan and Thenmozhi 2014).

Our results for deals in emerging capital markets are consistent with the outcomes of Singh et al. (2012), and Leepsa and Mishra (2013), who analyze Indian M&A

deals and employ value performance measures. Our findings are also in line with the results of empirical papers which employ accounting-based performance measures to assess the performance of M&A deals in India, Russia, ASEAN, and other different emerging capital markets (Mantravadi and Reddy 2008; Kumar 2009; Bertrand and Betschinger 2012; Narayan and Thenmozhi 2014; Rao-Nicholson et al. 2016).

The results that we obtain for the sample of deals initiated by firms from developed capital markets do not contradict the findings of Ghosh (2001), Sharma and Ho (2002), Yook (2004), Martynova et al. (2007), Dutta and Jog (2009), Papadakis and Thanos (2010), and Guest et al. (2010), who also find the impact of M&A deals on company performance measured by accounting- and value-based indicators to be insignificant.

In this study, we also examine the determinants of M&A performance. Analyzing the impact of the mode of payment, business similarity, and geographical diversification, we reveal that deals paid for with stock significantly outperform the cash transactions in developed capital markets for the 2-year period surrounding the deal and in emerging markets, also for the 2-year period and median values. We also find out that cross-border M&As in developed markets and focused deals in emerging economies provide significantly better value performance improvements than local and diversifying transactions, when a 4-year period is examined. Testing the effects of the economic crisis of 2007–2008 on the performance of M&A deals, we find that changes in economic profit values do not significantly differ for post- and pre-crisis acquisitions. For technological deals, low-tech acquisitions generate more value for shareholders than high-tech ones in developed capital markets. This result is in line with the findings of Porrini (2004), who also reveals that low-tech transaction are better, but find that both technological and non-technological deals are value-destroying. The opposite results were found for acquisitions in emerging capital markets. Our findings for this sample are supported by the results of other empirical studies, which also compare the performance of high- and low-tech deals (De Beule and Sels 2016; Yoon and Lee 2016).

We admit that the current study has some limitations; therefore, our results may not provide a comprehensive picture of the value effects of M&A deals in developed and emerging capital markets. Particularly, making the adjustment for industry trends, we do not control for size, pre-performance, and other characteristics of benchmark firms. In addition, we do not eliminate the M&A premium when calculating changes in performance; therefore, we cannot conclude whether high premiums, which are usually paid for targets, are the source of value destruction in M&A deals. In this study, we examine 2 years following M&As, but it is questionable whether the merged firms are able to realize all planned synergies in this period; thus, we suggest for future research to expand the time period of analysis. We also suggest examining more determinants of M&A performance, paying attention to target characteristics and the economic and institutional environment in the case of cross-border deals.

Appendix 1

Table 5 Sample description in the developed markets

Panel A: Completion year	No of deals	Percent
2004	13	8
2005	20	13
2006	23	15
2007	13	8
2008	21	14
2009	11	7
2010	15	10
2011	13	8
2012	11	7
2013	13	8
Panel B: Industries		
Consumer	59	39
Industrial	46	30
Technology and communications	38	25
Basic metals	10	7

Panel C: Acquirer country	No of deals	Percent
U.K.	40	26
Germany	20	13
France	19	12
Sweden	15	10
Switzerland	12	8
Netherland	9	6
Italy	7	5
Finland	6	4
Norway	4	3
Spain	4	3
Denmark	4	3
Greece	3	2
Austria	3	2
Portugal	2	1
Others	5	3

	No of deals	Percent
Panel D: Mode of payment		
Cash	126	82
Stock	27	18
Panel E: Location of deals		
Local	85	56
Cross-boarder	68	44
Panel F: Industry relatedness		
Related	47	31
Diversification	106	69
Panel G: Type of target's assets		
Low tech	74	51
High tech	79	49

Appendix 2

Table 6 Sample description in the emerging markets

	No of deals	Percent		No of deals	Percent		No of deals	Percent
Panel A: Completion year			Panel C: Acquirer country			Panel D: Mode of payment		
2003	6	5	China	18	14	Cash	86	69
2004	6	5	India	17	14	Stock	39	31
2005	8	6	Malaysia	15	12	Panel E: Location of deals		
2006	9	7	South Africa	12	10	Local	39	31
2007	11	9	Poland	10	8	Cross-boarder	86	69
2008	15	12	Brazil	8	6	Panel F: Industry relatedness		
2009	10	8	Thailand	7	6			
2010	14	11	Chile	5	4	Related	37	30
2011	19	15	Indonesia	5	4	Diversification	88	70
2012	11	9	Russia	4	3	Panel G: Type of target's assets		
2013	16	13	Turkey	4	3			
Panel B: Industries			Mexico	4	3	Low tech	89	29
Consumer	61	49	Philippines	3	2	High tech	36	71
Industrial	26	21	Vietnam	2	2			
Technology and communications	22	18	Others	11	9			
Basic metals	16	13						

Appendix 3

Table 7 Descriptive statistics

	Mean	Median	Maximum	Minimum	Std. Dev.
Panel A: Descriptive statistics of EP for companies in developed capital markets					
EP (−2)	248	63	7364	−559	812
EP (−1)	307	64	7809	−208	971
EP (+1)	550	97	23,406	−265	2417
EP (+2)	556	90	25,524	−427	2674
Panel B: Descriptive statistics of EP for companies in emerging capital markets					
EP (−2)	108	28	1502	−127	223
EP (−1)	185	31	2803	−436	457
EP (+1)	184	33	3456	−329	528
EP (+2)	95	40	1682	−1390	298

References

Al Rahahleh, N., & Wei, P. P. (2012). The performance of frequent acquirers: Evidence from emerging markets. *Global Finance Journal, 23*(1), 16–33.

Aybar, B., & Ficici, A. (2009). Cross-border acquisitions and firm value: An analysis of emerging-market multinationals. *Journal of International Business Studies, 40*(8), 1317–1338.

Benou, G., & Madura, J. (2005). High tech acquisitions, firm specific characteristics and the role of investment bank advisors. *The Journal of High Technology Management Research, 16*(1), 101–120.

Berger, P. G., & Ofek, E. (1995). Diversification's effect on firm value. *Journal of Financial Economics, 37*, 39–65.

Berkovitch, E., & Narayanan, M. (1990). Competition and the medium of exchange in takeovers. *Review of Financial Studies, 3*(2), 153–174.

Bertrand, O., & Betschinger, M.-A. (2012). Performance of domestic and cross-border acquisitions: Empirical evidence from Russian acquirers. *Journal of Comparative Economics, 40*, 413–437.

Bertrand, M., Mehta, P., & Mullainathan, S. (2002). Ferreting out tunneling: An application to Indian business groups. *Quarterly Journal of Economics, 117*(1), 121–148.

Bhagat, S., Malhotra, S., & Zhu, P. (2011). Emerging country cross-border acquisitions: Characteristics, acquirer returns and cross-sectional determinants. *Emerging Markets Review, 12*, 250–271.

Boateng, A., & Bi, X. (2014). Acquirer characteristics and method of payment: Evidence from Chinese mergers and acquisitions. *Managerial and Decision Economics, 35*(8), 540–554.

Boateng, A., Qian, W., & Tianle, Y. (2007). Cross-border M&As by Chinese firms: An analysis of strategic motivation and performance. *Thunderbird International Business Review, 50*(4), 259–270.

Bris, A., & Cabolis, C. (2008). The value of investor protection: Firm evidence from cross-border mergers. *The Review of Financial Studies, 21*(2), 605–648.

Bruner, R. F. (2004). *Applied mergers and acquisitions*. Hoboken, NJ: Wiley.

Bruner, R., Conroy, R., Estrada, J., Kritzman, M., & Li, W. (2002). Introduction to 'valuation in emerging markets'. *Emerging Markets Review, 3*(4), 310–324.

Canace, T. G., & Mann, S. V. (2013). The impact of technology-motivated M&A and joint ventures on the value of IT and non-IT firms: AA new examination. *Review of Quantitative Finance & Accounting, 43*(2), 333–366.

Chakrabarti, A., Hauschildt, J., & Suverkrup, C. (1994). Does it pay to acquire technological firms? *R&D Management, 24*(1), 47–56.

Chari, A., Ouimet, P., & Tesar, L. (2010). The value of control in emerging markets. *Review of Financial Studies, 23*(4), 1741–1770.

Datta, D. K., Pinches, G. E., & Narayanan, V. K. (1992). Factors influencing wealth creation from mergers and acquisitions: A meta-analysis. *Strategic Management Journal, 13*(1), 67–84.

De Beule, F., & Sels, A. (2016). Do innovative emerging market cross-border acquirers create more shareholder value? Evidence from India. *International Business Review, 25*, 604–617.

De Man, A., & Duysters, G. (2005). Collaboration and innovation: A review of the effect of mergers, acquisitions and alliances on innovation. *Technovation, 25*(12), 1377–1387.

Denis, D. J., & Denis, D. K. (1995). Performance changes following top management dismissals. *The Journal of Finance, 50*(4), 1029–1057.

Deshpande, S., Svetina, M., & Zhu, P. C. (2012). Analyst coverage of acquiring firms and value creation in cross-border acquisitions. *Journal of Multinational Financial Management, 22*(5), 212–229.

Dong, M., Hirshleifer, D., Richardson, S., & Hong Teoh, S. (2006). Does investor misvaluation drive the takeover market? *Journal of Finance, 61*, 725–762.

Dutta, S., & Jog, V. (2009). The long-term performance of acquiring firms: A re-examination of an anomaly. *Journal of Banking & Finance, 33*(8), 1400–1412.

Dutta, S., & Kumar, V. (2009). Mergers and acquisitions (M&As) by R&D intensive firms. *Journal of Risk and Financial Management, 2*, 1–37.

Dutta, S., Saadi, S., & Zhu, P. (2013). Does payment method matter in cross-border acquisitions? *International Review of Economics and Finance, 25*, 91–107.

Fauver, L., Houston, J., & Naranjo, A. (2003). Capital market development, international integration, legal systems and the value of corporate diversification: A cross-country analysis. *Journal of Finance and Quantitative Analysis, 38*(1), 135–157.

Francis, B. B., Hasan, I., & Sun, X. (2008). Financial market integration and the value of global diversification: Evidence for US acquirers in cross-border mergers and acquisitions. *Journal of Banking and Finance, 32*, 1522–1540.

Fukui, Y., & Ushijima, T. (2007). Corporate diversification, performance and restructuring in the largest Japanese manufacturers. *Journal of the Japanese and International Economics, 21*(3), 303–323.

Ghosh, A. (2001). Does operating performance really improve following corporate acquisitions? *Journal of Corporate Finance, 7*, 151–178.

Ghosh, A., & Ruland, W. (1998). Managerial ownership, the method of payment for acquisitions, and executive job retention. *Journal of Finance, 53*(2), 785–798.

Grigorieva, S., & Grinchenko, A. (2013). Impact of mergers and acquisitions in financial sector on bidder's returns in emerging capital markets. *Journal of Corporate Finance Research, 4*(28), 53–71. https://doi.org/10.17323/j.jcfr.2073-0438.7.4.2013.53-71.

Grigorieva, S., & Petrunina, T. (2015). The performance of mergers and acquisitions in emerging capital markets: New angle. *Journal of Management Control, 26*, 377–403.

Grigorieva, S., & Troitskiy, P. (2012). The impact of mergers and acquisitions on company performance in emerging capital markets. *Journal of Corporate Finance Research, 6*(3), 31–43. https://doi.org/10.17323/j.jcfr.2073-0438.6.3.2012.31-43.

Guest, P., Bild, M., & Runsten, N. (2010). The effects of takeovers on the fundamental value of acquirers. *Accounting and Business Research, 40*(4), 333–352.

Gugler, K., Mueller, D. C., Yurtoglu, B. B., & Zulehner, C. (2003). The effects of mergers: An international comparison. *International Journal of Industrial Organization, 21*, 625–653.

Haleblian, J., Devers, C. E., McNamara, G., Carpenter, M. A., & Davison, R. B. (2009). Taking stock of what we know about mergers and acquisitions: A review and research agenda. *Journal of Management, 35*(3), 469–502.

Hamza, T. (2009). Determinants of short-term value creation for the bidders: Evidence from France. *Journal of Management and Governance, 15*, 157–186.

Hansen, R. G. (1987). A theory for the choice of exchange medium in mergers and acquisitions. *The Journal of Business, 60*(1), 75–95.

Healy, P. M., Palepu, K. G., & Ruback, R. S. (1992). Does corporate performance improve after mergers? *Journal of Financial Economics, 31*, 135–175.

Hennart, J. F., & Reddy, S. (1997). The choice between mergers/acquisitions and joint ventures: The case of Japanese investors in the United States. *Strategic Management Journal, 18*, 1–12.

Hitt, M. A., King, D., Krishnan, H., Makri, M., Schijven, M., Shimizu, K., & Zhu, H. (2012). Creating value through mergers and acquisitions. In *The handbook of mergers and acquisitions*. Oxford: Oxford University Press.

Kan, K., & Ohno, T. (2012). Merger of major banks from the EVA standpoint. *Public Policy Review, 8*(5), 737–774.

Khanna, T., & Palepu, K. (1997, July–August). Why focused strategies may be wrong for emerging markets. *Harvard Business Review, 75*, 41–51.

Kohli, R., & Mann, B. J. S. (2012). Analyzing determinants of value creation in domestic and cross border acquisitions in India. *International Business Review, 21*, 998–1016.

Kohli, R., & Mann, B. J. S. (2013). Analyzing the likelihood and the impact of earnout offers on acquiring company wealth gains in India. *Emerging Markets Review, 16*, 203–222.

Kumar, N. (2009). Post-merger corporate performance: An Indian perspective. *Management Research News, 32*(2), 145–157.

Kumar, S., & Bansal, L. K. (2008). The impact of mergers and acquisitions on corporate performance in India. *Management Decision, 46*, 1531–1543.

La Porta, R., Lopez-de-Silanes, F., Shleifer, A., & Vishny, R. (2002). Investor protection and corporate valuation. *Journal of Finance, 57*, 1147–1170.

Lang, L., & Stulz, R. (1994). Tobin's q, Corporate diversification, and firm performance. *Journal of Political Economy, 102*, 1248–1280.

Lebedev, S., Peng, M. W., Xie, E., & Stevens, C. E. (2015). Mergers and acquisitions in and out of emerging economies. *Journal of World Business, 50*, 651–662.

Lee, K., Peng, M., & Lee, K. (2008). From diversification premium to diversification discount during institutional transitions. *Journal of World Business, 43*, 47–65.

Leepsa, N. M., & Mishra, C. S. (2013). Wealth creation through acquisitions. *Decision, 40*(3), 147–211.

Lins, K., & Servaes, H. (2002). Is corporate diversification beneficial in emerging markets? *Financial Management, 31*, 5–31.

Loughran, T., & Vijh, A. M. (1997). Do long-term shareholders benefit from corporate acquisitions? *Journal of Finance, 52*(5), 1765–1790.

Lu, Y., & Yao, J. (2006). Impact of state ownership and control mechanisms on the performance of group affiliated companies in China. *Asia Pacific Journal of Management, 23*, 485–503.

Lusyana, D., & Sherif, M. (2016). Do mergers create value for high-tech firms? The hounds of dotcom bubble. *Journal of High Technology Management Research, 27*, 196–213.

Mantravadi, P., & Reddy, A. V. (2008). Post-merger performance of acquiring firms from different industries in India. *International Research Journal of Finance and Economics, 22*, 192–204.

Martin, K. (1996). The method of payment in corporate acquisitions, investment opportunities, and management ownership. *Journal of Finance, 4*, 1227–1246.

Martynova, M., & Renneboog, L. (2011). The performance of the European market for corporate control: Evidence from the fifth takeover wave. *European Financial Management, 17*, 208–259.

Martynova, M., Oosting, S., & Renneboog, L. (2007). The long-term operating performance in European mergers and acquisitions. In G. N. Gregoriou & L. Renneboog (Eds.), *International mergers and acquisitions activity since 1990* (pp. 79–116). Cambridge, MA: Elsevier.

Mithas, S., Tafti, A., Bardhan, I., & Goh, J. M. (2012). Information technology and firm profitability: Mechanisms and empirical evidence. *MIS Quarterly, 36*(1), 205–224.

Moeller, S. B., & Schlingemann, F. P. (2005). Global diversification and bidder gains: A comparison between cross-border and domestic acquisitions. *Journal of Banking and Finance, 29*(3), 533–564.

Myers, S. C., & Majluf, N. S. (1984). Corporate financing and investment decisions when firms have information that investors do not have. *Journal of Financial Economics, 13*(2), 187–221.

Narayan, P. C., & Thenmozhi, M. (2014). Do cross-border acquisitions involving emerging market firms create value: Impact of deal characteristics. *Management Decision, 52*(8), 1451–1473.

Papadakis, V. M., & Thanos, I. C. (2010). Measuring the performance of acquisitions: An empirical investigation using multiple criteria. *British Journal of Management, 21*(4), 859–873.

Parrino, J. D., & Harris, R. S. (1999). Takeovers, management replacement, and post-acquisition operating performance: Some evidence from the 1980s. *Journal of Applied Corporate Finance, 11*, 88–97.

Porrini, P. (2004). Alliance experience and value creation in high-tech and low-tech acquisitions. *The Journal of High Technology Management Research, 15*, 267–292.

Powell, R. G., & Stark, A. W. (2005). Does operating performance increase post-takeover for UK takeovers? A comparison of performance measures and benchmarks. *Journal of Corporate Finance, 11*, 293–317.

Puranam, P., Singh, H., & Zollo, M. (2006). Organizing for innovation: Managing the coordination-autonomy dilemma in technology acquisitions. *Academy of Management Journal, 49*(2), 263–280.

Rao-Nicholson, R., Salaber, J., & Cao, T. H. (2016). Long-term performance of mergers and acquisitions of mergers and acquisitions in ASEAN countries. *Research in International Business and Finance, 36*, 373–387.

Rodionov, I., & Mikhalchuk, V. (2015). Review of major theoretical and empirical studies on M&A synergy. *Journal of Corporate Finance Research, 9*(3), 98–110.

Rossi, M., Tarba, S. Y., & Raviv, A. (2011). Mergers and acquisitions in the hightech industry: A literature review. *International Journal of Organizational Analysis, 21*(1), 66–82.

Sears, J. B., & Hoetker, G. (2014). Technological overlap, technological capabilities, and resource recombination in technological acquisitions. *Strategic Management Journal, 35*, 48–67.

Sharma, D. S., & Ho, J. (2002). The impact of acquisitions on operating performance: Some Australian evidence. *Journal of Business Finance & Accounting, 29*, 155–200.

Shimizu, K., Hitt, M. A., Vaidyanath, D., & Pisano, V. (2004). Theoretical foundations of cross-border mergers and acquisitions: A review of current research and recommendations for the future. *Journal of International Management, 10*, 307–353.

Singh, P., Suri, P., & Sah, R. (2012). Economic value added in Indian cross border mergers. *International Journal of Business Research, 12*(2), 160–164.

Sirower, M. L., & O'Byrne, S. F. (1998). The measurement of post-acquisition performance: Toward a value-based benchmarking methodology. *Journal of Applied Corporate Finance, 11*(2), 107–121.

Sudarsanam, S. (2003). *Creating value from mergers and acquisitions: The challenges, an international and integrated perspective*. Harlow: FT Prentice Hall.

Switzer, J. A. (1996). Evidence on real gains in corporate acquisitions. *Journal of Economics and Business, 48*, 443–460.

Thanos, I. C., & Papadakis, V. M. (2012). Unbundling acquisition performance: How do they perform and how can this be measured? In *The handbook of mergers and acquisitions*. Oxford: Oxford University Press.

Wan, W. P., & Yiu, D. W. (2009). From crisis to opportunity: Environmental jolt, corporate acquisitions, and firm performance. *Strategic Management Journal, 30*, 791–801.

Yook, K. C. (2004). The measurement of post-acquisition performance using EVA. *Quarterly Journal of Business and Economics, 42*(3,4), 67–83.

Yoon, H. D., & Lee, J. J. (2016). Technology-acquiring cross-border M&As by emerging market firms: Role of bilateral trade openness. *Technology Analysis & Strategic Management, 28*(3), 251–265.

Zaremba, A., & Plotnicki, M. (2016). Mergers and acquisitions: Evidence on post-announcement performance from CEE stock markets. *Journal of Business Economics and Management, 17*(2), 251–266.

Zollo, M., & Meier, D. (2008). What is M&A performance? *Academy of Management Perspective, 22*, 55–77.

What Drives the Control Premium? Evidence from BRIC Countries

Irina Ivashkovskaya and Elena Chvyrova

Abstract The literature on M&As provides ample evidence for the variability of premiums paid in M&A deals over time and in different types of deals. Most work has been done on the data from developed markets. Using a sample of M&A deals in the largest emerging markets (BRIC) for 2000–2015, we examine three types of factors (acquirer characteristics, target characteristics, deal characteristics). To measure the premium, the event study method is used; therefore the data on cumulative average abnormal returns (CAAR) is adjusted to the market movements in each respective country. We focus on three levels of acquired stakes ($>25\%$, $>50\%$, and 100%). The study contributes to a deeper understanding of the differences in the size of premiums among the countries and the interaction of the main determinants which influence the magnitude of the premium. The regression results document positive drivers of the size of the premium including the percentage of the stake and industry relatedness. Besides these stylized determinants, the premium increases if the deal is made in a crisis year and by a domestic bidder. The negative determinants include the target size, its financial leverage, and the pre-bid stake of the acquirer (toehold).

Keywords Mergers and acquisitions · Control premium · Event studies · Emerging capital markets

1 Introduction

The M&A literature provides ample evidence on the variability of premiums paid in M&A deals over time and in different types of deals. Research suggests several explanations for the magnitude of these premiums. First, the researchers agree that

I. Ivashkovskaya
Higher School of Economics, National Research University, Moscow, Russia
e-mail: iivashkovskaja@hse.ru

E. Chvyrova (✉)
Corporate Finance Center, Higher School of Economics, Moscow, Russia

© Springer Nature Switzerland AG 2020   137
I. Ivashkovskaya et al. (eds.), *Strategic Deals in Emerging Capital Markets*,
Advanced Studies in Emerging Markets Finance,
https://doi.org/10.1007/978-3-030-23850-6_6

the overall bidder premium is synergy-driven and, therefore, limited to the incremental value of benefits which can be derived from a controlling stake (Nenova 2003). Second, the premium can also be information-driven and reflect a reassessment of the target inspired by the recognition that the target was undervalued prior the deal (Sorwar and Sudarsanam 2010). Third, it can also be based on the potential private benefits for overconfident managers when they are very much motivated by bonuses and an opportunity to report the deal into their curriculum vitae (Harford and Li 2007; Loderer and Martin 1990). Therefore, the difference in M&A premiums may be due to different motivations driving the deals.

Most research has been done on samples from developed markets, and the magnitude of the premiums paid in emerging market deals is still not fully understood. What are the determinants that drive the size of the premium in these specific markets? Are they similar to the evidence from developed markets? To contribute to the literature, we study the deals for the sample of the firms from BRIC countries.

The chapter is organized as follows: Section 2 reviews the literature on the research methods and determinants of the premium. Section 3 discusses the hypotheses. The research model and the sample description are presented in Sects. 4 and 5, respectively. Section 6 presents the discussion and Sect. 7 conclusion.

2 Premiums in M&A Deals: Results in Empirical Studies in Developed and Emerging Markets

2.1 The Methods to Study the Size of Premiums

The empirical M&A literature suggests several methods for identifying premium values: deal approaches, dual-class stock, and block transactions.

2.1.1 Deal Approaches

The standard approach is based on the relationship between the premiums and the pre-announcement stock market price of the target, and it is equal to the ratio of the acquirer offer price per share over target share price as shown below:

$$CP = \frac{P_0 - P_m}{P_m},\tag{1}$$

where P_0 is the offer price per share paid by the acquirer and P_m is the target's market price per share before the deal.

The deal approach is used by Mergerstat, and the normal price of a company's shares is based on stock trade volumes. In empirical chapters, there are various definitions of the target's normal price as shown in Table 1. Nathan and O'Keefe (1989) and Betton and Eckbo (2000) applied the target's share price 60 days before

Table 1 Empirical studies of the size of premium

Authors	Countries	Years	Observations	Size of premium
Dual-class stock				
Nenova (2003)	18 countries	1997	618	USA, 2%; Korea, 47.72%
Ødegaard (2007)	Netherlands	1988–2003	206	7%
Caprio and Croci (2008)	Italy	1974–2003	1150	56.51%
Hong (2013)	20 countries	2002–2007	263	11.9–19.9%
Block transactions				
Barclay and Holderness (1989)	USA	1978–1982	63	20.40%
Maux and Francoeur (2014)	European countries	1998–2006	515	27.38%
M&A method				
Hanouna et al. (2001)	Countries G7	1986–2000	6119—USA 3447—others	20–30% (standard)
Wickramanayake and Wood (2009)	Australia, Canada	1997–2007	92, Australia; 103, Canada	Australia, 71.8%; Canada, 54.2% (standard)
Thraya and Hagendorff (2010)	European countries	1994–2001	231	44.39% (standard)
Raad (2012)	USA	1990–2005	190	24.39–44.9% (standard)
Alexandridis et al. (2013)	USA	1990–2007	3691	(1) 43.76%, 42.23% (standard) (2) 35.38%, 20.32% (event studies)
La Bruslerie (2013)	European countries	2000–2010	528	37.59% (event studies)
Simonyan (2014)	USA	1985–2005	2116	35.54% (standard)

the announcement date, while Moeller (2005) and Dong et al. (2006) use the share price 6 and 5 days before the announcement date (respectively). In his study of the US market for M&A 1990–2005, Raad (2012) used several definitions of the normal share market price of the target firm, 30, 15, and 10 days and 1 day before announcement date, and got a range of minimum and maximum premiums from 24.4% to 44.9%. On the sample of the deals in the G7, the normal price per share was defined 28 days prior the deal, and the premiums ranged from 20% to 30% depending on the country (Hanouna et al. 2001). Table 2 summarizes the empirical results based on different types of methods on samples from emerging markets.

The standard deal approach is not adjusted to overall market movements. An alternative definition is based on the cumulative average abnormal returns (CAAR) on the target stock. This method allows an adjustment of the data on the premiums to

Table 2 Empirical studies of the size of premium in emerging markets

Author	Countries	Years	Observations	Size
Dual-class stock				
Saito (2003)	Brazil	1994–2002	3591	−1.30%
Nenova (2003)	18 countries	1997	618	Brazil, 23%, Mexico, 36.42%
da Silva and Subrahmanyam (2007)	Brazil	1994–2004	141	−8.7 to 35.13%
Muravyev et al. (2014)	Russia	1997–2006	672	125.10%
Block transactions				
Evstafjeva and Fedotova (2008)	Russia	2005–2008	130	29%
Byrka-Kita et al. (1989)	Poland	1997–2009	139	−0.48%
Saito and Silveira (2010)	Brazil	1995–2006	87	+7.68%
da Silva and Subrahmanyam (2007)	Brazil	1994–2004	141	+65%
M&A method				
Dragota et al. (2007)	Romania	2002–2004	44	(1) 82.44% (standard) (2) 44.62% (event studies)
Sonenshine and Reynolds (2014)	Worldwide	2000–2010	553	34% (standard)
Dragota et al. (2013)	Romania	2000–2011	173	3–160% (standard)

changes in market returns, and it does not require the acquirer offer price for premium calculations. Thus, the method avoids the missing reliable data on the deal price. Studies based on alternative techniques also differ by the length of the period to calculate the CAAR and the adjustments to the market. Table 1 summarizes the major papers based on this technique. Simonyan (2014) uses 42 trading days before and 126 trading days after the announcement date for the sample of 2216 takeovers of public firms in the USA 1985–2005. He gets the average premium of 35.5% with the highest values of 53.5% in 2001 and lower values of 12.2% in 2004.

2.1.2 Dual-Class Stock Method

The dual-class stock method can be applied to firms issuing voting and non-voting stock. Two assets of the same risk that generate identical free cash flows will have equal values. The difference in the market prices for voting and non-voting stock of the same firm is a measure of the value of control rights assigned to voting shareholders.

The standard method measures the ratio of the difference between the price per voting stock and non-voting stock as shown below:

$$VP = \frac{P_{Csh} - P_{Psh}}{P_{Psh}}, \tag{2}$$

where P_{Csh} is the price of voting stock and P_{Psh} is the price of non-voting stock (or restricted stock).

With this standard technique, the average premium for Italian companies 1977–2003 was as high as 56.5% (Caprio and Croci 2008). Depending on the year of observation, some authors showed both negative and positive values for the premiums for European companies (Neumann 2003; Ødegaard 2007). The negative values were explained by liquidity and corporate governance risks. When applying dual-class standard techniques, chapters on emerging markets also demonstrate high result variability. For the Russian market 1998–2009, the average premium was 113% (Muravyev et al. 2014), and for Brazilian market 1995–2006, it varied from −2.8% to +17.9% (Saito and Silveira 2010). Given the existence of negative values, the authors commented on the role of the low liquidity of voting stock in some cases and the size of dividends paid to different classes of stock.

The dual-class method assumes that the difference in stock market prices is due to the voting power which approximates control rights, but it cannot eliminate additional factors which impact stock prices with different voting rights. Thus, the standard method should be adjusted (Zingales 1995):

$$VP = \frac{P_{csh} - P_{psh}}{P_{psh} - rP_{csh}} \tag{3}$$

where r is the ratio of the number of votes of the stock class with low voting power to the number of votes of the stock class with higher voting power.

Following this logic, Nenova (2003) applied the method to stock with voting power higher than 50%.

$$\frac{P_{Csh} - P_{Psh}}{(1 - k)} \times \frac{0.5x(N_{csh} - N_{psh} * k)}{N_{csh} * P_{Csh} + N_{psh} * P_{Psh}} \tag{4}$$

where k is the ratio of votes of shares with low voting power to the votes of shares with high voting power and N is the number of shares of the corresponding type.

2.1.3 Block Transactions

The block transaction method also relies on the private benefits of control based on the opportunities to directly receive benefits through higher cash flows from the stakes (dividends or the right to purchase the company's new issues at a special price) and indirect benefits (e.g., to push forward some investment project and contracts with related parties). The empirical results of this technique vary substantially due to the differences in the definitions of blocks and the date determining the normal market price per share as shown in Table 1 which summarizes the major chapters on the samples of developed markets.

Dyck and Zingales (2004) use a threshold of 10% of votes at the shareholder meeting and plus 2 days to the announcement date to determine the normal market price. To the standard calculations, they added adjustments for the market power of the target firm and for overall market trends. Based on a sample of developed and emerging markets, they demonstrate an average premium of 14%, and for the weighted average (by equity value), the size of the premium declines to 10%. The highest premiums are paid for the deals in emerging markets, and the chapter shows the average premium for the subsample of emerging markets exceeding 25% of the value of equity with the maximum of 65% in Brazil, while for the subsample of developed countries, it is much lower (less than 3%).

2.2 The Determinants for Premiums

2.2.1 Acquirer Characteristics

The size of the stake purchased may influence the level of the control premium. A greater fractional ownership gives controlling shareholders more power and influence over the current and future performance. The contribution to the firm's management can increase company value and, consequently, shareholder wealth. The stake size is indicated as the main determinant of the control premium in Rodionov and Perevalova (2012). Research conducted on the Romanian market also confirms the positive relationship between the stake size and the control premium (Dragota et al. 2013). However, some studies reveal that the possibility for an investor to diversify his/her portfolio decreases with the purchase of a large stake, which increases the costs of control (Barclay and Holderness 1989). This fact leads to a negative relationship between the premium and stake size, starting from a certain investment amount.

An acquirer with a pre-bid ownership stake in the target company (toehold) will have not only voting rights but also access to inside information about its strategy and organization, leading to a lower premium (Albuquerque and Schroth 2010). A bigger toehold may drive up the pre-announcement target share price because it already captures the benefits from the deal initiated by the insider bidder and therefore it may reduce the gap between the final price and the price before the announcement (Bris 2002). Betton et al. (2009) point out that for the mandatory disclosure of purchases of 5% or more shares, a toehold becomes too costly. Rational bidders avoid toeholds as a response to large costs also because of the entrenched management of the target to start defeating bidders. This successful management resistance may cause the target price to drop. The toehold-induced bidder cost creates some toehold threshold below which the optimal toehold must be zero. This argument can explain the bimodal distribution of actual toeholds centered on zero or large toeholds.

The empirical evidence on the assumed negative relationship between the size of toehold and the magnitude of the control premium is provided in Betton and Eckbo (2000). Later Simonyan (2014) documented a negative correlation between the pre-bid ownership and the size of the control premium for the US market. Similar results were obtained for the Romanian market (Dragota et al. 2013).

2.2.2 The Target Characteristics

The size of the target is one of the most obvious determinants influencing the size of the premium. Most chapters assume a negative relationship between these variables, since it is considered that the larger the company, the better its management and the greater its market power and it is expected to have higher bargaining power. The strengths of larger targets reduce the gains for the acquirer. In the case of small companies where the ownership will be more concentrated in hands of fewer shareholders, it is likely to be more difficult to convince them to sell their shares. Therefore, buyers will pay a higher premium to obtain control.

Empirical studies document a negative impact of target size on the control premium for developed countries. The greater the total equity capitalization of the target before the initial offer, the lower the initial and final offer premiums (Betton et al. 2008a, b; Alexandridis et al. 2013). Simonyan (2014) confirmed this for the US market, Nenova (2003) for a sample of 18 countries, and Ødegaard (2007) for the Norwegian market. Moeller et al. (2004) show higher premiums for smaller targets. The negative size premium relationship is also confirmed by research for some emerging markets (Trojanowski 2008; Dragota et al. 2013; Fan et al. 2012).

Many studies investigated the role of the financial leverage of the target in setting the premium. A high level of debt increases the probability of financial distress and the transfer of control to the debt holders; therefore, the premium decreases. In developed markets, a negative relationship between debt and the control premium has been documented (Dyck and Zingales 2004). Thraya and Hagendorff (2010) show a significant negative correlation between the leverage in the year prior to the deal and the premium in European markets. Empirical studies for emerging markets document an ambiguous effect of financial leverage. Saito (2003) found a nonlinear relationship between leverage and premiums for the Brazilian market: for companies with a low debt level, its increase has a positive effect on the size of the control premium, while for companies with an already high level of debt dependence, it was negative.

Another important driver is the performance of the target before the deal. When the target has high profitability, it is easier to derive the benefits from a controlling stake, and it could be less costly to capture the synergies, and a higher premium can be applied. Chapters on the determinants of the premium often include the profitability of the target company in the variables. da Silva and Subrahmanyam (2007) document a significant positive correlation in the Brazilian market. On the other hand, Dyck and Zingales (2004) using a sample of companies from 39 countries including emerging markets found a negative relationship. Liquidity ratios of the target company are also a determinant of the size for the premium: less liquid companies are less attractive for investors, so the premium for them is lower (Dragota et al. 2013).

Various characteristics of the target's corporate governance are documented to influence the control premium: the degree of concentration of ownership before the transaction and the types of owners (managers, outsiders, government) (Rodionov and Perevalova 2012). The higher the ownership concentration, the more difficult to buy a controlling stake. Dragota et al. (2013) and Muravyev et al. (2014) document a significant positive effect of ownership concentration on the control premium.

In addition to these standard determinants, the target's intellectual capital (IC) may affect the size of the control premium. IC represents a collection of unique assets valuable for gaining competitive advantages: human capital, the set of knowledge, skills, and unique human resources; relational capital, the structure of the relationship with external agents (suppliers, contractors, customers, investors, agents, etc.); and structural capital, the intellectual property, research and development, and any innovation which can be separated from human resources. There are few empirical studies on the impact of IC on the size of the control premium. Given the potential importance of different components of IC to the acquirer, research has focused on the size of the IC of the target company and on the ability to integrate IC after the deal.

Bena and Li (2014) on the sample of US transactions within 1984–2006 analyzed the intellectual capital by R&D expenditure and the availability of patents in the company as a proxy. The study confirmed the hypothesis that the increase in performance after the deal is more likely to occur in companies with similar technologies, since the likelihood of integration increases. Accordingly, the control premium in such transactions is higher, as shown in Marcelo (2008) and Alves (2008).

2.2.3 Deal Type

A large number of studies focus on the analysis of the type of transaction and its impact on the value of the control premium. Wickramanayake and Wood (2009) and Sonenshine and Reynolds (2014) argue that the control premium for hostile M&A deals will be higher. According to Dyck and Zingales (2004), deals with foreign buyers were characterized by a higher control premium. A similar study on the Romanian market found the reverse relationship (Dragota et al. 2013).

Transactions can also vary depending on whether the target and acquirer operate in the same industry or not. Thraya and Hagendorff (2010) found a significant positive relationship if the companies operate in the same industry for the European market. This is due to the greater synergies and a higher probability of realizing them; hence the premium for control of such transactions is higher.

2.2.4 Country/Residence

Many authors believe that country differences contribute to the differences in the value of the control premium. More developed markets tend to have a more developed legal environment and stronger protection of shareholder interests. Hence, the control premium will be lower for the target in more developed markets. A number of researchers (Nenova 2003; Dyck and Zingales 2004; Jurfest et al. 2015) outline the importance of the country and legislation factor.

3 The Hypotheses

In accordance with the results of empirical studies, the following hypotheses are introduced:

H1: *The estimated control premium will be positive for firms from all countries.*

As control premium is calculated as the CAAR, the hypothesis assumes a positive value. This hypothesis is also associated with previous studies (da Silva and Subrahmanyam 2007).

H2: *The higher the stake acquired, the higher the control premium.*

It is expected that a larger acquired stake gives a greater level of control. Therefore, the cost increases due to the gains from the acquisition of additional rights (Alexandridis et al. 2013; Dragota et al. 2013). The hypothesis is also backed by the results for the annual payments from the major deal's source Mergerstat.

H3: *The smaller the size of the company, the higher the control premium.*

Increasing the size of the target will reduce the number of potential buyers of the stake and will reduce the size of the control premium they are willing to offer. The lack of competition among buyers will reduce the amount of the premium. The hypothesis is based on studies (Trojanowski 2008; Fan et al. 2012; Dragota et al. 2013).

H4: *The control premium will be lower, if the acquirer already has an initial stake in the target company.*

The acquirer will be better acquainted with the industry or the specific business or will have some insider information if it already has shares in the target company. These benefits allow to estimate the control premium more accurately. Similar findings were shown in the studies for other samples (Dragota et al. 2013; Simonyan 2014; Trojanowski 2008).

H5: *The lower the target company's level of debt, the higher the control premium.*

It is assumed that the probability of moving control to the creditors will increase if the level of debt increases. Bankruptcy risk is higher in companies with high debt levels. Therefore, the value of the control premium is lower. This hypothesis is backed by previous research findings (Saito 2003; Thraya and Hagendorff 2010).

H6: *The control premium is higher, if the transaction is domestic.*

This hypothesis is based on the fact that inside investors are aware of the state of the market as a whole, the industry, and the company's position better than outsiders. Given lower information efficiency and transparency of the firms in emerging markets, the relationship must be positive. Similar findings are demonstrated in empirical research on other samples (Dragota et al. 2013).

H7: *The control premium is higher, if the acquirer and the target company operate in the same industry.*

Companies operating in the same industry know the market and the specifics of the industry better. Hence, the likelihood of synergies from the transaction will be higher which increases the control premium (Thraya and Hagendorff 2010).

H8: *The control premium is higher, if the deal is announced in a crisis.*

The acquirer determines the fair value of the target company based on the future cash flow of the business, but the market is undervalued during a crisis. Usually, the transaction price is significantly higher than the market value during a crisis. Therefore, the control premium will be higher (Simonyan 2014).

4 The Model and the Variables

Given the overview of the methods to determine the size of premium, the dual-class method is difficult to apply. First, the method reflects the difference between the two classes of shares and voting rights which cannot be considered as a perfect proxy for the measurement of control. Second, with this criterion of two types of shares in emerging markets, the sample may become very small, and the results of the study will be unrepresentative. The method of block transaction is also inappropriate for emerging markets, since this method investigates mainly the private benefits of control, so the results would also be unrepresentative. For these reasons, we use the deal method based on event studies to find out the size of the control premium. As the markets in these countries are very volatile, the adjustment for the general market movement is required before the calculation of the control premium. Jordan and Hoppe (2008) show that 96% of the difference between the control premiums, calculated using the Mergerstat methodology and event study methodology, was explained by the adjustment for market movement. Moreover, the event study method is the most widely used among the empirical studies on M&A performance (Eckbo 2009). We calculate CAAR of a target company to measure the control premium. Obviously, this indicator also includes synergies from the transaction and other adjustments. However, any method described above does not suggest a perfect proxy for the control premium especially for emerging markets. CAAR indicators do not contain general market movements and show only the effect of the transaction; therefore, they can be considered as the maximum possible control premium.

At step 1, the date of the event, the evaluation period, and the event window are determined. Trading days are counted from the date of announcement. The window should be wide because it should accommodate the full reaction of the stock market. On the other hand, the event window should be narrow because of potential effect of other significant corporate events on stock price movement. Some researchers state that only wide windows allow us to see the price of stock, without the effect of transaction (Eckbo 2009). For this work, we selected the window length following the empirical study by Schwert (1996) with the average cumulative excess return on the event window $(-124; 250)$ using the estimated range $(-250; -125)$ based only on trading days. According to the schedule of the accumulated excess returns for the entire sample, the day of the market reaction (t_1) is determined (a significant surge in the abnormal return). The average life of the transaction in the sample (the number of days between the announcement and the closing of the transaction) is used for detecting the day of closing the window (t_2). As a result, the event window lies between (t_1) and (t_2); the estimated period is $(-250, t_1 - 1)$. At step 2, the daily logarithmic stock returns of target companies are calculated:

$$R_t = \ln \left(\frac{P_t}{P_{t-1}} \right), \tag{5}$$

where P_t is the stock price of a target in time period t.

The expected (normal) return is derived with the market model at step 3:

$$R_{it} = \alpha_i + \beta_i R_{Mt} + \varepsilon_{it}, \tag{6}$$

R_{it} is the actual stock return of target company i in time period t.
R_{Mt} is market index return in time period t.

Estimated parameters $\widehat{\alpha}$ and $\widehat{\beta}$ are used for the expected stock return through the event window. Given the calculations of the abnormal returns (AR) for each day of the event window, the average excess returns for all transactions are computed as follows:

$$\overline{AR_t} = \frac{\sum_{i=1}^{N} AR_{it}}{N}, \tag{7}$$

where N is the number of deals in the sample.

Finally, the CAAR in the sample is found:

$$CAAR = \sum_{t=t_1}^{t_2} \overline{AR_t}, \tag{8}$$

t_1, t_2 are the frontiers of the event window.

The indicators of CAAR were calculated for shorter windows for a comparison of results. The significance of CAAR (when it is normally distributed) is tested by parametric technique (standard test statistic):

$$\frac{CAAR\,(t_1, t_2)}{\sqrt{L}\sigma}, \tag{9}$$

$\sigma = \sigma\left(\overline{AR_t}\right)$ is the standard deviation of the average abnormal return on estimated period.

$L = t_2 - t_1 + 1$ is the length of the event window.

t_1, t_2 are the frontiers of the event window.

Based on the literature review of the determinants of the control premium, the following variables are included in the model:

- The size of target company *(size)*—the natural logarithm of total assets of a target a year before the deal
- The purchased stake in percentage *(PSP)*
- Financial leverage of the target *(leverage)*—debt-to-equity ratio a year before the deal announcement
- Pre-bid shares owned by acquirer (toehold) *(D_IS)*—dummy variable, 1 when the acquirer owns target shares before the deal announcement, 0 otherwise
- Crisis environment *(D_Crisis)*—dummy variable, 1 when the deal was announced during an economic crisis,[1] 0 otherwise
- Type of the deal *(D_Country)*—dummy variable, 1 for a domestic acquirer and the target, 0 otherwise
- Industry *(D_Industry)*—dummy variable, 1 when the acquirer and the target operate in the same industry, 0 otherwise

The descriptive statistics of the variables is included in the model which is presented in Table 4.

A multiple regression model was used in order to identify the determinants of the size of the premium for control:

$$CAAR_i = \alpha + \beta_1 Size_i + \beta_2 PSP_i + \beta_3 Leverage_i + \beta_4 D\_IS_i + \beta_5 D\_Crisis_i$$
$$+ \beta_6 D\_Country_i + \beta_7 D\_Industry_i + \varepsilon_i. \tag{10}$$

---

[1]Crisis time considered: 01.07.2008–30.06.2009

Both broad and narrow windows are used for robustness checks. The quality of regression models was checked on the presence of multicollinearity (using the VIF calculation) and heteroskedasticity (White test).

5   The Sample

The sample was constructed using the database Bureau Van Dijk Zephyr; stock quotes, market indices, and financial performance indicators were obtained from the database S&P Capital IQ and Thomson Reuters. All financial figures are denominated in US dollars. The following criteria were used for the sample construction:

1. Deal announcement is within the period January 01, 2000–December 31, 2015.
2. Deal type: merger, acquisition, and minority stake.
3. Deal status: announced/completed/pending.
4. Type of a target company: public.
5. The residence of a target company: BRIC countries.
6. Acquired stake:

   (a) Acquirer has owned less than 50% of the target before the deal and more than 50% after the deal.
   (b) Acquirer has owned less than 25% of the target before the deal and more than 25% after the deal.
   (c) Minimal stake acquired in the deal is 10%.

The following market indices were chosen to estimate the market returns: Russian MICEX, Brazilian BOVESPA, Indian Sensex, and Chinese Shanghai and Shenzhen indices. The target company must be publicly traded due to the choice of the event study method.

For the purpose of the uniformity of the sample, we apply a benchmark of 25% ownership after the deal to identify a block of shares and 50% +1 for the acquisition of control. The owner of such a package of shares has the right to block significant decisions, namely, the issue of additional shares, the making of large transactions, the restructuring and liquidation of the company, etc. Therefore, three subsamples of transactions have been considered separately: higher than 50%, higher than 25%, and 100% of the shares. Transactions for which the share price of the target company in the required period was not available or shares were illiquid were excluded from consideration. Table 3 shows the sampling steps (the original sample size corresponds to the data from Bureau Van Dijk Zephyr) and Table 4 presents descriptive statistics.

After the application of the criteria, the sample consists of 418 deals, and the distribution of deals according to the percentage of the acquired shares is presented in Fig. 1.

Table 3 The steps of sample construction

Criterion	Russia	China	India	Brazil
Initial sample	10,627	14,147	7840	758
(1) No information about the value of the stake (no information about the ownership before or after the deal)	973	9365	3673	438
(2) No consolidation up to 25%+1 share or 50%+1 share	6911	1513	1016	163
(3) The acquired stake is less than 10%	810	2750	1270	52
(4) Illiquidity of target company stocks	1840	316	1787	77
Final sample	93	203	94	28

Table 4 Descriptive statistics of the sample

Variable	Mean	Median	Minimum	Maximum	St dev
Size	2.12	11.17	5.67	5.98	1.72
PSP (acquired stake)	6%	100%	30%	39%	21%
Leverage	0%	228%	15%	48%	94%
D_IS (initial stake)	0	1	0	0.38	0.49
D_Crisis	0	1	0	0.08	0.28
D_Country	0	1	1	0.74	0.44
D_Industry	0	1	0	0.31	0.46

Fig. 1 The number of transactions among subsamples

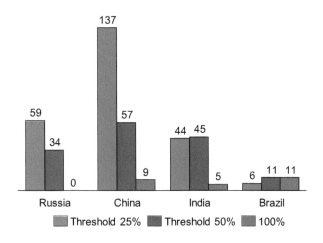

Target companies from the financial sector were excluded from the analysis. After the exclusion of this sector and deals with a lack of information, the final sample consisted of 348 deals: Russia, 89; China, 184; India, 47; and Brazil, 28.

6 Results and Discussion

6.1 M&A Premium Estimation Results

6.1.1 Results for the Whole Sample

The length of the period to study adjustments of the market is rather an important element of this method. To capture market reaction, it should not be too narrow and therefore should account for the level of information efficiency in the given markets. It also should not be too wide to escape the influence of other corporate events. Following the two-step approach from the literature to identify the period (Schwert 1996), at first the date of the market reaction has been determined. The second step aims to identify the length of the period to close the deal. To begin, we estimated CAAR on the wide window to find out the day when market starts to react to the transaction announcement (the evaluation period (250; 125); event window (−124; 250)). Figure 2 shows the plot of cumulative average abnormal returns and permits to demonstrate that the stock market starts to react at −40 trading day before the official announcement of the transaction. This indicates that insider information was reflected in the stock prices long before the official announcement.

Following the method (Schwert 1996), the second step is to identify the average length of the periods to close the deals, and it is 72 days for all countries as shown in Fig. 2. After selecting the event window, the predictive regression of the market model on the estimated period (−250; −40) has been restated. As a further step, CAAR was estimated on the chosen event window. The average control premium for the whole sample of all BRIC countries is 10.3%. To test the robustness of the results, narrow windows were applied as shown in Fig. 3. Table 5 presents the results for these narrow windows. Despite the varying length of the event window, the results remain significant at 1% and 5% significance levels.

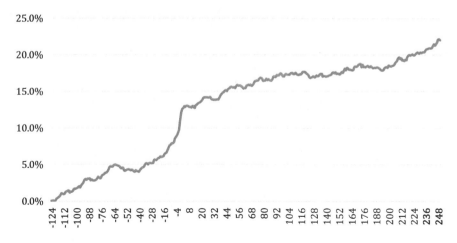

Fig. 2 CAAR dynamic for all countries on the wide event window (−124; +250)

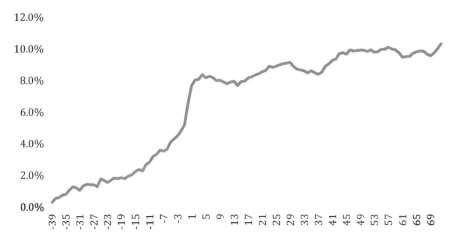

Fig. 3 CAAR dynamic for all countries for the event window (−39; +72)

6.1.2   Results for the Country Subsamples

Next, stock market reactions were examined separately for each country. For each national sample, we got a positive market reaction to the deal long before the official announcement for all countries. This fact strongly indicates the presence of insider information. The results are presented in Table 6. In general for the event window (−39; 72), we observe the highest CAAR of 12.9% in the Chinese M&A market (the result is significant at 1% level).

6.1.3   Results for Different Threshold Levels of the Acquired Stake

As mentioned, CAAR can be considered as a proxy for the control premium, but the reaction of the stock market includes not only the control premium but also, for example, synergies that can arise after the deal. However, the study of different subsamples based on the various thresholds proves the premium for control: the purchase of a blocking stake (25%), operational control (50%), and full control (100%). All results on the longer window are significant at 1% level. As shown in Fig. 4, the higher the threshold, the higher the CAAR.

Table 7 summarizes CAAR at various thresholds within different windows. At the 100% threshold, CAAR is higher than the average for the entire sample by 7% points. CAAR for the transactions for which the stake exceeds 50% are also higher than the average for the entire sample.

We can conclude that the higher the level of ownership after the transaction, the higher the size of the control premium. A similar relationship holds for the shorter window of observation.

Table 5 Event windows range (all transactions, BRIC countries)

Event window	(−39; +72)	(−39; +39)	(−20; +20)	(−10; +10)	(−5; +5)	(−3; +3)	(−1; +1)
CAAR	**10.3****	8.9%**	6.6%**	5.1%**	4.5%***	3.8%***	2.9%**

***, **, *Significance level of 1%, 5%, and 10%, respectively

Table 6 Event windows range (results by countries)

	Russia	China	India	Brazil
The number of transactions	93	203	94	28
CAR(−39; +72)	5.0%	12.9%***	10.2%***	10.3%*
CAR(−39; +39)	4.4%	10.2%***	10.3%***	10.3%**
CAR(−20; +20)	5.5%**	7.2%***	8.1%***	1.2%
CAR(−10; +10)	3.7%*	5.5%***	6.4%***	1.5%
CAR(−5; +5)	4.1%***	4.7%***	5.8%***	1.0%
CAR(−3; +3)	4.3%***	3.6%***	4.5%***	0.9%
CAR(−1; +1)	2.9%**	2.2%***	4.2%***	2.8%***

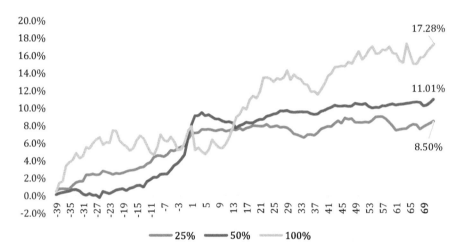

Fig. 4 CAAR dynamic for threshold levels of ownership after the transaction for the event window (−39; +72)

Table 7 Event windows range. Results for subsamples

	All transactions	Threshold 25%	Threshold 50%	Threshold 100%
The number of deals	418	177	216	25
CAR(−39; +72)	10.3%**	8.5%***	11.0%***	17.3%***
CAR(−39; +39)	8.9%**	7.6%***	9.6%***	12.1%**
CAR(−20; +20)	6.6%**	5.4%***	7.9%***	3.7%
CAR(−10; +10)	5.1%**	3.7%***	6.7%***	0.5%
CAR(−5; +5)	4.5%***	2.8%***	6.6%***	−1.4%
CAR(−3; +3)	3.8%***	2.1%**	5.7%***	−0.7%
CAR(−1; +1)	2.8%**	1.5%**	3.9%***	2.6%*

***At 1%; **at 5%; *at 10%

Table 8 Determinants of the size of control premium (all BRIC countries and by country)

Variables	BRIC countries	Russia	China	India	Brazil
Window (−39; +39)					
Size					
PSP					
Leverage	−0.039***		−0.028⁺	−0.236**	
D_IS		−0.159*			
D_Crisis	0.324***	0.886***			0.695***
D_Country					
D_Industry	0.221***		0.262***	0.213	
Window (−10; +10)					
Size		−0.017*			
PSP				0.231**	
Leverage	−0.02**		−0.016⁺	−0.102*	−0.090⁺
D_IS					
D_Crisis	0.156***	0.362***			0.444***
D_Country					
D_Industry	0.079***		0.115***		
Window (−1; +1)					
Size		−0.007⁺			
PSP	0.0413*	0.186***			
Leverage					
D_IS			−0.02*	−0.043*	
D_Crisis	0.032*				0.172***
D_Country	−0.024**			0.054**	
D_Industry	0.025**		0.02**		

***Significant at 1%; ** at 5%; * at 10%; + at 15%

6.2 The Determinants of the Size of Premium

6.2.1 Identifying the Factors Which Influence the Size of the Control Premium (Whole Sample)

To identify the determinants affecting the size of the control premium, we ran an OLS regression for the whole sample and for each country separately to capture the characteristics of the market. To check the robustness of the results, we employed three event windows: to capture the impact of the determinants, we used a wide window (−39; 39), a medium window (−10; 10), and a narrow window (−1; 1). At the first stage, the OLS regressions were built taking into account all the factors described above, and then insignificant variables were excluded. This procedure was applied to all windows. Table 8 presents at first the results for the *whole* sample.

Our empirical tests provide evidence that the results differ for the longer windows as compared to the shortest window. There is indeed positive impact of the announcement of the deal in a year of crisis and the industry relatedness on the size of control premium for the wide $(-39; +39)$ and smaller window $(-10; +10)$. But for the same windows, financial leverage negatively affects the size of the premium. The same country of residence of the target and the acquirer and the acquired stake size become significant for the shortest window. However, the financial leverage becomes insignificant. The changes in the significance of variables over time can be explained by the increase in the detailed information flow. The closer the date of the announcement, the higher the opportunities to capture a detailed picture of the target and to evaluate the potential influence of the package to be purchased and the value of the acquired control.

Given the results of the analysis, our findings provide support for hypothesis 1 on the existence of positive premium in M&A deals of the sample of firms in BRIC group. Our empirical tests show several positive drivers for the overall sample. First, we show that when the target and acquirer operate in the same industry, the premium increases. And these results hold for all event windows. The conclusion could be based on the argument that the likelihood to derive expected operating synergies from the transaction will be higher. Our results are consistent with the previous studies (Thraya and Hagendorff 2010). Therefore, hypothesis 7 is not rejected.

The second positive driver we document is the announcement of the deal during a crisis. The specific nature of this period has a positive effect on the value of the control premium. It is important that the effect holds for all investigated event windows. As the market is undervalued in times of crisis, the buyer pays a significantly higher price for the stake than the market value. The results are consistent with previous studies (Simonyan 2014). Thus, hypothesis 8 is not rejected.

The third positive factor we observe is the origin of the acquirer and the target from the same country. The size of the premium in BRIC overall sample will increase, if the acquirer and the target are both domestic firms. For emerging markets, it is important that a domestic buyer better understands specific features of business environment and networks due to the preliminary expertise in settling business problems. Thus, hypothesis 6 on the role of the same country residence is not rejected.

Our findings also show a negative determinant. The higher the target's financial leverage, the lower the premium (for the wide event windows). This can be justified by the fact that an increase in the level of debt leads to an increase in the indirect costs of financial distress of the target, when the firm becomes very sensitive to any unfavorable shifts in the market and is subject to debt overhang. The probability of transferring control to the debt holders due to covenants in the contracts or in case of bankruptcy increases with the increase of the debt burden. The results show that the magnitude of the premium for such a target with higher leverage will be lower. This result is consistent with the conclusions from previous studies (Thraya and Hagendorff 2010). Therefore, hypothesis 5 is not rejected.

The results on the impact of the acquired stake on the premium in the deals for the whole sample are controversial. As shown in Table 8, the positive effect holds only for the shortest event window at low level of significance and is not significant within longer windows. Thus, hypothesis 4 is not confirmed for the whole sample. At the same time, our findings for the overall sample do not provide support to hypotheses 4 on the impact of the toehold and 3 on the role of the firm size. Both factors are not significant for the whole sample.

6.2.2 Identifying the Factors Which Influence the Size of the Control Premium by Countries

The picture of determinants slightly differs in each stand-alone national sample. Table 7 presents significant positive and negative determinants for each country. Similar to abovementioned results for the overall sample of BRIC group, the announcement of the transactions within a crisis year becomes a positive driver for Brazilian and Russian M&A. During a crisis, the company is undervalued, while the price of the acquired stake and of the control is based on future cash flows expected beyond the crisis. Moreover, the opportunities to follow a growth strategy in such a period are very limited; therefore the purchase of a controlling stake becomes a valuable pattern of growth for the acquirer. The industry relatedness matters for the deals in Chinese M&A market for all windows, while for the deals in other national subsamples, it is not significant. However, this may be due to the small number of observations for the deals in related industries in Russian, Brazilian, and Indian subsamples. The positive influence of this type of driver can be explained by lower costs in the post-merger integration processes for Chinese firms. Finally, the size of the premium in deals made with a domestic acquirer is an important driver for the Indian market, which is characterized by high costs to acquire control due to the large number of legal requirements and restrictions. Thus, the likelihood that domestic investors will offer a greater control premium will be higher than for foreign investors, as they are more aware of the characteristics of the market and its environment.

We also find that financial leverage negatively affects the size of the premium for the Chinese, Indian, and Brazilian markets, but it is does not impact the premiums in the Russian subsample. In contrast to the whole sample, the existence of the toehold is among the determinants of the premium for the Russian, Chinese, and Indian subsamples. If the buyer has a toehold in the target company (d_IS), the control premium will be lower. The target company is more likely to agree on a deal with a known shareholder at a lower premium (Simonyan 2014; Dragota et al. 2013). The size of a target becomes significant only in the Russian market and negatively affects the magnitude of premium. It can be explained by the absence of a large number of potential buyers willing to acquire a large stake in a large company and by the complexity of integration with a large company. The size of the purchased package (D_PSP) is the common positive driver for Russian and Indian M&A markets. The larger the package, the greater the number of votes and the variety of rights and functions that can be exercised. This effect was demonstrated also by Trojanowski (2008) and Dragota et al. (2013).

7   Conclusions

Our research can be summarized in several findings. First, we confirm that M&A premiums were positive in the deals under study. We found a positive statistically significant control premium for BRIC countries of 10.3% for main event window $(-39; +72)$. We show that Chinese acquirers paid the highest control premium (12.9%), while Russian companies paid the lowest control premium (5%).

Second, the M&A premium in BRIC markets is affected by seven drivers: the number of acquired shares, the size of a target, the toehold, the financial leverage, the deal concluded by a domestic acquirer, the industry relatedness, and the announcement of the deal in a year of crisis. We documented key factors that drive the size of the premium up. It matters whether companies operate in the same sector and in the same country. Investors are ready to pay a higher premium if companies belong to the same industrial sector, due to the high potential synergy effects (the buyer will possibly have some insider information). The size of premium goes up if the announcement happens in a year of crisis. In the deals in the emerging markets, it is important whether the acquirer is domestic. The last positive driver we investigate is the size of the acquired stake. It was found that the acquisition of a 100% stake results in a 17.3% premium for control in the BRIC M&A market. In deals where the purchased stake is above 50% and 25%, the sizes of the premiums were 11 and 8.5%, respectively.

Third, we show the factors that decrease the premiums in M&A deals in large emerging markets. A highly leveraged target and a large target decrease the control premium. These results are largely consistent with the negative factors reported in earlier chapters on different emerging markets.

Acknowledgments I express my thanks to Elena Chvyrova—former member of Corporate Finance Research Center—for help in data collecting and processing.

References

Albuquerque, R. A., & Schroth, E. J. (2010). Quantifying private benefits of control from a structural model of block trades. *Journal of Financial Economics, 96*(1), 33–55.

Alexandridis, G., Fuller, K. P., Terhaar, L., & Travlos, N. G. (2013). Deal size, acquisition premia and shareholder gains. *Journal of Corporate Finance, 20*, 1–13.

Alves, J. M. (2008). Determining knowledge-intensive companies acquisition value for M&A purposes: An intellectual capital approach. *Portuguese Journal of Management Studies, 13* (3), 385–402.

Barclay, M. J., & Holderness, C. G. (1989). Private benefits from control of public corporations. *Journal of Financial Economics, 25*(2), 371–395.

Bena, J., & Li, K. (2014). Corporate innovations and mergers and acquisitions. *The Journal of Finance, 69*(5), 1923–1960.

Betton, S., & Eckbo, B. E. (2000). Toeholds, bid jumps, and expected payoffs in takeovers. *The Review of Financial Studies, 13*(4), 841–882.

Betton, S., Eckbo, B. E., & Thorburn, K. S. (2008a). *Markup pricing revisited.* Tuck School of Business at Dartmouth. Working chapter no. 2008-45. Retrieved from https://ssrn.com/abstract=1094946 or https://doi.org/10.2139/ssrn.1094946

Betton, S., Eckbo, B. E., & Thorburn, K. S. (2008b). Corporate takeovers. In B. E. Eckbo (Ed.), *Handbook of corporate finance: Empirical corporate finance* (Vol. 2, pp. 291–430). Amsterdam: Elsevier/North-Holland.

Betton, S., Eckbo, B. E., & Thorburn, K. S. (2009). Merger negotiations and the toehold puzzle. *Journal of Financial Economics, 91*(2), 158–178.

Bris, A. (2002). Toeholds, takeover premium, and the probability of being acquired. *Journal of Corporate Finance, 8*(3), 227–253.

Byrka-Kita, K., Czerwiński, M., & Zarzecki, D. (1989). Control premium on polish capital market. *Economics, 25,* 371–395.

Caprio, L., & Croci, E. (2008). The determinants of the voting premium in Italy: The evidence from 1974 to 2003. *Journal of Banking & Finance, 32*(11), 2433–2443.

da Silva, A. C., & Subrahmanyam, A. (2007). Dual-class premium, corporate governance, and the mandatory bid rule: Evidence from the Brazilian stock market. *Journal of Corporate Finance, 13*(1), 1–24.

Dong, M., Hirshleifer, D., Richardson, S., & Teoh, S. H. (2006). Does investor misvaluation drive the takeover market? *The Journal of Finance, 61*(2), 725–762.

Dragota, V., Dumitrescu, D., Ruxanda, G., Ciobanu, A., Brasoveanu, I., Stoian, A. M., & Lipară, C. (2007). Estimation of control premium: The case of Romanian listed companies. *Economic Computation and Economic Cybernetics Studies and Research., 41,* 55–72.

Dragota, V., Lipara, C., & Ciobanu, R. (2013). Agency problems and synergistic effects in Romania: The determinants of the control premium. *Czech Journal of Economics and Finance (Finance a Uver), 63*(2), 197–219.

Dyck, A., & Zingales, L. (2004). Private benefits of control: An international comparison. *The Journal of Finance, 59*(2), 537–600.

Eckbo, B. E. (2009). Bidding strategies and takeover premiums: A review. *Journal of Corporate Finance, 15*(1), 149–178.

Fan, L., Hu, B., & Jiang, C. (2012). Pricing and information content of block trades on the Shanghai Stock Exchange. *Pacific-Basin Finance Journal, 20*(3), 378–397.

Fedotova, M., Evstafjeva, E. (2008). The complex approach to control premium and liquidity adjustments for stock valuation. *Problemy Sovremennoy Economici, 3,* 356–362 (in Russian).

Hanouna, P., Sarin, A., & Shapiro, A. C. (2001). *Value of corporate control: Some international evidence.* West Lafayette, IN: Krannert Graduate School of Management, Purdue University.

Harford, J., & Li, K. (2007). Decoupling CEO wealth and firm performance: The case of acquiring CEOs. *The Journal of Finance, 62*(2), 917–949.

Hong, H. A. (2013). Does mandatory adoption of international financial reporting standards decrease the voting premium for dual-class shares? *The Accounting Review, 88*(4), 1289–1325.

Jordan, D., & Hoppe, P. (2008). Is the Mergerstat control premium overstated? *Journal of Business Valuation and Economic Loss Analysis, 3*(1), 1–13.

Jurfest, S. P., Paredes, R. D., & Riutort, J. (2015). Control premium and corporate regulatory changes: Theory and evidence. *The Developing Economies, 53*(3), 159–187.

La Bruslerie, H. (2013). Crossing takeover premiums and mix of payment: An empirical test of contractual setting in M&A transactions. *Journal of Banking & Finance, 37*(6), 2106–2123.

Loderer, C., & Martin, K. (1990). Corporate acquisitions by listed firms: The experience of a comprehensive sample. *Financial Management, 19*(4), 17–33.

Marcelo, A. (2008). Determining knowledge-intensive companies acquisition value for M&A purposes: An intellectual capital approach. *European Journal of Management Studies, XIII,* 385–402.

Maux, J. L., & Francoeur, C. (2014). Block premia, litigation risk, and shareholder protection. *European Financial Management, 20*(4), 756–769.

Moeller, T. (2005). Let's make a deal! How shareholder control impacts merger payoffs. *Journal of Financial Economics, 76*(1), 167–190.

Moeller, S. B., Schlingemann, F. P., & Stulz, R. M. (2004). Firm size and the gains from acquisitions. *Journal of Financial Economics, 73*(2), 201–228.

Muravyev, A., Berezinets, I., & Ilina, Y. (2014). The structure of corporate boards and private benefits of control: Evidence from the Russian stock exchange. *International Review of Financial Analysis, 34*, 247–261.

Nathan, K. S., & O'Keefe, T. B. (1989). The rise in takeover premiums: An exploratory study. *Journal of Financial Economics, 23*(1), 101–119.

Nenova, T. (2003). The value of corporate voting rights and control: A cross-country analysis. *Journal of Financial Economics, 68*(3), 325–351.

Neumann, R. (2003). Price differentials between dual-class stocks: Voting premium or liquidity discount? *European Financial Management, 9*(3), 315–332.

Ødegaard, B. A. (2007). Price differences between equity classes. Corporate control, foreign ownership or liquidity? *Journal of Banking & Finance, 31*(12), 3621–3645.

Raad, E. (2012). Why do acquiring firms pay high premiums to takeover target shareholders: An empirical study. *Journal of Applied Business Research (JABR), 28*(4), 725–734.

Rodionov, I., Perevalova V. (2012). The factors affecting the control premium size. *Journal of Corporate Finance Research, 5*(4), 112–121 (in Russian).

Saito, R. (2003). Determinants of the differential pricing between voting and non-voting shares in Brazil. *Brazilian Review of Econometrics, 23*(1), 77–109.

Saito, R., & Silveira, A. D. M. D. (2010). The Relevance of tag along rights and identity of controlling shareholders for the price spreads between dual-class shares: The Brazilian case. *BAR-Brazilian Administration Review, 7*(1), 01–21.

Schwert, G. W. (1996). Markup pricing in mergers and acquisitions. *Journal of Financial Economics, 41*(2), 153–192.

Simonyan, K. (2014). What determines takeover premia: An empirical analysis. *Journal of Economics and Business, 75*, 93–125.

Sonenshine, R., & Reynolds, K. (2014). Determinants of cross-border merger premia. *Review of World Economics, 150*(1), 173–189.

Sorwar, G., & Sudarsanam, S. (2010). Determinants of takeover premium in cash-financed takeover offers: An option pricing approach. *Journal of Business, Finance & Accounting, 37*(5–6), 687–714.

Thraya, M. F., & Hagendorff, J. (2010). *Controlling shareholders and the acquisition premiums paid in European takeover bids.* Cahier de recherche n° 2010-10 E2. Retrieved from https://halshs.archives-ouvertes.fr/halshs-00534763

Trojanowski, G. (2008). Equity block transfers in transition economies: Evidence from Poland. *Economic Systems, 32*(3), 217–238.

Wickramanayake, J., & Wood, A. (2009). *Determinants of acquisition premiums: Empirical evidence from mining industry in Australia and Canada.* In EFMA Annual Meetings, Chapter (No. 412).

Zingales, L. (1995). What determines the value of corporate votes? *The Quarterly Journal of Economics, 110*(4), 1047–1073.

Success Factors in M&As of Knowledge-Intensive Firms in Brazil: Evidence from Consulting Engineering Companies

Karla Motta Kiffer de Moraes and Luiz F. Autran M. Gomes

Abstract We present the critical success factors (CSFs) in mergers and acquisitions (M&A) integration processes based on the practices of consulting engineering companies in Brazil in the last 10 years. The relevance of this issue is inherent to the M&A processes, especially at the integration phase of the companies involved. In this phase, several actions should be taken to quickly define an integration approach that must effectively achieve operational synergies and value creation. A practical application using 2 classical ordinal ranking methods was held, and a group of 23 executives active in consulting engineering in Brazil in the last decades with experience in leadership, management, integration, and/or M&A processes was interviewed. The research included seven consulting engineering companies that developed M&A operations, with focus on the success factors, challenges, and risks. Eight critical success factors were ordered in the first ten positions according to both methods. Given the results, these critical success factors should be strongly considered and prioritized in the process of integration of knowledge-intensive companies to achieve their objectives and reach full success in M&A transaction.

Keywords Critical success · Mergers and acquisitions · Consulting engineering · Integration · Ordinal methods · Voting

K. M. Kiffer de Moraes (✉)
Arcadis, Rio de Janeiro, Brazil

Ibmec School of Business and Economics, Rio de Janeiro, Brazil
e-mail: karla.kiffer@arcadis.com

L. F. A. M. Gomes
Ibmec School of Business and Economics, Rio de Janeiro, Brazil
e-mail: luiz.gomes@ibmec.edu.br

© Springer Nature Switzerland AG 2020
I. Ivashkovskaya et al. (eds.), *Strategic Deals in Emerging Capital Markets*,
Advanced Studies in Emerging Markets Finance,
https://doi.org/10.1007/978-3-030-23850-6_7

1 Introduction

The goal of this chapter is to present the critical success factors (CSFs) that should be considered by consulting engineering companies in Brazil involved as acquirer, acquired, or partner in M&A processes, in order to maximize the chances of success through effective integration management, thus achieving M&A objectives. The main motivation behind reaching that goal starts with the following question: "What are the critical factors that determine the success of the integration process of consulting engineering companies in Brazil involved in mergers and acquisitions?" This broad question requires considering and analyzing the following objectives:

- To present an overview of M&A transactions involving consulting engineering companies in Brazil in the last 10 years focusing on the factors for the success of the transaction, challenges, and risks
- To select and order the CSF for M&A operations of consulting engineering companies in Brazil

The research is focused on the selection and ordering of CSF related to the management of the integration process in M&A transactions in the last 10 years related to Brazilian consulting engineering companies. The specific processes that involved construction engineering companies, assemblers, or developers were not considered in this study. Likewise, the CSFs of the stages prior to the formalization of the purchase and sale agreement, such as the selection of companies to be acquired, evaluations, and negotiations, among others, were not considered either. Based on the main trends in M&A market in Brazil described in Chap. 1, we proceed to the analysis with the summary of CSF main concepts in Sect. 2. Section 3 is focused on a literature review of ordinal ranking methods with emphasis on Borda and Condorcet methods. Section 4 provides a review of the literature on consulting engineering and its current situation in Brazil, including global and Brazilian rankings. The methodology of the research with the seven steps is explained in Sect. 5. We discuss the results in Sect. 6. Finally, Section 7 presents our conclusions.

2 Critical Success Factors (CSFs)

2.1 Concepts

The concept of success factors was initially developed by D.R. Daniel in 1961. This concept led to the more refined notion of CSF by J.F. Rockart (1979). The CSF approach has been used in a growing number of organizations (Bullen and Rockart 1981). Various applications of CSF have been available in the literature since then (Aquilani et al. 2016; Klimoski 2016; Molwus et al. 2017). In line with the authors, CSFs are understood as a relatively limited number of factors in which a satisfactory outcome ensures a good competitive performance for individuals, departments, and organizations. Critical factors are therefore the variables and areas of the company that have higher prevalence in achieving the desired results. Because these areas of activity are critical, the manager should have the appropriate information that will allow him/her to determine if events are occurring well enough in each area. The CSF interview method was designed to provide a structured technique to be used by the interviewer to be able to support managers from scratch until identification of their CSF and to determine the necessary resulting information.

CSFs have thus been taking up space along with other basic terms related to the management of an organization. Also according to Bullen and Rockart (1981), those are defined as follows:

1. CSF: a limited number of areas where satisfactory results will ensure a successful competitive performance for the individual, department, or organization. CSFs are the few areas where things must go right, that is, where things have to work, for business to thrive and for management goals to be achieved.
2. Strategy: the set of mission, objectives, policies, and plans of use of significant resources established to define what business the company is in and the type of company that is or will be. A full strategy statement will define the production line, the markets and market segments for which the products are designated, the channels by which those markets will be achieved, the means by which the operations will be financed, the profit objectives, the size of the organization, and the image to be designed for its employees, suppliers, and customers.
3. Objectives: general statements about the directions in which the organization intends to follow, without setting goals to be achieved in a certain period of time.
4. Goals: specific targets to be achieved in a given period of time. A goal is therefore an operational transformation of one or more objectives.
5. Actions: specific standards which allow the measurement of performance for each CSF, goal, or objective. Actions can be light, that is, subjective and qualitative, or heavy, which are objective and quantitative.
6. Problems: specific tasks that have become important because of poor performance or changes in the environment. Problems can affect achievement of goals or performance in a critical area of success.

2.2 General CSF Considerations

Given the current situation, managers need access to information relevant to their roles within the organization and their responsibilities. The CSF transforms the tacit areas into explicit ones, allowing them to be used to assist in the company's planning process, to improve communication between managers, and to develop communication systems within the company with a more centralized focus (Roldan et al. 2011). Some considerations can be made regarding the CSF:

- CSFs are vital elements for an organization's strategy to succeed.
- CSF pushes the strategy forward, making it happen or harming the success of the strategy and therefore being critical to the organization.
- Strategists should ask themselves "Why do our customers choose us?" The answer is typically a critical success factor.

Furlan et al. (1994) report that the CSF approach serves several levels of management, with the following benefits: (1) to help determine the factors that should be maintained and monitored; (2) to collect only the necessary information; (3) to allow the definition of relevant information on the factors of the individual or organization; and (4) to be used as a communication vehicle for management, facilitating integration around critical topics and ensuring synergy in pursuit of established goals. Regarding the importance of CSF, Bullen and Rockart (1981) consider that the number of truly important issues on which the manager should focus attention is relatively small. For this reason, the term CSF is appropriately used. It reflects few factors that are critical to the success of the manager concerned. There are, in the professional life of each manager, an unbelievable number of things that can divert his/her attention. The key to success for most managers is to focus their most limited resource (i.e., time) on those things that really make the difference between success and failure.

It is important to note that different managers identify different CSF and may therefore collect different decision-oriented information. The CSFs are related to the specifics of the particular situations of each manager. This means that they must be tailored to the industry, the organization, and each individual interviewed. CSF will also differ from manager to manager according to his/her position in the organization. In addition, they will often change in line with changes in the environment, with the organization's positioning on changes in the industry, or with particular problems or new opportunities for a specific manager.

It is also necessary to understand what the CSFs are not. They are not a standard set of actions, also called key performance indicators (KPI), which are applied to all divisions of the organization. They are not limited to factors that are reported as historical, consolidated, or accounting information. Instead, the CSF approach looks at the world from the manager's current operational point of view. CSFs are particular areas of particular importance to a particular manager of a particular division at a given time. They then demand specific and differentiated actions, many of which are evaluated as light subjective information not obtained explicitly.

According to Bullen and Rockart (1981), there are five main types of CSF: the industry, competitive strategy and positioning of the industry, environmental factors, temporal factors, and managerial positioning. These are explained below.

1. The industry: each industry has a set of CSF that are determined by characteristics of the same industry. Different industries will get specific CSF. A certain set of characteristics typical of each industry will define its own CSF. In fact, each organization has its own goals although there is a typical pattern for the industry, i.e., companies in the same industry do not have identical CSF. Some industry associations in the same industry may offer benchmarking about common CSF.

2. Competitive strategy and positioning of the industry: the nature of the positioning in the labor market or the adoption of strategy to obtain a greater market share indicates that the strategies of differentiation of CSF and positioning present different CSF. All companies in the same industry will not have the same CSF. A company's current position in the industry, its history, strategy, and capabilities will define its CSF. The values of an organization and its marketing goal, among others, will impact the CSFs that are appropriate for a given moment.

3. Environmental factors: environmental changes, whether economic, regulatory, political, or demographic, create specific CSF for an organization. These changes are related to environmental factors that are not under the control of the organization but which an organization should consider in the development of CSF. The organization must fulfill its mission while seeking to adapt to the course of changes in the environment in which it operates.

4. Temporal factors: motivated by short-term situations, very often by crises. Those factors are important, but usually of short duration. They are temporary CSF or related to extraordinary measures resulting in a specific event that makes it necessary to include them. Practically, with the evolution and integration of the markets due to globalization, the temporality of the factors can be questioned since they can exist in a regular way in the organizations.

5. Management positioning: the role of the individual should generate CSF in a specific area of responsibility. This is considered critical to the success of an organization. It is important if the CSF is considered from the point of view of the individual.

In short, CSFs are key points that, when well executed, define and guarantee the development and growth of a company and its business, achieving its objectives. In contrast, when these same factors are neglected or ignored, they contribute greatly to the failure of the organization. CSF must be found through an in-depth study of the company's own objectives, deriving from its mission, vision, and values, making it mandatory and fundamental references for the company to survive, be competitive, and have success, whatever the segment. It can be emphasized that CSF also helps managers to define the main guidelines for the implementation of plans and projects and processes, and, more specifically, they can be of great value in the integration processes of companies involved in M&A processes. Some CSFs of M&A processes that aim at value creation and operational synergies are related to organizational culture, strategic consistency, communication, knowledge management, stakeholder management, and integration management and can be exemplified to eliminate existing cultural differences; merge cultures; manage goals and objectives; manage expectations; manage skills; provide strategic alignment; create a favorable culture; manage changes and manage best practices; manage knowledge; achieve synergy and engagement; align the human resources programs with the values and targets of the corporation; integrate people and retain the best professionals; and provide and integrate work tools, among others.

According to Giusti (2000), the critical factors of post-operation success are related to the main activities required during the process of integration of companies considering (1) organizational structure, since in the first moment, there are great doubts about the imminent changes in the power structure and formal hierarchical structure; (2) communication, since they change the messengers and the way they deliver the messages, also considering the quality and reliability of the information; (3) integration of operational areas, considering their complexity given the inherent differences in each structure, including information technology, finance, human resources, sales and marketing, operations, and supplies; and (4) new mission and values, in order to answer questions such as "who will we be?" and "what will we do?"

3   Ordinal Ranking Methods

The two most classical and commonly used ordinal ranking approaches are Borda and Condorcet methods, and recent extensions of both methods have been made available in the literature (Danielson and Ekenberg 2017; Caklovic and Kurdija 2017).

3.1   Borda Method

A. The Classical Borda Aggregation Procedure

This ordinal ranking method considers a jury composed of several people. The idea of the method is to add up the rankings obtained by a given alternative with respect to each criterion. For a given criterion, a point is assigned to the alternative that comes first, two points to the second, three to the third, and so on. The social choice, or aggregated pre-order, is obtained by summing all the points obtained in all criteria for all alternatives and ranking first the one that has the lowest number of points, second the one that has points just above the first, and so on (Pomerol and Barba Romero 2000). In the analysis presented in this research, it was decided, for the sake of consistency, to slightly modify the basic idea so that the alternative that comes first will be the one with the greatest number of points, not the smallest, thus obtaining the equivalent to readings of a value function. Therefore, by assuming m alternatives, the integer numbers thus obtained will be number of points $k_1 > k_2 > k_3 \ldots > k_m \geq 0$, and those are called Borda coefficients. For each criterion j, the alternatives are ranked according to a complete pre-order and are called the rank of alternative i for the pre-order associated with criterion j. The alternatives, relative to criterion j, form a chain of preferences of the type

$$a_{i1} \succ a_{i2} \succ a_{i3} \approx a_{i4} \succ \ldots \succ a_{im-1} \succ a_{im}$$

where $\succ$ denotes strict preference and $\approx$ indifference. According to Pomerol and Barba Romero (2000), the Borda aggregation procedure solves ranking problems, generates a complete pre-order in a set of alternatives, and is purely ordinal.

B. Borda Voting

Given n complete pre-orders $\succ j$ for m alternatives $A_1, A_2, \ldots, A_m$, Borda voting is the procedure that, for a given alternative A_i, consists of realizing the sum of the votes (or $\sum_{k \neq j} v_{ik}$) resulting from all possible comparisons of A_i against A_k. The alternatives are then ranked according to the number of votes.

Borda voting is indeed related to the Borda method and is therefore a predecessor of the North American multicriteria analysis school. In essence it is a sum of points, having the great advantage of simplicity. Some of the Borda method's extensions are used in sporting competitions and can also be applied as an aid in evaluating an organization's suppliers. However, despite its simplicity and widespread use of its variations, the Borda method does not respect Arrow's axiom of independence of irrelevant alternatives (Pomerol and Barba Romero 2000). Both Borda and Condorcet ordinal ranking methods belong to the scientific field of Multicriteria Decision Aid (Pomerol and Barba Romero 2000).

3.2 Condorcet Method

In the Condorcet method, the alternatives are always compared two by two, and a graph is constructed that expresses the relation between them.

According to the simple majority voting of the Condorcet aggregation procedure given two alternatives (a_i, a_j), we can say that $a_i \succ a_j$ if and only if the number of criteria for which a_i dominates a_j is strictly greater than the number for which the reverse is true. We can also affirm that $a_i \approx a_j$ when the number of criteria in favor is equal to the number of criteria against.

This method has the advantage of preventing distortions by making the relative position of two alternatives independent of their positions relative to any other. However, it may lead to the so-called Condorcet paradox, or situation of intransitivity. This happens when alternative A overcomes alternative B, which surpasses C, which in turn overcomes alternative A. This situation can be exploited in certain problems, when the objective is to group alternatives. However, when it occurs, it makes it impossible to generate an ordering of the alternatives. When the intransitivity cycles do not appear and it is desired to obtain a total pre-order, the Condorcet method should be preferred to the Borda method (Mello et al. 2004). If the goal is to make a choice, even with intransitivity, the Condorcet method has the advantage of requiring interactive interventions with the decision-maker.

4 Consulting Engineering

4.1 Introduction

Consulting engineering companies offer intellectual, specialized, and customized services that optimize and offer solutions to investment projects in several sectors of the economy with an emphasis in industry, construction, and infrastructure, in all phases of a project, and also in the implementation and operation of these enterprises. However, the delimitation of the consulting engineering sector is much more complex. According to the Brazilian Association of Industrial Development (ABDI 2011), there are deep diversity and heterogeneity observed in the following aspects:

1. Heterogeneity of the nature of the service offered: going from basic design, detailing, implementation (including supplies), and management/operation. The companies offer services in isolation in each of these stages, in all of them in different projects, or in an integrated way, offering complete packages (of the type Engineering, Procurement, and Construction (EPC)) that involve engineering, procurement selection, and construction or that also include financing (design, finance, build, and operate (DFBO)).
2. Heterogeneity of the supplier company: independent companies of various sizes (composed of many or few engineers, local or highly internationalized) and specializations or departments/subsidiaries in the service of the applicants themselves, especially large construction companies.

Such heterogeneities imply difficulties in data collection and analysis, since there is a great overlap of information and, at the same time, information veiled by the integrated project, construction, and operation activity.

4.2 Main Features

It is possible to outline the main economic characteristics of the sectors as follows:

A. Economic Characteristics and Attributes of Competitiveness in Brazil

Until the mid-1980s, companies earned most of their revenue through engineering or architectural projects. With the interruption of major infrastructure projects and large industrial projects throughout the decade, companies in the sector started to work strongly in project management and even in construction and operation. Project design and development services demand more intense intellectual work, in which the experience, qualification, and creativity of engineers and designers become the company's main competitive assets. In recent years, this activity has provided smaller profit margins, since the percentage of the project represents 2–3% in the total costs of the projects (in the 1970s and 1980s, it was around 7%). In addition, the demand for projects is discontinuous over time, creating an intermittence that imposes strong obstacles to the maintenance of fixed costs. For this reason, billing and the number of employees, including highly skilled engineers, who are the main assets of a project company, are extremely volatile. However, project design and development services represent a fundamental step in determining the total costs of the project. Also, participation in the first stages of the project also allows companies to structure themselves to offer engineering services in later stages, making it possible to improve the competitiveness of the corporate scope of the company as a whole.

There are basically two types of products offered, namely, engineering design solutions and enterprise management and supervising solutions. In both cases, the company's ability to differentiate and compete would be associated with its reputation for competence, measured by the agility, efficiency, reliability, and quality of technical solutions previously proposed by its staff.

According to the association, successful companies in the competitive process would be those that have a curriculum vitae and a proven portfolio of efficient solutions in ventures in the particular area for which they are offering both projects and management solutions. This reputation is an intangible asset, which should have a low degree of absorption by competitors and therefore should constitute a strong attribute of competitiveness.

Some factors explain this argument: barriers to entry are low; the intra-sector rivalry is very intense; the market power of downstream links is quite significant; dominance is aggravated when the contractors are public companies, subject to the legislation of biddings that directs the decision of purchase for price and not for technical quality; the intermittent demand prevents the permanent remuneration of fixed costs; the growth in demand for projects is accompanied by a more than proportional increase in the main operating costs; and there are risks associated with contracts. For those reasons, the competition in the sector is large, mainly in prices. As a consequence, there is a great mortality (and birth) of companies in the sector and limited degree of learning and technological development. Survival strategies have included the downgrading of operations and the price war, factors that have been able to cause, on a growing scale, the loss of quality of services offered and have consequently damaged the reputation of the company and cast doubt on their future survival (ABDI 2011).

B. Importance of the Sector for the Various Downstream Segments

Again according to the ABDI report, the larger companies concentrate their activities on the steps that guarantee higher margins while subcontracting smaller firms to carry out the stages whose margins have been steadily declining, such as design and detailing. Smaller companies, on the other hand, usually focus on consulting engineering activities and depend on the level of outsourcing of activities adopted by large companies, which assume the role of the main service demanders.

Historically, the participation of local companies in the detailed stages of industrial projects was a crucial factor in accelerating the process of technological absorption and local development of the improvement and adaptation of existing technologies, demonstrating an important role of the sector in the dissemination of new technologies (Katz 2005). There is a close relationship between the insertion of consulting engineering companies in the design and detailing stages and a greater capacity to disseminate new technologies to the interior of the local productive chains, as well as the development of local producers. Likewise, the weakening of this chain link tends to increase technological dependence and cut an important link in the appropriation of new technologies. It can be inferred that the strengthening of consulting engineering activities contributes to the development of technological licensing packages and to increasing the availability of these packages, as well as reducing their costs and delivery times.

4.3 Current Situation

The historical series of the Brazilian engineering ranking of *O Empreiteiro* (The Contractor) magazine completed 20 years in 2014 (O Empreiteiro 2015). Considering the period from 1995 to 2014, it can be observed that all four segments—Construction, Industrial Assembly, Projects, and Consulting and Services Special Engineering—enter their fifth year of relative stagnation. The constant growth registered in the engineering and construction sector in recent years, bringing gross revenues from R\$ 42.3 billion in 2003 to R\$ 118.2 billion in 2013, showed an approximate decrease of 24% in 2014 with a revenue of R\$ 95.4 billion.

Considering the 20-year period between 1995 and 2014, it is estimated that the accumulated gross revenue of the construction and engineering sector, after its peak in 2013 with 249%, decreased to 182% in 2014 and the accumulated GDP in the same period of 20 years reached 73%. Regarding consulting engineering, it can be observed that the 40 largest projects and consulting companies recorded a reduction of 12.95% in the total revenues for 2014, totaling R\$ 8.6 million.

Table 1 displays the ranking of the 15 largest consulting engineering companies in Brazil, the comparison with their positions in 2013, their places of origin, gross revenues in 2014, and their domains. The first two places account for more than R\$ 1 billion of individual income. It is noteworthy, however, that both companies perform services other than engineering consulting services. It can be observed that the first three ranks did not change in ranking with respect to the year of 2013. It is also noted that the gross revenue of the three largest companies is equal to the sum of the gross revenues of the other companies that make up the group of 15 largest consulting engineering companies in the country.

Table 2 displays the 20 largest consulting engineering companies in the world, including the ranking position in 2014 and 2015, as well as the headquarters and the segments in which they operate. The ranking is compiled by *ENR* (2015) magazine, and, according to this source, the impact of uncertainties on the global market can be seen in *ENR*'s top 225 international design firm survey results. The top 225 companies generated US\$ 70.85 billion in gross revenue in 2014 from projects outside their countries of origin, a reduction of 1.1% when compared to the US\$ 71.63 billion generated in 2013. Billing from the host countries generated an amount of US\$ 73.48

Table 1 Fifteen largest projects and consulting companies

Ranking 2014/ 2013	Company	Headquarter	Gross revenue 2014 (R $ \times 100$)	Segments
1/1	Engevix Engenharia	SP	1150.28	ABCDEFGHIJKLMOPQRST
2/2	Concremat Engenharia e Tecnologia	RJ	1065.99	ABCDEFHIJKMNPQRS
3/3	Arcadis Logos	SP	742.73	ABCDEFHIJKMNOPQRSTU
4/6	Progen	SP	396.3	AEHIJKLMNOPQRST
5/5	WorleyParsons	SP	388.9	ABCDEFGHIJKLMNOPQRSTU
6/4	Promon Engenharia	SP	362.16	BCDFGHIJKMOPQRST
7/8	Ductor Implantação de Projetos	SP	253.48	Q
8/11	Leme Engenharia	MG	240.9	BCDEFJMPQR
9/10	Falcão Bauer	SP	238.37	ABDEFGHIJKMNOPQRST
10/17	Intertechne	PR	226.28	ABCEFGHIJKMQRS
11/9	Chemtech Serviços de Engenharia e Software	RJ	206.28	GHKOPRQ
12/14	Sondotécnica	RJ	179.92	ABCDEFGHIJKLMNOPQRST
13/13	Poyry Tecnologia	SP	167.16	FJKNPQRST
14/30	Qualidados Engenharia	BA	153.43	HILPQR
15/21	Sistema PRI Engenharia	SP	151.08	ABCDEGHIJKLMNPQRST

(A)/(H)/(O) Road works, oil installations, steel/metallurgy
(B)/(I)/(P) Hydroelectric plants, bridges and viaducts, industrial plants
(C)/(J)/(Q) Transmission line, airports, project management
(D)/(K)/(R) Sanitation works, pipelines, viability study
(E)/(L)/(S) Railway works, telecom, architecture
(F)/(M)/(T) Nuclear power plants, metro works, urban planning
(G)/(N)/(U) Offshore platforms, shopping centers, installation design
Source: O Empreiteiro (2015)

billion in 2014, against US$ 72.32 billion in 2014. The group's total revenues were US$ 144.34 billion, 0.3% above US$ 143.95 billion in 2013.

It can be observed that at least 15 of the 20 companies mentioned work or have already acted in the implementation of projects in Brazil. Nine companies have conducted M&A transactions in Brazil in the last 10 years. They are AECOM, Jacobs, WorleyParsons, Fluor, Arcadis NV, Fugro, SNC-Lavalin, Tetra Tech, and Mott MacDonald. In addition to the top 20, other companies, as reported in the media, performed M&A operations in Brazil.

Table 2 Twenty largest international project companies

Ranking 2015/2014	Company	Headquarter	Type
1/1	AECOM	EUA	EA
2/2	Jacobs	EUA	EAC
3/[a]	Power Construction Corp. of China	China	EAC
4/3	WorleyParsons	Australia	EC
5/5	AMEC plc	UK	EC
6/6	Fluor Corp.	USA	EC
7/10	Arcadis NV	Holanda	E
8/11	China Communications Construction Ltd	China	EAC
9/16	WSP Parsons Brinckerhoff	Canada	E
10/7	CH2M HILL	USA	EAC
11/9	Fugro NV	Holanda	GE
12/8	SNC-Lavalin International Inc.	Canada	EC
13/18	CB&I	USA	EC
14/15	Atkins	UK	EA
15/19	Dar Al-Handasah Consultants	Egito	EA
16/13	Tetra Tech Inc.	USA	E
17/17	Stantec Inc.	Canada	EAL
18/14	Bechtel	USA	EC
19/27	China Railway Construction Corp. Ltd	China	EC
20/20	Mott MacDonald Group Ltd	UK	E

(A)/(E)/(C)/(G)/(L) Architecture, engineering, constructor, geotechnical, landscaping
[a]Not ranked last year
Source: ENR (2015)

5   Research Methodology

5.1   Framework

The method used in this work was ordinal ranking through Borda and Condorcet methods. According to Levin and Nalebuff (1995), five constraints must be taken into account to solve a given ordinal ranking problem, namely, (1) level of complexity, which establishes that the method should be simple and transparent; (2) voter strategy, which goes against the former, in the sense that the less simple, the better; (3) the candidate's strategy; and (4) classification of several candidates or choice of a winner and minority and (5) of safe choice, where one seeks to know strong preferences over consensus. Tideman and Plassman (2008) also discuss the problem, stating that the comparison between the methods present in the literature is done by comparing the properties of the same. Since no method satisfies all properties and since there is no consensus on which properties are best, there is no consensus as to which method is best.

Both Borda and Condorcet methods are basis to all other succeeding methods that have been developed to tackle the ordinal ranking problem. Borda and Condorcet methods are indeed the classical methods, although each of them is not immune to criticism. Besides, their use is widely disseminated in various fields of application.

Regarding the methodology, this research is of an exploratory nature, since it intends to generate knowledge from a bibliographical survey and from interviews with professionals who had, or have, practical experiences with the problem researched and analysis of examples that stimulate the understanding about the addressed problem. From the point of view of data analysis, this research can be classified as qualitative research, since it presents qualitative data, analysis of questionnaire's responses, and interviews, based on information from articles and research related to CSF and M&A. The research question is the following: "What are the critical factors that determine the success of the integration process of consulting engineering companies in Brazil involved in mergers and acquisitions?" It is assumed that the application of effective integration management between the companies involved can mitigate the errors and maximize the chances of success in the M&A processes with generation of shareholder value. Specifically, the research aims to:

- Select and order the CSF specifically for M&A operations of consulting engineering companies in Brazil.
- Present analysis of M&A transactions involving consulting engineering companies in Brazil in the last 10 years, focusing on the factors for the success of the transaction, the challenges, and the risks.

5.2 Research Sample and Operationalization

The data required for the preparation of the present study consisted of the following steps:

1. Sample determination: survey of 11 consulting engineering companies (Table 3) that conducted mergers and acquisitions in the last 10 years in Brazil and group survey of 30 consulting engineering experts and/or mergers and acquisitions experience, with at least 10 years of experience in the sector.
2. Identification of 22 CSF: select specific CSF for the integration process in M&A. For that, a theoretical basis was used for M&A (in Brazil and in the world), CSF (specific for M&A and also for post-merger integration process), and other data collected in the literature (Table 4).
3. Elaboration of questionnaire and pre-test: elaboration of questionnaire and pre-test with professional of the area.
4. Analysis of results from the questionnaires: adjustments were made based on the face-to-face interview that tested the questionnaire and split it into two types. The Type 1 questionnaire was elaborated with a focus on the expert executive and his/her vision and preferences about the CSF for the integration process, and the Type 2 questionnaire focused on consulting engineering companies that underwent M&As in Brazil in the last 10 years.

Table 3 Consulting engineering companies

Item	Buyer	Acquired	Transaction year
1	AECOM (USA)	ENSR Brasil (Brazil)	2005
2	Arcadis (Netherlands)	Logos Engenharia (Brazil)	1999 and 2011
3	Hill (USA)	Engineering (Brazil)	2011
4	Jacobs (USA)	Guimar (Brazil)	2013
5	Arcadis Logos (Brazil)	ETEP (Brazil)	2012
6	SNC-Lavalin (Canada)	Minerconsult (Brazil)	2007
7	Tetra Tech (USA)	CRA (Canada)	2013
8	TPF (Belgium)	Projetec (Brazil)	2010
9	TUV (Germany)	Ductor (Brazil)	2007
10	TYPSA (Spain)	Engecorps (Brazil)	2009
11	WorleyParsons (Australia)	CNEC (Brazil)	2010

5. Conducting the interviews, in person, by telephone, and by electronic mail using the two types of questionnaire according to the respondent. Of the 30 Type 1 questionnaires, a return of 23 expert executives was obtained, equivalent to 77%. In relation to the 11 companies involved in mapped M&As, 9 were contacted, and a return of 7 transactions was received, highlighted in Table 5.
6. After data collection, the data were consolidated, the results were analyzed, and the CSFs of the process of integration of consultative engineering companies in Brazil, with the use of Borda and Condorcet methods, were ranked and analyzed. A critical analysis was then performed on the results and the similarities and divergences identified when comparing the results of the two methods.
7. Subsequently, the results of the questionnaires of the seven M&A transactions carried out between consulting engineering companies in Brazil in the last 10 years were analyzed.

6 Practical Application

6.1 Introduction

To better understand how M&A processes in Brazil are being carried out in the consulting engineering sector, especially in the integration process, a quantitative and qualitative research was conducted in the first quarter of 2016 with 23 executives in engineering consulting firms with relevant experience in the area and also in M&A transactions. In order to collect the quantitative data, the instrument of the questionnaire that served as the basis for the research was tested in a face-to-face interview and adjusted to reality. The questionnaire was also adapted for two types of respondents, executives and companies. The research was carried out through face-to-face interviews, by telephone, and by e-mail with the support of the specific questionnaire. The questionnaire for the expert executives was focused on the

Table 4 Critical success factors

	Critical success factors	Source
1	Vision and values of organization	Bullen and Rockart (1981)
2	Look at culture and organization	Barros (2001), Johann (2004)
3	Image with stakeholders	Bullen and Rockart (1981), Zollo and Meier (2008)
4	Physical location	Deloitte (2015)
5	Human resources policies (remuneration, training, bonuses, etc.)	Giusti (2000), Bullen and Rockart (1981), Zollo and Meier (2008)
6	Planning of integration actions	Giusti (2000), Bullen and Rockart (1981)
7	Internal communication	Orsi (2000), Giuti (2000), Buellen and Rockart (1981)
8	Characteristics of the development and implementation team	Giusti (2000), Zollo and Meier (2008)
9	Accounting principles and practice	Giusti (2000), Buellen and Rockart (1981), Zollo and Meier (2008)
10	Integration of financial data	Giusti (2000), Zollo and Meier (2008)
11	Knowledge management	Orsi (2000)
12	Strong support from executives	Deloitte (2015)
13	Develop a comprehensive project with risk governance, optimizing the use of budget and time resources	Orsi (2000), Deloitte (2015)
14	Have performed due diligence	Deloitte (2015)
15	Initiate integration planning during due diligence analysis	Bullen and Rockart (1981), Deloitte (2015)
16	Promote the involvement of the management of both	Giusti (2000), Deloitte (2015)
17	Make transparent and constant communication with employees	Orsi (2000), Giusti (2000), Deloitte (2015)
18	Create a dedicated team for integration	Deloitte (2015)
19	Assess and address the cultural fit between the two organizations	Barros (2001), Johann (2004), Deloitte (2015)
20	Develop a robust synergy plan	Giusti (2000), Deloitte (2015), Motta et al. (2013), Camargos and Barbosa (2010)
21	Allocate an appropriate budget for integration	Giusti (2000), Deloitte (2015)
22	Hire an outside company to assist with integration	Orsi (2000), Deloitte (2015)

selection and ranking of the CSF in integration processes. The questionnaire for companies was more comprehensive, seeking to better understand the post-operation process, M&A motivations, and future intentions of new transactions, among others. Thirty consultant experts in consulting engineering were selected and contacted, with a return of 23 responses. Eleven consulting engineering companies were

Table 5 Consulting engineering companies' participants of the survey

Item	Buyer	Acquired	Transaction year
1	AECOM (USA)	ENSR Brasil (Brazil)	2005
2	Arcadis (Netherlands)	Logos Engenharia (Brazil)	1999 and 2011
3	Hill (USA)	Engineering (Brazil)	2011
4	Jacobs (USA)	Guimar (Brazil)	2013
5	Arcadis Logos (Brazil)	ETEP (Brazil)	2012
6	SNC-Lavalin (Canada)	Minerconsult (Brazil)	2007
7	Tetra Tech (USA)	CRA (Canada)	2013
8	TPF (Belgium)	Projetec (Brazil)	2010
9	TUV (Germany)	Ductor (Brazil)	2007
10	TYPSA (Spain)	Engecorps (Brazil)	2009
11	WorleyParsons (Australia)	CNEC (Brazil)	2010

identified that underwent the M&A process in Brazil in the last 10 years. Nine of them were contacted, and seven of those companies participated in the research.

The sample enables a profile of M&A operations involving consulting engineering firms in the country. The qualitative research included seven interviews with the companies, as well as four consulting experts, representing the main organisms related to consulting engineering in Brazil; those have started the operation for at least 2 years and a maximum of 10 years before and provide information requested in the questionnaire. It is shown next how the results of all questionnaires were consolidated and analyzed.

6.2 Analysis of the Results

Type 1: Expert Executives in Consulting Engineering and M&A Processes
The 23 most respondents, 96% work for consulting engineering firms, and 4% have worked, with the average time spent in consulting engineering being 29.6 years. One hundred percent of the interviewers occupy or hold an executive position, having an average of 14.8 years in the current position. Ninety percent of the respondents are male. More than 87% have already been involved in M&A operations, with 35% being chief executive officers, 60% as directors, and 5% as managers.

Table 6 shows the results for identifying the level of criticality of the CSF presented in columns 1 and 2. The factors considered as very critical that stand out are those related to the vision and values of the organization (64%) and to the fact of having executed due diligence (62%). In the sequence, it can be observed that there is a strong support of the executives in the integration process (57%), as well as the cultural alignment and planning of the integration actions, both with a rate of 45%. When we look at the CSF considered as critical and very critical, we perceive that 94% of respondents consider organizational view and values to be as critical as 95%. At this level, there is also the support of executives and the execution of due

Table 6 Criticality of CSF with respect to integration

1. Factors	2. Group on critical factors				3. Group on Borda method			4. Group on Condorcet method		
What are the CSFs that can be related to the success of an integration M&A process?	Criticality				Number of votes	Total	Borda order	Number of votes	Total	Condorcet order
	1	2	3	4						
1. Vision and values of the organization	0%	5%	32%	64%	17	134	1	17	19	3
2. Look to the culture and to the organization	0%	5%	50%	45%	16	92	3	16	18	4
3. Image with stakeholders	0%	9%	68%	23%	9	44	8	9	9.5	
4. Physical location	27%	50%	18%	5%	2	5		2	1	
5. Human resources policies (remuneration, training, bonuses, etc.)	0%	18%	73%	9%	8	20		8	8	
6. Planning of integration actions	0%	9%	45%	45%	15	73	5	15	17	5
7. Internal communication	5%	9%	59%	27%	13	57	6	13	15.5	6
8. Characteristics of the development and implementation team	5%	19%	67%	10%	2	4		2	1	
9. Accounting principles and practice	14%	27%	45%	14%	7	33		7	6.5	
10. Integration of financial data	14%	5%	59%	23%	11	45	7	11	13.5	8
11. Knowledge management	5%	27%	45%	23%	6	23		6	4.5	
12. Strong support from executives	0%	5%	38%	57%	19	84	4	19	21	1
13. Develop a comprehensive project with risk governance, optimizing the use of budget and time resources	0%	24%	57%	19%	4	18		4	3	
14. Have performed due diligence	5%	0%	33%	62%	18	116	2	18	20	2
15. Initiate integration planning during due diligence analysis	15%	20%	55%	10%	10	27		10	11.5	10
16. Promote the involvement of the management of both companies, acquirer and acquired	5%	33%	24%	38%	12	41	9	12	15	7
17. Make transparent and constant communication with employees	0%	10%	48%	43%	10	34		10	11.5	
18. Create a dedicated team for integration	0%	19%	48%	33%	9	35	10	9	9.5	

(continued)

Table 6 (continued)

19. Assess and address the cultural fit between the two organizations	5%	29%	43%	24%	6	34	6	4.5	
20. Develop a robust synergy plan	0%	10%	67%	24%	11	29	11	13.5	9
21. Allocate an appropriate budget for integration	5%	38%	43%	14%	7	17	7	6.5	
22. Hire an outside company to assist with integration	24%	43%	33%	0%	2	5	2	1	

(1)/(2)/(3)/(4) Not Critical, uncritical, critical, very critical

diligence. The sums of votes for each of the 22 CSF are presented, since voters should select from among the 22 proposed CSF the 10 most important ones, numbering them in the order of 1–10, where the first position represents the most important and the tenth position the least important. Column 3 in Table 6 presents also the ranking according to the Borda method: in first place, vision and values; in second place, have executed due diligence; in third place, look at culture and organization; in fourth place, have a strong support of the executives; in fifth place, planning of integration actions; in sixth place, internal communication; in seventh place, integration of financial data; in eighth place, image with stakeholders; in ninth place, promote the involvement of the management of both companies, acquirer and acquired; and, in tenth place, create a dedicated team for integration.

The critical success factors ordered by the Condorcet method are given in column 4 of Table 6. Thus, the ranking established by the voting of the 23 respondents according to Condorcet gives a priority to strong support by the executives, and the second place is given to the executed due diligence; in the third place, vision and values; in the fourth place, the look at the culture and the organization; in the fifth place, planning of integration actions; in the sixth place, internal communication; in the seventh place, promotion of the management of both companies' involvement (acquirer and acquired); in the eighth place, the integration of financial data; in the ninth place, to develop a robust plan of synergy, and in the tenth place, to start integration planning during the analysis of due diligence.

Table 7 presents results related to the characteristics of the organizations surveyed, where 1 equals totally disagree, 2 equals disagree, 3 equals neither disagree nor agree, 4 equals agree, and 5 equals fully agree. A 100% of respondents agree that their organization conducts their activities with a sense of responsibility and quality, ethical posture, and respect for the market and society.

Table 8 presents the consolidated answers to the question "What is the degree of importance of CSF for successful integration?" focusing on more effective exploration of the activities that must be prioritized for successful integration. While only seven items related to the communication and human resources management areas are listed, dissemination of best practices obtained 100% of the votes considering the relevant or very relevant topics. Effective communication reached 95%, and

Table 7 Characteristics of the organization

Which option most closely matches your organization?	1	2	3	4	5
Conducts its activities with a sense of responsibility and quality, ethical posture, and respect for the market and society	0%	0%	0%	18%	82%
Respect for the environment	0%	0%	9%	23%	68%
Support for social causes and contribution to the development of society	5%	0%	18%	41%	36%
Open and transparent in relation to its stakeholders	0%	5%	0%	41%	55%
Conduct your business ethically	0%	0%	5%	9%	86%
Promotes equal opportunities in the workplace	0%	0%	18%	36%	45%

(1)/(2)/(3)/(4)/(5) Totally disagree, disagree, neither disagree nor agree, agree, totally agree

Table 8 Degree of relevance of CSF in communication and human resources management

How important is CSF to a successful integration?	1	2	3	4
Effective communication	0%	5%	32%	64%
Integration of IT systems	9%	18%	64%	9%
Standardization of administrative processes	5%	32%	41%	23%
Standardization of HR policies	5%	9%	50%	36%
Dissemination of best practices	0%	0%	59%	41%
Team integration activities	0%	9%	32%	59%
Creation of a single brand	14%	27%	32%	27%

(1)/(2)/(3)/(4) Irrelevant, reasonably relevant, relevant, very relevant

completion of team integration activities obtained 91% in the same analysis. Next come standardization of human resources policies with 86% and integration of information technology systems with 73% relevant or very relevant. From these specific CSFs, it can be inferred that in the integration phase, the standardization of administrative processes and the creation of a single brand need not be prioritized.

Table 9 presents the three most significant factors to be prioritized in the case of a future transaction, duly ordered by the Borda method, which are (a) the best change management program, (b) more focus on cultural adequacy or better cultural alignment, and (c) better communication strategy with clients. The total value for each factor was obtained from the weighting, where the most important has weight 2, the second most important has weight 1, and the third most important does not score.

By the Condorcet method, in a future transaction, the three factors to be prioritized are (a) best change management program, (b) gradual/phased approach to integration, and (c) more planning before the agreement is announced (Table 10).

Type 2: Consulting Engineering Companies that Have Operated M&A

Among the 11 M&A transactions involving consulting engineering companies carried out in the last 10 years, contacts were made with 9 organizations and realized interviews with 7 of them, equivalent to 64% of the total operations identified. Regarding the sectors that the organization operates or has operated, 86% of them provide services in the infrastructure, environment, and transportation areas; 71% in water, buildings, and energy; and 57% in mining. Less than half surveyed (43%) provide services in steel and oil and gas. Five companies have between 100 and 499 employees, one has 500–1000 employees, and one company has over 1000 employees. All 100% of the companies interviewed were acquired by others, 43% of which were partially acquired and 57% were fully acquired. In all cases, the shareholding control was transferred to the purchasers, being 71% of these publicly held. The buyers are from Australia, Belgium, Spain, the USA, and the Netherlands. The company Arcadis Logos, buyer of the company ETEP, is Brazilian with 100% foreign capital. Tetra Tech acquired 100% of the CRA (Canadian) environment operation. The other acquired companies that have transferred their shareholding control, partial or total, to the buyers, are Brazilian. The operations were carried out

Table 9 Significant factors for future transaction according to the Borda method

In the case of a new transaction in the future, rank in order of importance the actions below	No. of votes	1	2	3	P2	P1	P0	Total	Ranking
Best change management program	10	6	3	1	12	3	0	15	1
Gradual/phased integration approach	10	4	1	5	8	1	0	9	
More rigorous selection of a leader/integration team	5	4	1	0	8	1	0	9	
More planning ahead of agreement announcement	6	3	2	1	6	2	0	8	
More focus on cultural adequacy or better cultural alignment	11	4	6		8	6	0	14	2
Faster pace of integration	2	0	1	1	0	1	0	1	
More planning as to the date of day 1—the day of the conclusion of ownership transfer between seller and buyer	3	0	1	2	0	1	0	1	
Initiate due diligence integration planning for better understanding of risk and integration efforts	6	1	3	2	2	3	0	5	
Best communication strategy with employees	12	2	5	5	4	5	0	9	
Biggest budget for integration	2	1	0	1	2	0	0	2	
Best communication strategy with customers	9	3	5	1	6	5	0	11	3
Best communication strategy with suppliers/distributors	3	0	1	2	0	1	0	1	
Others—HR policy	1	0	1	0	0	1	0	1	
Others—financial management	1	0	0	1	0	0	0	0	

1/(2)/(3) More important, second most important, third most important

from 3 to 7 years ago or from 2009 to 2013 obeying the maximum limit of 10 years established in the research criteria.

In terms of geographic performance, 89% of companies operate or have operated throughout the country, 100% in Latin America, and less than half (43%) in other countries.

The integration process between companies, post-formalization of M&A, had an average duration of 13.1 months, and 71% of transactions had a formal plan for integration. In 57% of operations performed, 80% of integration goals were achieved in less than 2 years.

Regarding the catalysts that led consulting engineering companies to carry out M&A transactions in Brazil, the survey identified that 100% of the respondents first indicated obtaining market share/increased market share/access to new markets as the main reason. In the survey conducted by Deloitte in 2015 considering all segments in the country, this was also the main reason for companies in Brazil with a percentage of 76%. This is the reason most cited by several authors (Bradley et al. 1987; Kimura and Suent 1997; Rossetti 2001; Barros et al. 2003).

Table 10 The most important factors for a future M&A operation

In the case of a new transaction in the future, rank in order of importance the actions below	No. of votes		1	2	3	4	5	6	7	8	9	10	11	12	13	14	Total	Ranking
Best change management program	10	1		0.5	1	1	0	1	1	1	0	1	1	1	1	1	10.5	1
Gradual/phased integration approach	10	2	0.5		1	1	0	1	1	1	0	1	1	1	1	1	10.5	2
More rigorous selection of a leader/integration team	5	3	0	0		0	0	1	1	0	0	1	0	1	1	1	6	
More planning ahead of agreement announcement	6	4	0	0	1		0	1	1	0.5	0	1	0	1	1	1	7.5	3
More focus on cultural adequacy or better cultural alignment	11	5	1	1	1	1		1	1	1	0	1	1	1	1	1	12	
Faster pace of integration	2	6	0	0	0	0	0		0	0	0	0.5	0	0	1	1	2.5	
More planning as to the date of day 1—the day of the conclusion of ownership transfer between seller and buyer	3	7	0	0	0	0	0	1		0	0	1	0	0.5	1	1	4.5	
Initiate due diligence integration planning for better understanding of risk and integration efforts	6	8	0	0	1	0.5	0	1	1		0	1	0	1	1	1	7.5	
Best communication strategy with employees	12	9	1	1	1	1	1	1	1	1		1	1	1	1	1	13	
Biggest budget for integration	2	10	0	0	0	0	0	0.5	0	0	0		0	0	1	1	2.5	
Best communication strategy with customers	9	11	0	0	1	1	0	1	1	1	0	1		1	1	1	9	
Best communication strategy with suppliers/distributors	3	12	0	0	0	0	0	1	0.5	0	0	1	0		1	1	4.5	
Others—HR policy	1	13	0	0	0	0	0	0	0	0	0	0	0	0		0.5	0.5	
Others—financial management	1	14	0	0	0	0	0	0	0	0	0	0	0	0	0.5		0.5	

1/(2)/(3) More important, second most important, third most important

Another reason that led the companies in the consulting engineering sector to carry out M&A activity was the development of new products and services/build new business capabilities with a 57% index, while in the consulting survey, this was also the second more selected reason with 39%. Less than half of respondents (42%) considered obtaining strategic and intangible assets such as technology, brand, distribution channels, brand image patents, experienced management, diversification, and market position as relevant reasons to engage in the M&A operation.

The average approximate value of 43% of the transactions carried out was up to US$ 100 million, the others being aligned with the research done by Barros et al. (2003), who concluded that M&A operations as a growth strategy are not limited to large companies.

Regarding the level of success of the integration phase, 85% of the respondents considered the process to be very successful or successful. Regarding due diligence, one of the respondents was not able to report on the services that were included in the scope of the same. The other companies performed due diligence. Of these, 100% included in the analysis the finance/accounting, labor/trade, and commercial analysis; 83% included tax and operational; half of the enterprises included human resources; and one third included information technology. In order to mitigate tax risk, 57% of operations used escrow accounts, and 43% worked with guarantees until risk prescription.

Members of the integration team in 86% of cases continued to perform their normal functions within the company while devoting part of their time to integration activities. The others had part of the team assigned full time.

Still in 86% of the companies, the alignment of cultures was very important for the success of the integration, and in 14%, it was misconducted prejudicing the integration. The point that strengthened the cultural alignment was the communication to the employees of both companies in a timely and transparent manner. The influence of organizational culture on M&A operations in general is confirmed by the high percentage of importance in consulting engineering companies in Brazil.

When questioned about synergies, only one third of executives indicated they had exceeded their synergy goals, while 43% were below expectations. In addition, one company is still in the process of measuring synergies, and another was not sure if it had achieved its objectives.

The functional areas with the greatest need for skills and competences for integration are, in this order, finance and accounting (cited by more than half of the respondents), sales and marketing (43%), and information technology and production in 28% of cases. Areas such as human resources, change management, operations, supplies, and communications have also been cited by at least one company. When comparing the results of the consulting engineering sector in Brazil against all other segments, according to Deloitte survey, sales and marketing is also the second most cited area, but information technology for all segments has a greater impact on integration of competences, coming first.

Factors such as capturing synergies and standardizing information systems were those that required more effort than initially expected in 43% of companies. Other factors mentioned in 28% of the cases each were managing cultural differences, adapting employees to the new scenario, and retaining key personnel. In the consulting survey, for all segments in Brazil, the most pressing action is to standardize information systems in 52% of cases, followed by manage cultural differences in 41% and capture synergies in 32% of companies. The action adapting employees to the new scenario was very close to the survey with 26%, and retaining key personnel was also identified as an important action in 23% of the cases.

7   Final Considerations

When ordinal ranking methods were applied in order to identify the ten main CSFs in post-merger integration and acquisition of consulting engineering companies in Brazil, in a total of 22 suggested CSFs, the results generated by Borda and Condorcet voting methods were similar in 80% of the CSF, that is, eight of them listed by the Borda were also considered within the order of the ten most relevant by the Condorcet method, regardless of the position occupied in the ranking. Therefore, 80% of the CSFs that are simultaneously related to the orders by the two methods should be prioritized and receive special attention in the integration process of consulting engineering companies in Brazil for the deals. The ten main factors of success in integration processes of consulting engineering companies in Brazil confirm their relevance in the phase in question, after formalization of the operation. The eight CSFs that were ordered in both methods are:

- Vision and values of organizations (first by Borda and third by Condorcet methods)
- Performed due diligence in the previous phase (second in both methods)
- Have strong support from executives (fourth by Borda but first by Condorcet methods)
- Look at culture and organization (third by Borda and fourth by Condorcet methods)
- Have a strong planning of integration actions (fifth in both methods)
- Internal communication (sixth place in both methods)
- Financial data integration (seventh in Borda and eighth in Condorcet methods)
- Promote the involvement of the management of both companies (in ninth by Borda and in seventh by Condorcet methods)

There are four CSFs that appear in only one of the methods. In Borda, the CSF image with stakeholders was ranked eighth and creation of a dedicated team for integration in tenth place. Under the Condorcet method, developing a robust synergy plan was ranked ninth, and integration planning during due diligence is at tenth place. Since they were also identified as the ten most impacting in at least one of the methods, it is concluded that they must also be considered in the integration process.

The results also suggest that integration process following the top ten CSFs can mitigate the errors and weaknesses detected in the processes and increase the chances to capture operational synergies and generate value. Given our analysis of the success factors, the challenges, and the risks, some fundamental points were observed:

- The main reason that led the consulting engineering companies in Brazil to M&A transactions was the acquisition of market share (products, services, geographic location, customers).
- The minor part of executives recognized that they had exceeded their synergy and about 43% of them have not reached their expectations.
- Regarding the level of success of the integration phase, 85% considered it to be very successful or successful.
- The duration of the integration process in this knowledge-based sector lasted on average 13.1 months, which was shorter than the national average for all industries that revolve around 2 years.
- Eighty-six percent of companies carried out due diligence demonstrating a trend of greater maturity in performing their integration plans in this sector.
- Capturing synergies and standardizing information systems became those factors that required more effort than initially expected in 43% of companies.

An important aspect found in the research and reinforced by the existing literature is the importance of the alignment of organizations' cultures.

The results of the CSFs identified by the two methods for consulting engineering firms suggest that these companies mainly employ the knowledge of their professionals to develop and commercialize intangible solutions for clients. Therefore, we can conclude that the same CSF can be attributed to other knowledge-intensive companies for M&A.

References

ABDI (Industrial Development Brazilian Association). (2011). *Relatório: Engenharia Consultiva no Brasil* (report: Consulting engineering in Brazil). São Paulo: ABDI.

Aquilani, B., Silvestri, C., Ruggieri, A., & Gatti, C. (2016). A systematic literature review on total quality management critical success factors and the identification of new avenues of research. *The TQM Journal, 29*, 184–213.

Barros, B (coordenação). (2001). *Fusões, aquisições & parcerias*. Atlas: São Paulo.

Barros, B., Souza, H., & Steuer, R. (2003). Gestão nos processos de fusões e aquisições (Merges and acquisitions processes management). In B. Barros (Ed.), *Fusões e aquisições no Brasil – Entendendo as razões dos sucessos e fracassos (Mergers and Acquisitions in Brazil—Understanding Reasons for Successes and Failures)*. São Paulo: Atlas.

Bradley, M., Desai, A., & Kim, E. (1987). Synergistic gains from the stockholders of target and acquiring firms. *Journal of Financial Economics, 1*, 3–40.

Bullen, C., & Rockart, F. (1981). *A primer on critical success factors*. Cambridge Center for Information Systems Research, Sloan School of Management, Massachusetts Institute of Technology, Massachusetts, USA.

Caklovic, L., & Kurdija, A. (2017). A universal voting system based on the potential method. *European Journal of Operational Research, 259*(2), 677–688.

Camargos, M., & Barbosa, F. (2010). Fusões e Aquisições de Empresas Brasileiras: Sinergias Operacionais, Gerenciais e Rentabilidade. *Revista de Contabilidade Vista & Revista, UFMG, Belo Horizonte, 21*(1), 69–99.

Danielson, M., & Ekenberg, L. (2017). Trade-offs for ordinal ranking methods in multi-criteria decisions. In D. Bajwa, S. Koeszegi, & R. Vetschera (Eds.), *Group decision and negotiation. Theory, empirical evidence, and application. GDN 2016* (Lecture notes in business information processing) (Vol. 274). Cham: Springer.

Deloitte. (2015). *Pesquisa de Integração Brasil 2015 – Entendendo os desafios para maximizar o investimento em M&A* (Brazil 2015 integration research project – Understanding the challenges to maximize investment in M&A), [online]. Retrieved April 12, 2016, from https://www2. deloitte.com/content/dam/Deloitte/br/Documents/mergers-acquisitions/Pesquisa-de-Integracao-Brasil-2015.pdf

ENR – Engineering News Record. (2015). *The 2015 Top 225 International Design Firms* [online]. Retrieved January 23, 2016, from http://www.enr.com/toplists/2015_Top_225_International_ Design_Firms1

Furlan, J., Ivo, I., & Amaral, F. (1994). *Sistemas de Informação Executiva (Executive information systems)*. São Paulo: Makron Books.

Giusti, M. (2000). *Fatores críticos de sucesso em operações de fusões e aquisições: A captura de valor através de sinergia (critical success factors in mergers and acquisitions: Capture value through synergies)*. São Paulo: FGV.

Johann, S. L. (2004). *Gestão da Cultura Corporativa: como as organizações de alto desempenho gerenciam sua cultura organizacional*. Saraiva: São Paulo.

Katz, J. (2005). A dinâmica do aprendizado tecnológico no período de substituição de importações e as recentes mudanças estruturais no setor industrial da Argentina, do Brasil e do México [The dynamics of technological learning in the period of import substitution and the recent structural changes in the industrial sector of Argentina, Brazil and Mexico]. In L. Kim & R. Nelson (Eds.), *Tecnologia, aprendizado e inovação: as experiências das economias de industrialização recente (Technology, learning and innovation: The experiences of the economies of recent industrialization)*. Unicamp: Campinas.

Kimura, H., & Suen, A. (1997). Fusões e aquisições Como estratégia de entrada no mercado brasileiro (mergers and acquisitions as an entry strategy in the Brazilian market). *Caderno de Pesquisas em Administração, 2*, 54–60.

Klimoski, R. (2016). Critical success factors for cybersecurity leaders: Not just technical competence. *People and Strategy, 39*(1), 14–18.

Levin, J., & Nalebuff, B. (1995). An introduction to vote-counting schemes. *The Journal of Economics Perspectives, 9*, 3–26.

Mello, M., Quintella, H., & Mello, J. (2004). Avaliação do desempenho de alunos considerando classificações obtidas e opiniões dos docentes (Evaluation of student performance considering classifications obtained and opinions of teachers). *Investigação Operacional, 24*, 187–196.

Molwus, J., Erdogan, B., & Ogunlana, S. (2017). Using structural equations modelling (SEM) to understand the relationships among critical success factors (CSF) for stakeholder management in construction. *Engineering, Construction and Architectural Management, 24*, 426–450.

Motta, L. F. J., Oliveira, P. V. C., Cavazotte, F. S. C. N., Pinto, A. C. F., & Klotzle, M. C. (2013). Criação de valor em fusões e aquisições brasileiras. *Revista de Administração FACES Journal, 12*(4), 100–119.

O Empreiteiro. (2015). *Ranking da Engenharia Brasileira (Brazilian engineering ranking)* [online]. Retrieved January 23, 2013, from https://www.revistaoempreiteiro.com.br

Orsi, A. (2000). Gestão do conhecimento – os modos de conversão do conhecimento nas incorporações de bases externas. *FACEF Pesquisa, 7*(2), 2004.

Pomerol, J., & Barba-Romero, S. (2000). *Multicriterion decision in management: Principles and practices*. Dordrech: Kluwer Academic Publishers.

Rockart, J. (1979). Chief executives define their own data needs [online]. *Harvard Business Review*. Retrieved May 03, 2016, from https://hbr.org/1979/03/chief-executives-define-their-own-data-need

Roldan, L., Hansen, P., & Dalé, L. (2011). Modelo de identificação de fatores críticos de sucesso na gestão de cadeias de suprimentos (Identification model of critical success factors in the management of supply chains). In *XIV Simpósio de Administração da Produção, Logística e Operações Internacionais* (XIV Symposium on Production, Logistics and International Operations Administration), São Paulo.

Rossetti, J. (2001). Fusões e aquisições no Brasil: As razões e os impactos (Mergers and acquisitions in Brazil: The reasons and impacts). In B. Barros (Ed.), *Fusões, Aquisições & Parcerias (Mergers, acquisitions and partnerships). Fundação Dom Cabral (Dom Cabral Foundation).* Belo Horizonte: Atlas.

Tideman, N., & Plassman, F. (2008). Evaluating voting rules by their probability of success: An empirical analysis. *Journal of Economic Literature*. Classification code: C4 D72.

Zollo, M., & Meier, D. (2008). What is M&A performance? *Academy of Management Perspectives, 22*, 55–75.

Domestic M&As in Russia: Performance and Success Factors

Ivan Rodionov and Vitaly Mikhalchuk

Abstract This research develops an approach to synergy analysis in domestic Russian mergers and acquisitions (M&As), tests potential success factors, and evaluates two types of operating and three types of financial synergies. This chapter makes two primary contributions to the literature. First, this chapter is related to the recent research that investigates M&As in emerging markets. Our chapter is unique in that we study domestic Russian M&As based on long-term firm accounting data. This approach captures private companies and small deals that make up the majority of the Russian M&A market. The second contribution is to estimate the structure of operating and financial synergies for every deal and test the significance of potential success factors. The scope is limited to domestic Russian M&As closed between January 2006 and September 2015. The sample is based on the Mergermarket database and includes 171 deals. Our analysis shows that after M&As, firms achieve -0.1% capital expenditure efficiency and -0.2% operating margin compared to the industry benchmark. Deals lead to 11.7% abnormal reduction of capital expenditures and cause 3.1% cost of debt growth. Deals create small tax benefits: the median for the whole sample is 87.5 million rubles, or 1.4% of the median deal value.

Keywords Mergers and acquisitions · Synergy · Company valuation · Emerging markets · Strategy · Economies of scale

1 Introduction

Mergers and acquisitions (M&As) remain one of the main ways companies develop and sustain competitiveness in developed and emerging markets. Because of the economic instability in 2014–2015, Russian companies are motivated to find successful domestic M&As.

I. Rodionov (✉) · V. Mikhalchuk (✉)
Department of Finance, National Research University Higher School of Economics, Moscow, Russia

© Springer Nature Switzerland AG 2020
I. Ivashkovskaya et al. (eds.), *Strategic Deals in Emerging Capital Markets*,
Advanced Studies in Emerging Markets Finance,
https://doi.org/10.1007/978-3-030-23850-6_8

Little research has been dedicated to studying domestic deals in developing countries mostly because there is no ready-to-use data available. Research about M&As in developing countries often focuses on deals made in BRICS countries. Existing research does not study different components of financial and operating synergies and the structure of synergies after M&As.

However, companies seek M&A opportunities for various reasons. Companies may be looking to reduce production costs, improve market position, buy new technologies, or lower cost of capital. Without analyzing the structure of synergies, many practical questions remain unanswered: Are some types of synergy easier to achieve than others? What success factors affect different types of synergy? Are operating and financial synergies correlated?

The second important aspect is industry analysis. Kenneth and Harford (2014) noted the significance of industry relations for the timing and incidence of merger waves. They found that merger activity in one industry leads to increased merger activity in other related industries. In this chapter, we analyze the synergies for M&As in Russian industries—manufacturing, telecoms, retail, and extraction of natural resources—merger timings, and the structure of synergies in these industries.

This research develops an approach to synergy analysis in domestic Russian M&As, tests potential success factors, and evaluates five types of operating and financial synergies. Operating synergies include economies of scale and market power. Financial synergies include tax benefits, new investment opportunities, and increased debt capacity. The scope is limited to deals between Russian companies.

The rest of this chapter is organized as follows. In Sect. 2 we derive a research hypothesis based on the existing literature on M&A synergies in developed and emerging markets. Section 3 presents a hypothesis for empirical tests. In Sect. 4 we develop a methodology for synergy valuation and an econometrical model for hypothesis tests. Section 5 describes industry and merger data. Section 6 presents a synergy valuation, and Sect. 7 presents the analysis of synergy structure. We test the hypothesis about M&A success factors in Sect. 8 and discuss major Russian mergers in Sect. 9. Section 10 concludes.

2 Derivation of Hypotheses for Russian Companies

2.1 Operating Synergies

Operating synergies are the synergies that allow companies to improve profitability, increase growth, or both. Recent research by Garzella and Fiorentino (2016) includes three main operating synergies:

- *Economies of scale* are usually created in mergers of companies in the same industry. They make the combined company more cost-efficient.

- Greater *market power* results in profitability growth from reduced competition and higher market share. This synergy is likely to arise in the concentrated industries or after large mergers.
- Synergistic combination of *functional strengths* after the M&As.

In this chapter we consider two types of operating synergies: economies of scale and market power.

Economies of scale are estimated with changes in capital expenditure (CAPEX) efficiency after M&As. This method is based on the assumption that the bidder will outperform the CAPEX efficiency benchmark. Applying this method, Maksimovic and Phillips (2001) and Kwoka and Pollitt (2010) concluded that M&As in the USA do not create economies of scale.

Nevertheless, scholars have recently provided some contrasting evidence. Zschille (2015) showed that the abnormal CAPEX efficiency improved after deals in Germany between 2006 and 2008. Agrell et al. (2015) reached the same conclusion for deals in Norway from 1995 to 2004.

There are several methods of estimating increased market power. The first method is based on market share analysis. It is assumed that the market structure has a direct effect on the financial results of competing companies. In concentrated markets, companies can earn more profits than companies in highly competitive markets.

Blonigen and Pierce (2016) used this method for M&As in the USA from 1997 to 2007 and Kyriazopoulos and Drumbetas (2015) for M&As in Europe between 1996 and 2010. Both chapters concluded that market share growth after M&As leads to an improvement in profitability for the bidder.

Some authors rely on the comparison of prices for the major goods and services of the bidder before and after the deal. If prices go up after the deal in a competitive market, the bidder has increased its market power. Similarly, abnormal growth of EBITDA, EBIT, or net income margins can be used as a proxy of increased market power.

Kim and Singal (1993) found abnormal growth of airplane ticket prices after large M&As in the industry. Sapienza (2002) found a reduction in deposit rates after M&As between commercial banks. On the other hand, several chapters (Berger et al. 1998; Eckbo 1983; Fee and Thomas 2004; Shahrur 2005; and others) did not find significant changes in prices after M&As.

In a perfect market, prices on goods and services would be one of the most precise proxy variables to estimate a change in market position. However, this method is hardly applicable for diversified companies in terms of products, services, or local markets.

Research of operating synergy with accounting methods in emerging markets has appeared since 2010. For M&As in the Philippines between 1994 and 2003, Cabanda and Pajara (2011) estimated 7.7% abnormal CAPEX efficiency reduction for the bidder after the deal closure. Pazarskis et al. (2006), Greece and Visic (2013), and Grigorieva and Petrunina (2015) looked at BRICS countries using profitability margins, and all concluded that M&As do not increase the bidder's market power.

2.2   Financial Synergies

The payoffs from financial synergies are either higher cash flows or a lower cost of capital. Damodaran (2005) includes the following financial synergies:

- *Tax benefits* from the net operating losses or faster amortization of the acquired company.
- *Investment opportunities* from the combination of the company with excess cash (and limited investment opportunities) and the company with high-return projects (and limited cash).
- *Lower cost of debt*, or increased debt capacity, if the combined company has more stable and predictable cash flows. This reduces the average cost of capital or allows the combined firm to borrow more, increasing its tax benefits.

Research of M&As on tax benefits is sparse even for developed countries. Hayn (1989), based on 640 deals in the USA in 1970–1985, showed that an abnormal return of the bidder's shares and accumulated deficit in the target company balance sheet have a strong positive correlation. Recent research (e.g., Chow et al. 2016) also used stock market data to analyze synergy from M&As driven by tax savings.

Devos et al. (2009) estimated the average tax benefit growth after M&As in the USA between 1980 and 2004 to be 1.6%. Elgemark (2014) on M&As in Denmark and Sweden estimated the average tax benefit growth to be 1.4%.

The most common approach to estimate investment opportunities for a company is *Tobin's q* coefficient, calculated as the ratio of its equity market value to equity book value. Recent chapters demonstrate that companies with low *Tobin's q* will seek M&A opportunities (Nguyen et al. 2012; Boyson et al. 2017). However, in emerging markets equity market value is often unavailable; therefore, *Tobin's q* can be applied to very few deals.

The method with abnormal CAPEX growth developed in Bruner (2002) and Rhodes-Kropf and Viswanathan (2004) is more suitable for emerging markets. This method assumes that the bidder had access to investment opportunities after the deal if its CAPEX growth is higher than the industry benchmark. Ovtchinnikov (2013), based on 7858 deals in the USA between 1980 and 2008, estimated this decline to be 0.2%. Agliardi et al. (2016) based on 1121 deals larger than $100 million in the USA between 1980 and 2010 estimated this decline as 4.3%.

Debt capacity after M&As has been researched with the analysis of the correlation between bidder and target company free cash flows (Lewellen 1971) or with cost of debt estimation (Damodaran 2005).

Recent chapters based on Lewellen's approach (e.g., Mooney and Shim 2015) show that debt capacity will not increase if the correlation between cash flows is positive. M&As between companies with a negative correlation between cash flows have a significant positive effect on debt capacity. It is difficult to apply this method to emerging markets, because there is usually not enough financial data to calculate free cash flows for private companies.

Damodaran (2005) proposed using cost of debt as a proxy variable for debt capacity. Data about the cost of debt is taken from public or synthetic credit ratings. The latter is based on the interest coverage ratio that is available from profit and loss statements. With this method, Karampatsas et al. (2014) found that deals between companies with investment grade credit rating in the USA between 1998 and 2009 increased debt capacity.

The research of financial synergies is mostly based on data from China and India as the largest emerging M&A markets. Tao et al. (2017) found that companies with low leverage in China tend to adjust their leverage ratios and increase tax benefits with M&As. Bhagat et al. (2011) and Du and Boateng (2015) used the correlation of cash flows as a proxy variable for cost of debt and, similar to developed countries, found that companies with low correlation of cash flows create better financial synergy in emerging markets.

2.3 Synergy Success Factors

There is a vast amount of literature about factors and conditions of synergy creation in M&As. The majority study deals in developed countries, especially the USA as the largest market. Studies of developing markets in the last 10–15 years have mostly focused on Eastern Europe and BRICS countries.

Significant company-specific factors include industry (Lin and Chou 2016), size (Grigoryeva and Grinchenko 2014; Rogova and Luzina 2015), concentration of ownership (Bhaumik and Selarka 2012), type of ownership (Rani et al. 2012), and others. Significant deal-specific factors include deal value (Grigoryeva and Troitsky 2012), type of merger (Healy et al. 1992), and others. Macroeconomic factors, such as GDP and industry growth, are significant for synergy as well.

Overall, evidence on the impact of many factors in emerging markets is not consistent and depends on the features of particular countries.

3 Hypotheses

Our hypotheses are based on previous research for developed and emerging markets. We test nine hypotheses on each type of operating and financial synergy—economies of scale, market power, tax benefits, investment opportunities, and cost of debt.

We test the hypotheses on the whole sample of 171 deals and separately on 2 smaller samples: one for deals completed during Russian M&A market growth (2006–2007 and 2010–2012, 101 deals total) and one during crisis (2008–2009 and 2013–2015, 70 deals total). The growth and crisis split is based on the annual Russian M&A volume. In 2013 the Russian M&A market shrunk to $115 billion from $136 billion. In 2014 the market size reduced further to $71 billion (KPMG 2015).

Hypothesis 1 *Deals create higher synergies if both the target and the bidder operate in the same industry.*

Existing research has mixed results about testing this hypothesis. Moeller and Schlingemann (2005) showed that being part of the same industry helps in creating synergies, although this variable is not significant in all countries and industries. On the other hand, Chatterjee (2007) provides several well-known examples of unsuccessful M&As between companies in the same industry, notably, AOL/Time Warner and Hewlett-Packard/Compaq.

For Hypothesis 1 we test the significance of the dummy variable *industry*. Industry is taken from the SPARK database as the bidder's dominant activity according to the Russian National Classification of Economic Activities. If both the target and the bidder have the same dominant industry, the variable is equal to 1 and 0 otherwise.

Hypothesis 2 *Vertical deals create higher synergies than horizontal deals.*

Eckbo (1983) and Grigoryeva and Grinchenko (2014) tested this hypothesis with a regression model based on cumulative average returns and Healy et al. (1992) with a regression model based on financial data.

For Hypothesis 2 we test the significance of the dummy variable *type*. The type of deal is equal to 1 if the deal is vertical and 0 if the deal is horizontal. Deal types are taken from the Mergermarket database. According to Mergermarket methodology, a deal is considered horizontal if the companies compete at least in one market. The deal is considered vertical, if companies operate on a different stage of production.[1]

Hypothesis 3 *Smaller companies achieve higher synergies in M&As.*

In recent chapters, the effect of the bidder company size was studied in Johnston et al. (2014) using the number of employees as a proxy variable and in Dionne et al. (2015) using a natural logarithm of total assets. Both chapters showed that smaller companies integrate targets easier and achieve better results in the acquisitions.

In terms of economies of scale, small companies should achieve potentially greater synergy from M&As than the large ones. For Hypothesis 3 we test the significance of the variable *lnassets*—natural logarithm of bidder's assets 1 year before the deal closure (million rubles).

Hypothesis 4 *Deals with public targets create higher synergies than deals with private targets.*

Asymmetric information between the bidder and the target has a significant impact on the decision to complete M&As (Myers and Majluf 1984). With more information available about public targets, bidders will be able to make better forecasts about the outcome of their M&As.

---

[1] See methodology at https://data.bvresources.com/pdf/CPS-FAQ.pdf.

For Hypothesis 4 we test the significance of the dummy variable *tpublic*. It is equal to 1 for public targets and 0 for private targets.

Hypothesis 5 *Deals initiated by private bidders create higher synergies than deals initiated by public bidders.*

The majority of chapters that research this hypothesis conclude that public bidders offer considerably higher premiums than private bidders. For example, Bargeron et al. (2008) in 1667 deals in the USA estimated the average premium by public bidders as 63%. This extra premium reduces potential synergy, and therefore public bidders have worse results than private bidders.

For Hypothesis 5 we test the significance of the dummy variable *bpublic*. It is equal to 1 for public bidders and 0 for private bidders.

Hypothesis 6 *Larger deals create lower synergies than smaller deals.*

Following several recent chapters (e.g., Grigoryeva and Troitsky 2012), we assume that larger expenses for completing a deal (both absolute and relative to bidder's annual revenue) reduce potential synergy.

For Hypothesis 6 we test the significance of variables *lndealval* (natural logarithm of deal value in million dollars) and *prevenue* (ratio of deal value to bidder's annual revenue).

Hypothesis 7 *Bidders with a higher concentration of ownership create lower synergies.*

Companies with a higher concentration of ownership have less developed corporate management and control systems (Yasser et al. 2017). In developed markets these companies have worse results in M&As than companies with a more diversified ownership structures (Rossi and Volpin 2004).

For Hypothesis 7 we test the significance of the variable *conc*, calculated as the sum of the top 3 shareholder shares in bidder's total equity capital (%).

Hypothesis 8 *Bidders with better accounting performance create higher synergies.*

Recent academic (Madsen and Wu 2016) and practical (Bain & Company 2014) chapters suggest that bidders with better accounting performance (profitability, employee productivity, CAPEX efficiency, etc.) achieve better results in M&As. Bidders with poor performance usually cannot improve their position by buying another company.

For Hypothesis 8 we test the significance of several lagged variables related to the accounting measures of performance: CAPEX efficiency, EBIT margin, the cost of debt for economies of scale, market power, and debt capacity models, respectively. Hypothesis 8 is not tested for tax benefits and new investment opportunity models.

Hypothesis 9 *Deals completed during economic and industry growth create higher synergies.*

GDP or industry growth is used very often in research as one of the explanatory variables. Normally M&As during economic or industry growth have significantly better results. Recent research related to this problem includes Ray (2014) and Levine et al. (2015).

For Hypothesis 9 we test the significance of several macroeconomic variables, such as real Russian GDP growth, average CAPEX efficiency for the bidder's industry, average EBIT margin for the bidder's industry, and CAPEX growth rate for the bidder's industry.

4 Methodology

4.1 Economies of Scale

We analyze the effect of M&As on economies of scale with the abnormal growth of CAPEX efficiency as the main metric. By CAPEX efficiency we understand the sum of capital investments required to generate 1 dollar of revenue, or CAPEX-to-revenue ratio.

The model is stated as:

1. Calculate CAPEX efficiency for the bidder and its industry for the year before and the year after the deal closure using:

$$CAPEX\ efficiency = \frac{CAPEX}{Revenue}$$

2. Calculate the change in CAPEX efficiency for the bidder and industry.
3. Calculate the economies of scale as the difference between the bidder and the industry CAPEX efficiency performance:

$$Economy\ of\ scale = \Delta CAPEX\ efficiency_{bidder} - \Delta CAPEX\ efficieny_{industry}$$

4. Hypothesis testing is based on linear regression model (Eq. 1):

$$
\begin{aligned}
Wecapex_{i,t+1} = {}&\alpha_i + \beta_0 Wecapex_{i,t-1} + \beta_1 industry_{i,t} + \beta_2 type_{i,t} \\
&+ \beta_3 lnassets_{i,t-1} + \beta_4 tpublic_{i,t} + \beta_5 bpublic_{i,t} + \beta_6 gdp_{i,t} \\
&+ \beta_7 lndealval_{i,t} + \beta_8 prevenue_{i,t} + \beta_9 conc_{i,t} + \beta_{10} iecapex_{i,t} \\
&+ \varepsilon_{i,t}
\end{aligned}
\tag{1}
$$

where *Wecapex* is the bidder's CAPEX efficiency (corrected for outliers with winsorizing, %); *industry* is a dummy variable, equal to 1 if both companies operate in the same industry and 0 otherwise; *type* is a dummy variable, equal to 1 for vertical deals and 0 for horizontal deals; *lnassets* is the natural logarithm of the bidder's assets the year before the deal closure (million rubles); *tpublic* is a dummy variable, equal to 1 for a public bidder and 0 otherwise; *bpublic* is a dummy variable, equal to 1 for a public target and 0 otherwise; *gdp* is real Russian GDP growth in 2008 prices according to the Russian Federal State Statistics Service (%); *lndealval* is the natural logarithm of the deal value (million USD); and *prvalue* is the relative deal value calculated as the ratio of the deal value to the bidder's annual revenue for the year before the deal closure (%). If needed, the average annual exchange rate for the year before the deal closure is used for ruble to USD conversion; *conc* is the concentration of ownership for the bidder, calculated as the sum of the top three shareholder shares in total equity capital (%); *iecapex* is the industry CAPEX efficiency (%); β is a regression coefficient; α is the intercept term; ε_i is an error term; t is the year of the deal closure; and i is the index of a deal in the sample.

4.2 Market Power

We estimate the effect of M&As on market power with the abnormal growth of EBIT margin as the main metric.

The model is stated as:

1. Calculate the EBIT margin for the bidder and its industry for the year before and the year after deal closure using:

$$EBIT\ margin = \frac{EBIT}{Revenue}$$

2. Calculate the change in the EBIT margin for the bidder and the industry.
3. Calculate the effect on the market power as the difference between the bidder and the industry EBIT margin performance:

$$Effect\ on\ market\ position = \Delta EBIT\ margin_{bidder} - \Delta EBIT\ margin_{industry}$$

4. Hypotheses testing is based on linear regression model (Eq. 2):

$$\begin{aligned}
Webitm_{i,t+1} = {} & \alpha + \beta_0 Webitm_{i,t-1} + \beta_1 industry_{i,t} + \beta_2 type_{i,t} + \beta_3 lnassets_{i,t-1} \\
& + \beta_4 tpublic_{i,t} + \beta_5 bpublic_{i,t} + \beta_6 gdp_{i,t} + \beta_7 lndealval_{i,t} \\
& + \beta_8 prevenue_{i,t} + \beta_9 conc_{i,t} + \beta_{10} iebitm_{i,t} + \varepsilon_{i,t}
\end{aligned} \tag{2}$$

where *Webitm* is the bidder's EBIT margin (corrected for outliers with winsorizing, %) and *iebitm* is the industry EBIT margin (%). Other explanatory variables are the same as in Eq. (1) for economies of scale.

4.3 Tax Benefits

The tax benefit is estimated with total debt, risk-free rate, and effective tax rate for the bidder. For the risk-free rate calculation, we use yield to maturity of 10-year Russian government bonds from cbonds.ru.

The model is stated as:

1. Calculate the tax benefit for the bidder for the year before and the year after the deal closure using the formula:

$$Tax\ shield = Total\ debt \times Effective\ tax\ rate \\ \times YTM\ of\ 10\ years\ Russian\ government\ bonds$$

2. Calculate the synergy from the tax benefit as the difference between the tax benefit after and before the deal:

$$\Delta Tax\ shield = Tax\ shield_{after\ deal} - Tax\ shield_{before\ deal}$$

3. Hypotheses testing is based on the linear regression model (Eq. 3):

$$Wtax_i = \alpha_i + \beta_1 industry_{i,t} + \beta_2 type_{i,t} + \beta_3 lnassets_{i,t-1} + \beta_4 tpublic_{i,t} \\ + \beta_5 bpublic_{i,t} + \beta_6 gdp_{i,t} + \beta_7 lndealval_{i,t} + \beta_8 prevenue_{i,t} + \beta_9 conc_{i,t} \\ + \varepsilon_{i,t} \tag{3}$$

where $Wtax$ is the change in tax benefit for the bidder between the year before and after the deal (corrected for outliers with winsorizing, mln rubles). Other explanatory variables are the same as in Eq. (1) for economies of scale.

4.4 Investment Opportunities

We estimate the effect of M&As on investment opportunities with the abnormal CAPEX growth as the main metric.

The model is stated as:

1. Calculate the CAPEX growth rate for the bidder and its industry between the year before and the year after the deal closure using:

$$CAPEX\ growth = \frac{CAPEX_{t+1}}{CAPEX_{t-1}} - 1$$

2. Calculate the effect on investment opportunities as the difference between the bidder and the industry CAPEX growth performance:

$$Effect\ on\ investment\ opportunities = \Delta CAPEX\ growth_{bidder} \\ - \Delta CAPEX\ growth_{industry}$$

3. Hypotheses testing is based on the linear regression model (Eq. 4):

$$Wecapexg_i = \alpha_i + \beta_1 industry_{i,t} + \beta_2 type_{i,t} + \beta_3 lnassets_{i,t-1} + \beta_4 tpublic_{i,t}$$
$$+ \beta_5 bpublic_{i,t} + \beta_6 gdp_{i,t} + \beta_7 lndealval_{i,t} + \beta_8 prevenue_{i,t}$$
$$+ \beta_9 conc_{i,t} + \beta_{10} icapexg + \varepsilon_{i,t} \tag{4}$$

where *Wecapexg* is the bidder's CAPEX growth rate between the year before and after the deal (corrected for outliers with winsorizing, %) and *icapexg* is the industry CAPEX growth rate between the year before and after the deal (%). Other explanatory variables are the same as in Eq. (1) for economies of scale.

4.5 Debt Capacity

We estimate the effect of M&As on debt capacity using Damodaran's (2005) approach based on the cost of debt as the main metric. The cost of debt is estimated with credit ratings. If the credit rating for the bidder is unavailable, a synthetic credit rating is assigned according to its interest coverage ratio.

The model is stated as:

1. Calculate the interest coverage ratio for the bidder for the year before and the year after the deal closure using the formula:

$$ICR = \frac{EBIT}{Interest\ expenses}$$

2. Assign a synthetic credit rating to the interest coverage ratio according to Damodaran's data (Tables 1 and 2). Steps 1 and 2 are redundant if the bidder already has a credit rating by one of the international rating agencies.
3. Calculate the cost of debt for the bidder 1 year before and 1 year after the deal closure as the sum of YTM of 10-year Russian government bonds and the default spread.

Cost of debt = YTM of 10 *years Russian government bonds + Default spread*

4. Calculate the effect on debt capacity as the difference between the bidder's cost of debt after and before the deal.

Effect on debt capacity = Cost of debt$_{after\ deal}$ − Cost of debt$_{before\ deal}$

5. Hypotheses testing is based on the linear regression model (Eq. 5):

Table 1 Ratings, interest coverage ratios, and default spread for large companies with market cap > $5 billion

Interest coverage ratio	Rating	Default spread, %
>8.5	Aaa/AAA	0.75
6.5–8.5	Aa2/AA	1.00
5.5–6.5	A1/A+	1.10
4.5–5.5	A2/A	1.25
3.0–4.25	A3/A−	1.75
2.5–3.0	Baa2/BBB	2.25
2.25–2.5	Ba1/BB+	3.25
2–2.25	Ba2/BB	4.25
1.75–2.0	B1/B+	5.50
1.5–1.75	B2/B	6.50
1.25–1.5	B3/B−	7.50
0.8–1.25	Caa/CCC	9.00
0.65–0.8	Ca2/CC	12.00
0.2–0.65	C2/C	16.00
<0.2	D2/D	20.00

Source: http://pages.stern.nyu.edu/~adamodar/New_Home_Page/datafile/ratings.htm

Table 2 Ratings, interest coverage ratios, and default spread for smaller companies with market cap <$ 5 billion

Interest coverage ratio	Rating	Default spread, %
>12.5	Aaa/AAA	0.75
9.5–12.5	Aa2/AA	1.00
7.5–9.5	A1/A+	1.10
6.0–7.5	A2/A	1.25
4.5–6.0	A3/A−	1.75
4.0–4.5	Baa2/BBB	2.25
3.5–4.0	Ba1/BB+	3.25
3.0–3.5	Ba2/BB	4.25
2.5–3.0	B1/B+	5.50
2.0–2.5	B2/B	6.50
1.5–2.0	B3/B−	7.50
1.25–1.5	Caa/CCC	9.00
0.8–1.25	Ca2/CC	12.00
0.5–0.8	C2/C	16.00
<0.5	D2/D	20.00

Source: http://pages.stern.nyu.edu/~adamodar/New_Home_Page/datafile/ratings.htm

$$Debt_{i,t+1} = \alpha_i + \beta_0 Debt_{i,t-1} + \beta_1 indindustry_{i,t} + \beta_2 type_{i,t} + \beta_3 lnassets_{i,t-1}$$
$$+ \beta_4 tpublic_{i,t} + \beta_5 bpublic_{i,t} + \beta_6 gdp_{i,t} + \beta_7 lndealval_{i,t}$$
$$+ \beta_8 prevenue_{i,t} + \beta_9 conc_{i,t} + \varepsilon_{i,t} \tag{5}$$

where *Debt* is the bidder's cost of debt (%). Other explanatory variables are the same as in Eq. (1) for economies of scale.

5 Sample

We used the Mergermarket M&A database with several restrictions:

- Deal type: acquisition or merger.
- Deal was completed between 1 January 2006 and 16 September 2015.
- Dominant geography of operations for target and bidder: Russia.
- Type of ownership for target and bidder: public and/or private.
- Type of payment: shares and/or cash.
- Type of deal: vertical or horizontal.
- Database has information about all deal-specific characteristics (deal value, date, type of deal, etc.).

The following deals were excluded from the sample:

- Bidder has no public financial statements for the year before and the year after deal closure.
- Bidder ceased operations 2 years or less after the deal (because of acquisition, bankruptcy, etc.). These deals do not provide enough financial data to estimate synergy with our approach.
- Deal value is less than 5% of bidder's revenue.
- Target and bidder operate in utilities or financial industries.

There are 171 deals in the final sample. Financial data was collected from SPARK Interfax database, Bloomberg, and official company websites. Macroeconomic and industry data was collected from the Russian Federal State Statistics Service and the Central Bank of Russia.

The description of the variables and their descriptive statistics are provided in Table 3.

6 Synergy Valuation

Table 4 summarizes the valuation of the five synergy components during Russian M&A market growth (2006–2007 and 2010–2012) and crisis (2008–2009 and 2013–2015) and over the whole period from 2006 to 2015. All numbers are medians to overcome the asymmetric distribution of data.

Domestic deals in Russia do not create operating synergies: bidders achieve −0.1% CAPEX efficiency and −0.2% EBIT margin compared to the industry benchmark. In every period the deals lead to significant reduction of CAPEX after the deal—from 9.1% for "growth deals" up to 20.3% for "crisis deals." Similarly,

Table 3 Descriptive statistics

Variable	Description	Units	N	Max.	Min.	Mean	25%	50%	75%	Std. deviation
Wecapex (t+1)	CAPEX efficiency for the bidder 1 year after the deal closure	%	171	0.330	0.000	0.095	0.004	0.054	0.165	0.102
Wecapex (t−1)	CAPEX efficiency for the bidder 1 year before the deal closure	%	171	0.320	0.000	0.093	0.005	0.065	0.156	0.096
Webitm (t+1)	EBIT margin for the bidder 1 year after the deal closure	%	171	0.434	−0.033	0.175	0.054	0.160	0.272	0.138
Webitm (t−1)	EBIT margin for the bidder 1 year before the deal closure	%	171	0.523	−0.015	0.195	0.065	0.157	0.313	0.153
Wtax	Change in tax benefit after the deal closure	mln rubles	171	3,517,576	−263,147	515,184	3488	87,547	497,894	976,779
Wcapexg	Growth of CAPEX for the bidder after the deal closure	%	171	3.717	−0.991	0.456	−0.296	0.036	0.759	1.222
Debt(t+1)	Cost of debt for the bidder 1 year after the deal closure	%	171	0.270	0.073	0.154	0.108	0.138	0.203	0.056
Debt(t−1)	Cost of debt for the bidder 1 year before the deal closure	%	171	0.249	0.073	0.125	0.085	0.103	0.174	0.051
Industry	1, if both the target and the bidder operate in the same industry; 0 otherwise	Dummy	171	1	0	0.497	0	0	1	0.501
Type	1 for vertical deals, 0 for horizontal deals	Dummy	171	1	0	0.345	0	0	1	0.477
lnassets	Natural logarithm of assets (bidder company) at the end of the year of deal closure	mln rubles	171	23	10	17	15	17	19	2.303
tpublic	1 for the public target companies; 0 for the private target companies	Dummy	171	1	0	0.298	0	0	1	0.459
bpublic	1 for the public bidder companies; 0 for the private bidder companies	Dummy	171	1	0	0.719	0	1	1	0.451
lndealval	Natural logarithm of deal value	mln USD.	171	10.240	1.609	5.203	3.761	5.081	6.633	1.842

Prevenue	Ratio of deal value to the bidder's annual revenue	%	171	132	0.046	2.994	0.126	0.272	0.837	14
conc	Concentration of ownership for the bidder (sum of shares for top 3 shareholders)	%	171	1.000	0.240	0.832	0.675	0.980	1.000	0.214
gdp	Annual real Russian GDP growth (2008 prices)	%	171	0.085	−0.078	0.036	0.013	0.043	0.052	0.039
iecapex	CAPEX efficiency for the bidder's industry	%	171	0.732	0.004	0.184	0.065	0.170	0.223	0.149
iebitm	EBIT margin for the bidder's industry	%	171	0.482	−0.010	0.190	0.092	0.145	0.289	0.113
icapexg	Growth of CAPEX for the bidder's industry	%	171	1.245	−0.255	0.317	0.085	0.293	0.469	0.296

Source: authors' analysis

Table 4 Synergy valuation by components during growth and crisis

Period (number of deals)	Median abnormal CAPEX efficiency growth, %	Median EBIT margin growth, %	Median abnormal CAPEX growth, %	Median tax benefits growth, million rubles	Median reduction (−) or growth (+) of cost of debt, %
Growth (101)	−1.3	−0.5	−9.1	87.8	0.6
Crisis (70)	0.5	0.1	−20.3	80.2	4.5
Total (171)	−0.1	−0.2	−11.7	87.5	3.1

Source: authors' calculations

Table 5 Synergy valuation by components in different industries

Industry (number of deals)	Median abnormal CAPEX efficiency growth, %	Median EBIT margin growth, %	Median abnormal CAPEX growth, %	Median tax benefits growth, million rubles	Median reduction (−) or growth (+) of cost of debt, %
Manufacturing (45)	−1.4	3.5	−19.1	153.6	2.9
Telecoms (32)	0.9	−0.4	5.7	124.0	3.3
Extraction of natural resources (31)	−1.0	−0.1	30.6	470.9	3.0
Retail (25)	0.1	1.7	−29.3	57.2	2.2
Total (171)	−0.1	−0.2	−11.7	87.5	3.1

Source: authors' calculations

deals cause growth of the cost of debt for bidder companies, and this effect is more severe for "crisis deals." Deals create tax benefits; however, they are small—only 87.5 million rubles for the whole sample (about 1.4% of median deal value).

Table 5 summarizes the valuation of the five synergy components for manufacturing, telecoms, extraction of natural resources, and retail industries.

In the manufacturing industry deals are relatively more successful in increasing market power compared to other industries. Only 40% of the deals in the manufacturing industry create investment opportunities, and bidders experience 19.1% abnormal CAPEX decline after the deal.

In contrast, deals in telecoms are more successful in creating investment opportunities. The search for new investments is one the major motives for M&As in this industry because of the quickly developing technologies and large R&D spending. A significant portion of deals in telecoms are motivated by getting access to new technologies by competitors.

Deals in the extraction of natural resources (mining, oil, and gas) are the most successful in Russia. Bidders in this industry outperform, or at least match, both the industry benchmark and bidders in other industries. A lot of deals in mining and oil and gas are aimed at large mining or extraction assets and lead to abnormal growth of CAPEX. Deals is this industry are also larger on average (2643 million USD vs 558 million USD for other industries) and create bigger tax benefits.

In retail deals often aimed at direct competitors and increase bidder's market power. Deals in this industry lead to significant abnormal decline of CAPEX (−29.3%) and moderate growth of cost of debt (2.2%).

7   Analysis of Synergy Structure

To get a better picture of operating and financial synergies we introduce ranking for deals in the sample. The ranking goes as follows:

- For every deal, we estimate the value of operating and financial synergy components according to the approach described in the "Methodology" section. The next two steps apply to every synergy component.
- Deals with positive synergy are split into five equal 20-percentile groups. Deals in the top 20 percentile get a score of "5," deals in second 20-percentile group get a score of "4," and so forth until score "1" for deals in the bottom 20-percentile group.
- Deals with negative synergy are also split into five equal 20-percentile groups. Deals in the bottom 20 percentile get a score of "−5," deals in the second 20-percentile group get a score of "−4," and so forth until score "−1" for deals in the top 20-percentile group.
- For operating synergies, the maximum score for the deal is 10 (two components with a maximum score of 5 each).
- For financial synergies, the maximum score for the deal is 15 (three components with a maximum score of 5 each).
- The total score for each deal is −25 to 25, inclusive.

Operational synergy is plotted on x-axis and financial synergy is plotted on y-axis. Deals that create both types of synergy are located in quadrant I; deals that create financial synergy and destroy operational synergy are located in quadrant II; deals that destroy both types of synergy are located in quadrant III; deals that create operational synergy and destroy financial synergy are located in quadrant IV.

The structure of synergies in domestic Russian M&As during growth and crisis is illustrated in Fig. 1.

During crisis operating synergies prevail: 63% of the deals create operating synergy and only 42% create financial synergies. During growth the picture is almost the opposite: only 44% of the deals create operating synergies, and 61% create financial synergies.

It is also interesting that during crisis very few deals lead to the exchange of operating synergies for financial synergies (only 7%, quadrant II) and during growth

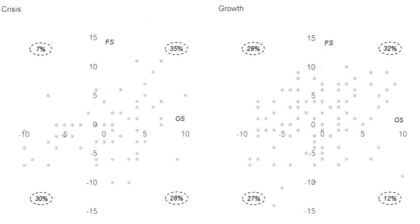

Fig. 1 Synergy structure in domestic Russian M&As during growth and crisis

very few deals lead to the exchange of financial synergies for operating synergies (12%, quadrant IV).

The structure of synergies in domestic Russian M&As for major industries is illustrated in Fig. 2.

The extraction of natural resources industry has the highest percentage of deals with an exchange between financial and operating synergies (54% of the total number of deals). In telecoms, on the other hand, only 28% of deals feature this exchange between synergies. The majority of deals either create both types of synergy (45%) or none (27%).

In manufacturing, 62% of the deals create financial synergies. Very few deals have positive operating synergies and negative financial synergies (quadrant IV). In retail, the majority of deals are clustered around (0,0) score. There are only a few particularly successful deals in the first quadrant.

8 Synergy Success Factors

8.1 Economies of Scale

Equation (2) for economies of scale has a good fit with the data (minimal $R^2 = 0.54$). For the entire period (Table 6), several factors significantly affect economies of scale: favorable macroeconomic conditions (both GDP and industry), the bidder's CAPEX efficiency before the deal, and the type of ownership for both the bidder and the target.

During M&A market growth, bidders overpay for deals as the coefficient for relative deal value is negative and strongly significant. During crisis, vertical M&As are more successful.

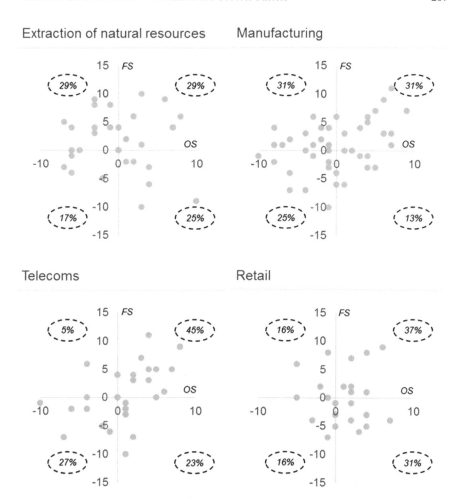

Fig. 2 Synergy structure in domestic Russian M&As for major industries

8.2 Market Power

Applying Eq. (2) to the data shows that the lagged EBIT margin is consistently significant for increasing market power during all periods (Table 7).

During growth and crisis, significant factors are quite different. During growth, possible successful deal profiles are large companies involved in horizontal deals or smaller companies involved in relatively large deals for their size. During crisis, the deal size and the concentration of ownership in the bidder's capital have a negative effect on synergy. The latter means that bidders with more diversified ownership structure can estimate potential synergy better.

Table 6 Economies of scale model

Variable	Whole sample (2006–2014)	Growth (2006–2007, 2010–2012)	Crisis (2008–2009, 2013–2014)
Wecapex (t−1)	0.762*** (0.063)	0.895*** (0.074)	0.698*** (0.085)
Industry	−0.011 (0.011)	−0.024 (0.016)	0.013 (0.012)
Type	0.003 (0.012)	−0.002 (0.018)	0.035*** (0.012)
lnassets	0.000 (0.004)	0.004 (0.005)	0.004 (0.005)
tpublic	0.035*** (0.012)	0.023 (0.016)	0.030* (0.016)
bpublic	−0.044** (0.018)	−0.056* (0.030)	−0.026 (0.017)
lndealval	−0.002 (0.005)	−0.006 (0.006)	−0.007 (0.005)
Prevenue	−0.001 (0.001)	−0.003*** (0.000)	0.000 (0.000)
conc	−0.048 (0.032)	−0.025 (0.050)	−0.031 (0.029)
gdp	0.213* (0.129)	0.104 (0.400)	−0.228 (0.158)
iecapexg	0.240** (0.110)	0.261 (0.187)	0.079 (0.091)
_cons	0.091 (0.062)	0.050 (0.083)	−0.017 (0.072)
R^2	0.54	0.54	0.75
N	171	101	70

The standard deviation of coefficients is in the brackets
***Significant at the 1% level
**Significant at the 5% level
*Significant at the 10% level

8.3 Tax Benefits

Larger deals consistently generate larger tax benefits, according to Eq. (3). These deals significantly affect financial statements of bidders, their tax benefit, in particular.

A second interesting observation is that deals closed during economic growth generate larger tax benefits (Table 8). This is likely because during crisis target companies accumulate a balance sheet deficit that bidders convert into tax synergy after the deal.

Table 7 Market power model

Variable	Whole sample (2006–2014)	Growth (2006–2007, 2010–2012)	Crisis (2008–2009, 2013–2014)
Webitm (t-1)	0.555*** (0.061)	0.545*** (0.096)	0.640*** (0.068)
Industry	0.007 (0.017)	0.030 (0.024)	−0.016 (0.026)
Type	−0.008 (0.017)	−0.039* (0.022)	0.036 (0.026)
lnassets	0.009 (0.007)	0.019** (0.008)	−0.016* (0.009)
tpublic	0.010 (0.021)	0.021 (0.028)	−0.003 (0.030)
bpublic	0.001 (0.023)	−0.013 (0.033)	0.023 (0.027)
lndealval	−0.009 (0.009)	−0.019* (0.011)	0.009 (0.012)
Prevenue	0.001 (0.001)	0.003*** (0.001)	−0.001*** (0.000)
conc	−0.041 (0.041)	−0.006 (0.054)	−0.113* (0.061)
gdp	0.217 (0.206)	0.673 (0.556)	−0.176 (0.242)
iebitm	−0.036 (0.085)	−0.040 (0.128)	0.058 (0.126)
_cons	−0.013 (0.098)	−0.164 (0.111)	0.329** (0.125)
R^2	0.40	0.37	0.64
N	171	101	70

The standard deviation of coefficients is in the brackets
***Significant at the 1% level
**Significant at the 5% level
*Significant at the 10% level

8.4 Investment Opportunities

Deals capture more investment opportunities during economic growth (Table 9), according to Eq. (4). Public bidders show worse results during crisis compared to private bidders. This indicates that private companies can more precisely estimate investment opportunities from the deal. Larger deals between companies in one industry also achieve good results in crisis.

Table 8 Tax benefits model

Variable	Whole sample (2006–2014)	Growth (2006–2007, 2010–2012)	Crisis (2008–2009, 2013–2014)
Industry	−74,917	−8756	−204,918
	(122,881)	(148,263)	(199,051)
Type	41,506	1616	482
	(133,722)	(163,298)	(232,245)
lnassets	93,965**	83,210	115,091
	(45,785)	(54,465)	(114,761)
tpublic	28,481	50,994	−79,211
	(171,242)	(192,161)	(338,466)
bpublic	−32,026	−165,986	145,141
	(118,677)	(133,850)	(266,832)
Prevenue	−2441	−3681	1154
	(5212)	(2525)	(8335)
lndealval	226,767***	227,113***	249,056**
	(47,647)	(52,341)	(103,466)
conc	171,425	53,258	199,051
	(310,743)	(283,643)	(662,793)
gdp	2,344,081	12,637,119***	2,509,139
	(1,669,787)	(3,963,289)	(2,791,884)
_cons	−2441,010***	−2,770,070***	−2,792,845*
	(734,857)	(1,026,086)	(1,589,569)
R^2	0,37	0,46	0,39
N	171	101	70

The standard deviation of coefficients is in the brackets
***Significant at the 1% level
**Significant at the 5% level
*Significant at the 10% level

8.5   Debt Capacity

Applying Eq. (5) to the data shows that the lagged cost of debt is consistently significant for increasing the debt capacity after the deal during all periods (Table 10). GDP growth is also a positive and significant coefficient in the model in all periods. Deals initiated by a large private bidder for the target in the same industry are the most successful in increasing debt capacity during crisis.

The results of econometric analysis for Eqs. (1–5) are consolidated in Table 11.

The first important result of hypothesis testing is significant differences between synergy creation factors for different types of synergies. This suggests that top management should focus on one main source of synergy before and after the deal to achieve maximum value for the company.

However, there are two factors with positive effect on synergies: economic growth and the bidder's financial performance. The latter may suggest that attempts to improve financial performance with M&As are not feasible. Besides, M&As during economic crisis should be planned and valued with extra caution.

Table 9 Investment opportunities model

Variable	Whole sample (2006–2014)	Growth (2006–2007, 2010–2012)	Crisis (2008–2009, 2013–2014)
Industry	−0.039	0.148	−0.047
	(0.202)	(0.297)	(0.204)
Type	0.133	0.074	0.485**
	(0.196)	(0.289)	(0.198)
lnassets	−0.094	−0.194*	0.208**
	(0.071)	(0.106)	(0.091)
tpublic	0.339	0.308	0.115
	(0.225)	(0.311)	(0.269)
bpublic	0.099	0.398	−0.455*
	(0.240)	(0.350)	(0.268)
Prevenue	−0.001	−0.011*	0.016
	(0.007)	(0.006)	(0.012)
lndealval	0.112	0.203	−0.155
	(0.094)	(0.139)	(0.108)
conc	−0.446	−0.707	−0.104
	(0.515)	(0.730)	(0.542)
gdp	5.997**	21.151**	−1.111
	(2.436)	(8.632)	(2.224)
icapexg	0.316	−1.190	0.731
	(0.377)	(0.750)	(0.467)
_cons	1.335	2.424	−2.623*
	(1.073)	(1.649)	(1.441)
R^2	0.11	0.16	0.26
N	171	101	70

The standard deviation of coefficients is in the brackets
***Significant at the 1% level
**Significant at the 5% level
*Significant at the 10% level

Secondly, hypothesis testing shows that the concentration of ownership in Russian bidders does not affect synergy in M&As. In other emerging markets, such as China and India, deals initiated by the bidders with one large owner (holding company or government) achieve higher abnormal stock returns than the deals initiated by the bidders with diversified ownership structure (e.g., Bhaumik and Selarka 2012).

Thirdly, larger deals create more tax benefits and increase the bidder's market power during economic growth. On the other hand, during crisis deals aimed at smaller companies achieve better results because bidders have difficulties with integrating larger targets into their normal operations.

Table 10 Debt capacity model

Variable	Whole sample (2006–2014)	Growth (2006–2007, 2010–2012)	Crisis (2008–2009, 2013–2014)
Debt (t−1)	0.663*** (0.099)	0.663*** (0.099)	0.775*** (0.102)
Industry	−0.002 (0.007)	−0.002 (0.007)	0.020** (0.010)
Type	−0.000 (0.008)	−0.000 (0.008)	0.002 (0.011)
lnassets	0.000 (0.003)	0.000 (0.003)	0.001 (0.004)
tpublic	−0.005 (0.009)	−0.005 (0.009)	0.006 (0.011)
bpublic	−0.006 (0.011)	−0.006 (0.011)	−0.024* (0.012)
Prevenue	−0.000 (0.000)	−0.000 (0.000)	0.001*** (0.000)
lndealval	0.001 (0.005)	0.001 (0.005)	0.002 (0.004)
conc	0.024 (0.017)	0.024 (0.017)	0.087*** (0.026)
gdp	0.624*** (0.200)	0.624*** (0.200)	0.563*** (0.127)
_cons	0.001 (0.047)	0.001 (0.047)	−0.025 (0.045)
R^2	0.46	0.46	0.65
N	101	101	70

The standard deviation of coefficients is in the brackets
***Significant at the 1% level
**Significant at the 5% level
*Significant at the 10% level

9 Application of the Methodology to the Major Domestic Russian Deals

To check how the model captures practical M&A results, we analyze in more detail four major domestic deals in different industries: manufacturing, telecoms, oil and gas, and IT.

9.1 MMK and Belon Group (October 2009)

Magnitogorsk Iron and Steel Works OJSC (MMK) is engaged in steel and iron production and Belon Group OJSC is engaged in production of metallurgical and

Table 11 Consolidated results of econometric analysis

Hypothesis	Economies of scale	Market power	Tax benefits	Investment opportunities	Debt capacity
1. Deals create higher synergies if both the target and the bidder operate in the same industry					Accepted during crisis
2. Vertical deals create higher synergies than horizontal deals	Accepted during crisis			Accepted	
3. Smaller companies achieve higher synergies		Depends on economic growth	Rejected	Depends on economic growth	
4. Deals with public targets create higher synergies than deals with private targets	Accepted				
5. Deals initiated by private bidders create higher synergies than deals initiated by public bidders	Accepted			Accepted during crisis	Accepted during crisis
6. Larger deals create lower synergies than smaller deals		Depends on economic growth	Rejected		Depends on economic growth
7. Bidders with a higher concentration of ownership create lower synergies		Accepted during crisis			Rejected during crisis
8. Bidders with better accounting performance create higher synergies	Accepted	Accepted	Not tested	Not tested	Accepted
9. Deals completed during economic and industry growth create higher synergies	Accepted		Accepted	Accepted	Accepted

Note: The hypothesis is "accepted" if the corresponding coefficient has expected sign and is significant at 10% significance level or better. Hypothesis is "rejected" if the corresponding coefficient has the opposite sign and is significant at 10% significance level or better. Empty cells indicate insignificant coefficients (significance level is worse than 10%)

steam coals. MMK acquired a 41.3% stake in Belon Group for an undisclosed consideration, estimated to be around 10.45 billion rubles (586 million USD).

The results of the deal according to the model are consolidated in Table 12.

As a result of this deal, MMK secured stable coking coal supplies for its steel smelting operations, including supplies of deficit coal grades. The share of long-term coal supply contracts increased from 14% at the beginning of 2008 to 50% at the end of 2010. This, in turn, protected MMK's margins from changes in coal prices: the cost of debt reduced by 2.4% (down to 9.2%) and the EBIT margin outperformed the industry by 7.0%.

Table 12 Results of Belon Group acquisition by MMK

Type of synergy	Proxy variable	Change in proxy variable after the deal
Economies of scale	Abnormal CAPEX efficiency growth, %	+9.9
Market power	Abnormal EBIT margin growth, %	+7.0
Tax benefits	Change in tax benefit, million rubles	+270.4
Investment opportunities	Abnormal CAPEX growth, %	+75.3
Debt capacity	Change in cost of debt, %	−2.4

Source: authors' analysis

The transaction also allowed MMK to take part in Belon's investment program aimed at increasing the production of coking coal. MMK's CAPEX increased by 50% the following year (in the non-ferrous metal industry they fell by about 25%), and they generated more revenue than the industry average.

9.2 Megafon and Scartel (October 2013)

Megafon is a telecommunications services operator covering all regions in Russia. Scartel is a Russian provider of Internet 4G services operating under the brand name Yota and is the only company with a multicity 4G network covering 27% of the Russian population. Megafon acquired Scartel for a cash consideration of 1180 million USD.

The results of the deal according to the model are consolidated in Table 13.

The acquisition was in line with Megafon's strategy to increase 4G network capacity and quality. The transaction allowed Megafon to reduce the costs of data transmission and expand 4G network development. The number of 4G stations owned by Megafon in Russia grew by 84%, from 10,100 in 2013 to 18,600 in 2014, and 4G network coverage increased from 36% of Russian population in 2013 to 51% in 2014.

The most noticeable impact was on Megafon CAPEX growth due to investments in 4G network development. The deal also led to significant growth of the cost of debt and additional tax benefits after Megafon consolidated 600 million USD net debt owned by Scartel.

9.3 Independent Petroleum Company and Alliance Oil (April 2014)

Independent Petroleum Company (IPC) is a Russian private oil and gas company owned by ex-Rosneft president Eduard Khudainatov. IPC grew mostly via

Table 13 Results of Scartel acquisition by Megafon

Type of synergy	Proxy variable	Change in proxy variable after the deal
Economies of scale	Abnormal CAPEX efficiency growth, %	+2.2
Market power	Abnormal EBIT margin growth, %	+1.2
Tax benefits	Change in tax benefit, million rubles	+3.35
Investment opportunities	Abnormal CAPEX growth, %	+24.1
Debt capacity	Change in cost of debt, %	+6.5

Source: authors' analysis

acquisitions of smaller oil companies operating near Eastern Siberia-Pacific Ocean (ESPO) oil pipeline. IPC had oil and gas extraction assets in the Saratov Region and the Taymyr Peninsula. Alliance Oil is a small Russian oil company with Khabarovsk refinery in the Far East region, at that time not connected to the ESPO pipeline.

The acquisition consideration was estimated to be around 2.4 billion USD. The goal was to integrate Alliance Oil refinery in Khabarovsk with IPC oil extraction assets and build more efficient vertically integrated oil company.

The results of the deal according to the model are consolidated in Table 14.

The deal achieved no operating synergies in 2014. IPC assets were located more than 3000 km from Khabarovsk refinery, which was supplied with crude oil via expensive railroad. IPC connected Khabarovsk refinery to the ESPO pipeline only in August 2015.

IPC raised significant debt to finance this deal. Total IPC debt grew from 53 billion rubles (about 1.7 billion USD) in 2013 to 86.3 billion rubles (2.7 billion USD) in 2014 with 8.6 billion rubles (270 million USD) operating profit. The cost of debt increased by 12.3% (up to 24.9%).

The acquisition of Alliance Oil was the last large deal of IPC (as of December 2016), despite announced plans to participate in the privatization of Bashneft in 2016.

9.4 Mail.ru and VKontakte (September 2014)

Mail.ru Group Limited (Mail.ru) is a Russian Internet company engaged in providing communication tools and Internet value-added services. VKontakte Ltd. (VK) is an operator of a popular Russian social networking website. Mail.ru paid 1.47 billion USD in cash for the acquisition of the remaining 48.01% stake in VK. Including payment for the initial 51.99% stake, the total acquisition cost for VK was 2.07 billion USD.

Table 14 Results of Alliance Oil acquisition by IPC

Type of synergy	Proxy variable	Change in proxy variable after the deal
Economies of scale	Abnormal CAPEX efficiency growth, %	−6.0
Market power	Abnormal EBIT margin growth, %	−9.2
Tax benefits	Change in tax benefit, million rubles	+1.23
Investment opportunities	Abnormal CAPEX growth, %	−97.8
Debt capacity	Change in cost of debt, %	+12.3

Source: authors' analysis

Table 15 Results of VKontakte acquisition by Mail.ru

Type of synergy	Proxy variable	Change in proxy variable after the deal
Economies of scale	Abnormal CAPEX efficiency growth, %	−0.4
Market power	Abnormal EBIT margin growth, %	−15.7
Tax benefits	Change in tax benefit, million rubles	+417.5
Investment opportunities	Abnormal CAPEX growth, %	−38.6
Debt capacity	Change in cost of debt, %	+5.8

Source: authors' analysis

Mail.ru already controlled several other popular Russian social networks, including Odnoklassniki, and this acquisition increased Mail.ru domination in the Russian social network space.

The results of the deal according to the model are consolidated in Table 15.

Despite further consolidation of Russian social networks, the EBIT margin of Mail.ru actually dropped by 15.7% compared to the industry average. This deal had a negative effect on financials, as Mail.ru was unable to apply existing online advertising and integrated value-added services products due to the differences in user behavior. In fact, VK with the largest number of users generated three times less revenue than other Mail.ru social networks.

Low VK margins (for instance, Mail.ru ended 2014 with 53% EBITDA margin and VK with 37% EBITDA margin) required new monetization and cost efficiency programs from Mail.ru. The effect of these programs will be reflected in Mail.ru financial statements no earlier than in 2017.

New 585 million USD debt (raised to finance this deal) increased Mail.ru leverage and the cost of debt by 5.8%.

To sum up these examples, the model correctly captures important short-term M&A results, such as new investment opportunities, changes in debt capacity, tax benefits, and operating synergies. However, it does not reflect specific industry features (Mail.ru and VK case) and long-term M&A perspectives (IPC and Alliance Oil case).

10   Conclusion

We estimate separate synergy components and find significant factors of synergy creation in 171 domestic Russian M&As in 2006–2015. The analysis is based on the financial data of involved companies, macroeconomic data for Russian economy and separate industries, and qualitative and quantitative features of M&As.

There are restrictions on this analysis. First, it depends on the features of Russian accounting standards, as many Russian companies do not use GAAP or IFRS. Second, not every Russian company discloses beneficiaries or owners, so some deals may be a way of rearranging the portfolio of assets and not market deals. Third, this method is not applicable if actual profit center is outside of the bidder's legal entity. We corrected the sample for these issues where possible.

Our analysis and results develop existing research of M&As in emerging markets in several ways. First, this approach to synergy valuation can be applied to private companies and small deals that make up the majority of M&As in emerging markets. Splitting synergy into five operating and financial types helps to better understand the structure of synergy and significant factors affecting it.

Second, we estimated the structure of synergy for every deal and found features of synergies in major Russian industries. Third, we tested the significance of potential synergy creation factors and found similarities and features of domestic Russian M&As compared to developed and emerging markets.

This research can be expanded with the analysis of other industries, addition of potentially better explanatory success factors, and the application of this method to other emerging M&A markets.

References

Agliardi, E., Amel-Zadeh, A., & Koussis, N. (2016). Leverage changes and growth options in mergers and acquisitions. *Journal of Empirical Finance, 37*, 37–58.

Agrell, J., Bogetoft, P. & Grammeltvedt, T. (2015). The efficiency of the regulation for horizontal mergers among electricity distribution operators in Norway. *12th International Conference on the European Energy Market,* [online] pp. 1–5. Retrieved May 08, 2017, from https://www. researchgate.net/profile/Per_Agrell/publication/281645825_The_Efficiency_of_the_Regula tion_for_Horizontal_Mergers_among_Electricity_Distribution_Operators_in_Norway/links/ 55f2a09308ae0af8ee1f9097.pdf

Bargeron, L., Schlingemann, P., Stulz, M., & Zutter, J. (2008). Why do private acquirers pay so little compared to public acquirers? *Journal of Financial Economics, 89*(3), 375–390.

Berger, N., Saunders, A., Scalise, M., & Udell, F. (1998). The effects of bank mergers and acquisitions on small business lending. *Journal of Financial Economics, 50*(2), 187–229.

Bhagat, S., Malhotra, S., & Zhu, P. (2011). Emerging country cross-border acquisitions: Characteristics, acquirer returns and cross-sectional determinants. *Emerging Markets Review, 12*(3), 250–271.

Bhaumik, K., & Selarka, E. (2012). Does ownership concentration improve M&A outcomes in emerging markets? Evidence from India. *Journal of Corporate Finance, 18*(4), 717–726.

Blonigen, A. & Pierce, R. (2016). Evidence for the effects of mergers on market power and efficiency. *National Bureau of Economic Research* [online] pp. 1–36. Retrieved May 08, 2017, from https://www.researchgate.net/profile/Justin_Pierce2/publication/309163412_Evidence_for_the Effects_of_Mergers_on_Market_Power_and_Efficiency/links/5812aeca08ae1f5510c2b46e.pdf

Boyson, N., Gantchev, N., & Shivdasani, A. (2017). Activism mergers. *Journal of Financial Economics, 126*, 54–73 [online]. Retrieved May 08, 2017, https://www.activistinsight.com/research/Activism%20mergers%20-%20Nicole%20Boyson,%20Nickolay%20Gantchev,%20Anil%20Shivdasani_021116031253.pdf

Bruner, R. (2002). Does M&A pay? A survey of evidence for the decision-maker. *Journal of Applied Finance, 12*, 48–68.

Cabanda, E., & Pajara, M. (2011). Merger in the Philippines: Evidence in the corporate performance of shipping companies. *Journal of Business Case Studies, 3*(4), 87–100.

Chatterjee, S. (2007). Why is synergy so difficult in mergers of related businesses? *Strategy & Leadership, 35*(2), 46–52.

Chow, T., Klassen, K., & Liu, Y. (2016). Targets' tax shelter participation and takeover premiums. *Contemporary Accounting Research, 33*(4), 1440–1472.

Damodaran, A. (2005). The value of synergy [online]. *SSRN.* Retrieved May 08, 2017, from https://chapters.ssrn.com/sol3/chapters.cfm?abstract_id=841486

Devos, E., Kadapakkam, P., & Krishnamurthy, S. (2009). How do mergers create value? A comparison of taxes, market power, and efficiency improvements as explanations for synergies. *Review of Financial Studies, 22*, 1179–1211.

Dionne, G., La Haye, M., & Bergeres, A. (2015). Does asymmetric information affect the premium in mergers and acquisitions? *Canadian Journal of Economics, 48*(3), 819–852.

Du, M., & Boateng, A. (2015). State ownership, institutional effects and value creation in cross-border M&A by Chinese firms. *International Business Review, 24*(3), 430–442.

Eckbo, E. (1983). Horizontal mergers, collusion, and stockholder wealth. *Journal of Financial Economics, 11*(1), 241–273.

Elgemark, A. (2014). Estimating merger synergies and the impact on corporate performance. *Journal of Copenhagen Business School* [online], 1–98. Retrieved May 08, 2017, from http://studenttheses.cbs.dk/bitstream/handle/10417/5470/anders_elgemark.pdf?sequence=1

Fee, E., & Thomas, S. (2004). Sources of gains in horizontal mergers: Evidence from customer, supplier, and rival firms. *Journal of Financial Economics, 74*(3), 423–460.

Garzella, S., & Fiorentino, R. (2016). *Synergy value and strategic management: Inside the black box of mergers and acquisitions* (Contributions to Management Science Series). Switzerland: Springer.

Grigorieva, S., & Petrunina, T. (2015). The performance of mergers and acquisitions in emerging capital markets: New angle. *Journal of Management Control, 26*(4), 377–403.

Hayn, C. (1989). Tax attributes as determinants of shareholder gains in corporate acquisitions. *Journal of Financial Economics, 23*(1), 121–153.

Healy, P., Palepu, K., & Ruback, R. (1992). Does corporate performance improve after mergers? *Journal of Financial Economics, 31*(2), 135–175.

Johnston, W., Oh, J., & Peters, D. (2014). Who's acquiring whom?—Experimental evidence of firm size effect on B2B mergers and marketing/sales tasks. *Industrial Marketing Management, 43*(6), 1035–1044.

Karampatsas, N., Petmezas, D., & Travlos, N. (2014). Credit ratings and the choice of payment method in mergers and acquisitions. *Journal of Corporate Finance, 25*, 474–493.

Kenneth, A., & Harford, J. (2014). The importance of industry links in merger waves. *The Journal of Finance, 69*(2), 527–576.

Kim, E., & Singal, V. (1993). Mergers and market power: Evidence from the airline industry. *The American Economic Review, 83*(3), 549–569.

Kpmg.com. (2015). Russian M&A Review 2015. *KPMG Official Website* [online], pp. 1–32. Retrieved May 08, 2017, from https://assets.kpmg.com/content/dam/kpmg/pdf/2016/03/ru-en-russian-ma-review-2015.pdf

Kwoka, J., & Pollitt, M. (2010). Do mergers improve efficiency? Evidence from restructuring the US electric power sector. *International Journal of Industrial Organization, 28*(6), 645–656.

Kyriazopoulos, G., & Drymbetas, E. (2015). Do domestic banks mergers and acquisitions still create value? Recent evidence from Europe. *Journal of Finance, 3*(1), 100–116.

Lewellen, W. (1971). A pure financial rationale for the conglomerate merger. *The Journal of Finance, 26*(2), 521–537.

Levine, R., Lin, C. & Shen, B. (2015). Cross-border acquisitions and labor regulations. *National Bureau of Economic Research* [online] (pp. 1–60). Retrieved May 08, 2017, from http://www.hertig.ethz.ch/content/dam/ethz/special-interest/gess/law-n-economics/professor-of-law-hertig-dam/documents/W%26L%20Series/Fall%202015/Levive_Labor_Regulations_2015.pdf

Lin, H., & Chou, Y. (2016). The impact of industry commonality on post-merger performance. *Advances in Economics and Business, 4*(6), 297–305.

Madsen, S., & Wu, Y. (2016). Marketing and globalization of the brewing industry. In I. Cabras, D. Higgins, & D. Preece (Eds.), *Brewing, beer and pubs: A global perspective* (1st ed., pp. 34–53). New York: Springer.

Maksimovic, V., & Phillips, G. (2001). The market for corporate assets: Who engages in mergers and asset sales and are there efficiency gains? *Journal of Finance, 56*(6), 2019–2065.

Moeller, B., & Schlingemann, P. (2005). Wealth destruction on a massive scale? A study of acquiring-firm returns in the recent merger wave. *The Journal of Finance, 60*(2), 757–782.

Mooney, T., & Shim, H. (2015). Does financial synergy provide a rationale for conglomerate mergers? *Asia-Pacific Journal of Financial Studies, 44*(4), 537–586.

Myers, C., & Majluf, S. (1984). Corporate financing and investment decisions when firms have information that investors do not have. *Journal of Financial Economics, 13*(2), 187–221.

Nguyen, H., Yung, K., & Sun, Q. (2012). Motives for mergers and acquisitions: Ex-post market evidence from the US. *Journal of Business Finance & Accounting, 39*(9–10), 1357–1375.

Ovtchinnikov, A. (2013). Merger waves following industry deregulation. *Journal of Corporate Finance, 21*, 51–76.

Pazarskis, M., Vogiatzogloy, M., Christodoulou, P., & Drogalas, G. (2006). Exploring the improvement of corporate performance after mergers – The case of Greece. *International Research Journal of Finance and Economics, 6*(22), 184–192.

Rani, N., Surendra, Y., & Jain, P. (2012). Impact of mergers and acquisition on returns to shareholders of acquiring firms: Indian economy in perspective. *Journal of Financial Management and Analysis, 25*(1), 1–24.

Ray, G. (2014). Cross-border mergers and acquisitions: Modelling synergy for value creation. *Advances in Mergers and Acquisitions, 12*, 113–134.

Rhodes-Kropf, M., & Viswanathan, S. (2004). Market valuation and merger waves. *The Journal of Finance, 59*, 2685–2718.

Rossi, S., & Volpin, P. (2004). Cross-country determinants of mergers and acquisitions. *Journal of Financial Economics, 74*(2), 277–304.

Sapienza, P. (2002). The effects of banking mergers on loan contracts. *The Journal of Finance, 57*(1), 329–367.

Shahrur, H. (2005). Industry structure and horizontal takeovers: Analysis of wealth effects on rivals, suppliers, and corporate customers. *Journal of Financial Economics, 76*(1), 61–98.

Tao, Q., Sun, W., Zhu, Y., & Zhang, T. (2017). Do firms have leverage targets? New evidence from mergers and acquisitions in China. *The North American Journal of Economics and Finance, 40*, 41–54.

Višić, J. (2013). Impact of takeovers on profitability of target companies: Evidence from Croatian companies. *Communist and Post-Communist Studies, 46*(4), 455–461.

Yasser, Q., Mamun, A., & Hook, M. (2017). The impact of ownership structure on financial reporting quality in the east. *International Journal of Organizational Analysis, 25*(2), 178.

Zschille, M. (2015). Consolidating the water industry: An analysis of the potential gains from horizontal integration in a conditional efficiency framework. *Journal of Productivity Analysis, 44*(1), 97–114.

Translation of References in Russian into English

Grigoryeva, S., & Grinchenko, A. (2014). Impact of mergers and acquisitions in financial sector on bidder's returns in emerging capital markets. *Journal of Corporate Finance Research, 7*(4), 53–71.

Grigoryeva, S., & Troitsky, P. (2012). The impact of mergers and acquisitions on company performance in emerging capital markets. *Journal of Corporate Finance Research, 6*(3), 31–43.

Rogova, E., & Luzina, D. (2015). The effect of mergers and acquisitions on companies' fundamental values in emerging capital markets (the case of BRICS). *Journal of Corporate Finance Research, 9*(3), 27–50.

Part III
Diversification Strategies via M&As: New Evidence from BRIC

Corporate Diversification-Performance Puzzle in BRIC

Svetlana Grigorieva

Abstract Researchers have long tried to define the impact of corporate diversification on firm value. Academic papers mainly concentrate on the effects of corporate diversification in mature markets, while its consequences in emerging capital markets are less explored. This article presents the results of an empirical analysis of corporate diversification strategies of a sample of companies from BRIC countries that expanded via acquisitions during 2000–2013. We contribute to the existing literature by examining the effects of corporate diversification on firm value during the pre- and post-crisis periods. In line with other studies, we distinguish between related and unrelated diversification, and in contrast to them, we single out and separately analyze horizontal, conglomerate, and vertical acquisitions. Based on a sample of 319 deals initiated by companies from BRIC countries, we found positive (3.32% and 9.01%) and statistically significant cumulative abnormal returns for conglomerate acquisitions during the pre- and post-crisis periods, correspondingly. We also found that the market reacts positively and statistically significantly to the announcements of horizontal and vertical integration only during the pre-crisis period.

Keywords Corporate diversification · Firm value · Conglomerate acquisitions · Vertical integration · Emerging markets · Capital markets

This chapter revises and updates the results contained in Ivashkovskaya I. and Shamraeva (Grigorieva) S. Corporate Diversification Effect on Firm Value in Emerging Markets: Evidence from BRIC Countries. Global Business and Technological Association. 11th International Conference. Readings Book. Business Strategies and Technological Innovations for Sustainable Development: Creating Global Prosperity for Humanity. Edited by N. Delener—New York—2009, pp. 565–571.

S. Grigorieva (✉)
Corporate Finance Center, Department of Finance, National Research University Higher School of Economics, Moscow, Russia

© Springer Nature Switzerland AG 2020
I. Ivashkovskaya et al. (eds.), *Strategic Deals in Emerging Capital Markets*,
Advanced Studies in Emerging Markets Finance,
https://doi.org/10.1007/978-3-030-23850-6_9

1 Introduction

Each company moving across its life cycle is faced with the choice of expansion strategy. A company may invest in the same industry (related diversification) or enter new markets (unrelated diversification). The latter option may be a very attractive way for a company to develop and improve its prospects. A diversification strategy may allow firms to generate synergies, increase market power, reduce investment risk, increase debt capacity, and efficiently allocate capital through an internal capital market. At the same time, corporate diversification significantly increases the costs of coordination and control, exacerbates managerial agency problems, leads to inefficient allocation of capital, and requires special skills and knowledge to operate diversified firms. Thus, the decision about expansion, the direction of this expansion, and the level of corporate diversification are the most important decisions that are taken by management and boards.

According to the principles of corporate finance, the performance of diversification strategy is always assessed by its impact on shareholder value. Is corporate diversification beneficial in developed and emerging capital markets? While there is a great body of literature that examines the effects of corporate diversification in mature markets, its consequences in emerging capital markets are less explored. We contribute to the existing literature by analyzing the corporate diversification phenomenon using a sample of companies from BRIC countries that expanded via acquisitions. In line with other studies, we distinguished between related and unrelated diversification, and in contrast to them, we singled out and separately analyzed the market reaction to horizontal, vertical, and conglomerate deals. To reveal diversified firms in related and unrelated industries, researchers always employ SIC code, Herfindahl-Hirschman index, or entropy measure. But these methods do not allow distinguishing between vertically integrated firms and conglomerates and always mix them in one group that is called unrelated diversification. But these are two different strategies that have their own sources of value. Vertical integration allows firms to benefit mainly from operating synergy and technical and coordination efficiency (Sudarsanam 2003), while conglomerate acquisitions allows companies to gain from financial synergy, increasing debt capacity and effective resource allocation through an internal capital market. According to institution-based theory, conglomerates may become more efficient in emerging capital markets—providing a superior ability to raise capital, allocating this capital among divisions more efficiently than the external market does, diversifying investors' portfolios, guaranteeing the fulfillment of contracts, and preparing and training promising management (Khanna and Palepu 1997; Khanna and Palepu 2000a, b). Thus these underline the importance of distinguishing between vertical and conglomerate deals when analyzing the efficiency of diversification, especially in emerging economies.

We also contribute to the existing literature by concentrating on the pre- and post-crisis periods, providing the opportunity to compare the market reaction to the announcements of diversified acquisitions, and understanding whether the value of corporate diversification has changed. The global economic crisis of 2008–2009 led to more severe financial constraints in emerging markets, suggesting that the affiliation with big diversified companies is more attractive.

The reminder of this chapter is organized as follows: Section 2 reviews the recent developments in the literature on corporate diversification concentrating on research in emerging markets. Section 3 defines the methodology. Section 4 describes the sample selection procedure. Section 5 provides the discussion of the results. Section 6 concludes this study.

2 Literature Review

Phenomenon of corporate diversification has been actively discussed in financial academic literature. For a long time, such a business strategy was viewed as a rational and effective model, but many countries have taken the "return to focus" as wholesome and compelling corporate doctrine (Sudarsanam 2003). According to the empirical results in developed countries, the prevailing wisdom among financial researchers is that diversified firms are sold at a discount and the level of corporate diversification is trending downward (Berger and Ofek 1995; Lang and Stulz 1994; Lins and Servaes 1999; Fukui and Ushijima 2007; Grigorieva 2010). Value-decreasing investments and the inefficient allocation of funds among divisions of diversified firms via the internal capital market are viewed as the main sources of value destruction (Rajan et al. 2000; Scharfstein and Stein 2000). Even if capital allocation among divisions within a diversified company leads to economic benefits, it also creates the conditions for an increase in agency costs (Gautier and Heider 2009; Inderst and Laux 2005; Brusco and Panunzi 2005; Grigorieva 2010; Erdorf et al. 2013).

However, recent research questions both mentioned results. A number of studies suggest that the observed discount is attributable to factors others than diversification or may be a result of improper measurement techniques. There is a substantial body of empirical evidence that proves that the diversification discount is not due to the diversification strategy per se but may be connected to the target's characteristics or the endogeneity of the diversification decision (Graham et al. 2002; Campa and Kedia 2002; Pal and Bohl 2006; Beckmann et al. 2006; Dastidar 2009; Glegg et al. 2010). In some cases, the corporate diversification discount was related to the premium. According to Villalonga (2000), there is no diversification discount. Using the Business Information Tracking Series (the BITS) database instead of Compustat, which has been used by most authors, she shows that diversified firms trade at a significant premium. In contrast to a linear relationship between diversification and firm value, some of the latest empirical studies reveal significant curvilinear effects, suggesting that diversification in developed countries creates value at low and moderate levels (when companies move from single-segment to related diversification) and destroys value at moderate and high levels of diversification (Palich et al. 2000). This dependence forms a so-called inverted-U model

(Dess et al. 1995; Palich et al. 2000; Galvan et al. 2007; Kistruck et al. 2013; Andres et al. 2014).

"Whereas the majority of empirical research shows the negative impact of corporate diversification on firm value for companies based in developed countries, this strategy may be more valuable for companies that operate in emerging capital markets (Khanna and Palepu 1997; Benito-Osorio et al. 2012; Caudillo et al. 2015). These markets are characterized as a rule by a dominance of diversified companies. The specific features of emerging markets, to some extent, can affect the effectiveness of integration strategy. In developed countries, well-developed structures in capital markets, competitive product markets and labor markets—as well as strong contract enforcement—guarantee similar rules of play for both diversified and focused firms. In these conditions the benefits of integration may be reduced. On the contrary, in an imperfect institutional environment like emerging markets and with weak enforcement of contracts, diversified firms may be of value. They can mimic the beneficial functions of various institutions that are present in developed markets and thereby create a potential source of value growth for integrated firms (Khanna and Palepu 1997). On the other hand, severe market imperfections, which increase the potential agency costs resulting from higher information asymmetry, can lead to value destruction in firms that undertake such strategies" (Ivashkovskaya and Shamraeva 2009, p. 566).

"Fauver et al. (2003) suggest that the value of diversification is negatively related to the level of capital market development. For companies that operate in developed and internationally integrated capital markets the authors find a statistically significant diversification discount, which is consistent with the findings of Berger and Ofek (1995) and Lang and Stulz (1994). But for companies that operate in emerging and segmented capital markets, a diversification premium is found. Furthermore, authors suggest that the financial, legal and regulatory environment have an important influence on the firm's value in case of diversification, and the optimal organizational structure depend on where the company operates. These results are consistent with Khanna and Palepu's evidence that the evolution of the institutional environment alters the value-creating potential of business groups (Khanna and Palepu 2000a, b). Comparing diversified companies in Hong Kong, Malaysia, Indonesia, Singapore, Korea, Thailand, Taiwan, and the Philippines with diversified companies in US and Japan, Claessen et al. (2001) suggest that diversification diminishes corporate value for US firms, but it does not have the same effect for most East Asian firms. In their later study, using a sample of 2000 Asian companies they found that a group affiliation was more positive for mature, slow-growing firms than for young and high-growth companies (Claessen et al. 2006). Similar results were obtained by Bae et al. (2002) and Khanna and Palepu (2000a, b) using evidence from Korean business groups and evidence from Indian business groups, respectively. Khanna and Palepu (2000a, b) found that diversified Indian business groups often outperform their stand-alone counterparts and there is no diversification discount in the value of diversified business groups. The efficiency of affiliation with business groups in India is also confirmed by George and Kabir (2012). The role of Russian financial-industrial groups (FIG) and their impact on capital allocation among the group's firms was examined by Perotti and Gelfer (2001). The authors suggest that FIG allocate capital comparatively better than stand-alone firms" (Ivashkovskaya and Shamraeva 2009, p. 566). Wong et al. (2009) identify value increase for acquiring firms and value decrease for target firms in diversification deals, based on a sample of companies from different developed and emerging countries for the period of 2000–2007. A recent study presented by McKinsey (Caudillo et al. 2015) also demonstrates the efficiency of diversified firms. Employing the data of more than 4500 firms from developed and emerging countries from 2002 to 2012, the authors find that the highly diversified firms in emerging capital markets generate higher excess returns (3.6%) than focused firms (0%) and pure players (−2.8%). In developed economies, there is almost no difference in excess TRS for diversified and pure players. The authors explain the positive linkage between diversification and performance by the ability of diversified firms to reinvest retained earnings in new businesses, to easily interact with governmental and regulatory officials, to attract talent, and to attract capital.

The opposite results were obtained by Lins and Servaes (2002) on the efficiency of corporate diversification. Comparing the value of diversified and focused firms within and across seven emerging markets at the end of 1995, the authors find that diversified companies trade at a discount of approximately 8% compared to focused firms. According to the authors, the discount may be partially explained by less profitability of diversified firms than single-segment firms, affiliation with industrial groups, and ownership concentration. Lu and Yao (2006) and Bertrand et al. (2002) confirm the discounts in China and India correspondingly. Lee et al. (2008) extend the institution-based theory by examining the instability of diversification premium in South Korea from 1984 to 1996. The authors argue that with the development of the institutional environment, a diversification premium in emerging capital markets turns into a diversification discount.

In spite of how much the phenomenon of corporate diversification has been discussed in financial academic literature, the evidence is still controversial. The observed divergence in the results can be explained by different samples, databases, empirical methods, and home country environment. A significant role is also played by the examined time period (Benito-Osorio et al. 2012). Analyzing the linkage between corporate diversification and firm value during the global financial crisis of 2007–2009, Kuppuswamy et al. (2014) reveal that diversification strategy becomes attractive for US companies under external financial constraints. The authors argue that the debt coinsurance effect allows diversified companies to gain the competition for scarce financial resources of the compared stand-alone firms and allocate them more efficiently through an internal capital market. Rudolph and Schwetzler (2013) also demonstrate the reduction in diversification discount during the financial crisis for companies that operate in countries with a perfect institutional environment (developed Asia Pacific, British Isles, and North America). But for firms from countries with the least developed capital markets and the lowest legal investor protection (continental Europe), the authors do not find significant results, suggesting that in these countries, the effect of the crisis on the efficiency of diversified companies would not be strong since raising funds in an imperfect institutional environment is difficult for firms even during non-crisis periods. The results of these papers also indirectly confirm that corporate diversification is a more attractive strategy in emerging countries than in developed ones and may create additional sources of value for shareholders.

In this chapter, we shed additional light on the impact of diversification on firm value in emerging economies. Following the institution-based theory (Khanna and Palepu 1997; Peng and Delios 2006), we expect that the institutional environment of emerging capital markets positively influences the value creation process in diversified firms. But in contrast to existing studies, we (1) distinguish between different types of acquisition deals (horizontal, vertical, conglomerate) and (2) examine the efficiency of diversification deals during the pre- and post-crisis periods. We believe that the value of diversification would change as a result of the crisis. Going along with Kuppuswamy et al. (2014), we expect that under more severe external financial constraints following the crisis, the unrelated diversification strategy (pure conglomerates) would be more attractive for shareholders since this strategy allows firms to benefit from financial synergy, providing risk reduction, increased debt capacity as a result of the "coinsurance effect," and efficient resource allocation through an internal capital market.

3 Methodology

3.1 Announcement-Period Abnormal Stock Return

To study the link between corporate diversification and firm value on the sample of companies from BRIC countries, we applied the standard event study method.

We examined only the acquirer's returns due to the fact that most target firms in our sample are non-public. The normal (predicted) returns were generated using the market model:

$$R_{jt} = \alpha_j + \beta_j R_{mt} + \varepsilon_{jt} \qquad (1)$$

where R_m is return on a market index on day t; β_j measures the sensitivity of firm j to the market; α_j measures the mean return over the period not explained by the market; $t \in (t_1; t_n)$ is the estimation period, ε_{jt}—statistical error; and $E(\varepsilon_{jt}) = 0$, var $(\varepsilon_{jt}) = \sigma^2$.

The abnormal return here is $AR_{j\tau} = R_{j\tau} - \hat{\alpha}_j + \hat{\beta}_j R_{m\tau}$, where, $R_{j\tau}$ is the actual return and $\tau \in (T_1; T_m)$ is the event window.

For the sample of Russian companies, we used the RTS index; for Brazilian companies, the Bovespa; for Indian companies, the Sensex; and for Chinese companies, the Shanghai Composite.

We employed a 41-day event window, comprised of 20 pre-event days, the event day, and 20 post-event days and also varied it, decreasing the number of days. So the choice of the window did not affect its explanatory character. We took 80 trading days prior to the event window as the estimation period to calculate predicted return to each firm. We cumulated the average residuals for each day over the event window and got a cumulative abnormal return (CAR). The market reaction to an event is positive if CAR is higher than zero ($CAR \geq 0$). The statistical significance of the results is the integral part of the analysis. The general test used for all hypotheses is the following (Weston et al. 2002; Kothari and Warner 2007):

$$H_0 : CAR = 0 \tag{2}$$

Test statistics are defined as follows:

$$t = \frac{CAR(T_1; T_m)}{\sqrt{m\sigma^2(t_1; t_n)}}, \text{where } \sigma^2(t_1; t_n) = \sum_{t=t_1}^{t_n} \sigma^2(AR_t) \tag{3}$$

where m is the length of the event window and n is the length of the estimation period.

3.2   Construction of Vertical Measures

To reveal the deals that lead to vertical integration, we followed the methodology suggested by Fan and Lang (2000). This methodology allows constructing vertical measures at industry and firm level.

At industry level:

$$V_{ij} = \frac{1}{2}\left(v_{ij} + v_{ji}\right) \tag{4}$$

where V_{ij} is the proxy for the opportunity for vertical integration between industries i and j; v_{ij} the dollar value of industry i's output required to produce 1 dollar's worth of industry j's output; and v_{ji} the dollar value of industry j's output required to produce 1 dollar's worth of industry i's output.

$$\text{At firm level}: V = \sum_{j}\left(w_j \times V_{ij}\right) \tag{5}$$

where V is a firm-level vertical relatedness measure and w_j represents sales weight equal to the ratio of the j secondary segment sales to the total sales of all secondary segments.

4 Sample Characteristics

We used the Zephyr Mergers and Acquisitions database from Bureau van Dijk to identify an initial pre-crisis sample of 3172 publicly traded deals that fit into the categories of complete, announced, or pending transaction during the period of 2000–mid-2008. Using the same database, we obtained a sample of 3026 deals for the post-crisis period of mid-2009–2013. We further required that (1) only acquirers are publicly traded firms, (2) the acquiring firm controls less than 50% of the shares of the target firm before the announcement, (3) the relative transaction size is higher than 5%, (4) the acquirer's closed prices are available for us, and (5) there is a lack of significant corporate events in the estimation period, such as shares buyback, other mergers and acquisitions, and joint ventures.

Our requirements yielded a sample of 198 transactions for the pre-crisis period and 121 deals for the post-crisis period. Table 1 presents the distribution of deals among BRIC countries.

We grouped the firms according to their diversification type—related and unrelated—using the SIC code system. This classification approach is consistent with the approach used by Berger and Ofek (1995) and Denis et al. (1997). If the acquirer and the target have no commonality in first three digits of four-digit SIC codes, the acquisition is classified as unrelated. Other deals are classified as related diversification. For our sample, 90 of the acquisitions are related, and 108 are unrelated deals during the pre-crisis period, while during the post-crisis period, there are 85 related and 36 unrelated deals in the sample. In Table 2, we present a time series of diversification deals for the aggregate sample as well as for related and unrelated diversification subsamples. The number of diversification announcements appears to pick up in 2004. The number of related deals decreased, while the number of unrelated M&As increased over the pre-crisis period. But after 2009, the number of related deals showed stable growth.

Unfortunately, the SIC code system does not allow singling out vertically inte-grated firms and often refers them to unrelated diversification. Thereby this approach as a rule mixes conglomerate and vertically integrated firms in one group, which is called unrelated diversification. Based on SIC data, it is impossible to find and analyze separately pure conglomerate and vertically integrated companies. To iden-tify such firms, we followed the methodology of Fan and Lang (2000), which provided us with the detailed information about the construction of vertical measures at both industry and firm levels (4), (5). We use the input-output tables at the US

Table 1 Distribution of diversification deals by BRIC countries

Country	No. of deals in pre-crisis period	No. of deals in post-crisis period
Brazil	30	19
Russia	38	24
India	73	38
China	57	40
Total	198	121

Table 2 Distribution of diversification deals by year

Announcement year	No. of announcements	Related diversification	Unrelated diversification
2000	2	1	1
2001	4	3	1
2002	5	3	2
2003	20	12	8
2004	46	26	20
2005	27	7	20
2006	34	16	18
2007	39	15	24
Mid-2008	21	7	14
Mid-2009	3	0	3
2010	22	16	6
2011	28	21	7
2012	32	22	10
2013	36	26	10
Total	319	175	144

Table 3 Types of mergers and acquisitions in BRIC countries

M&A type	Pre-crisis period	Post-crisis period
Horizontal	87	46
Vertical	42	57
Conglomerate	69	18
Total	198	121

Bureau of Economic Analysis to create a matrix of relatedness at the industry level (Fan and Lang 2000; Claessen et al. 2001). Researchers often use the input-output tables for the US economy, examining the effects of vertical integrations on firm value in emerging capital markets, based on the assumption that the specificity of industries does not depend on national particularities (Claessen et al. 2001). Industries are considered vertically related if they receive at least 5% of their inputs from another industry or supply more than 5% of their own outputs to one other industry (Schoar 2002). As a result, 42 acquisitions are considered as vertical, 69 as conglomerate, and 87 as horizontal M&As during the pre-crisis period. After 2009 almost half of the sample (57 deals) is considered as vertical acquisitions, 18 deals as conglomerate deals, and 46 as horizontal M&As (Table 3).

In Fig. 1, deals are classified by the acquirer's industry affiliation for the pre-crisis sample. The most common industry is chemical and pharmaceutical (20.2%) followed by metals and mining (12.6%), software (9.1%), and light industry (9.1%).

The industry affiliation structure is rather consistent during the post crisis-period (Fig. 2) with chemical and pharmaceutical (15%) and metals and mining (14%) as the most common industries which are followed by light industry (12%) and machinery (10%). The number of acquirers from the software industry dropped to 7%.

M&A classification by industry affiliation

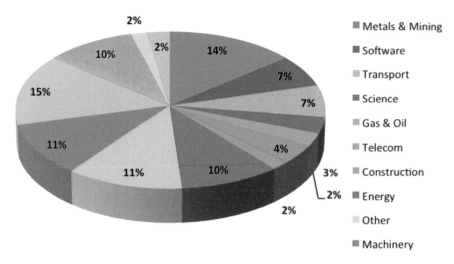

Fig. 1 Distribution of M&As by industry affiliation during the pre-crisis period

M&A classification by industry affiliation

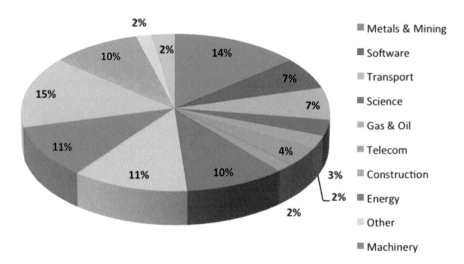

Fig. 2 Distribution of M&As by industry affiliation during the post-crisis period

Table 4 CARs for diversification deals on different event windows and for different subsamples during pre-crisis period

Event window				
	[−20;+20]	[−15;+15]	[−2;+2]	[−1;+1]
BRIC—whole sample				
CAR	5.98%***	5.34%***	1.8%***	1.53%**
Number of observations	198			
BRIC—horizontal M&As				
CAR	6.68%***	6.10%***	2.13%**	1.00%†
Number of observations	87			
BRIC—vertical M&As				
CAR	8.92%***	7.59%***	1.44%†	1.92%**
Number of observations	42			
BRIC—conglomerate M&As				
CAR	3.32%*	3.03%*	1.61%*	1.95%**
Number of observations	69			
BRIC—related diversification				
CAR	6.72%***	6.14%***	2.12%**	1.00%†
Number of observations	90			
BRIC—unrelated diversification				
CAR	5.36%***	4.68%***	1.54%**	1.98%**
Number of observations	108			

***Significant at the 1% level
**Significant at the 5% level
*Significant at the 10% level
†Significant at the 15% level

5 Empirical Findings and Results

By analyzing the results for each country separately, we get similar tendencies in market reaction to the announcements of corporate diversification. So, we present results for the entire sample. The aggregation BRIC countries data seems to be the most interesting because it allows testing our hypotheses on a large sample and to get typical results for emerging markets within the BRIC group. The results for the entire sample of diversification deals and for different subsamples during the pre-crisis period are shown in Table 4.

For the whole sample, the mean 41-, 31-, and 5-day announcement period abnormal returns are positive and statistically significant at 1% level, and 3-day abnormal returns are also positive and statistically significant at 5% level. These results indicate that shareholders of the sample firms experience significant wealth gains from diversification deals. The CARs for 41-day event window are graphed in Fig. 3.

The plot shows that the market learns about the deals a few days before the announcement, which may indicate to some extent the insider nature of the examined markets. Table 4 also reports that corporate diversification does not destroy the

CARs for diversification deals in BRIC

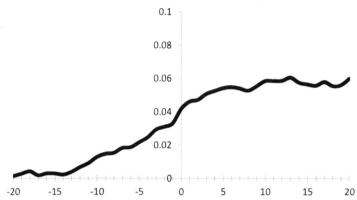

Fig. 3 Plot of CARs for all diversification deals for 41-day event window during the pre-crisis period

value of acquirers from BRIC countries irrespective of diversification type. The lack of high significant returns in the shorter announcement periods indicates that the market does not capitalize on the information contained with the M&A announcement at the time of the announcement. This situation is typical for developing markets due to their lower efficiency. The market needs additional time to capitalize on the information; therefore using a longer announcement period may be more justified. The highest CARs are associated with vertical and horizontal integration. The announcements of conglomerate acquisitions cause also positive and statistically significant (at 10% level) returns for acquirers. But the CARs for these deals are two and a half times less than for vertical acquisitions, indicating that vertically integrated firms may create a sustainable competitive advantage, achieve technical and coordination efficiency, and create new resources and capabilities. Our findings are consistent with outcomes of Claessen et al. (2001, 2006), Khanna and Palepu (2000a, b), and Fauver et al. (2003). But in contrast to Claessen et al. who argue that vertical integration leads to the reduction of shareholder's value in countries with weak financial systems, we obtained positive and statistically significant CARs for acquirers in BRIC countries indicating that vertical relatedness increases firm value.

Considering the post-crisis period, the results for the total sample and different subsamples are shown in Table 5.

For the whole sample, the cumulative average abnormal returns for all event windows are statistically insignificant. These results indicate that after the financial crisis, shareholders of acquirers from the sample cannot extract substantial wealth gains from diversification deals. Table 4 shows that corporate diversification is no more irrelevant to the diversification type. Thus, the CARs for related deals are statistically insignificant, while for unrelated acquisitions, they are positive and statistically significant at 5 and 10% level for 41- and 31-day event windows (6.51% and 5.76%, correspondingly). Market reaction to horizontal deals is positive

Table 5 CARs for diversification deals on different event windows and for different subsamples during post-crisis period

Event window				
	[−20; +20]	[−15; +15]	[−2; +2]	[−1; +1]
BRIC—whole sample				
CAR	2.22%	1.25%	−0.13%	0.37%
Number of observations	121			
BRIC—horizontal M&As				
CAR	3.02%*	1.62%	−0.42%	−0.46%
Number of observations	46			
BRIC—vertical M&As				
CAR	−0.57%	−1.04%	−0.08%	0.41%
Number of observations	57			
BRIC—conglomerate M&As				
CAR	9.01%**	7.51%*	0.13%	2.33%
Number of observations	18			
BRIC—related diversification				
CAR	0.41%	−0.67%	−0.33%	−0.03%
Number of observations	85			
BRIC—unrelated diversification				
CAR	6.51%**	5.76%*	0.33%	1.30%
Number of observations	36			

***Significant at the 1% level
**Significant at the 5% level
*Significant at the 10% level
†Significant at the 15% level

and statistically significant only for 41-day event window, while for vertical acquisitions, the stock market reaction becomes negative and statistically insignificant. The highest CARs are associated with conglomerate deals. Their announcements cause significant (at 5% and 10% level) abnormal returns equal to 9.01% for 41-day event window and 7.51% for 31-day window. The results indicate that a market reacts more favorably for conglomerate acquisitions following the crisis (9.01% compared with 3.32% before the crisis), confirming our expectation that under the more severe external financial constraints, the conglomerate acquisitions become more efficient since they allow firms to reduce risk, increase debt capacity as a result of "coinsurance effect," and allocate scarce financial resources through an internal capital market.

6 Conclusion

According to Khanna and Palepu (1997), diversified companies in emerging markets have the potential to add value. This evidence is supported by a number of empirical studies (Fauver et al. 2003; Khanna and Palepu 2000a, b; Claessen et al. 2001, 2006). Our empirical study contributes to the existing literature by examining the link between different types of corporate diversification and firm value for companies from BRIC countries. Our results indicate the predominance of positive effects of corporate diversification in emerging markets supporting the institution-based theory. For the pre-crisis period, we found positive and statistically significant returns for acquirer's shareholders for different event windows. We got the highest returns for vertical deals and the lowest for conglomerate ones. By analyzing diversification effects on firm value after the crisis, we revealed that more severe external financial constraints make conglomerates more efficient for shareholders. But the results are statistically significant only for two event windows. Cumulative abnormal returns for vertical acquisitions show no statistically significant difference from zero. We also found that shareholders received the lower returns in horizontal acquisitions after the crisis than before it, suggesting that it may be difficult for companies to obtain benefits from operating synergy. But the results for horizontal acquisitions are not robust for different event windows, indicating that we cannot make a final conclusion.

"The existence of opportunities to create value does not mean that diversified companies automatically become efficient and can create value. It depends to a large extent on how the company is managed and what potential it has. Having the correct management model is one of the main factors of successful diversification. A skillful management system that allows for a complete understanding of which businesses in the company's portfolio are value-creators or value-destructors, what investments are efficient, how to coordinate and control the activities of business-units and how to make the company more transparent to investors can lead the success of diversified companies in any market" (Ivashkovskaya and Shamraeva 2009, p. 569).

Our study does not pretend to be complete and detailed in providing a comprehensive picture of the impact of different types of corporate diversification on firm value in emerging capital markets. In particular, our sample consists of 319 M&A deals in BRIC over the period of 2000–2013, including only 18 conglomerate deals in post-crisis period. Thus, future studies should try to expand the sample by analyzing deals in more developing countries over broader time period. In addition, this study examined the effects of corporate diversification on firm value in short-run period based on the event study method. We suggest that future research should look to undertake an analysis of the efficiency of different types of corporate diversification in long-run period. Moreover, in this study, we examined the impact of diversification on firm value during the pre- and post-crisis periods, but did not analyze the crisis itself, which may also open a direction for further research.

Acknowledgments I express my sincere thanks to research fellow Georgii Gorbatov for his help with data collection and calculations.

References

Andres, P., Fuente, G., & Velasco, P. (2014). Growth opportunities and the effect of corporate diversification on value. *The Spanish Review of Financial Economics, 12*(2), 73–81.

Bae, K. H., Kang, J. K., & Kim, J. M. (2002). Tunneling or valued added: Evidence from mergers by Korean business groups. *Journal of Finance, 57*(6), 2695–2740.

Beckmann, P., Fechtel, A., & Heuskel, D. (2006). Managing for value. How the world's top diversified companies produce superior shareholder returns. *BCG Report* [online]. Retrieved December 31, 2017, from http://www.bcg.com/documents/file14912.pdf

Benito-Osorio, D., Guerras-Martín, L. A., & Zuniga-Vicente, J. A. (2012). Four decades of research on product diversification: A literature review. *Management Decision, 50*(2), 325–344.

Berger, P. G., & Ofek, E. (1995). Diversification's effect on firm value. *Journal of Financial Economics, 37*, 39–65.

Bertrand, M., Mehta, P., & Mullainathan, S. (2002). Ferreting out tunneling: An application to Indian business groups. *Quarterly Journal of Economics, 117*(1), 121–148.

Brusco, S., & Panunzi, F. (2005). Reallocation of corporate resources and managerial incentives in internal capital markets. *European Economic Review, 49*(3), 659–681.

Campa, J. M., & Kedia, S. (2002). Explaining the diversification discount. *Journal of Finance, LVII*(4), 1731–1762.

Caudillo, F., Houben, S., & Noor, J. (2015). Mapping the value of diversification. *McKinsey on Finance, 55*, 10–12.

Claessen, S., Djankov, S., Fan, J., & Lang, L. (2001). The pattern and valuation effects of corporate diversification: A comparison of the US, Japan, and Other East Asian economies. *World institute for development economics research* (Discussion chapter. № 2001/127).

Claessen, S., Fan, J., & Lang, L. (2006). The benefits and costs of group affiliation: Evidence from East Asia. *Emerging Markets Review, 7*, 1–26.

Dastidar, P. (2009). International corporate diversification and performance: Does firm self-selection matter? *Journal of International Business Studies, 40*, 71–85.

Denis, D. J., Denis, D. K., & Sarin, A. (1997). Agency problems, equity ownership and corporate diversification. *Journal of Finance, 52*, 135–160.

Dess, G. G., Gupta, A., Hennart, J. F., & Hill, C. W. L. (1995). Conducting and integrating strategy research at the international, corporate and business levels: Issues and directions. *Journal of Management, 21*(3), 357–393.

Erdorf, S., Hartmann-Wendels, T., Heinrichs, N., & Matz, M. (2013). Corporate diversification and firm value: A survey of recent literature. *Financial Markets and Portfolio Management, 27*(2), 187–215.

Fan, J., & Lang, L. (2000). The measurement of relatedness: An application to corporate diversification. *Journal of Business, 73*(4), 629–660.

Fauver, L., Houston, J., & Naranjo, A. (2003). Capital market development, international integration, legal systems and the value of corporate diversification: A cross-country analysis. *Journal of Finance and Quantitative Analysis, 38*(1), 135–157.

Fukui, Y., & Ushijima, T. (2007). Corporate diversification, performance and restructuring in the largest Japanese manufacturers. *Journal of the Japanese and International Economics, 21*(3), 303–323.

Galvan, A., Pindado, J., & Torre, C. (2007). *Diversification: Value-creating or value-destroying strategy? Evidence from using panel data* (Working Chapter No. DT04/07).

Gautier, A., & Heider, F. (2009). The benefits and costs of winner-picking: Redistribution vs. incentives. *Journal of Institutional and Theoretical Economics, 165*, 622–649.

George, R., & Kabir, R. (2012). Heterogeneity in business groups and the corporate diversification firm performance relationship. *Journal of Business Research, 65*(3), 412–420.

Glegg, C., Harris, O., & Buckley, W. (2010). When does diversification add value: Evidence from corporate governance and abnormal long-term stock performance. *Corporate Ownership & Control, 7*(3), 325–342.

Graham, J. R., Lemmon, M. L., & Wolf, J. G. (2002). Does corporate diversification destroy value? *The Journal of Finance, LVII*(2), 695–719.

Grigorieva, S. (2010). Empirical research of corporate diversification strategy in developed and emerging markets: An overview. *Journal of Corporate Finance Research, 1*(1), 111–144.

Inderst, R., & Laux, C. (2005). Incentives in internal capital markets: Capital constraints, competition, and investment opportunities. *RAND Journal of Economics, 36*(1), 215–228.

Ivashkovskaya, I., & Shamraeva (Grigorieva), S. (2009). Corporate diversification effect on firm value in emerging markets: Evidence from BRIC countries. Global business and technological association. *11th international conference. Readings book. Business strategies and technological innovations for sustainable development: Creating global prosperity for humanity* (pp. 565–571). – Edited by N. Delener. New York.

Khanna, T., & Palepu, K. (1997). Why focused strategies may be wrong for emerging markets. *Harvard Business Review, 75*(4), 41–51.

Khanna, T., & Palepu, K. (2000a). Is group affiliation profitable in emerging markets? An analysis of diversified Indian business groups. *The Journal of Finance, LV*(2), 867–889.

Khanna, T., & Palepu, K. (2000b). The future of business groups in emerging markets: Long-run evidence from Chile. *The Academy of Management Journal, 43*(3), 268–285.

Kistruck, G. M., Qureshi, I., & Beamish, P. W. (2013). Geographic and product diversification in charitable organizations. *Journal of Management, 39*(2), 496–530.

Kothari, S. P., & Warner, J. B. (2007). Econometrics of event studies. In B. E. Eckbo (Ed.), *Handbook of corporate finance* (pp. 3–36). Amsterdam: Elsevier.

Kuppuswamy, V., Serafeim, G., & Villalonga, B. (2014). The effect of institutional factors on the value of corporate diversification. *Advances in Strategic Management: Finance and Strategy, 32*, 37–68.

Lang, L., & Stulz, R. (1994). Tobin's q, corporate diversification, and firm performance. *Journal of Political Economy, 102*, 1248–1280.

Lee, K., Peng, M., & Lee, K. (2008). From diversification premium to diversification discount during institutional transitions. *Journal of World Business, 43*, 47–65.

Lins, K., & Servaes, H. (1999). International evidence on the value of corporate diversification. *Journal of Finance, 54*, 2215–2239.

Lins, K., & Servaes, H. (2002). Is corporate diversification beneficial in emerging markets? *Financial Management, 31*, 5–31.

Lu, Y., & Yao, J. (2006). Impact of state ownership and control mechanisms on the performance of group affiliated companies in China. *Asia Pacific Journal of Management, 23*, 485–503.

Pal, R., & Bohl, M. (2006). *Discount or premium? New evidence on corporate diversification of UK firms* (SSRN Working chapter).

Palich, L. E., Cardinal, L. B., & Miller, C. C. (2000). Curvilinearity in the diversification performance linkage: An examination of over three decades of research. *Strategic Management Journal, 21*(2), 155–174.

Peng, M. W., & Delios, A. (2006). What determines the scope of the firm over time and around the world? An Asia Pacific perspective. *Asia Pacific Journal of Management, 23*(4), 385–405.

Perotti, E., & Gelfer, C. (2001). Red barons or robber barons? Governance and Investment in Russian Financial-Industrial Groups. *European Economic Review, 45*(9), 1601–1617.

Rajan, R., Servaes, H., & Zingales, L. (2000). The cost of diversity: The diversification discount and inefficient investment. *Journal of Finance, LV*(1), 35–80.

Rudolph, C., & Schwetzler, B. (2013). Conglomerates on the rise again? A cross-regional study on the impact of the 2008–2009 financial crisis on the diversification discount. *Journal of Corporate Finance, 22*, 153–165.

Scharfstein, D. S., & Stein, J. C. (2000). The dark side of internal capital markets: Divisional rent-seeking and inefficient investment. *Journal of Finance, LV*(6), 2537–2564.

Schoar, A. (2002). Effects of corporate diversification on productivity. *The Journal of Finance, 57* (6), 2379–2403.

Sudarsanam, S. (2003). *Creating value from mergers and acquisitions: The challenges, an international and integrated perspective* (p. 613). London: FT Prentice Hall.

Villalonga, B. (2000). Diversification discount or premium? New evidence from BITS establishment-level data. *Journal of Finance, 59*, 475–503.

Weston, F., Siu, A., & Johnson, B. A. (2002). *Takeovers, restructuring and corporate governance* (pp. 171–184). London: Prentice Hall.

Wong, A., Cheung, K. Y., & Mun, T. (2009). The effects of merger and acquisition announcements on the security prices of bidding firms and target firms in Asia. *International Journal of Economics and Finance, 1*(2), 274–228.

Corporate International Diversification and Performance: An Economic Profit Viewpoint—Evidence from BRIC Companies

Irina Ivashkovskaya, Dmitry Shcherbakov, and Pavel Yakovenko

Abstract In recent years, corporate international diversification has become a widely used growth strategy for companies from both developed and emerging markets. Nevertheless, academic papers provide contradictory results on whether the influence of international diversification on firm performance is positive or negative. This chapter presents the results of an empirical analysis of corporate international diversification—performance relationship on a sample of companies from BRIC countries, which expanded geographically in 2005–2015. We contribute to the existing literature by applying a new methodology to identify the performance effects of corporate international diversification based on an economic profit measure. The results indicate that there is a nonlinear relationship between the degree of international diversification and economic profit spread. Additionally, for BRIC companies, international diversification on average does not have a significant impact on expected long-term performance, measured by Tobin's Q.

Keywords International diversification · Economic profit · Diversification-performance relationship

1 Introduction

One of the most popular directions of research about corporate international diversification is identifying the patterns in the relationship between the degree of internationalization (DOI) and firm performance; however, in the economic and financial literature, there is no consensus on how internationalization affects firm

I. Ivashkovskaya
Higher School of Economics, National Research University, Moscow, Russia

D. Shcherbakov
Bain&Co, Moskva, Russia

P. Yakovenko (✉)
National Research University, Higher School of Economics, Moscow, Russia

© Springer Nature Switzerland AG 2020
I. Ivashkovskaya et al. (eds.), *Strategic Deals in Emerging Capital Markets,*
Advanced Studies in Emerging Markets Finance,
https://doi.org/10.1007/978-3-030-23850-6_10

performance. This is because of the trade-off between the costs and benefits of international diversification. Companies benefit from competitive advantages that are not accessible in their home market; however international diversification brings various risks, transactional costs, and agency problems. Some research demonstrates an increase of performance for firms involved in internationalization (Cardinal 2011; Hennart 2011, etc.). Others find a negative impact of international diversification on corporate performance (Zaheer and Mosakowski 1997; Singla and George 2013, etc.). Most recent studies illustrate a more complicated nonlinear pattern of the DOI-performance relationship (Hitt et al. 1997; Lu and Beamish 2004; Xiao et al. 2013).

This chapter contributes to the analysis of the relationship between DOI and performance. On the data of firms from BRIC markets, we investigate the form of the DOI-performance relationship applying different DOI measures as well as performance metrics that capture effects in the long run and short run. We also study the impact of product diversification on the effectiveness of internationalization.

Given that companies internationally diversify by both M&As and organic growth, it is difficult to determine the degree of international diversification attributed only to organic growth or only to M&As. Thus, current chapter provides insights on efficiency of internationalization strategies, achieved by both M&As and organic growth. These insights should be considered by executives for formulating cross-border M&A strategies in a broader context of determining an optimal level of international diversification. Our results can be used in predictions of internationalization performance.

2   Theoretical Background and Hypotheses

2.1   Research Approach

The DOI-performance relationship is typically studied in two paradigms[1]: event studies and accounting studies. While the first is based on the analysis of corporate performance change within a time window around a cross-border M&A deal, the second approach is based on the identification of the relationship between corporate performance (typically accounting-based measures) and DOI. A thorough review of research literature of both event-based and accounting-based internationalization studies can be found in Bruener (2004) and Hitt et al. (2006). Current research contributes to accounting-based approach but differs from the existing ones significantly in the use of different performance indicators and measures of DOI.

---

[1]There exists the third paradigm of case studies analysis, but it remains a rather niche study field.

2.1.1 Choice of DOI Measures

Depending on the choice of DOI measure, it is possible to investigate different internationalization patterns. Usually international diversification is classified into two classes—diversification of assets and diversification of markets. The most commonly used measures of these types are the foreign-assets-to-total-assets (FATA) ratio and the foreign-sales-to-total-sales (FSTS) ratio, respectively. In contrast to the event studies approach, the use of FATA and FSTS allows the analysis of both nonorganic foreign growth (cross-border M&As) and foreign greenfield investments.

The mentioned variables are well-studied and frequently used; however, they have a significant weakness: they do not account for the number of regions or countries in which a firm operates. We would expect different performance from firms if they operate in a different number of countries even with equal FSTS or FATA, since the companies have to get adapted to different economic conditions in different countries and adopt different organizational models. As Hitt et al. stated (1997), addition of the number of countries of operations as a control variable to the model is likely to create a multicollinearity problem as the number of countries is correlated with both FSTS and FATA (the more countries the firm operates in, the higher the FSTS and FATA ratios). One possible solution for this problem is to use the Herfindahl-Hirschman Index (HHI) as a proxy for DOI. The Herfindahl-Hirschman Index can be calculated as follows:

$$HHI = 1 - \sum_{i=1}^{N} p_i^2 \tag{1}$$

where p_i is the share of sales of country i (or share of assets, if the measure is asset-based) in the overall sales volume (overall assets value) of the company and N total number of countries. HHI incorporates not only the foreign share of sales or assets but also the distribution of these measures among countries. An example of HHI usage is in Elif (2015).

One more frequently used measure is an Entropy Index (Hitt et al. 1997), calculated as:

$$Entropy = \sum_{i=1}^{N} \left(P_i * \ln \left(\frac{1}{P_i} \right) \right) \tag{2}$$

where P_i is the share of revenue from country i in total revenue of the firm and N overall number of countries. This index considers both diversity (how many countries the firm operates in) and the intensity (the weight of revenue from a single country in the overall revenue) of firm's revenue.

Following Grigorieva (2007), the Entropy Index illustrates both the number of countries or regions where the company operates and the distribution of sales or

Table 1 Accounting studies by the types of corporate performance measures

Type of measure	Type of corporate performance	Examples of measures	References
Book value-based	Current operational efficiency (expected performance change is not considered)	Revenue, operating cash flow, EBIT-based measures (EBIT margin, ROS, ROE, ROA, etc.)	Qian and Li (2002), Gulger et al. (2003), Moeller and Schlingemann (2005), Lu and Beamish (2004), Contractor et al. (2007), Bobillo et al. (2010), Rugman and Chang (2010), Wu (2012), Tian and Buckleya (2017)
Market value-based	Expected operational and financial efficiency (measures incorporating expectations)	Tobin's Q, PE, market-to-book ratio	Bodnar et al. (2003), Chang and Wang (2007), Rugman and Chang (2010), Elif (2015), Bany-Ariffin et al. (2016)
		WACC and other cost-of-capital-related measures	Singh and Najadmalayeri (2004), Joliet and Hubner (2006)

assets among geographic segments. Hitt et al. (1997) argue that entropy is the most efficient index for international diversification as it is strongly correlated with FSTS and FATA but at the same time captures both intensity and diversity of international diversification. The implication of this measure can be also found in research by Bany-Ariffin et al. (2016).

2.1.2   The Choice of Performance Indicators

The usage of various corporate performance indicators allows to study different effects of internationalization over different time horizons. A classification of typically used performance measures is described in Table 1.

As can be seen from Table 1, accounting studies typically use the following two types of corporate performance measures:

1. The current corporate performance during a particular period of time (usually 1 year), which does not incorporate expectations of potential efficiency changes in the future (usually benefits from internationalization are fully realized over several years)
2. The expectations of the future corporate performance by combining different valuation multiples and in some papers weighted average cost of capital (WACC), which also captures expected returns

The weakness of the first group of measures is that they do not simultaneously account for the risk generated by internationalization. In fact, the change in operational efficiency measures should be compared to the change in opportunity costs measured by the change in the cost of capital. Therefore, we follow the approach of a simultaneous analysis of operational efficiency and required returns for the risk of investments related to corporate international diversification. The research model is based on the concept of economic profit spread. Since economic profit spread comprises the cost of capital, which represents the required return on overall capital based on risks associated with a firm and its internationalization decisions, it is an appropriate measure of strategic performance (Shcherbakov 2013; Ivashkovskaya 2008). The economic profit spread is measured as follows:

$$Economic\ profit\ spread_{it} = ROCE_{it} - WACC_{it} \qquad (3)$$

where $ROCE_{it}$ is the return on capital employed of company i in period t and $WACC_{it}$ is the weighted average cost of capital. Both $ROCE$ and $WACC$ are functions of DOI. While the factors, which define the impact of DOI on $ROCE$ (such as cost reduction effects, commercial synergies, local culture-specific effects, etc.), are widely discussed and well-studied in the economic literature (see Grigorieva 2007; Shcherbakov 2013), the factors of $WACC$ in the context of internalization are covered less. We will discuss these factors in the next section.

2.1.3 The Impact over Required Rates of Return

In the context of internationalization, scholars identify three factors that may affect required rate of return: change in capital structure, change in the cost of equity, and change in the cost of debt. Singh and Najadmalayeri (2004) identified an increase of financial leverage related to international diversification. This fact is motivated by a corresponding increase in debt supply in capital markets, which is driven by the diminishing bankruptcy risks of internationalizing firms due to country-specific risk diversification. Other studies show that the decrease in debt supply related to corporate internationalization is due to the following factors (see, e.g., Doukas and Pantzalis 2003):

(a) Typically, internationalization is associated with higher growth rates and growing organizational complexity, both of which increase the agency costs of debt holders.
(b) The amount of intangible assets is likely to increase with international diversification, which means additional risks to debt holders as these assets cannot be monetized in case of bankruptcy.

DOI influences the cost of equity through the following three factors:

(a) A change in the level of risk: there may be a nonlinear relationship between DOI and the level of risk to shareholders due to the addition of new internationalization-specific risks at the initial stage of international diversification. At later stages, a decrease of shareholder risk due to diversification could be expected.
(b) A rise of shareholder agency costs: it is supposed that as DOI grows, the costs of monitoring and controlling the management also increase.

(c) A change in capital structure: different levers are described above.

Singh and Najadmalayeri (2004) state that a higher risk from internalization for shareholders is reflected in higher beta coefficients of multinational corporations (MNCs).

The most significant debt-specific factors are:

(a) A change in debt maturity: MNCs typically raise longer-term debt than domestic firms do (Singh and Najadmalayeri 2004). This results in a higher cost of debt.
(b) A change in the effective tax rate driven by the move of a company's profit center to countries with different corporate taxation: this factor directly influences the after-tax cost of debt.

2.1.4 Prior Results

Using the measures of internationalization and efficiency listed above, researchers obtained different and often contradictory results. An overview of the recent studies devoted to the analysis of the companies from developing markets is presented in Table 2. There are a large number of studies on international diversification efficiency of Chinese firms, and their results vary from linear relationship to S-shaped

Table 2 The results of the analysis of companies from developing countries

Research	Sample	Performance variable	DOI variable	Relationship
Thomas (2005)	500 Mexican firms	ROS	FSTS	U-shaped curve
Chen, Tan (2012)	887 Chinese firms	Tobin's Q	FSTS	Linear negative
			RSTS (regional sales to total sales)	U-shaped curve
			RSTS (intra-Greater China)	S-shaped curve
Wu (2012)	318 Chinese firms	ROA	Entropy Index	S-shaped curve
Singla and George (2013)	237 Indian firms	ROA, Tobin's Q	FSTS	No relationship
			Composite index (FSTS, FATA, OSTS, scope)	Linear negative
Xiao et al. (2013)	114,398 Chinese firms	ROA	FSTS	S-shaped curve
Chen et al. (2014)	685 Chinese firms	ROA	FSTS	Inverse U-shaped curve
Borda (2016)	103 Latin American firms (Brazil, Chile, Mexico)	ROA	FSTS	Inverse U-shaped curve

Table 3 Meta-analytical researches on diversification performance

Research	Sample	Explanatory variable	Relationship
Bausch and Pils (2009)	104 studies	FSTS, product diversification	Positive
Carney and Gedajlovic (2011)	141 studies	Number of foreign affiliates, FSTS, product diversification	Positive with moderating effect (form of the relationship affected by other factors)
Kirca et al. (2011)	111 studies	FSTS, firm-specific assets	Positive

curve pattern even for the companies from the same sample depending on the choice of measures of internationalization (see Chen and Tan 2012). The analysis of Indian companies, which uses both operational and financial measures of efficiency, shows no relationship between FSTS and performance but linear relationship for composite index of several DOI measures. For Latin American companies, a nonlinear form of relationship was found with more recent study (Borda et al. 2017) having an inverted U-shape pattern, while earlier research (Thomas 2005) done for the Mexican firms only found a U-shaped pattern between DOI and performance measure.

A generalization of a larger set of studies is presented in meta-analyses, which also study the patterns of relationship between international diversification and corporate performance. The results of selected meta-analytical research are presented in Table 3. These research aggregate studies, which use both book and market value-based performance measures. The main difference between these studies is in the choice of explanatory variables. Bausch and Pils (2009) and Kirca et al. (2011) used FSTS as a DOI measure and found that it has a positive influence on performance. Carney and Gedajlovic (2011) used a number of firm's foreign affiliates as a proxy for DOI, while share of exports and product diversification were used as control variables. In their study, the overall impact of DOI on the performance measures was positive, but the form of this relationship was affected by several control variables including FSTS and measure of product diversification.

2.1.5 Side Factors

Scholars suggest that there is also a wide array of side factors, also called moderators, which affect the DOI-performance relationship. These factors include firm-, industry- and country-specific factors. Firm-specific factors consist of marketing and technological resources (Chen et al. 2014), R&D level (Kotabe et al. 2002), financial capabilities, and managerial competencies. Industry-specific factors include the degree of competition, the industry policies, and the technology levels within the industry. Both home and host country-specific factors can also affect the DOI-performance relationship (Wan and Hoskisson 2003).

Firms balance their growth between geographical and product diversification. Thus, another factor, which has an impact on internationalization-performance, is the level of product diversification (Bausch and Pills 2009; Oh et al. 2015; Ref 2015,

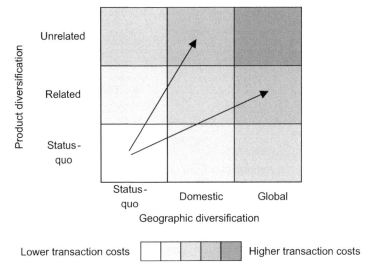

Fig. 1 Transaction costs in diversification matrix (Shcherbakov (2013))

Hashai and Delios 2013; Chen et al. 2014). Scholars divide the directions of product diversification into related diversification (expanding to industries, which are similar to the firm's core competencies) and unrelated diversification (expanding to industries dissimilar to the firm's core competencies). While expanding into related foreign markets, firms transfer home business capabilities and intellectual capital and combine it with local technologies and resources, increasing their competitive advantage in both local and foreign markets. Firms following an unrelated diversification strategy in foreign markets are unable to effectively apply these advantages. Moreover, the unrelated international diversification is likely to increase organizational complexity and transaction costs (Shcherbakov 2013) (Fig. 1). Thus, these firms will incur additional costs, related to both internationalization and developing new products, which can exceed the benefits of diversification (Chen et al. 2014).

Based on the literature, the most frequently mentioned side factors and their effects on the DOI-performance relationship are given in Table 4.

2.2 Hypotheses

Based on existing studies as well as on our analysis of internationalization processes in BRIC countries, we formulated several research hypotheses for a sample of Chinese, Indian, Brazilian, and Russian companies.

Table 4 Frequently studied side effects (moderators) on DOI-performance relationship

Factor	Moderating effect	Research examples
Degree of product diversification	Positive	Riahi-Belkaoui (1998), Hitt et al. (1997)
	Negative	Vermeulen and Barkema (2002), Chen et al. (2014)
Share of intangible assets	Positive	Lu and Beamish (2004)
R&D intensity	Positive	Zahra et al. (2000), Kotabe et al. (2002)
Company size	Positive	Dragun (2002)
Overall risk level	Positive	Hejazi and Santor (2010)

2.2.1 Performance Indicator-DOI Relationship

As stated, economic profit spread depends on two elements: ROCE (operational efficiency) and WACC (cost of capital). Both of them are subject to synergies and risks associated with internationalization. Prior research shows that internationalization has stronger impact on operational performance (ROCE) and lower impact on cost of capital (WACC) (Shcherbakov 2013); thus we assume that the relation between economic profit spread and DOI mostly follows the ROCE to DOI relationship.

The majority of DOI-performance research finds a nonlinear relationship between DOI and operational performance measures for firms from developed economies. Lu and Beamish (2004) identified the most general pattern of this relationship represented by a horizontal S-shaped curve which was also supported by Bobillo et al. (2010), Rugman and Chang (2010), and Oh et al. (2015). The S-shaped curve consists of three sequential intervals:

(a) At a low level of DOI, the operating performance decreases with an increase in DOI since internationalization-related costs (learning costs, costs of the coordination and the control of foreign divisions, and other transaction costs) are too high in comparison with the low marginal increase in efficiency and foreign sales.

(b) At a medium level of DOI, the firm gains significant benefits including those derived from economies of scale and scope, the diversification of country risks, an access to foreign knowledge and cheaper resources, and an increase of market power, which are higher than the transaction costs. Therefore, there is an increase in performance.

(c) At a high level of DOI, performance may start declining again due to the unmanageable complexity of international organizations (the over-internationalization stage) and the resulting high transaction costs.

Another pattern of DOI-operating performance relationship has been identified for India by Contractor et al. (2007) and for Chinese companies by Chen and Tan (2012). These studies demonstrated a U-shaped pattern for DOI-performance relationship and showed that nonlinear relationship between performance and DOI measures was found for both short-term (ROA) and long-term (Tobin's Q) performance indicators. It is assumed that companies from emerging markets typically do not reach a high degree of complexity related to over-internationalization. Therefore, we expect a U-shaped pattern in the relationship between performance (measured by both economic profit spread and Tobin's Q) and DOI for companies from BRIC countries.

Hypothesis 1 *The relationship between the degree of international diversification and firm performance follows a U-shaped curve pattern for BRIC countries.*

In order to test that the companies in our sample on average do not reach the over-internationalization phase, and thus are not characterized by S-shaped relationship between performance and DOI, we also tested the hypothesis of S-shaped curve pattern. As the S-shaped curve hypothesis was not confirmed by estimations (see Appendix 1 for more details), we consider the U-shaped curve to be our main hypothesis.

2.2.2 The Choice of DOI Measure

As mentioned above, there are studies which emphasize the advantages of using an Entropy Index as a DOI measure (Hitt et al. 1997). It incorporates both an intensity factor of internationalization (the share of all foreign sales in total sales), measured by FSTS, and a diversity factor (the number of countries and the sales distribution among them), which is commonly measured with HHI. That fact positively distinguishes an Entropy Index from others in terms of economic sense. That is why we expect it to have the same accuracy as the combination of FSTS and HHI in measuring the relationship between DOI and performance.

Hypothesis 2 *The Entropy Index has the same power in firm performance estimation as the combination of FSTS and HHI.*

Testing Hypothesis 2 will allow us to choose for the further analysis either the models with Entropy or those with the combination of FSTS and HHI as a measure of DOI.

2.2.3 The Impact of Internationalization in the Long Run and the Short Run

Prior research states that the benefits and costs of internationalization can have different impact in the short term versus the long term (Thomas and Eden 2004). For example, investments in R&D have a negative impact in the short term, as the costs are incurred in favor of future benefits. The benefits from investments in intangible assets are also reflected in the long-run performance. Internationalizing enterprises should adopt new mechanisms, and consequently, they increase organizational complexity, raising their overall costs over time (Hitt et al. 1997). Firms also learn to manage the new processes and adapt to the changes (Vermeulen and Barkema 2002). Because the benefits are more likely to be longer term in nature relative to the costs (Thomas and Eden 2004), we hypothesize that:

Hypothesis 3 *The impact of international diversification on long-run performance is stronger than on short-run performance.*

2.2.4 The Impact of Product Diversification

The papers of Chang and Wang (2007), Hitt et al. (1997), and Chen et al. (2014) have demonstrated that the performance-internationalization relationship is also affected by the level and type of the product diversification of a company. Typically, the internationalization effect is more positive when the company has a higher level of related product diversification (Chang and Wang 2007). It is described by the organizational design of product-diversified companies, which are usually better adapted to international diversification. Hence, the degree of unrelated product diversification can have a stronger negative effect on efficiency of international diversification. As stated above, high levels of both internationalization and unrelated product diversification are likely to increase organizational complexity and transaction costs. On a sample of Chinese manufacturing firms, Chen et al. (2014) find that unrelated product diversification reduces efficiency of internationalization. Thus, we hypothesize that:

Hypothesis 4 *Unrelated product diversification has a negative effect on the relationship between internationalization and performance.*

3 Methods

3.1 The Sample

We use a sample of 109 companies from BRIC countries. Overall, there are 40 - Russian, 29 Chinese, 25 Brazilian, and 15 Indian companies in the sample. All companies satisfy the following criteria:

1. The company is public and discloses all the key information.
2. The company closed at least one acquisition of a foreign company worth more than $10 million between 2005 and 2015.
3. The company discloses distribution of its foreign sales.
4. The company is not a financial institution.

While the first criterion is rather natural and controls for the availability of data, the second one ensures that companies in the sample have foreign businesses that are large enough to be disclosed in their financial statements. However, it does not necessarily mean that all companies in the sample have a subsidiary in other countries since we do not specify the share of the company bought in the deal, so both strategic and financial deals may be included in the sample. The third criterion is required to calculate the Entropy Index and HHI based on foreign and domestic revenue. If company discloses only export sales, there is not enough information to analyze the sources of foreign revenue.

The data set is derived from the Bloomberg database for the period 2005–2015. All financial figures are given in USD million. Overall, we have an unbalanced panel of 440 observations for Russian, 330 for Chinese, 187 for Indian, and 308 for Brazilian companies. The descriptive statistics of all the variables by country after the exclusion of outliers are depicted in Table 5. The sample includes companies from several industries following the NAICS standard (including mining, manufacturing, transportation and public utilities, and services sector). The majority of firms in the sample are manufacturing companies.

The Indian firms have the highest average value of both performance variables—economic profit spread and Tobin's Q. Russian and Chinese companies have almost the same mean value of economic profit spread, but Tobin's Q is significantly higher for Chinese companies (1.92 versus 1.46 for Russian companies). Chinese companies are less internationally diversified than Russian (measured by all the DOI variables), while Indian companies have the highest degree of international diversification.

3.2   The Model

We use two different performance variables to test the efficiency of international diversification. The short-run performance is represented by economic profit spread, which is calculated as follows:

$$Economic\ profit\ spread = ROCE - WACC \tag{4}$$

Economic profit spread captures both the operational results and impact of the riskiness of international diversification on the company's performance.

Long-run performance is measured by Tobin's Q, one of the most common metrics, which reflects firm's long-term growth and investor expectations. It is calculated as the ratio of the market value to the book value of its assets. We choose this variable among different market multiples for the following reasons:

- The denominator of Tobin's Q (book value of assets) is far less volatile than other operating variables (like EBITDA, revenue, etc.), and thus it is less exposed to short-term industry and macroeconomic fluctuations.
- It reflects the expectations of investors focused on the stable growth of the company.

Table 5 Variable's description and statistics for the sample

Variable	Description	Russia			China			India			Brazil		
		Obs	Mean	S. D.	Obs	Mean	S. D.	Obs	Mean	S. D.	Obs	Mean	S. D.
Dependent variables													
Spread	Economic profit spread (%)	286	9.47	13.49	233	9.46	11.49	113	16.26	13.02	147	2.00	11.21
Q	Tobin's Q	299	1.46	1.05	265	1.92	1.72	151	2.21	1.44	262	1.33	0.60
Internationalization measures (DOI)													
Entropy	Entropy Index	422	0.54	0.64	302	0.33	0.49	169	0.86	0.55	280	0.57	0.58
FSTS	Ratio of foreign sales to total sale	422	0.29	0.35	302	0.23	0.35	169	0.59	0.38	280	0.35	0.37
HHI	Herfindahl-Hirschman Index	422	0.27	0.30	302	0.18	0.26	169	0.45	0.27	280	0.30	0.29
Company-specific control variables													
Ln_sales	Company size (log of sales)	383	8.00	1.84	285	7.33	285	151	7.20	1.98	273	7.70	1.71
Asset_turnover	Asset turnover ratio	372	0.83	0.55	281	0.59	28-	141	0.91	0.36	269	0.80	0.69
Int_assets	Intangibles to total assets, %	422	0.07	0.12	297	0.03	297	169	0.13	0.13	280	0.12	0.15
ROE	3-year average return on equity, %	314	14.55	18.52	261	15.39	261	129	17.90	17.54	240	11.09	17.22
Ebit_sales	EBIT/sales, %	383	14.80	31.52	285	15.45	285	150	11.80	10.15	273	9.24	22.48
Unrelated	Unrelated product diversification measure	422	0.71	0.43	302	0.67	0.45	169	0.82	0.37	280	0.69	0.46
Country-specific variables													
Log_GDP	Natural logarithm of country's GDP	422	28.69	0.24	302	30.12	0.34	169	29.29	0.28	280	28.64	0.15
Curr	% change of national currency exchange rate over the previous year	422	0.08	0.19	302	−0.03	0.03	169	0.03	0.07	280	0.03	0.16
Industry dummies (NAICS)													
NAICS1	Mining industry dummy	422	0.21	0.41	302	0.07	0.25	169	0.00	0.00	280	0.04	0.19
NAICS2	Manufacturing industry dummy	422	0.45	0.50	302	0.32	0.47	169	0.62	0.49	280	0.75	0.43
NAICS3	Transportation and public utilities dummy	422	0.13	0.33	302	0.21	0.41	169	0.13	0.34	280	0.09	0.29
NAICS4	Services sector dummy	422	0.11	0.31	302	0.10	0.30	169	0.20	0.40	280	0.00	0.00

Based on the hypotheses proposed in Sect. 2, the following regression equations will be estimated:

Spread-Entropy model	$Spread_{itc} = \beta_0 + \beta_1 * X + \beta_2 * entropy_{itc} + \beta_3 * unrelated_{itc}$ $* entropy_{itc} + \beta_4 * GDP_{tc} * entropy_{itc} + \beta_5$ $* Curr_{tc} * entropy_{itc} + \beta_6 * entropy_{itc}^2 + \epsilon_{itc}$	(10.5)
Q-Entropy model	$Q_{itc} = \beta_0 + \beta_1 * X + \beta_2 * entropy_{itc} + \beta_3 * unrelated_{itc}$ $* entropy_{itc} + \beta_4 * GDP_{tc} * entropy_{itc} + \beta_5$ $* Curr_{tc} * entropy_{itc} + \beta_6 * entropy_{itc}^2 + \epsilon_{itc}$	(10.6)
Spread-FSTS model	$Spread_{itc} = \beta_0 + \beta_1 * X + \beta_2 * FSTS_{itc} + \beta_3 * unrelated_{itc}$ $* FSTS_{itc} + \beta_4 * Curr_{tc} * FSTS_{itc} + \beta_5 * FSTS_{itc}^2$ $+ \beta_6 * HHI_{itc} + \beta_7 * unrelated_{itc} * HHI_{itc} + + \beta_8$ $* Curr_{tc} * HHI_{itc} + \beta_9 * HHI_{itc}^2 + \epsilon_{itc}$	(10.7)
Q-FSTS model	$Q_{itc} = \beta_0 + \beta_1 * X + \beta_2 * FSTS_{itc} + \beta_3 * unrelated_{itc} * FSTS_{itc}$ $+ \beta_4 * Curr_{tc} * FSTS_{itc} + \beta_5 * FSTS_{itc}^2 + \beta_6$ $* HHI_{itc} + \beta_7 * unrelated_{itc} * HHI_{itc} + + \beta_8$ $* Curr_{tc} * HHI_{itc} + \beta_9 * HHI_{itc}^2 + \epsilon_{itc}$	(10.8)

where i, t, and c stand for company, year, and country, respectively. As *GDP* and *Curr* measures are similar for companies from one country, these variables have only year and country notations.

We use the Hausman-Taylor method which controls for the possible endogeneity of data caused by potential simultaneity problem (e.g., more profitable firms have higher resources to participate in international diversification), as well as potential correlation of explanatory variables with unobserved factors (e.g., DOI can be correlated with unobserved quality of management team). To check the presence of endogeneity, we run a Hausman test for each model.

In all equations, X is the matrix of control variables described in Table 5. Control variables are the basic factors, associated with corporate performance and international diversification (see Bruener 2004; Hitt et al. 2006). The X matrix also includes country-specific dummies, natural logarithm of GDP as a proxy of economic activity in a particular country, and the percentage year-to-year change of the national currency exchange rate since all financial figures are in USD. Industry dummies based on the NAICS codes are also included in the X matrix.

Our hypotheses are tested based on the results of the estimation of the four models. Hypothesis 1 is tested by the significance of the coefficients for the squared variables in each model (β_6 in Entropy models and β_5 and β_9 in FSTS models). To

Table 6 Forecast efficiency measures

Forecast efficiency measure	Formula
Mean error	$ME_t = \frac{\sum_{t=1}^{N} E_t}{N} = \frac{1}{N}\sum_{t=1}^{N}(F_t - A_t)$, where F_t is the forecast at moment t, A_t actual value at moment t, and E_t forecast error
Mean average percentage error (MAPE)	$MAPE = \frac{100}{N}\sum_{i=1}^{N}\left| \frac{A_t - F_t}{A_t} \right|$
Forecast bias	$Bias = \sum_{t=1}^{N} E_t$
Mean absolute deviation	$MAD = \frac{\sum_{t=1}^{N}|E_t|}{N}$
Tracking signal	$TS = \frac{Bias}{MAD}$
RMSE (root mean standard error)	$RMSE = \sqrt{\frac{\sum_{t=1}^{N} E_t^2}{N}}$

test Hypothesis 2, we compare the forecasting power of the models that have the same dependent variable (*Spread* or *Q*) but different DOI variables (*Entropy* or *FSTS* and *HHI*). We should mention here that our models are not identical in terms of explanatory variables (the models with *FSTS* and *HHI* miss the joint products of *FSTS* and *HHI* with GDP measure because of multicollinearity problem). But since the effect of DOI on the performance is distributed between several variables in the models (DOI, DOI times GDP, DOI times unrelated product diversification, and DOI times national currency exchange rate change), removing one of these products from the model makes a moderate change. To measure the forecasting power, we employ several statistics, which compare the efficiency of the forecasts of two competing models. The description of these statistics is presented in Table 6. The closer the value of each statistic to zero, the more efficient the forecast is. Additionally, to test Hypothesis 2, we run a Diebold-Mariano (DM) test, which statistically compares the forecasting power of the two models with the same dependent variable (see Appendix 2 for more details).

Hypothesis 3 is tested by analyzing the impact of an average degree of internationalization on each of the performance measures (*Spread* and *Q*). Thus, for each model, we calculated the predicted firm performance of an "average firm" in two scenarios: the first scenario assumes that the firm operates only on domestic market, while the second scenario supposes that the firm has average values of DOI and moderating variables (unrelated product diversification, GDP, change in currency exchange rate). We then calculate the difference in performance between the second and the first scenarios.

Hypothesis 4 is tested by estimation of the sign and the significance of the coefficient of the joint product of unrelated product diversification measure and DOI variables (β_3 in Entropy models and β_3 and β_7 in FSTS models). Product diversification is measured by HHI based on the sales from different industries following the NAICS standard. If the first two digits of the industry NAICS code do not coincide with the first two digits of the major industry NAICS code (defined as the industry with the largest revenue), then the firm's product diversification would be unrelated.

4 Findings

4.1 Multi-country Models

The results of multi-country models are presented in Table 7.

All models are estimated using the Hausman-Taylor method of the panel data estimations with random effects and the presence of endogeneity. For each model, a Hausman test is done in order to control for the possible endogeneity. In each model, we assume that both the linear and quadratic parts of the DOI variable (*Entropy* and *Entropy2* in Spread-Entropy and Q-Entropy models an, *FSTS2* and *HHI2* in Spread-

Table 7 Results of multi-country models

Model	Spread-Entropy	Q-Entropy	Spread-Intensity	Q-Intensity
LN_SALES	-1.196^{***}	-0.508^{***}	-1.284^{***}	-0.505^{***}
ASSET_TURNOVERR	8.435^{***}	0.736^{***}	8.664^{***}	0.725^{***}
INT_ASSETS	7.743^{*}	-1.799^{***}	7.575^{*}	-1.824^{***}
ROE	0.397^{***}	0.003^{*}	0.396^{***}	0.003^{*}
EBIT_SALES	0.297	0.156	-0.632	0.185
UNRELATED	-1.876	0.299	-0.753	0.263
LOG_GDP	-11.542^{***}	-0.089	-11.035^{***}	-0.013
CURR	0.229^{***}	0.008^{***}	0.221^{***}	0.008^{***}
ENTROPY*UNRELATED	-3.214	0.134		
ENTROPY*GDP	2.633^{*}	-0.079		
ENTROPY*CURR	-1.691	-0.221		
ENTROPY	-78.538^{**}	2.404		
ENTROPY2	2.866^{*}	-0.077		
NAICS1	3.681	1.309^{**}	3.597	1.311^{**}
NAICS2	6.617^{***}	0.501	6.809^{***}	0.499
NAICS3	5.673^{**}	1.278^{***}	6.211^{**}	1.267^{***}
NAICS4	8.952^{***}	1.389^{***}	8.897^{***}	1.396^{***}
RUSSIA	-5.439^{**}	-0.447	-5.123^{*}	-0.436
CHINA	-1.898	-0.491	-1.753	-0.477
BRAZIL	-11.365^{***}	-0.261	-11.483^{***}	-0.239
FSTS*UNRELATED			7.811^{*}	-0.512
HHI*UNRELATED			-13.007^{**}	0.812^{*}
FSTS*CURR			-15.071	0.371
HHI*CURR			10.831	-1.035
FSTS2			-4.153	0.409
HHI2			10.843^{**}	-0.596
INTERCEPT	55.114	-4.225	22.962	-3.227
Number of observations	711	890	711	890
Wald chi-squared	519.170	210.670	518.160	213.380
p-value	0.00	0.00	0.00	0.00

Note: $^{*}p < 0.1$; $^{**}p < 0.05$; $^{***}p < 0.01$

Table 8 Results of Hausman test for endogeneity

Model	Spread-Entropy	Q-Entropy	Spread-Intensity	Q-Intensity
P-value	0.000	0.000	0.050	0.000
Conclusion	Null hypothesis is rejected	Null hypothesis is rejected	Null hypothesis is rejected	Null hypothesis is rejected

FSTS and Q-FSTS, respectively) as well as joint products of DOI measures with control variables can be endogenous. The results of the Hausman test are presented in Table 8.

This test compares the estimates of the two models: the Hausman-Taylor model and the one with random effects. Under the null hypothesis, there is no significant difference in the estimates of these two models, and thus we should not confirm endogeneity and should choose a simple random effect model. But if we reject the null hypothesis of the Hausman test, it means that there is endogeneity in the data, and we thus should choose the Hausman-Taylor model. According to the results, the null hypotheses (absence of endogeneity) are rejected in all models at 10% level. There are several possible reasons for endogeneity in the data: the omission of some significant variables, measurement error, or simultaneity (when the dependent and some independent variables are codetermined). In our case, the most possible reason for endogeneity is simultaneity, which means that international diversification affects firm performance and performance has an impact on DOI.

The findings indicate that unrelated product diversification measure and GDP dynamics in Q models have no significant influence on firm performance, but other control variables are significant. Firm size has a negative effect on performance in each specification, which indicates that on average, large firms tend to be less efficient in terms of operating performance and risk consequences as these firms are more complex and thus harder to manage. Another result is that the ratio of intangible assets to total assets has a significant positive effect on economic profit spread but a significant negative on Tobin's Q, which can be explained by potentially higher cost of financial distress in long term.

4.1.1 The Performance-DOI Pattern for BRIC Firms

Given the results in Table 7, Hypothesis 1 is rejected. We can see from the empirical results that there is no significant impact of DOI measures (both *Entropy* and combination of *FSTS* and *HHI*) on *Q*. However, there is statistically significant and nonlinear influence of DOI measures on *Spread*. This result means that on average in short term, BRIC companies' value is affected when company expands its sales abroad, but in the long run, market expectations might be based on convergence to a common for the market international profile; thus a firm's market capitalization is not significantly affected by international diversification advantages and risks.

Table 9 Linear and quadratic coefficients for models with two DOI variables (for mean values of variables)

Performance variable	Spread	Q
Linear coefficient for FSTS	5.78	−0.39
Quadric coefficient for FSTS	−4.15	0.41
Linear coefficient for HHI	−10.24	0.6
Quadric coefficient for HHI	10.84	−0.6
Linear coefficient for Entropy	−4.18	0.18
Quadric coefficient for Entropy	2.87	−0.08

In order to visually represent the effect of DOI on performance measures, we need to account for the joint products with control variables, as these variables will affect the form of the linear dependence of DOI and firm performance. For instance, in the Q-FSTS model:

$$Q_{itc} = \beta_0 + \beta_1 * X + \beta_2 * FSTS_{itc} + \beta_3 * unrelated_{itc} * FSTS_{itc} + \beta_4 * GDP_{tc}$$
$$* FSTS_{itc} + \beta_5 * Curr_{tc} * FSTS_{itc} + \beta_6 * FSTS_{itc}^2 + \beta_7 * HHI_{itc} + \beta_8$$
$$* unrelated_{itc} * HHI_{itc} + \beta_9 * GDP_{tc} * HHI_{itc} + \beta_{10} * Curr_{tc} * HHI_{itc}$$
$$+ \beta_{11} * HHI_{itc}^2 + \epsilon_{itc} \tag{8}$$

the linear coefficient for *FSTS* will be:

$$\beta_2 + \beta_3 * unrelated_{itc} + \beta_4 * GDP_{tc} + \beta_5 * Curr_{tc} \tag{9}$$

Under assumption of applying mean values of unrelated diversification, GDP, and currency dynamics, we calculate the coefficients for the linear and quadratic DOI factors of the models (see Table 9).

FSTS and *HHI* have different signs in different models, but also they change signs with different performance measures. Since these variables capture different aspects of international diversification (intensity and diversity), this result is quite natural. The form of the relationship and the influence of international diversification highly depend on the choice of DOI measure. This conclusion corresponds to the meta-analytical studies on this topic (see Kirca et al. (2011) and Yang and Driffield 2012).

The results of Hypothesis 1 can be also presented graphically. Figure 2 presents the outcome pattern of the Spread-Entropy relationship on average for BRIC companies and separately for companies from Russia and China (countries with the highest number of observations in the sample). The general model predicts that for Russian companies, international diversification is value destroying and leads to a decline in economic profit spread of up to almost 3 percentage points, while for Chinese companies, international diversification is more profitable and results in up to 4 percentage point increase in economic profit spread for highly internationalized companies. On average, international diversification has moderate impact on the short-term performance for the sample of BRIC companies.

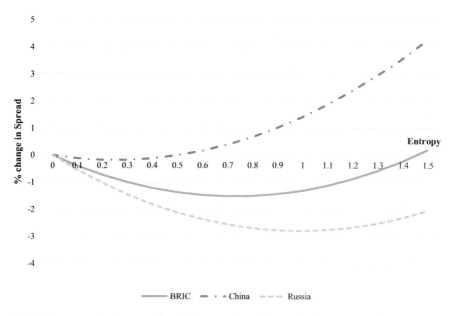

Fig. 2 The pattern of Entropy—change in economic profit spread relationship. Note: this graph is plotted for mean value of all variables except for DOI measure. The equation is $y = \alpha * x + \beta * x^2$, where y and x are performance variable and DOI measure, correspondingly

Table 10 Forecast efficiency measures

Measure	Spread-Entropy	Spread-FSTS	Q-Entropy	Q-FSTS
ME	−0.03	−0.1	0.04	0.05
MAPE	1.86	1.79	−0.18	−0.18
Bias	−23.56	−70.97	38.44	39.75
MAD	6.47	6.43	0.88	0.88
TS	−3.64	−11.04	43.82	45.25
RMSE	8.82	8.84	1.25	1.25

4.1.2 The Choice of DOI Measure

Hypothesis 2 on the similar power of Entropy Index in firm performance estimation compared to the combination of FSTS and HHI is not rejected. We calculate several measures of efficiency of forecasts. The results are presented in Table 10.

We can see that general models with *Entropy* (columns 1 and 3) are more efficient than models with *FSTS* and *HHI* (columns 2 and 4), but this difference is small and can be insignificant. To test this difference and to provide another way to validate Hypothesis 2, we performed a DM test based on the results of the forecast we obtained after the estimation of each model. This test compares the efficiency of the forecasts of competing models (Spread-Entropy versus Spread-FSTS and Q-Entropy versus Q-FSTS). The results of the test are presented in Table 11.

Table 11 Results of DM test for forecast efficiency

Performance variable	Test statistics value	Critical value	Conclusion
Spread	−0.39	1.96	Null hypothesis is not rejected
Q	0.023	1.96	Null hypothesis is not rejected

Table 12 Average change in performance variables attributed to the average level of Entropy (in multi-country model)

Performance measure	BRIC	China	Russia
Average change in *Spread*	−1.42*	−0.18*	−2.27*
Average change in *Q*	0.07	0.03	0.09

Note: $^*p < 0.1$; $^{**}p < 0.05$; $^{***}p < 0.01$

In both cases, we do not reject the null hypotheses about the equal forecasting power of competing models. Thus, we conclude that *Entropy* and the combination of *FSTS* and *HHI* have equal forecasting power for firm performance, and therefore Hypothesis 2 is not rejected. According to the DM test, the difference in forecast efficiency measures is statistically insignificant. However, the Entropy Index can be more convenient since the application of one DOI measure instead of two makes it easier to interpret and graphically represent the results and decreases the level of multicollinearity. Thus, we will base our further analysis on the models with *Entropy* as a DOI measure.

4.1.3 The Impact of International Diversification in Short Run and Long Run

The results of tests for Hypothesis 3 are presented in Table 12.

When we use average values of *Entropy* and other Entropy-related values in Spread-Entropy and in Q-Entropy multi-country models, we can see that compared to the zero level of international diversification (i.e., compared to the firm that operates only on the domestic market), *Spread* slightly declines on average, while *Q* change is insignificant. It means that international diversification can be value destroying in the short term. This result can also be seen on Fig. 2. Thus, we conclude that international diversification has a more positive influence on long-term performance, since in the short term, a company generally bears additional costs of transforming its business structure and integrating new international assets. However, this decrease in short-term efficiency is compensated by the long-term benefits of international diversification, and investors already incorporate these effects of international diversification in the company's market price. This can explain why in Q-Entropy model, the coefficients for DOI variables are statistically insignificant as can be seen in Table 7.

This value destruction performance effect in short run holds for all countries in our sample, but it differs in magnitude. For example, for Chinese companies, the change in *Spread* is negative, but less than 1 percentage point (the average value of *Entropy* variable for China is 0.33 as can be seen from Table 5). For Russian companies, *Spread* decreases much stronger (-2.27 percentage points on average).

4.1.4   The Impact of Product Diversification

Given the findings from Table 7, Hypothesis 4 is rejected. In *Entropy* models, joint products of unrelated product diversification and *Entropy* are not significant. There are various costs and benefits of unrelated product diversification—positive effects are derived from diversification of risks across product markets, while negative effects are due to complication of organization model and lack of synergies. Therefore, we can say that on average these effects compensate each other which makes coefficient for unrelated product diversification insignificant.

4.2   The Results for Single-Country Models

To perform a robustness check for the multi-country models, we run country-specific regressions. The comparison of the results of single- and multi-country models allows us to conclude whether the multi-country model produces the same pattern of the DOI-performance relationship as a single-country model and, thus, whether it captures the country-specific factors that affect this pattern.

We performed this analysis for Russian and Chinese companies as these countries have the highest number of observations in our sample. For India and Brazil, there are not enough observations to run statistical tests. For each country, we run the same regressions as we did for all BRIC companies. The results for selected single-country models are presented in Table 13. Figure 3 illustrates comparison for country-specific models for Russian companies with multi-county model outcomes. We make this comparison for the Spread-Entropy model only as the Q-Entropy multi-country model shows no significant relationship between *Q* and *Entropy*.

The results indicate that for the Russian companies, the relationship patterns between *Spread* and *Entropy* predicted by single-country and multi-country models follow the similar U-shaped curve and are very close in values. The largest difference between these two models occurs at very high values of *Entropy* (the biggest difference between these two curves is 1.3 percentage points when *Entropy* equals to 1.5).

Overall, the graphical analysis of our results allows us to conclude that multi-country models estimated for the sample of all four BRIC countries capture the country-specific factors that affect the DOI-performance relationship pattern and thus can be used for the analysis of specific features of DOI-performance relationship of the firms from different BRIC markets.

Table 13 Results of single-country models

Model	Spread-Entropy_R	Spread-Entropy_C	Q-Entropy_R	Q-Entropy_C
LN_SALES	−1.514**	−0.953	−0.281**	−1.053***
ASSET_TURNOVER	9.536***	4.745*	0.093	1.172***
INT_ASSETS	6.619	25.555***	−4.229***	0.032
ROE	0.214***	0.195***	0.006	0.002
EBIT_SALES	0.412***	0.277***	0.001	0.011**
UNRELATED	−3.384	0.471	−0.343	−0.367
LOG_GDP	2.829	−2.692	−1.292***	1.743***
CURR	−12.088**	−20.871	−0.259	1.241
ENT*UNREL	4.976	−3.361	−0.021	1.221***
ENT*CURR	−4.247	−8.763*	0.173	−1.107**
ENT*GDP	2.053	52.127	0.197	1.336
ENTROPY	108.774	278.328**	−4.738	33.333**
ENTROPY2	5.709*	−4.937	−0.177	−0.491
NAICS1	4.133	1.839	0.208	0.262
NAICS2	7.029	3.252	−0.061	0.591
NAICS3	4.031	5.321	−0.445	2.451***
NAICS4	5.561	5.396	1.106	−0.325
Intercept	−80.511	80.729	41.242***	−44.316***
Number of observations	247	217	266	257
Wald chi-squared	149.130	142.62	106.360	82.510
p-value	0.000	0.000	0.000	0.000

Note: $^*p < 0.1$; $^{**}p < 0.05$; $^{***}p < 0.01$. C and R stand for models run for Chinese and Russian companies, correspondingly

5 Conclusion

This chapter contributes to the literature on the DOI-performance relationship by shedding light on the measurement of this relationship for companies from BRIC markets. We used the concept of economic profit spread, which allows us to take into account the effects of international diversification on both operating efficiency and required rates of returns. We applied this methodology to a sample of 109 companies from BRIC countries. We also used Tobin's Q as a proxy of firms' long-run performance. The degree of international diversification was measured by three types of variables—the Entropy Index, the FSTS ratio, and the Herfindahl-Hirschman Index—and the latter two were used simultaneously.

Based on results of panel data random effect models, estimated using the Hausman-Taylor method, we conclude that in the short run, international diversification tends to be value destroying for the majority of the companies in our sample, having a negative effect on economic profit spread. This result differs between companies, depending on country- and firm-specific characteristics. For example,

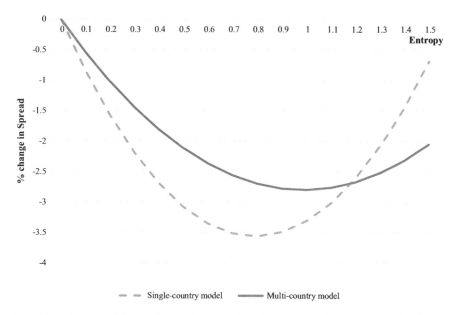

Fig. 3 The pattern of Entropy—change in economic profit spread relationship predicted by single- and multi-country models for Russian companies. *Note: this graph is plotted for mean value of all variables except for DOI measure. The equation is* $y = \alpha * x + \beta * x^2$, *where y and x are performance variable and DOI measure, correspondingly*

while for the Russian companies international diversification mostly reduces economic profit spread, it can have a positive effect on that of the Chinese companies. At the same time, the impact of internationalization on the long-run performance, measured by Tobin's Q, has a lower level of statistical significance and for some model specifications no statistical impact at all.

Another important result is the comparison of the estimation power of different measures of international diversification. Our findings demonstrate that the Entropy Index and the combination of FSTS and HHI have the same predictive power in forecasting short-run and long-run performance. Thus, it is possible to use either the combination of FSTS and HHI or Entropy Index. Still we suggest to use Entropy Index given that it simplifies interpretation and reduces the level of multicollinearity.

One more result of our research considers the predictive power of the general model for all BRIC countries compared to single-country models. In our analysis, we used two country-level variables to take into account differences in economic conditions of BRIC countries: the logarithm of country's GDP and the percentage change in national currency exchange rate. The results show that the pattern of DOI-performance relationship obtained from general multi-country model is close to the one from the model, estimated for companies from only one country (tested for Russian and Chinese companies). This fact can be treated as a robustness check for the multi-country model and demonstrates that the mechanism of influence of international diversification on firm performance depends on common macroeconomic factors for different BRIC countries. At the same time, there are still multiple country-specific factors related to institutional and macroeconomic environment, which influence efficiency of internationalization, but could not be accounted in the current model. Thus, our recommendation would be to use the results of both multi-county models and country-specific models in combination to draw more balanced conclusions.

The research can be used by corporate decision-makers for developing solutions about the optimal degree of international diversification or the prediction of international diversification performance effects in both short run and long run. However, the results of this research should be treated with some caution, as there are certain limitations. First, current research is conducted on a relatively small sample of companies, limited by the requirements of M&A activity between 2005 and 2015, as well as availability of data about international business. Further extension of the data set would potentially allow to overcome statistical insignificance of estimations. Second, inclusion of additional variables, characterizing cultural, political, and economic traits of the countries as well as firm-specific characteristics, could improve the results of both multi-country and single-country models. Future research in this area can focus on these limitations.

Appendix 1. Estimation of S-Shaped Curve Pattern

On the initial step of our analysis, we decided to test the S-shaped pattern hypothesis. The results of this estimation are presented in Table 14.

Generally, these models do not produce significant results of DOI-performance pattern (although there are some DOI variables that are significant in these models). This fact allows us to test the hypothesis that DOI-performance relationship follows the U-shaped curve pattern in the main text of the chapter.

Appendix 2. Diebold-Mariano Test for Predicting Better Forecasting Power of DOI Measures

Diebold-Mariano (DM) (Diebold and Mariano (1995)) test statistically compares the forecasting power of two models with the same dependent variable. Under the null hypothesis that two models have the same forecasting power, the distribution of the differences of the forecast errors of the two models is a standard normal distribution. Test statistics for DM test are calculated as follows:

Let $e_{ip}(s)$ be a forecast error of model s for company i at moment p. Then $d_{ip} = e_{ip}(1) - e_{ip}(2)$ is the difference in the errors of the two competing models. If the two models gave the same forecasting power, then $E(d_{ip}) = 0$, and the test statistic has a standard normal distribution. The test statistic is:

Table 14 Results of multi-country models

Model	Spread-Entropy	Q-Entropy	Spread-Intensity	Q-Intensity
LN_SALES	-1.244^{***}	-0.501^{***}	-1.307^{***}	-0.511^{***}
ASSET_TURNOVERR	8.636^{***}	0.726^{***}	8.723^{***}	0.734^{***}
INT_ASSETS	7.269^{*}	-1.801^{***}	7.233^{*}	-1.817^{***}
3ROE	0.396^{***}	0.002^{*}	0.398^{***}	0.002^{*}
EBIT_SALES	0.037	0.164	-0.704	0.193
UNRELATED	-0.615	0.243	-0.616	0.272
LOG_GDP	-11.984^{***}	-0.072	-13.357^{***}	-0.237
CURR	0.221^{***}	0.007^{***}	0.219^{***}	0.007^{***}
ENTROPY*UNRELATED	-7.525	0.252		
ENTROPY*CURR	10.944^{*}	-0.296		
ENTROPY	-3.059	0.076		
ENTROPY2	-2.906	0.122		
ENTROPY3	-1.111	-0.231		
NAICS1	4.078	1.290^{**}	3.507	1.347^{**}
NAICS2	7.415^{***}	0.477	6.793^{***}	0.504
NAICS3	6.413^{**}	1.244^{***}	6.258^{**}	1.296^{***}
NAICS4	9.331^{***}	1.378^{***}	8.855^{***}	1.383^{***}
RUSSIA	-5.773^{**}	-0.447	-4.995^{*}	-0.431
CHINA	-2.565	-0.459	-1.927	-0.490
BRAZIL	-11.876^{***}	-0.258	-11.492^{***}	-0.239
INTENSITY*UNRELATED			-6.861	-1.605
DIVERSITY*UNRELATED			2.477	1.793^{*}
INTENSITY2			13.194	1.149
INTENSITY3			-2.557	-1.546
DIVERSITY2			7.303^{*}	-0.275
DIVERSITY3			-12.417^{**}	0.492
INTERCEPT	19.141	-2.671	19.193	-3.462
Number of observations	711	890	711	890
Wald chi-squared	507.260	210.540	512.220	215.42
p-value	0.000	0.000	0.000	0.000

Note: $^{*}p < 0.1$; $^{**}p < 0.05$; $^{***}p < 0.01$

$$DM = \overline{d_{..}}\sqrt{N/\hat{V}_e}, \qquad (10)$$

where:

$$\overline{d_{..}} = \frac{1}{NP}\sum_{i=1}^{N}\sum_{p=1}^{P}d_{ip} \qquad (11)$$

and

$$\hat{V}_e = \frac{1}{N-1} \sum_{i=1}^{N} \left(\overline{d_{i.}} - \overline{d_{..}} \right)^2 . \tag{12}$$

If DM is less than the critical value (5% level of significance), we conclude that the *Entropy* and the combination of *FSTS* and *HHI* give the same forecasting power. If DM is greater than the critical value, we reject the null hypothesis and choose the DOI measure with the highest forecasting power based on the measures of the forecast efficiency stated in Sect. 3.2.

References

Bausch, A., & Pils, F. (2009). Product diversification strategy and financial performance: Meta-analytic evidence on casualty and construct multidimensionality. *Review of Managerial Science, 3*, 157–190.

Bany-Ariffin, A. N., Matemilola, B. T., Wahid, L., & Abdullah, S. (2016). International diversification and firm's value: Evidence from developing nations. *Review of International Business and Strategy, 26*(2), 166–183.

Bobillo, A., Lopez-Iturriaga, F., & Tejerina-Gaite, F. (2010). Firm performance and international diversification: The internal and external competitive advantages. *International Business Review, 19*, 607–618.

Bodnar, G., Tang, C., & Weintrop, J. (2003). *The value of corporate international diversification* (NBER Working Chapter, 2003).

Borda, A., Geleilate, J.-M. G., Newburry, W., & Kundu, S. K. (2017). Firm internationalization, business group diversification and firm performance: The case of Latin American firms. *Journal of Business Research, 72*(2017), 104–113.

Bruener, R. F. (2004). *Applied mergers and acquisitions*. New Jersey: Wiley.

Cardinal, L. B., Miller, C. C., & Palich, L. E. (2011). Breaking the cycle of iteration: Forensic failures of international diversification and firm performance research. *Global Strategy Journal, 1*, 175–186.

Carney, M., & Gedajlovic, E. (2011). Business group affiliation, performance, context and strategy: A meta-analysis. *Academy of Management Journal, 54*, 437–460.

Chang, S., & Wang, C. (2007). The effect of product diversification strategies on the relationship between international diversification and firm performance. *Journal of World Business, 42*, 61–79.

Chen, S., & Tan, H. (2012). Region effects in the internationalization-performance relationship in Chinese firms. *Journal of World Business, 47*(2012), 73–80.

Chen, Y., Jiang, Y., Wang, C., & Hsu, W. C. (2014). How do resources and diversification strategy explain the performance consequences of internationalization? *Management Decision, 52*(5), 897–915.

Contractor, F., Kumar, V., & Kundu, S. (2007). Nature of the relationship between international expansion and performance: The case of emerging market firms. *Journal of World Business, 42*, 401–417.

Diebold, F. X., & Mariano, R. (1995). Comparing predictive accuracy. *Journal of Business and Economic Statistics, 13*, 253–265.

Doukas, J., & Pantzalis, C. (2003). Geographic diversification and agency costs of debt of multinational firms. *Journal of Corporate Finance, 9*, 59–92.

Dragun, D. (2002). Challenging the rhetoric: Internationalisation, size and financial performance. *European Retail Digest, 36*, 25–33.

Elif, A. S. (2015). Corporate diversification and firm value: Evidence from emerging markets. *International Journal of Emerging Markets, 10*(3), 294–310.

Grigorieva, S. A. (2007). Empirical research of corporate diversification strategy in developed and emerging markets: An overview. *Journal of Corporate Finance Research, 1*(1), 111–144.

Gugler, K., Mueller, D., Yurtoglu, B., & Zulehner, C. (2003). The effects of mergers: An international comparison. *International Journal of Industrial Organization, 21*, 625–653.

Hashai, N., & Delios, A. (2013). Balancing growth across the geographic and product diversification domains – A Contingency approach. *International Business Review, 21*, 1052–1064.

Hejazi, W., & Santor, E. (2010). Foreign asset risk exposure, and performance: An analysis of Canadian banks. *Journal of International Business Studies, 41*, 845–860.

Hennart, J. F. (2011). A theoretical assessment of the empirical literature on the impact of multinationality on performance. *Global Strategy Journal, 1*, 135–151.

Hitt, M. A., Tihanyi, L., Miller, T., & Connelly, B. (2006). International diversification: antecedents, outcomes, and moderators. *Journal of Management, 32*(6), 831–867.

Hitt, M., Hoskisson, R., & Kim, H. (1997). International diversification: Effects on innovation and firm performance in product-diversified firms. *The Academy of Management Journal, 40*(4), 767–798.

Ivashkovskaya, I. V. (2008). *Finansovye izmereniya korporativnyh strategij*. Stejkholderskij podhod. INFRA-M.

Joliet, R., & Hubner, G. (2006). *Corporate international diversification and the cost of equity: European evidence* (Working chapter of Ecole de Gestion de l'Universite de Liege #200605/01).

Kirca, A. H., Hult, G. T. M., Roth, K., Cavusgil, S. T., Perryy, M. Z., Akdeniz, M. B., & White, R. C. (2011). Firm specific assets, multinationality, and financial performance: A metaanalytic review and theoretical integration. *Academy of Management Journal, 54*(1), 47–72.

Kotabe, M., Srinivasan, S. S., & Aulakh, P. S. (2002). Multinationality and firm performance: The moderating role of R&D and marketing capabilities. *Journal of International Business Studies, 33*, 79–89.

Lu, J., & Beamish, P. (2004). International diversification and firm performance: The S- curve hypothesis. *The Academy of Management Journal, 47*(4), 598–609.

Moeller, S., & Schlingemann, F. (2005). Are cross-border acquisitions different from domestic acquisitions? Evidence on stock and operating performance for U.S. acquirers. *Journal of Banking and Finance, 29*, 533–564.

Oh, C. H., Sohl, T., & Rugman, A. M. (2015). Regional and product diversification and the performance of retail multinationals. *Journal of International Management, 21*(3), 220–234.

Qian, G., & Li, J. (2002). Multinationality, global market diversification and profitability among the largest US firms. *Journal of Business Research, 55*, 325–335.

Ref, O. (2015). The relationship between product and geographic diversification: A fine-grained analysis of its different patterns (2015). *Journal of International Management, 21*(2), 83–99.

Riahi-Belkaoui, A. (1998). The effects of the degree of internationalization on firm performance. *International Business Review, 7*, 315–325.

Rugman, A., & Chang, O. (2010). Does the regional nature of multinationals affect the multinationality and performance relationship? *International Business Review, 19*, 479–488.

Singla, C., & George, R. (2013). Internationalization and performance: A contextual analysis of Indian firms. *Journal of Business Research, 66*, 2500–2506.

Singh, M., & Najadmalayeri, A. (2004). Internationalization, capital structure, and cost of capital: Evidence from French corporations. *Journal of Multinational Financial Management, 14* (2004), 153–169.

Shcherbakov, D. (2013). *Diversification strategies effectiveness of emerging economies firms*. Dissertation for the degree of candidate of economic sciences, Moscow, 2013.

Tian, X., & Buckleya Peter, J. (2017). Internalization theory and the performance of emerging-market multinational enterprises. *International Business Review, 26*, 976–990. https://doi.org/10.1016/j.ibusrev.2017.03.005.

Thomas, D. E., & Eden, L. (2004). What is the shape of the multinationality-performance relationship? *Multinational Business Review, 12*(1), 89–99.

Thomas, D. (2005). International diversification and firm performance in Mexican firms: A curvilinear relationship? *Journal of Business Research, 59*, 501–507.

Vermeulen, F., & Barkema, H. (2002). Pace, rhythm, and scope: Process dependence in building a profitable multinational corporation. *Strategic Management Journal, 23*, 637–653.

Wan William, P., & Hoskisson Robert, E. (2003). Home country environments, corporate diversification strategies, and firm performance. *The Academy of Management Journal, 46*(1), 27–45.

Wu, D., Wu, X.-b., & Zhou, H.-j. (2012). International expansion and firm performance in emerging market: Evidence from China. *Chinese Management Studies, 6*(3), 509–528.

Xiao, S., Jeong, I., Moon, J., & Chung, C. (2013). Internationalization and performance of firms in China: Moderating effects of governance structure and the degree of centralized control. *Journal of International Management, 19*, 118–137.

Yang, Y., & Driffield, N. (2012). Multinationality-performance relationship. *Management International Review, 52*(1), 23–47.

Zaheer, S., & Mosakowski, E. (1997). The dynamics of the liability of foreignness: A global study of survival in financial services. *Strategic Management Journal, 18*, 439–463.

Zahra, S. A., Ireland, R. D., & Hitt, M. A. (2000). International expansion by new venture firms: International diversity, mode of market entry, technological learning, and performance. *Academy of Management Journal, 43*, 925–950.

Conclusion: M&As in Emerging Markets— The Lessons Learned

Eugene Nivorozhkin and Irina Ivashkovskaya

Keywords M&A premium · Cross-border M&A · International diversification · Economic profit

This book compares M&A performance for companies in developed and emerging economies over short-run and long-run periods.

Previous research on domestic acquisitions in developed and emerging capital markets suggests that target shareholders gain significantly from these deals regardless of the type of the capital market. These conclusions hold for studies based on the most widely used techniques, such as event studies and accounting studies. Nevertheless, for acquiring shareholders, the type of the market matters. Event studies do not prove value creation effects in deals in developed capital markets, but in most cases, they capture positive market reactions to the announcements of M&A deals in emerging capital markets. With book value-based measures, which reflect operating performance, the results are mixed in both types of capital markets. The research models with value-based performance measures allow the identification of the effects of M&A deals for a longer perspective, and they show value-destroying performance of domestic M&A for most deals in developed and emerging capital markets. These chapters do not show that domestic M&As are beneficial for emerging markets in most cases.

What have this book added to the studies on M&A performance? First, the authors have contributed to value creation studies by focusing on value-added measures for performance or *economic profit* adjusted to industry. We consider this to be the leading measure capable of capturing both components of fundamental value creation: the changes in operating performance and the impact on company

E. Nivorozhkin
Associate University College London, School of Slavonic and East European Studies, University College London, London, UK

I. Ivashkovskaya (✉)
Higher School of Economics, National Research University, Moscow, Russia
e-mail: iivashkovskaja@hse.ru

© Springer Nature Switzerland AG 2020
I. Ivashkovskaya et al. (eds.), *Strategic Deals in Emerging Capital Markets*,
Advanced Studies in Emerging Markets Finance,
https://doi.org/10.1007/978-3-030-23850-6_11

risk. The analysis in Chap. 5 finds that industry-adjusted economic profit significantly decreases after deals in emerging capital markets. The findings show that value destruction was the prevailing trend in emerging capital markets from 2002 to 2013. The sample firms did not succeed in extracting the synergies by bettering the operating performance and risk management of the combined firms. For companies in developed markets, statistically insignificant improvements in economic profit following M&A are observed. Nevertheless, when the effects of M&A deals on company value are compared in both markets, the authors arrive at an important conclusion. In the 2-year period surrounding M&A in developed markets, more value for shareholders is created than in deals in emerging economies. The difference in the results may be explained by the imperfect institutional environment in emerging capital markets which prevent companies from extracting benefits from M&A deals in the long run.

Second, in contrast to most published chapters, this book studies the impact of the economic crisis of 2007–2008 on the performance of M&A deals. The authors show that changes in performance due to M&A in emerging capital markets for deals completed during the pre-crisis period are negative and statistically significant, indicating that such deals decrease value for shareholders. While comparing the value effects of M&A deals in the post-crisis and pre-crisis periods, the study does not demonstrate statistically significant results in either developed or emerging capital markets.

Third, this book provides meta-analysis of chapters on emerging market deals and thus contributes to a deeper understanding of whether the drivers of performance in deals are common in both types of markets. This specific approach allows us to summarize the results obtained from different samples of emerging markets used in published and working chapters and with different methods of performance measurement. Using meta-analysis methodology, the authors identified the most widespread determinants of M&A performance in emerging markets. Among them are the method of payment, the size of the acquirer, the deal size, cross-border deals, a private target company, ROE, industry relatedness, state ownership of the target company, ROA and the financial leverage of the acquirer. Therefore, this book demonstrates that the driving forces in strategic deals are very similar regardless of the capital market. The meta-analysis also allows to show what the strongest drivers of performance for emerging capital markets are: method of payment, acquirer size, ROA and industry relatedness. Given the heterogeneity of the sample, an effect size was identified for the method of payment, acquirer size, and public companies, but it was not possible to identify a significant average effect size for industry relatedness or state ownership.

Fourth, this book compares the influence of typical deal characteristics on acquisition performance in both types of markets. Given the impact of the method of payment, the study reveals that deals paid for with stock significantly outperform the transactions paid for in cash in developed capital markets for the 2-year period surrounding the deal. A similar effect was found for the sample of deals in emerging markets. For geographical diversification, the study provides significant results only for companies from developed markets, indicating that they experience higher performance improvements following cross-border M&A than for local deals.

Analysing diversification effects in both types of markets, the authors revealed significant results only in emerging markets, suggesting that focused deals outperform diversification strategies, when the 2-year period surrounding the deal is examined.

Fifth, the book provides a better understanding of the link between different types of corporate diversification and firm value. On a sample of companies from BRIC countries, the authors demonstrate the predominance of positive effects of corporate diversification in emerging markets. The empirical findings clearly show that vertical deals create higher value added compared to conglomerate ones. In addition, this book provides an evidence on the impact of the crisis on diversification-performance relationship. It is shown that after the crisis, with more severe external financial constraints, conglomerates are more efficient for shareholders, but cumulative abnormal returns for vertical acquisitions show no statistically significant difference from zero, suggesting that it may be difficult for companies to obtain benefits from operating synergies.

Sixth, this book presents interesting results for technological deals, indicating that high-tech M&A deals show better performance than low-tech ones in emerging capital markets, while in developed capital markets, the opposite is true. Low-tech deals in developed markets generate more value for shareholders than high-tech ones, suggesting that such deals, regardless of their attractiveness for acquirers, may not lead to value creation for a number of reasons including the high level of uncertainty, difficulties in integration and a lack of disclosed information about the acquired technology.

The book identifies the most relevant factors of success in the deals of knowledge-intensive firms following the study of post-merger integration and the acquisition of engineering consulting companies in Brazil which mainly employ the knowledge of their professionals to develop and commercialize intangible solutions for clients. The results of the survey reported in Chap. 7 demonstrate that only one-third of executives indicated that they had exceeded their synergy goals, while 43% were below expectations, and the duration of the integration process was on average 13.1 months, which is well below the national average in Brazil for all segments. The respondents from these high-tech firms clearly show that capturing synergies and standardizing information systems were the most effort-consuming factors compared to the initial expectations of the firms in the sample. Based on questionnaires, the eight main factors for successful integration processes for these specific types of deals were confirmed by the Borda and Condorcet methods. Both techniques simultaneously showed that synergy extraction depends on the vision and values of organizations, due diligence in the previous phase, strong support from executives, planning the integration processes, culture and organization, internal communication, financial data integration and deep involvement of the management teams of both companies. In addition the study reveals the factors which are derived only by one type of applied analytical technique. For example, to succeed in managing the post-M&A integration process, a dialogue with stakeholders, the creation of a dedicated integration team and the development of a robust synergy plan are considered important. The findings suggest that accounting for these factors can mitigate errors and weaknesses in the integration processes and increase the chances of generating value for knowledge-intensive companies.

Additional contribution is made in this book to the synergy effects in large emerging markets. Based on the analysis of separate synergy components in 171 domestic M&As in Russia from 2006 to 2015, this study shows the structure of synergy effects for every deal and key factors that drive synergy creation. The analysis of domestic deals in the Russian market proves the existence of similar driving forces in these deals compared to developed and other emerging markets. Splitting synergy into five operating and financial types helps to better understand the value creation process. This approach to synergy estimation can be applied to closely held companies and small-cap deals that make up the majority of M&A in emerging markets.

While examining the dimensions of the M&A premium in BRIC markets, this book shows a positive control premium and how it differs among national M&A markets in the BRIC group. The findings suggest that Chinese acquirers paid the highest control premium, while Russian companies paid the lowest. In emerging markets, investors are ready to pay a higher premium if companies belong to the same industrial sector due to the high potential synergy. In deals in emerging markets, it is also important whether the acquirer is domestic. An additional interesting finding is that the size of premium goes up if the M&A announcement happens in a crisis year. The size of the acquired stake also has a positive impact. A large and highly leveraged target decreases the premium for control in the large emerging markets. These results are largely consistent with the negative factors reported in earlier chapters on different emerging markets.

Finally, this book contributes to the literature on cross-border deals initiated by firms from emerging markets by showing that they create value and produce gains for both parties involved in the transaction, compared to domestic M&A. The findings on the relationship between performance and international diversification shed new light on the mechanism of this relationship for BRIC companies. The concept of economic profit allows to take into account two types of international diversification effects, namely, the impact on financial and operating performance of the firm. On a sample of 109 companies from BRIC countries, the authors demonstrate the difference in the impact of international diversification on fundamental value-based performance and expectation-based performance measures. The findings reveal that international diversification has a smaller impact on economic profit and in some cases can be even value destroying, while performance based on expectations and measured by Tobin's Q increases significantly. Besides these effects, the research demonstrates the forecasting power of different measures of international diversification. Despite these measures take into account different aspects of international diversification and reveal different patterns in performance—international diversification relationship—they predict the change in the performance with the same quality. In addition, the findings suggest that the mechanism of the influence of international diversification on firm performance is the same for different BRIC countries. Based on three country-level variables, to account for differences in economic conditions of BRIC countries, this book provides an evidence that the general model for the four BRIC countries produces the same pattern in the performance—international diversification relationship—as the model predicts for the subsample companies from only one country.

The strategic deals initiated by the firms from emerging markets will continue attracting the researchers from different countries at times of structural shifts in the technologies and capital markets and the turbulence of competitive landscapes. This book makes a contribution and suggests new possible lenses for future research.

Printed by Printforce, the Netherlands